The French Revolution, 178

**European History in Perspective**
General Editor: Jeremy Black

Benjamin Arnold  *Medieval Germany*
Ronald Asch  *The Thirty Years' War*
Nigel Aston  *The French Revolution, 1789–1804*
Christopher Bartlett  *Peace, War and the European Powers, 1814–1914*
Robert Bireley  *The Refashioning of Catholicism, 1450–1700*
Donna Bohanan  *Crown and Nobility in Early Modern France*
Arden Bucholz  *Moltke and the German Wars, 1864–1871*
Patricia Clavin  *The Great Depression, 1929–1939*
Paula Sutter Fichtner  *The Habsburg Monarchy, 1490–1848*
Mark Galeotti  *Gorbachev and his Revolution*
David Gates  *Warfare in the Nineteenth Century*
Alexander Grab  *Napoleon and the Transformation of Europe*
Martin P. Johnson  *The Dreyfus Affair*
Paul Douglas Lockhart  *Sweden in the Seventeenth Century*
Graeme Murdock  *Beyond Calvin*
Peter Musgrave  *The Early Modern European Economy*
J. L. Price  *The Dutch Republic in the Seventeenth Century*
A. W. Purdue  *The Second World War*
Christopher Read  *The Making and Breaking of the Soviet System*
Francisco J. Romero-Salvado  *Twentieth-Century Spain*
Matthew S. Seligmann and Roderick R. McLean
   *Germany from Reich to Republic, 1871–1918*
Brendan Simms  *The Struggle for Mastery in Germany, 1779–1850*
David Sturdy  *Louis XIV*
David J. Sturdy  *Richelieu and Mazarin*
Hunt Tooley  *The Western Front*
Peter Waldron  *The End of Imperial Russia, 1855–1917*
Peter G. Wallace  *The Long European Reformation*
James D. White  *Lenin*
Patrick Williams  *Philip II*
Peter H. Wilson  *From Reich to Revolution*

---

**European History in Perspective
Series Standing Order
ISBN 0–333–71694–9 hardcover
ISBN 0–333–69336–1 paperback**
(*outside North America only*)

You can receive future titles in this series as they are published by placing a standing order. Please contact your bookseller or, in the case of difficulty, write to us at the address below with your name and address, the title of the series and the ISBN quoted above.

Customer Services Department, Palgrave Ltd
Houndmills, Basingstoke, Hampshire RG21 6XS, England

# The French Revolution, 1789–1804

## Authority, Liberty, and the Search for Stability

NIGEL ASTON

© Nigel Aston 2004

All rights reserved. No reproduction, copy or transmission of this publication may be made without written permission.

No paragraph of this publication may be reproduced, copied or transmitted save with written permission or in accordance with the provisions of the Copyright, Designs and Patents Act 1988, or under the terms of any licence permitting limited copying issued by the Copyright Licensing Agency, 90 Tottenham Court Road, London W1T 4LP.

Any person who does any unauthorised act in relation to this publication may be liable to criminal prosecution and civil claims for damages.

The author has asserted his right to be identified as the author of this work in accordance with the Copyright, Designs and Patents Act 1988.

First published 2004 by
PALGRAVE MACMILLAN
Houndmills, Basingstoke, Hampshire RG21 6XS and
175 Fifth Avenue, New York, N.Y. 10010
Companies and representatives throughout the world

PALGRAVE MACMILLAN is the global academic imprint of the Palgrave Macmillan division of St. Martin's Press, LLC and of Palgrave Macmillan Ltd. Macmillan® is a registered trademark in the United States, United Kingdom and other countries. Palgrave is a registered trademark in the European Union and other countries.

ISBN 0–333–61175–6 hardback
ISBN 0–333–61176–4 paperback

This book is printed on paper suitable for recycling and made from fully managed and sustained forest sources.

A catalogue record for this book is available from the British Library.

Library of Congress Cataloging-in-Publication Data
Aston, Nigel.
 The French Revolution, 1789–1804 : authority, liberty and the search for stability / Nigel Aston.
   p. cm. — (European history in perspective)
 Includes bibliographical references and index.
 ISBN 0–333–61175–6 — ISBN 0–333–61176–4 (pbk.)
 1. France—History—Revolution, 1789–1799.  2. France—Politics and government—1789–1815.  I. Title.  II. European history in perspective (Palgrave Macmillan (Firm))

DC148.A8 2004
944.04—dc22
                                                                2004046889

10  9  8  7  6  5  4  3  2  1
13 12 11 10 09 08 07 06 05 04

Printed in China

For Malcolm Crook

# Contents

| | |
|---|---|
| *List of Maps* | x |
| *Preface* | xi |
| *Timeline* | xiii |

**Introduction** — 1

## PART I: THE UNFOLDING OF THE REVOLUTION, 1789–1804

**1 The End of the Monarchy, 1789–1792** — 9
The Prelude to the Estates-General, May 1789 — 9
The Meeting of the Estates-General — 19
The Reform Agenda of the National Assembly — 24

**2 The Convention, 1792–1795** — 31
The Convention Established — 31
The Destruction of the Brissotins, 1793 — 36

**3 An Attempt at Moderation: the Directory and the Consulate, 1795–1804** — 47
The Directory, 1795–1799 — 47
The Coming of the Consulate, 1799 — 60
Success and Stability: the Consulate, 1799–1804 — 64
Conclusion — 68

## PART II: THE CREATION OF A NEW POLITICAL CULTURE

**4 The Language and Signs of Revolution and Counter-Revolution**   **73**
Introduction   73
Language, Ideologies and Revolution   75
The Revolution and the Arts   82
The French Revolution and Antiquity   89
Napoleon and the Signs and Symbols of Revolutionary France   93
Conclusion   95

**5 The Transformation of Institutions**   **97**
Introduction   97
Central Government Power and Performance in the French Revolution   101
The Revolutionary Renewal of Local Government   106
The Machinery of Justice   110
The Subordination of the Church   113

**6 Changing Patterns of Political Participation**   **119**
The Political Nation Defined   119
The Power of Opinion   125
The Patterns of Participatory Politics in the 1790s   130
The Limits to Revolutionary Involvement   139

## Part III: THE REVOLUTION AND ITS SOCIAL IMPACT

**7 The Militarisation of France: the Nation in Arms**   **145**
The Army, Autocracy and Ending the Revolution   145
The Unmartial Opening of the Revolution, 1789–92   151
The Nation Goes to War   154
The Wars of the Revolution   158
The Consequences of Incessant Warfare   163

**8 Violence, Vandalism and Coercion**   **168**
Violence   168
The Great Terror   175
Terrorism and Lawlessness after 1795   181

Vandalism 183
Conclusion 188

## 9  The Economy and Society 191
Introduction 191
Economic Liberalism and the Market Economy 192
The Predominance of Property 195
Economic Egalitarianism 196
The Changing Rural Picture 200
The Impact of the War 205
Summary 208

## Part IV:  THE REVOLUTION AND THE WIDER WORLD

### 10  The Impact on Europe 213
An International Dimension 214
An Authoritarian turn in Europe? 225
Conclusion 232

### 11  The French Diaspora and the Wider World 236
Introduction 236
A France Beyond the Frontiers: the *Émigrés* and Their Varied Worlds 237
The French Revolution in the Atlantic World 245

## Conclusion 254

*Notes* 261

*Glossary* 282

*Select Annotated Bibliography of Publications in English* 285

*Index* 294

# Maps

1 France in 1789   8
2 The expansion of France after 1791   233

# Preface

I was invited by the general editor, Jeremy Black, to produce a volume on the French Revolution only a few years after the *bicentennaire* of 1989. I have pursued the writing in fits and starts, often daunted by the constant flow of fascinating new research on the Revolution and the onerous challenge of both keeping up to date with it and summarising it for a wide audience. It is a highly competitive market and if my writing tends to revert to the darker side of the 1790s, then the reader who prefers a longer credit sheet for the Revolution has plenty of alternative choices. Jeremy Black has coaxed this book along when it seemed like imploding and I'm most grateful to him for his unfailing advice, support and friendship. His insistence that the fruits of archival research should be available in any work of historical scholarship rather than confined to a monograph has inspired me and continues to do so. For over two decades I have been struck by the wealth of unpublished primary source references to the Revolution in British archives and I have tried at every point in the book to include a fair slice of such references to give all my readers a sense of what there is out there still relatively under-utilised. I have also drawn heavily on the courteous and considerate staff at several institutions, notably the Bibliothèque nationale de France, the James Marshall and Marie-Louise Osborn Collection, Beinecke Rare Book and Manuscript Library (Yale University), the British Library, Cambridge University Library and University of Leicester Library. I wish to record my gratitude to the owners and custodians of manuscript collections who have allowed me to consult and quote from items in their possession: the trustees of the National Library of Scotland; Hampshire Record Office; Lord Sackville and the Centre for Kentish Studies; Staffordshire Record Office; the Earl of Onslow and the Surrey History

Centre; Edinburgh University Library. Colin Jones has read over the entire manuscript and made several constructive suggestions for alteration and improvement. His exact knowledge of the Revolution has no parallel and, though his view of the Revolution is very different to mine, it is typical of his generosity that he welcomes alternative readings of events. Clarissa Campbell Orr, Darrin MacMahon and John McManners have allowed me, sometimes unwittingly, to try out some of my wilder ideas on them. At Palgrave, Terka Acton, Felicity Noble and Sonya Barker were models of patience and professionalism in confronting and encouraging an author always on the brink of reaching the finishing post, while Penny Simmons of Password Publishing Services was a very helpful copy-editor. I'm also grateful to the third-year undergraduates at the University of Leicester who have taken my special subject in the Revolution in the last few years and have heard my arguments and have habitually improved them or caused me to reject them. My wife, Caroline Aston, amazingly, still puts up with my absence upstairs and her own lecturing style never ceases to show me that history can and should be enjoyable, amusing as well as exact and measured. Above all, I want to register my overwhelming debt to the scholars of all nationalities and all opinions whose work keeps this great topic to the forefront. Even counter-revolutionaries, it seems, can in the twenty-first century comfortably form part of this welcoming *fraternité*.

Nigel Aston
*Rutland*

# Timeline 1789–1804

| | | |
|---|---|---|
| 1789 | March–April | Elections to the Estates-General |
| | 5 May | Opening of the Estates-General at Versailles |
| | 17 June | Third Estate declares itself constituted as the National Assembly |
| | 20 June | Tennis Court oath |
| | 23 June | 'Royal Session' in which the king commands the three orders to continue meeting apart |
| | 11 July | Dismissal of Jacques Necker as first minister |
| | 14 July | Fall of the Bastille |
| | 16 July | Recall of Necker |
| | July–August | *Grande Peur* and peasant unrest in much of rural France |
| | 4 August | National Assembly provisionally proclaims the abolition of all surviving privileges |
| | 26 August | Declaration of the Rights of Man and of the Citizen approved |
| | 11 September | Vote in the National Assembly on the king's veto |

|      |                  |                                                                                                              |
|------|------------------|--------------------------------------------------------------------------------------------------------------|
|      | 5–6 October      | Revolutionary *journée* – march on Versailles – National Assembly and the royal family are brought back to Paris and the latter is installed in the Tuileries |
|      | 10 October       | Louis XVI declared 'King of the French'                                                                      |
|      | 2 November       | Clerical property placed at the disposal of the nation                                                       |
|      | 14–22 December   | Local government reorganised                                                                                 |
|      | 19 December      | First issue of *assignats*                                                                                   |
| 1790 | 13 February      | Suppression of monastic vows and most religious orders                                                       |
|      | 22 May           | National Assembly repudiates 'wars of conquest'                                                              |
|      | 13–14 June       | The 'Bagarre' of Nîmes                                                                                       |
|      | 19 June          | Abolition of noble titles                                                                                    |
|      | 12 July          | Civil Constitution of the Clergy approved by the National Assembly                                           |
|      | 14 July          | Festival of the Federation to celebrate the first anniversary of the fall of the Bastille                    |
|      | 16 August        | Decree reorganising the judiciary                                                                            |
|      | 31 August        | Repression at Nancy of mutiny by the Châteauvieux Regiment                                                   |
|      | 4 September      | Necker leaves the government                                                                                 |
|      | 29 October       | Slave rebellion begins in San Domingo                                                                        |
|      | 27 November      | Oath of acceptance of the Civil Constitution required of all public officials, including the clergy          |
| 1791 | April            | Louis XVI and royal family prevented from taking Easter communion from a refractory priest at Saint-Cloud    |

|  |  |  |
|---|---|---|
| | 13 April | Pius VI condemns the Civil Constitution in the bull *Caritas quae* |
| | 15 May | Black inhabitants of French colonies born of free parents are declared to possess the same civil rights as whites |
| | 14 June | *Loi Le Chapelier* banning workers' combinations |
| | 20 June | The king and queen and children quit Paris on the 'flight to Varennes' |
| | 15 July | The king's prerogatives are restored to him |
| | 17 July | Massacre of the Champ de Mars |
| | 27 August | Declaration of Pillnitz |
| | 14 September | Louis XVI accepts the Constitution of 1791; annexation of Avignon and the Comtat Venaissin |
| | 30 September | Dissolution of the National Assembly |
| | 1 October | Legislative Assembly convenes |
| | November | Decrees against *émigrés* and non-juring clergy |
| 1792 | 20 April | Declaration of war on the 'king of Hungary and Bohemia', that is Austria |
| | 12 June | Louis XVI dismisses his Girondin ministers |
| | 20 June | Parisian crowds invade the Tuileries and force the king to wear the *cockarde* |
| | 25 July | Publication of the Brunswick Manifesto |
| | 9 August | Revolutionary commune assumes the government of Paris |
| | 10 August | Storming of the Tuileries, massacre of the Swiss Guards and suspension of the monarchy |
| | 19 August | Lafayette defects to the Austrians |

# TIMELINE

|      |                |                                                                              |
|------|----------------|------------------------------------------------------------------------------|
|      | 2 September    | Verdun occupied by the Prussians                                             |
|      | 2–6 September  | September Massacres                                                          |
|      | 20 September   | French victory over the Prussians at Valmy                                   |
|      | 21 September   | National Convention convenes for the first time                              |
|      | 6 November     | Victory at Jemappes – Belgium invaded                                        |
|      | 19 November    | Edict of fraternity passed                                                   |
| 1793 | 21 January     | Execution of Louis XVI                                                       |
|      | 1 February     | Declaration of war on Britain and the United Provinces (Holland)             |
|      | March          | Recruitment quotas set for all local communities                             |
|      | 7 March        | Declaration of war on Spain                                                  |
|      | 9 March        | First représantants-en-mission sent to the provinces                         |
|      | 10 March       | Creation of the revolutionary tribunal                                       |
|      | 11 March       | Beginning of insurrection in the Vendée                                      |
|      | 18 March       | French army defeated at Neerwinden                                           |
|      | 4 April        | Dumouriez defects to the Austrians                                           |
|      | 6 April        | First Committee of Public Safety established                                 |
|      | 29 May         | Anti-Jacobin insurrection in Lyon                                            |
|      | 31 May–2 June  | Invasion of the Convention and fall of the Girondins                         |
|      | 7 June         | Federalist revolts in Bordeaux and the Calvados (Normandy)                   |
|      | 24 June        | Constitution of the Year I approved                                          |
|      | 13 July        | Assassination of Marat by Charlotte Corday                                   |
|      | 17 July        | Final abolition of all seigneurial dues without compensation                 |

|  |  |  |
|---|---|---|
|  | 27 July | Robespierre appointed to the Committee of Public Safety |
|  | August | Institution of the *levée en masse* |
|  | 1 August | Adoption of the metric system |
|  | 27 August | Toulon handed over to British naval forces under Lord Hood |
|  | 17 September | Law of Suspects passed |
|  | 29 September | Introduction of the *general maximum* on prices and wages |
|  | 10 October | Revolutionary government decreed until the return of peace |
|  | 16 October | Execution of Marie-Antoinette |
|  | 18–19 October | Republicans lose control of Cholet to the 'Royal and Catholic Army' |
|  | 24 November | Adoption of the revolutionary calendar |
|  | December | Defeat of the Vendéen rebels at Le Mans and Savenay |
|  | 4 December | Revolutionary government decreed: law of 14 *frimaire* |
|  | 19 December | British forces evacuate Toulon |
| 1794 | January | Repression in western France with use of the *colonnes infernales* |
|  | 4 February | Abolition of slavery in French colonies |
|  | 4 March | Attempted insurrection by the Cordelier Club |
|  | 13–24 March | Arrest and execution of the Hébertistes |
|  | 30 March–6 April | Arrest and execution of Danton and his followers |
|  | 1 June | Naval defeat in the 'Glorious First of June' but vital grain convoy still reaches Brest safely |

|  |  |  |
|---|---|---|
|  | 8 June | Festival of the Supreme Being in Paris |
|  | 10 June | Law of 22 prairial speeds up the work of the Revolutionary Tribunal |
|  | 26 June | French victory at Fleurus and the reconquest of Belgium |
|  | 26 July | Robespierre's last speech in the Convention |
|  | 27 July | Nine thermidor and overthrow of Robespierre |
|  | 30–31 July | Reorganisation of the Committee of Public Safety |
|  | 12 November | Closure of the Jacobin Club |
|  | 24 December | Abolition of the general maximum |
| 1795 | 21 February | Decree separating Church and state |
|  | February | Treaty of La Jaunaye with the Vendéens |
|  | April | Treaty of La Prevalaye with the *Chouans* |
|  | 1 April | Germinal *journée* in Paris |
|  | 5 April | Treaty of Basle with Prussia |
|  | April–May | 'White Terror' begins in Lyon and other parts of south-eastern France |
|  | 16 May | Peace with Holland and the Batavian Republic constituted |
|  | 20 May | Prairial *journée* in Paris – Convention invaded |
|  | 6 June | Death of Louis XVII in captivity; succeeded by his uncle as the titular Louis XVIII |
|  | 21 July | *Émigré* army defeated at Quiberon Bay |
|  | 22 July | Peace completed with Spain |
|  | 22 August | The Convention accepts the Constitution of the Year III |
|  | 5 October | Royalist rising of vendémiare in Paris |

|      |                |                                                                                                |
|------|----------------|------------------------------------------------------------------------------------------------|
|      | 26 October     | Convention dissolved                                                                           |
|      | 3 November     | Directory installed in office                                                                  |
| 1796 | 19 February    | Withdrawal of the *assignats*                                                                  |
|      | 2 March        | Napoleon Bonaparte appointed Commander-in-Chief of the Army of Italy                           |
|      | 10 May         | Babeuf arrested                                                                                |
|      | December       | Failure of expedition to Bantry Bay, Ireland, because of exceptional winter storms             |
| 1797 | March–April    | Royalists make electoral gains                                                                 |
|      | 27 May         | Execution of Babeuf                                                                            |
|      | 4 September    | Fructidor coup against the royalist threat, beginning of the 'Second Directory'                |
|      | 17 October     | France and the Austrian Empire sign the Treaty of Campo Formio                                 |
| 1798 | 11 May         | Coup of Floréal with purging of the legislative bodies                                         |
|      | 19 May         | Bonaparte departs from Toulon on his Egyptian campaign                                         |
|      | 1 August       | Nelson's victory at the battle of the Nile (Aboukir Bay)                                       |
|      | 5 September    | Jourdan's law on military conscription                                                         |
| 1799 | March          | War of the Second Coalition begins                                                             |
|      | April          | Legislative election results produce a Jacobin revival                                         |
|      | 23 August      | Bonaparte leaves Egypt for France                                                              |
|      | 9–10 November  | Coup of brumaire overthrows the Directory                                                      |
|      | 13 December    | Bonaparte, Cambacérès and Lebrun named Consuls                                                 |
|      | 15 December    | Proclamation of a new constitution                                                             |

| | | |
|---|---|---|
| 1800 | 17 February | Office of prefect instituted |
| | 18 March | Reorganisation of the judicial system |
| | June | Moderate press censorship restored |
| | 14 June | Battle of Marengo |
| | November | Sinking fund established |
| | 24 December | 'Infernal machine' assassination attempt against the First Consul |
| 1801 | February | Peace of Lunéville with Austria |
| | July | Concordat signed between France and the papacy |
| 1802 | 2 April | Bonaparte declared consul for life |
| | 18 April | The Concordat proclaimed publicly |
| 1803 | 28 March | *Franc de Germinal* created |
| 1804 | 21 March | Abduction and execution of the duc d'Enghien |
| | 4 December | Bonaparte crowned Emperor Napoleon I |

# Introduction

> Far from being a bloc, the Revolution is possibly the most complex phenomenon that has ever existed. It is an essentially multiple phenomenon, diverse in its causes, in its elements, in its development, in its consequences.
>
> Albert Vandal, quoted in John McManners, 'The Revolution and its antecedents (1774–94)', in ed. J. M. Wallace-Hadrill and J. McManners, *France: Government and Society* (London, 1957), 161–87, at 161.

The appearance of yet another book on the French Revolution undoubtedly requires a forceful defence from its author, especially when some fine new texts from authors such as David Andress, Peter McPhee, and Don Sutherland have all been published within the last few years, while the second edition of William Doyle's acclaimed *Oxford History of the French Revolution* is also newly available. This is, by any standard, a crowded market filled with some distinguished products and consumer choice is appreciable. Public curiosity about what is available on a subject of compelling interest for any educated person is striking. It suggests that the Revolution continues to be consensually identified as the starting point of the modern world and has been an inspiration and source of division to successive generations in France in life and literature. The revolutionaries found it hard to stop the Revolution, and historians have re-fought the conflicts. Early twenty-first century scholars seek to anchor it in an eighteenth-century context, but it keeps breaking loose from those moorings and is still doing so.

The late François Furet, the leading modern historian of the Revolution, spent much of his professional life attempting to declare the Revolution 'over' and to treat it exclusively as a historical phenomenon. His efforts were widely respected but he was up against the decision of President François Mitterand to commemorate the Revolution, the *whole* of the Revolution, in just one year – 1989. This tactic conveniently served to focus attention on the opening 'liberal' (the fact that it occurred under the aegis of a monarchy was ignored by the Fifth Republic) era of the Revolution, but it could not prevent the debate escaping Mitterand's control. Within France, there was a sizeable minority of the public (including a number of those descended from those who died in the Vendée) which denied there was anything to celebrate and, on the international stage, the British Premier, Margaret Thatcher, famously denied that France had been the first state to be founded on a statement of public liberties, the Declaration of the Rights of Man. Had Mitterand forgotten, she enquired, the English Bill of Rights of exactly a century earlier? Historians also reflected and shaped the disquiet generated by the bicentennial anniversary of the Revolution. Wrecking the determination of the Republic to use 1989 as a focus of national harmony, there were counterblasts from a number of scholars in which scholarship and polemic were sometimes hard to distinguish.[1] Reynald Secher returned to his thesis first published in 1986 that France had 'invented' genocide in its repression of the Vendée royalists[2] and Simon Schama with his best-selling *Citizens!*, argued that violence was an intrinsic and ever-present part of the Revolution as it developed and an ineradicable stain on its memory.[3]

Schama's contention helped set the agenda of debate for much of the 1990s (it was many years before his book found a translator and a publisher in France) though other topics also established themselves as no less central than violence. The political interpretation of the Revolution was confirmed as the principal interpretative tool for understanding its causes and its course, while the role of women, the press, and the Counter-Revolution also moved to the fore. At last, the distinctive contribution of British and American historians to the study of the Revolution was recognised by the French establishment, especially that of Alfred Cobban whose *The Social Interpretation of the French Revolution* (1964) destroyed the foundations of the Marxist social interpretation of events that under Lefevbre and Soboul was very much historical orthodoxy at the Sorbonne 40 years ago, and Richard Cobb, whose disdain for politicians and their rhetoric inspired him to write about the impact of the Revolution (often very little) on the lives of the ordinary men and women of France as he encountered them in his archival forays.

Books from publishers across the world appeared in profusion in the aftermath of the bicentenary. Whatever else it did, it showed that interest in the Revolution was still high and there was a market for books and discussion. Meanwhile, historians have an amended range of preoccupations, partly born out of '1989'. Life-expired concepts like Marxism litter the landscape of debate and in due course the recent obsession with reading the Revolution as a series of 'speech-acts' will undoubtedly join it in limbo. A reaction against the negative readings of the Revolution by revisionists has set in without endangering an open spirit of enquiry through academic wrangling and party politics. It has been suggested that revolution historiography is returning to the mainstream of the liberal and democratic tradition, away from symbolic and ideological concerns, in a way which might be described as 'neodemocratic' or 'neo-Jacobin'. It is attempting to regain a place in the history of liberalism and democracy from which revisionism had threatened to displace it.[4] One reliable gauge to this altered climate came in 2002 when Lynn Hunt, one of the outstanding American scholars in the field since the 1970s, gave her presidential address 'The World We Have Gained: The Future of the French Revolution' to the American Historical Association and the contents, though typically subtle, mirrored the quietly affirmative title. She called for a truce in saying (p. 3) that 'the interpretive forebears need not be wrong for me to be right'. This is far from a postmodern escape clause. It reflects the sense within the profession, again to quote Professor Hunt, that all historians are currently trying to achieve is 'a partial, provisional, and always revocable agreement on what needs to be explained, if not on how to explain it'.

It is in this spirit that the essay which follows has been written. The rediscovery of social history has been one of the most satisfying aspects of the writing of the last 15 years, freed as it is from its Marxist shadow, in its current expression an outgrowth of the ubiquitous vogue for cultural history writing. It is particularly refreshing that scholars of the calibre of Colin Jones and Jean-Pierre Hirsch are making us look again for a revolutionary bourgeoisie.[5] Similarly, scholarly interest in Napoleonic topics (partially fuelled by a host of commemorations to come between now and 2021) gathers pace. This is as it should be: the 1790s have been exhaustively studied from a variety of angles; consideration of the next decade, the 1800s, has been less thorough and less recent. It is with that consideration in mind that this book makes no apology for extending the Revolution into the nineteenth century and treating the Consulate as a period of attempted closure. This approach is a provisional, perhaps artificial exercise, some might say; the Revolution began suddenly and the speed with which events unrolled startled and excited contemporaries; ending it, by contrast, has been an unceasing task that has yet to be completed. Perhaps, but here at least I end with the Consulate.

Readers can also expect to find this book wary of treating the Revolution as an artificial entity, despite its rhetorical convenience as such for both contemporaries and subsequent scholars. 'The French Revolution' is a received historical construction, useful as an explanatory tool, but its meanings (where it had one) for those living through it were bewilderingly diverse and personal. It is in that spirit of respect for those living through these years of momentous and unpredictable change (the effect of the Revolution for most lives was to shorten rather than improve them) that my book is wary of offering any all-embracing theoretical framework, and it is not committed to any particular form of historical interpretation. It emphasises the contingent nature of the Revolution as it developed. It could so easily have ended differently, in as much as an 'ending' was feasible in the first place. The Revolution was in many respects fortunate to survive until 1799 given the ever- present prospect of a military coup which loomed large in the minds of the politicians almost from the early sessions of the Estates-General. Most never trusted the military men, who in turn came to despise their stumbling and usually divisive attempts to lead the French republic. The book also respects the growth in interest in the Counter-Revolution as topic in its own right, and accepts the proposition that the Counter-Revolution (in all its variant forms for in that respect it mirrored its Revolutionary opposite) was at least as popular as the Revolution with the bulk of the French population, and incontestably attracted the allegiance of most women. I have also attempted to consider the Revolution as it appeared to foreigners, as well as placing it within the wider context of revolutionary outbreaks in the later eighteenth century. Foreign perceptions have been accorded a separate chapter, but they also figure (often by reference to a primary source) throughout the book. A reflective narrative is offered for the first third of the book followed by thematic discussions. There is a recurrent and underlying stress on the difficulty of reconciling liberty with authority until the climate of uncertainty and instability of the Revolutionary decade made those who had gained by it desperate for the liquidation that only Bonaparte seemed able to provide.

To revert to my original question, what does this book offer that the others do not? The answer is simply a difference in emphasis to those of other scholars (if only to keep duplication to a minimum) without turning the book into a historiographical exercise, for details about the way in which the Revolution has been written up are readily available today. I have tried to limit my engagements with other historians to those currently working in the field. This has seemed to me most useful for my prospective readers' angle. I doubt that I shall return to the French Revolution as a subject for a book, so this one is inevitably something of a valedictory personal testament. After 30 years studying it, my underlying sympathy for the people who managed to live through the Revolution and, above all, for the millions who died because of it, continues to increase. These were supremely disruptive times in which a quiet life was not easily had. Whatever else it was, the Revolution was not in practice about peaceful change. Its ideals were considered nonnegotiable by the series of politicians who proclaimed them and to question them soon showed – whatever the Declaration of the Rights of Man proclaimed – the limits of pluralism.

PART I

*The Unfolding of the Revolution, 1789–1804*

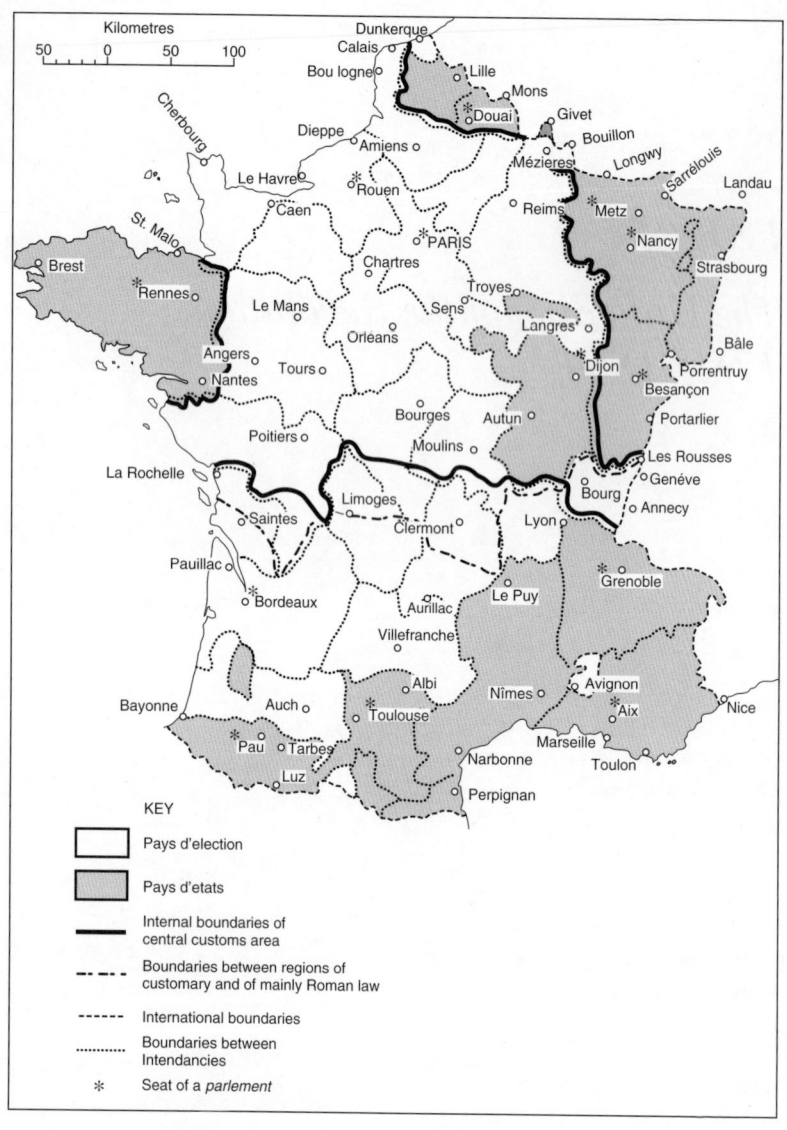

Map 1　France in 1789

# Chapter 1: The End of the Monarchy, 1789–1792

## The Prelude to the Estates-General, May 1789

The French Revolution of 1789 was the product of medium-term political and financial crises within the state and the destabilising efforts made to resolve them. Recognition of the stress points in the French polity pre-dated the start of Louis XVI's reign in 1774, and tended to centre on taxation, the viability of France's institutional framework, and the need for a more effective working relationship between the royal government and the governed. An educated, well-intentioned king had, more than a decade into his reign, been unable to discharge the formidable sovereign responsibilities that it was his ancestral right to operate, in a manner that suggested those problem areas might be progressively remedied. The king himself was temperamentally ill-suited to rule as a Louis-Quatorzian style absolutist: for the first decade after his accession he depended heavily on the ill-matched guidance of veterans such as Maurepas and Vergennes and newcomers to government such as Turgot and Necker, and gave no impression of personal decisiveness akin to his dynamic brother-in-law, the Emperor Joseph II (1780–90). His reign down to the mid-1780s had been remarkable for high political instability and factional squabbling, and there were signs that both the public and (some) politicians were ready to look at the alternatives if the executive monarchy did not possess the resourcefulness or the resources to regenerate the state and public life within it. The stakes were high, even France's survival as a major European power. The defeat of Britain in the American War of Independence (1778–83) temporarily added a lustre to France's foreign policy, but setbacks between 1783 and 1787 quickly blew away any sense of complacency.

It increasingly appeared that the absolutist dimension of the monarchy had failed France and was no longer appropriate to the times. Such sentiments were first glimpsed when the War of the Spanish Succession (1702–13) brought France close to collapse, but the perception really became both entrenched and articulated from the 1750s onwards as a loose alliance of magistrates, *philosophes*, and Jansenists emerged with demands for constitutional changes that would bring the monarchy into closer, formalised partnership with the wider French elite on the British model, and temper or dismantle its absolute power. The good sense of legitimising the authority of the state in a framework that was wider and more representative of the French people than just the person of the monarch had become generally admitted and took expression in demands for the Estates-General to be convened. The Crown was ready in principle to respond constructively and waste no further time on adapting and updating the workings of government both nationally and locally. On the other hand, the well-meaning monarch, ever conscious of what he owed to his ancestors, was wary of committing himself to any plan that might be seen as a betrayal of his royal inheritance. Calling the Estates-General would be a risky venture that might well end in further destabilisation rather than its opposite; on the other hand, the fiscal crisis that threatened to overwhelm the monarchy after the end of the American War left little room for inaction. Moreover, the majority of Louis's ministers still believed that it was for the monarchy alone to design and to introduce reforms. They did not intend to have the pace of change set by the magistrates in the thirteen *parlements* who, encouraged by Montesquieu's famous *L'Esprit des lois* (first published 1748), and in the absence since 1614 of the Estates-General, regarded themselves as the most important 'intermediary Order' guarding the king's subjects from the unbridled operation of his prerogative, and had legislative pretensions based on their claim to 'represent' the nation. The suppression of the *parlements* between 1771 and 1774 by Chancellor Maupeou was viewed by the government as an indispensable precondition of reform, by most of Louis XV's politically informed subjects (Voltaire was the most famous exception and sympathised with the monarchy's actions) as a reminder of how powerful the Crown remained and how flimsy were the liberties of Louis's subjects.

The *parlements* were marginalised for only three years. In 1774 a new king, Louis XV's 20-year-old grandson, recalled them in a goodwill gesture and also gave France a *philosophe* as Controller-General in the shape of Turgot. Brimful of reform schemes, he lacked the skills required either to implement them or persuade the majority of his colleagues to back him, not least the septuagenarian First Minister, Maurepas, possessed of a cautionary conservatism to match his age: he stayed in office until his death in 1781, Turgot was forced out five years earlier having accomplished little; his career a striking reminder that no minister could be a reformer without having a secure power base among the Court factions. He was eventually replaced by the Swiss Protestant banker, Jacques Necker, in itself a sign of the government's openness to Enlightenment influences. He was a masterly politician, an Anglophile, and as conscious of the growing power of public opinion as he was over-conscious of his own consummate skills. No friend to the French status quo, he attempted to introduce a new professionalism into the royal treasury, and inaugurated the first two provincial assemblies.

Necker saw wide consultation of the propertied in the heartlands of France as essential if reform was to be effective, achieved on the basis of consensus rather than imposed from above. He hoped to court provincial opinion and involve its leaders in a new relationship with the monarchy via the creation of provincial assemblies and the revival of provincial estates. His successor after 1783, the former *intendant* Alexandre de Calonne, disagreed with this diagnosis and these initiatives. Under his auspices, political life returned to its Court base, major upheavals were avoided, and reform initiatives discouraged. Calonne, however, incurred the displeasure of some of the leading noble dynasties in the kingdom (many of whom hankered after the sort of official place in public life granted to the British peerage) by his failure to offer them adequate offices at Court, and he could not avoid a running battle in the press with Necker and his supporters over the extent of the public deficit created by French participation in the American War. After three years of successfully raising credit on the European financial markets and rather overheating the French economy, Calonne was ready for a daring initiative that would enable him to introduce a new, universally applicable land tax that he hoped would both reduce the existing public debt and place government finances on a steadier basis in future.

That initiative took the form of summoning an Assembly of Notables (the first since 1626) to Versailles to 'advise' the king on policy. It was non-elected, and though Calonne permitted fellow ministers to put forward their nominees to fill the 144 seats it was not enough to win their wholehearted commitment to his scheme. Conservative colleagues such as the marquis de Castries, the navy minister, and Miromesnil, Keeper of the Seals (the *de facto* head of the judiciary even though Maurepas on paper remained Chancellor), feared that such an assembly undermined the sovereign authority vested exclusively in the monarch and could have been avoided completely had Calonne not been so unpopular with the Paris *parlement*. Unfortunately for Calonne, his most important ally, the Foreign Minister Vergennes, died on the eve of the final convening of the Assembly in February 1787, leaving him with only the king as an ally.

Calonne was relying on the Notables to give him their approval of new taxation on behalf of the wider nation; with that consent secure, Calonne reckoned his position in the government would be unassailable. However, his calculation that the Notables would quickly 'rubber-stamp' his plans proved well wide of the mark. With a membership drawn predominantly from the Court nobility, the bishops of the Gallican Church, and administrators and mayors from some of the main cities in France, the Notables settled down swiftly into what they assumed was a genuine legislative role. In each bureau of the Assembly, the form of Calonne's land tax and the rest of his reform package was expertly scrutinised by informed critics who were ready to submit alternatives adjudged both fairer and more viable. They were not well-born reactionaries selfishly refusing reforms that were demonstrably in the best interests of France; they accepted the desirability of changes that would increase the stake of propertied men in decision-making processes but, having thoroughly absorbed their Montesquieu, they denied the admissibility of reforms imposed by the Crown unilaterally.[1] These leading noblemen and prelates argued that the rights of Frenchmen needed protecting from an over-powerful and wayward executive. Indeed, the resistance to Calonne's plans once and for all indicated that, although respect for the institution of monarchy remained high, French notables (i.e. the political elite drawn from all three Estates) were insistent that the exercise of royal authority along absolutist lines was quite unacceptable: 'ministerial despotism' had to give way to what was presented as an earlier model of monarchy based on consultation of the king's most important subjects.

This thinking lay behind the insistence of the Assembly of Notables that, since they were non-elected, they were not empowered to consent to new taxation, especially when, straining incredulity, Calonne reluctantly revealed the extraordinary size of the deficit. Instead, ministers were asked to summon the representatives of the nation to meet in an Estates-General (none had convened since 1614) that could, in partnership with the Crown, give France a constitution that would at last bring her into line with the unwritten, but on the whole libertarian, conventions of Westminster and the brand new written settlement for the United States of America drawn up in Philadelphia and resoundingly proclaimed in 1787. Reluctant both to yield up any of their own power or to venture into completely unfamiliar but in all likelihood very choppy waters, the government only caved into the demand for the Estates-General over a year later, in July 1788, by which date Calonne had crossed to England and was trying to vindicate himself against his numerous detractors. The refusal of the Assembly of Notables to sanction his reform proposals had effectively forced him out of office in April 1787 and one of his principal enemies in the Assembly, Loménie de Brienne, archbishop of Toulouse, eventually replaced him as First Minister (his official title from August 1787). Despite the unprecedented authority accorded him, Brienne was no more successful than Calonne in coaxing the Notables into co-operation. The Assembly was dissolved in May 1787, and Brienne returned to the customary method of taking royal edicts through the *parlements*, in this case, an amended version of Calonne's land tax.

It did not work. With ministers unwilling to divulge full budgetary information to satisfy their critics and the *parlementaires* resolute in their argument that the Estates-General was the only organ in a position to consent to this financial resettlement, an impasse was soon reached. Failure to make progress drove Brienne back on the expedient of extending the existing *vingtièmes*, which was at least acceptable to the magistrates. Resentments festered over the winter of 1787–8, but there was a lingering reluctance among ministers to give in gracefully. Notorious incidents like the king's insistence on registration of financial edicts because that was 'his will', and the May Edicts of 1788, which drastically curtailed the power of the *parlements*, lent force to the arguments of those who denied that the Crown was really interested in working with its leading subjects, and pointed to the absolutist preferences of policy brokers like Lamoignon, Miromesnil's successor as Keeper of the Seals. The latter's kinsman and ex-minister, Malesherbes, was one of many who advocated a volte-face. In a memoir of June 1788, he urged the king to be bold and accept the out-of-doors demand for a constitution: 'The time is past when one can seek to mislead the Nation.... Let us speak clearly'.[2] Under pressure, archbishop Brienne gave ground and appeared to abandon authoritarian tactics. His consent to the Estates-General in July 1788 was the final admittance that the government could not dictate a constitutional and fiscal reordering. It inaugurated a period of executive drift that had momentous consequences. The frustration of ministerial initiatives in

1786–8 was one of the principal reasons behind the Crown's crucial reluctance to take the lead in making further proposals once the Estates-General gathered in May 1789. There was an expectation of royal leadership that never materialised until the Estates-General gave up waiting, developed a taste for independence, and unilaterally converted itself into the National Assembly – with impunity.

Financial necessity made the government vulnerable to political pressure in this pre-revolutionary period and negated the possibility of France going to war against Britain and Prussia in late summer 1787 to defend its political interests and allies in the Dutch United Provinces,[3] the supreme manifestation of what Bailey Stone has grandiloquently called 'a gradually developing crisis of governmental legitimacy in the domestic sphere paralleling and eventually interacting with the gradually developing crisis of French credibility in the international strategic sphere'.[4] Debt threatened to overwhelm the state and cripple existing expenditure schemes. Hence the justification for a new land tax and the eventual grudging acceptance that the changes must be overseen by the Estates-General. Tax reform and representation for taxpayers were, by the second half of the eighteenth century, the two sides of the same coin, as the *philosophes*, drawing their inspiration from the English 'Revolutionary' settlement of 1689, had often pointed out. The difficulties experienced by Brienne in 1788 in raising loans on foreign capital markets were tied up with the public reluctance of ministers to admit that this was now the only practicable way forward. No doubt demand for consensual government in France could have been resisted slightly longer had the financial crisis been less acute and so propelled the pace of change. That crisis had, as is well known, been aggravated through the decision to enter the American War of Independence in 1778; by how much was vigorously debated by partisans of Necker and Calonne in pamphlet warfare after the former's famous *Compte rendu* (1781) insisted that France was in slight surplus. More to the point, France embarked on fresh hostilities only 15 years after her previous global engagement with Britain in the Seven Years War had concluded. But the difference between the two powers was that whereas Britain possessed an efficient machinery of public credit through such institutions as the Bank of England and a public debt guaranteed by Parliament, in France arrangements ultimately depended on the honour of the monarchy and the goodwill of ministers to pay their creditors – eventually. It was small comfort that Louis XVI was known to be averse as a matter of personal honour to repudiating the national debt given his proven capacity for being pressured by interested parties into changing his mind.

For centuries the Bourbon monarchy had weathered the financial problems caused by the cost of wars. The French Revolution occurs, indeed, six years after the Treaty of Versailles (1783) rather than after the Treaty of Paris (1763). The Seven Years War left a deficit of 16 million *livres* that within three years had been reduced to just under three million, and that was achieved without resort to the sort of constitutional changes which, a quarter of a century on, ended the traditional monarchical order. The question as to what made the difference in the 1780s is therefore fundamental. The will of the elite to perpetuate what would soon be referred to as the *ancien régime* had weakened. The American example undoubtedly kindled interest in France imitating her junior, republican ally and internally negotiating a revised constitutional settlement that would, of course, be monarchical (a republican government was never a serious political option for France in the 1780s even if republican values were lauded) and could be presented, to a greater or lesser degree, as on all-fours with an earlier, now recovered model of government and governing that was pre-absolutist in character. And, given that royal power was constrained by the huge fiscal shortfalls that followed soon after the signing of peace with Britain in 1783, ministers like Calonne and Brienne saw little to lose by going along with the fashionably insistent demands for representative government, particularly if the prize in the medium term was sound state finances.

Such thinking underscored Brienne's announcement in July 1788 that the Estates-General would meet – though admittedly not for a further five years. The decision was accompanied by a request to members of the public that they offer their advice about the form the assembly should take and the issues it should discuss. It was a concession to the storm of protest aroused by the May Edicts, but not enough in itself to disarm the suspicions of the ministry's opponents in Paris and the provinces. Neither did it persuade the capital markets that Brienne and Lamoignon were in charge of the situation. In the late summer of 1788 the government was unable to secure the advance of further loans to meet its immediate needs, and in August 1788 the French treasury was obliged to suspend payments to its creditors. It was bankruptcy in all but name.

There is broad agreement among recent historians that this single event was the point of no return for the traditional monarchy. The government no longer had any choice except to stand by the tokens of constitutionalist intention it had offered the previous month. Its last 'despotic' attempt to impose change through the May Edicts was nullified, and the *parlementaires* returned from exile. It was finally accepted in most quarters that the situation could only be retrieved by bringing forward the date of the Estates-General to January 1789, and by Brienne offering his resignation to be replaced (much to the distaste of Louis personally) by the darling of the nation and the financiers, Jacques Necker. Absolutism could only have been salvaged by the monarchy repudiating its debts entirely, and some conservative politicians had argued in favour of it without convincing the king, as ever acutely aware of his obligations to his subjects and unwilling to incur the odium of bad faith.

The sense of what was appropriate in a civic society where responsible and patriotic conduct was required at every level was so widely diffused in late eighteenth-century France that it was even respected by the head of state. With the Estates-General imminent, the country could expect to receive the updated institutional infrastructure in which his subjects' sense of civic virtue (a quality Enlightenment authors like Montesquieu customarily associated with a republic) could be given ample expression. The idea rather than the practicalities of the Estates-General was perhaps what made it so desirable in people's minds; they did not necessarily know what the Estates-General would entail, but they knew that they wanted it. At the heart of such patriotic sentiments lay a desire for the renewal of public life that owed a lot to the writings of Rousseau and his popularisers. Expectations of what could be achieved were high within a nation whose political sophistication demanded new forms of expression. It could be accommodated within the organs of the existing order, but the archaic legal theory that they operated in isolation looking only to the Crown and without necessary reference to a public domain was no longer sustainable.

Public interest in constitutionalism went so deep by the 1780s that the few apologists for a revamped absolutist monarchy such as Moreau found an audience hard to come by. Absolutism may have been increasingly adjudged outmoded, but at least it had allowed the nurturing of fresh political outlooks and led to an emerging consensus that any 'solution' was to be found within the monarchy's own heritage in a new appeal to history, one that would return France to a mode of ruling that was recognisably in accordance with Bourbon tradition and offered a precedent capable of adaptation in difficult times. Pamphleteers claimed that the nation was entitled through the Estates-General to retrieve constitutional rights that were as old as the French Crown, and only recently overlain by an alternative model of monarchy. The impetus to change grew out of a public rhetoric which had long stressed the 'rights' of corporate bodies like the sovereign Courts, and stood ready to endow a much wider constituency – the entire French nation – with similar prescriptive powers. It had its roots in the tradition of aristocratic constitutionalism that had surfaced during the Fronde in the mid-seventeenth century and during the Regency (1715–23), and now incorporated into it participatory rights for all property holders. The British example (however imperfectly understood) remained a constant source of inspiration, but it had been the creation of the United States and the events leading up to it that had really caught the imagination of the French elite. And where nations had been created, so they could be recreated with a government genuinely accountable to a legislature representative of citizen–subjects.

In all this, public opinion had come to be seen as the final court of appeal rather than the Crown. The Revolution would confirm the importance of this 'public sphere' that had been evident to practising politicians, pamphleteers, and *philosophes* since at least the mid-century and, it has been argued, really been an aspect of national life since the minority of Louis XIII in the 1610s.[5] In his *Essai sur les Moeurs* of 1763 Voltaire talked of 'opinion' as the main mechanism by which societies made and observed laws, changed and modernised, and conferred legitimacy on their rulers. Although elusive and hard to define precisely, politicians of Louis XVI's reign were ready to cultivate public opinion, particularly Necker. He fought out in pamphlets his dispute with Calonne over the existence of a budget deficit, at stake the chance of a return to government irrespective of the king's preference. Public opinion duly ensured that Necker 'stormed the closet' in August 1788, a minister foisted on Louis much as Fox and North had been on George III in Britain five years previously when they formed their notorious Coalition. Such a verdict underlined the point that royal policies generally, let alone a new constitutional settlement, could not be imposed.

Whatever the wishes of his more conservative advisers, Louis XVI had no intention of doing so. His personal conversion to consultative government had been apparent as early as June 1788 when he requested that the public be welcome to forward its views about the elections and format of the Estates-General. Few considered that reproducing the arrangements of 1614 would be either appropriate or possible, and they had not been followed when reviving the Provincial Estates in the Dauphiné in July 1788 where the First and Second Estates received only half the places. The *parlementaire* critics of the government remained watchful. Their main objective was to ensure that the Estates-General had a weight that would guard against its ministerial manipulation. It was this line of thinking which lay behind the well-known remonstrances issued by the Parlement of Paris in September 1788 asking that the Estates-General should be arranged according to the forms and precedents of 1614. The recommendation was not popular with the public. If it was followed, the 95 per cent of Frenchmen who were neither clerics nor noblemen would receive only one-third of the seats. And whatever their apprehensions about the use of royal power, these members of the Third Estate had an increasingly sharp sense of what was due to them. Keen though most remained to present a united front with the two other Orders, they thought in terms of an equitable partnership. Inspired by brilliant polemics, including Sieyes's *Qu'est-ce que le Tiers Etat?*, the non-nobles defended their own interests rather than rely any longer on the protection of the 'Intermediary Orders' of the clergy and nobility (as Montesquieu had defined them), who might be more inclined to protect their own 'privileges'. Interestingly, this militancy was not without influential aristocratic sympathisers up to and including the cadet royal house of Orléans, and great nobles like Biron, Lafayette and La Rochefoucauld. Late Enlightenment forms of clubbability, not least the Masonic lodges, led to all kinds of informal exchanges that unavoidably had a high political content in the winter of 1788–9. And Sieyes was also member of the influential Society of Thirty, a patriotic political caucus lobbying hard for change in the run-up to May 1789.

The division of France for electoral purposes into three distinguishable Orders was a clumsy device that had a limited relation to the social reality of the upper reaches of society, but any attempt to treat nobles and senior clergy as one as in the British model was off the agenda: ministers had no wish to be accused of 'despotism' by abandoning the legal precedents of 1614. But they were able to identify the political maturity of the bourgeoisie by 1788, and were ready to acknowledge the fact, not least because the traditional elite had seemed (from the Crown's angle) so recalcitrant in the unfolding crisis since 1786. There was nevertheless much trepidation in official circles at the consequences of giving the Third Estate half the seats in the Estates-General. Necker havered for most of the autumn, and summoned a second Assembly of Notables to advise the government. It submitted a majority recommendation against doubling the Third Estate that increased rather than reduced the pressures on him. On 27 December 1788, after a full consultation among ministers, there was a narrow majority (including the king and queen) in favour of the *doublement*. It was a major concession to the nationwide agitation on behalf of the Third Estate, and earned Louis XVI and Necker immense personal gratitude (Louis was unofficially hailed as the 'restorer of French liberty' for a few months) despite the disappointment that voting arrangements had been declared a matter for the Estates-General itself to determine.

After this daring alignment of the Crown with the aspirations of the majority, Necker was not frightened of electoral adjustments that complemented the concessions to the Third Estate and were calculated to enhance his popularity further. There were few surprises as regards the nobility. All were eligible to vote in the electoral assemblies and stand for election to Versailles in accordance with the practice of 1614. Yet the lumping together of everyone, from impoverished provincial aristocrats with nothing but a blue-blooded descent, to the wealthy Court elite interested in a British-style House of Lords that guaranteed places for themselves, was courting trouble. In the Church, ripples were created on 24 January 1789 when it was announced that bishops and lower clergy were automatically entitled to vote, but only a proportion of the higher clergy and monastic orders. The decision ran counter to the hierarchical assumptions of the First Estate that had held good for centuries, and was, if anything, more radical than the concessions made to the Third Estate the previous month.

## The Meeting of the Estates-General

This was always going to be a spectacular adventure, a journey into unknown country, for no one living could have had any experience of running the Estates-General and the monarchy in tandem. Nevertheless, the indicators for the Crown were encouraging. The constitutional concessions to date had won it immense popular goodwill; those familiar ingredients of political crisis – aristocratic factionalism and financial penury – had been met by calling on the whole propertied nation to contain them; and so long as the provincial discontent at the meagre harvest of 1788 could be contained until the late summer, it was quite possible that the prize of an efficient, modernised monarchical state could have been achieved.

When it finally convened on 4 May 1789, the Third Estate was given every opportunity for taking the initiative. Few deputies could ever have foreseen the chance coming by default. And yet, amid splendid ceremonial, ministers had neither offered a package of reform measures in the opening speeches nor offered guidance about the format of proceedings. It reflected the extent to which the Crown was imaginatively as well as fiscally bankrupt, but still more the unwillingness of Necker and his colleagues to risk the charge of 'despotism' even if the consequence was abandoning government-led reform initiatives entirely. Deputies were just left to their own devices. It was at least clear to the socially respectable, politically inexperienced Third Estate deputies that reforms would need the co-operation of the other two Orders, but that could not be at the price of conceding vote by Order rather than by head (i.e. individually). They insisted that before substantive business could be discussed, deputies should verify their powers – their electoral mandates – as one body rather than as separate Estates. Whatever was decided would set a decisive precedent for the conduct of proceedings thereafter.

Despite a sizable liberal minority prepared to temporise, the nobility called their numbers over and declared their house constituted. Thereupon the divisions among the clergy were crucial, for the First Estate held the key to resolving the deadlock. The bishops and higher clergy had fought hard enough in the elections to ensure nearly a quarter of the places, and while most of them were reluctant to abandon the nobility, equally the necessity of restraining the restless *curés-députés* from a precipitant junction with the 'Commons' made them ready to listen sympathetically to delegations from the Third Estate appealing to their conciliatory sense. No collective decision was taken before the first priests in early June left their own chamber to join the 'Commons', and every day saw more of them do likewise. Tired of waiting for a formal response from their colleagues, the Third Estate had meanwhile unilaterally declared itself on 11 June to be the 'National Assembly' and ready to begin work. Historians have usually seen this as one of the key revolutionary moments in 1789, echoing the English commentator Arthur Young, who wrote that 'The step the commons have taken . . . is in fact an assumption of all the authority in the kingdom. They have at one stroke converted themselves into the long parliament of Charles I'.[6] It was certainly a brave gesture with rhetorical echoes of the American Declaration of Independence in 1776, and was another act of disobedience against the Crown. But it was born out of frustration rather than the politically heroic. Deputies were sensitive to the pent-up irritation of their constituents that procedural obfuscations were stunting the great expectations of reform, and coming to terms with a political landscape where the Crown had abdicated responsibility to the nation. They nevertheless hoped Louis was still on their side.

The king, urged on by advisers close to his wife and brothers, and numbed by private tragedy (the Dauphin had just died), responded to developments by ordering a 'Royal Session' [*Séance royale*] at Versailles, at which he could belatedly lay down the ground rules for reform. As each day brought more clergy – and some bishops – and noblemen to sit down with the Third Estate, rumours flew round Versailles that the king was under pressure to suspend the Assembly rather than give the lead. It was typical of the broken lines of communication that when deputies found themselves locked out of their normal meeting place on 20 June they should see this as the first stage in a royal coup and take refuge in an indoor tennis Court, vowing not to go home until France had received a constitution. Meanwhile ministers quarrelled over the contents of the king's speech at the 'Royal Session' and Necker deliberately absented himself from the occasion on 23 June rather than be publicly seen as party to a limited reform initiative that no longer corresponded to the national mood as expressed by the Third Estate. Having just become used to the absence of royal authority, deputies were not prepared to tolerate its revival when directed against 'the nation'. The king's speech announced the end of the Crown – Third Estate alliance that had endured for six months, and it prompted arguably the most heroic incident in the Revolution to date when Third Estate deputies refused to return to their own chamber.

Louis lacked the commitment to his publicly stated policy to enforce it, even if he could have relied on the army to use force against their fellow countrymen. With Necker back in place, for the second time within a year Louis 'deserted' the conservative majorities in the First and Second Estates and ordered them on 29 June to join the *tiers état* in forming a National Assembly. Gratitude and relief characterised the response of the majority at having the king behind them once more, and any hopes of the traditionalist minority that voting by Order had survived were soon dashed. Within days, it was plain that the awkward, archaic revival of the historic Orders for electoral purposes would not survive the junction: nobility and clergy were subsumed within the nation when it was decreed that voting 'by head' should be standard practice. It was at this point (second week of July) that, looking to his youngest brother, Necker's enemies, the comte d'Artois and the baron de Breteuil, finally succeeded in driving the Genevan out of office. And when Hussars appeared in the Tuileries Gardens on 12 July it seemed as if the long-rumoured royalist counterstroke was at hand. If it was, the demolition of the Bastille on 14 July by a Parisian crowd pre-empted it. The infant National Assembly was secure, but at the price of protection from the *menu peuple* rather than the monarchy.

Did the monarchy pose a threat to what was identifiably a Revolution in 1789? Having let slip the scope for leadership offered by the convening of the Estates-General, Louis was ill placed to recover it at the end of June when his intelligence admitted the nation's wishes and his temperament was averse to coercion. On the other hand, he was sensitive to the fears of his family and their wishes coincided over the removal of Necker. His dismissal amounted to an ill-timed attempt to revive the royal prerogative of selecting ministers (latterly so circumscribed) when Louis was no more willing than he had ever been to back his judgment with force. The incident sent out all the wrong signals to the revolutionaries, and precipitated the fall of the Bastille, the failure of the 'Ministry of the hundred hours' and Necker's return within four days. The latter was as essential to the credibility of government in July 1789 as he had been in August 1788, his vindication a token symbol of the monarchy's reluctant goodwill towards the Third Estate and their allies on the streets. Additional confirmation was given on 17 July when Louis visited his capital in person and blessed by adoption the new revolutionary colours of red, white and blue. The dramatic significance of these developments cannot be overstated. As one British minister observed: 'I believe it is...the only instance that two such changes have happened in the Government of any nation in the course of one week'.[7] None of these gestures could disguise the fact that Louis's shuffling conduct had eaten into the reserve of popular goodwill he had accumulated over the previous year, especially when Artois sped over the frontier to Brussels. There was no republican alternative at this early stage, but the contrast with his cousin, the dissipated but libertarian Philippe, duc d'Orléans, was stark. The duc's Parisian base, the Palais Royal, had long been a foyer for reformers, and Philippe's backers (if not the duc personally) presented him as a ready-made alternative monarch; his opponents as the furtive architect of the Revolution, intent on becoming king instead of Louis. Orléans was motivated less by desire for the throne than an uncomplicated wish to revenge himself on the king and express his biting, enduring distrust of Marie-Antoinette. If there was a throne lined up for him in 1789–90 it was that of Belgium, the Austrian Netherlands being in revolt against the centralising policies of the Emperor Joseph II. Letters from Montmorin to Orléans when the latter had been sent on a phantom diplomatic mission to Britain in late 1789 make clear that such a solution would have been very acceptable to Louis XVI, keeping his troublesome cousin out of France while recovering influence on the north-eastern frontier.[8]

Louis had no intention of resigning his throne. Whatever his private misgivings and resentments (and they were substantial), he acquiesced in the creation of a new constitutional order by the National Assembly over a two-year period from August 1789 and his diminished role in it as 'king of the French'. The two most recent biographers of Louis XVI, Evelyn Lever and John Hardman, have tended to deprecate the changes imposed on the monarchy and stress the limitations on royal power under the Constitution of 1791,[9] but this view is less convincing than it sounds. For a start, the Revolution merely speeded up the conversion of absolute into constitutional monarchy, a process that many modern scholars argue had started no later than the 1750s. Sovereignty indeed passed officially from the monarch to his people but the former remained as head of state, shorn of divine sanction but now, at least as usefully, the embodiment of the popular will. In the name of the nation, Louis retained room for political manouevre. Admittedly, he could no longer initiate legislation, but his approval was required to pass it and his power of suspensive veto was a formidable weapon, one that could be used far more flexibly than the absolute veto possessed by the British monarch, George III. In terms of power, the kings of France and Britain were relatively well-matched from 1789 to 1791. Both selected their ministers, could not dismiss the judges without legislative consent, sanctioned legislation, and disposed of formidable patronage in Church and state.[10] As Philip Mansel has shown, French Court life survived the onset of the Revolution, even the enforced move from Versailles to the Tuileries in October 1789.[11] Arguably, in widening Court circles the Revolution invigorated formalities, a trend enhanced by the monarchy's desire to display its dignity under pressure. The dress code remained uncompromising. The young Countess of Sutherland, wife of the new British envoy Earl Gower, complained to a friend in July 1790 that she had 'to go a miserable criminal to the Tuileries in a Court hoop, ... I hope by the power of habit to accustom my *état physique & morale* so much to these novelties that I may be in time an excellent *Cortessiana* (not to say *Courtessiana*)'.[12] Royal protocol during the constitutional monarchy compared colourfully with the staid, domestic flavour of Windsor Castle. The crucial difference between the two countries lay surely in this, that whereas George worked within a constitutional framework that was a century old, Louis had to come to terms with a new polity lacking in established conventions and ground rules. This was the real test of statesmanship for the king, and one that he might have passed.

## The Reform Agenda of the National Assembly

The remodelling of royal authority in the early autumn was seen by deputies as the foundation of those which affected virtually every other institution in what was coming to be identified as the 'Old Order'. The piecemeal network of agencies and jurisdictions was replaced by rationalised, graduated power structures with national application in accordance with the general principles laid down in the Declaration of the Rights of Man and of the Citizen (26 August 1789). American influences counted for much in its production. The federal and state constitutions were widely read by deputies and several suggested these and the states' bills of rights as models; Thomas Jefferson, minister to France, was consulted frequently on successive drafts of the Declaration.[13] The *parlements* and the other sovereign courts were abolished, as their existence was incompatible with the authority of the National Assembly. Deputies regarded the doctrine of the separation of powers as a preservative against corruption (particularly originating from the executive), and while the king retained the right to appoint ministers they could not be members of the legislature. Local government was completely overhauled with a strong emphasis on decentralisation. Not just intendants and governors were abolished. So were the provinces and *généralités* they administered to be replaced by departments, districts, communes and cantons. The structures of the judiciary were also reordered and the abolition of venality transformed the composition of the bench. Two informing principles underpinned the National Assembly's enactments. First, the supremacy of law in French public life and, second, land ownership as a passport to participation in affairs of state at any level and status as an active citizen. In other words, beneath the rhetoric of national rejuvenation that had its echoes throughout provincial France, the politicians of 1789–91 were intent on creating a state governed by men of substance. It was impressively wide by late eighteenth-century standards, but still recognisably an elite. Though a majority of French citizens were granted the franchise and were deemed 'active' citizens, they were not consulted as the men of 1789 made the constitution.[14] In fact the binding mandates deputies had been given by their constituents when they first went to Versailles were promptly discarded at the junction of the three Orders, and the suggestion on 7 July that deputies should secure new instructions from the electorate was overruled.

The Assembly also did little to ease the tax burden on the majority of citizens, and acted quickly to restore contributions following the brief 'tax holiday' that was the product of the collapse of institutional life in July–August 1789. Legislation confirmed the recommendations found in the Cahiers of all three Orders: the abolition of exemptions and the related principle of contributions according to wealth. Tax farming was abandoned, along with the *gabelle* and the internal tariffs which had restricted the flow of goods around the country. But the advent of the Revolution could not in itself alter the structural and organisational problems that worked against fiscal efficiency. Necker certainly had no panacea. He pinned his hopes on the traditional expedient of raising loans on the foreign capital markets and a satisfactory grain harvest in 1789. He was fortunate in both, but his inability to propose innovatory and equitable tax policies was fatal to his popularity in the winter of 1789–90.

Faced with a deficit that grew despite Revolution, the politicians needed a desperate expedient or risk the burden of debt overwhelming the new constitutional order much as it had the traditional monarchy in August 1788. The key to control was reckoned to be making that debt genuinely national much as had occurred in England after the 'Glorious Revolution' of 1689, and that in turn required guarantees on a scale that would satisfy government creditors. The security was to hand in the form of Church lands, and these were taken over by the state in December 1789. The Church, despite having voluntarily sacrificed its tithes during the heady proceedings of 4 August, further offered a voluntary 'patriotic' contribution in September but that was not enough to satisfy the Assembly. The nation's needs brooked no delay and the Church lost every acre it owned.

There was no compensation, no meaningful attempt at negotiation. Deputies were persuaded that the merger of the Orders in July at a stroke deprived the Church of its corporate status, and refused to concede that the Church, while no longer the First Estate, had a visible, sacerdotal character that transcended its legal definition. This was the stance throughout 1790 as the Assembly, driven by a moderate anticlericalism, proceded to abolish monasticism without compensating the Church by declaring Catholicism the religion of the majority of the French. These Erastian developments culminated in the Civil Constitution of the

Clergy, a lay-imposed reorganisation of the Gallican Church that redrew diocesan boundaries in line with the departmental ones, disbanded cathedral chapters, and accorded the clergy a uniform salaried structure. Senior prelates, in their *Exposition of Principles* (October 1790) made out a strong case for obtaining clerical consent via a national council and, though this plea was ignored, it had the effect of sharpening resistance to the imposition of the Civil Constitution by oath early in the New Year.

This legislation was a testimony to the dominance in debate of the moderate radicals, and their persuasiveness over the majority of uncommitted deputies. The wholesale renunciation of privilege on the night of 4 August gave these reformers such a fillip that they gained a momentum that endured for the duration of the National Assembly. The organisation of the reformers was on factional lines that corresponded loosely to membership of clubs like the Cordeliers and the Jacobins, but it had a slight – though sufficient – superiority to the conservative constitutional monarchists. On issues like bicameralism and the veto in the autumn of 1789, majority opinion found the latter too willing to empower the higher clergy and nobles, precisely those whose loyalty to the recent changes was questionable. With their proposals spurned and the king intimidated and removed to the Tuileries, some of the leading moderate monarchists (often called the *Monarchiens*) returned in dudgeon to the provinces. Most stayed on, and while comforting each other in clubs like the *Impartiaux*, saw the need for tighter unity in the Assembly. The result was that during 1790 the Right often attracted a high turn-out in the division lobbies. Nevertheless, their supporters could be so diffident and defensive about change that the uncommitted turned by default to the radicals. At least these men appeared uncompromising in their attachment to revolutionary principles.

The Civil Constitution of the Clergy appeared to underline as much. The subsequent passing of an oath requiring all clergy to accept its provisions generated a crisis of loyalty inside the Church. There was a simple choice: accept legislation that had received no independent acceptance at any level of the Church, or refuse it and be branded a Counter-Revolutionary. Many years before François Furet talked in terms of the Revolution 'skidding off course', John McManners argued that 'If there was a point at which the Revolution "went wrong"', it was with the imposition of the oath. 'This marked the end of national unity and the beginning of civil war'.[15] It was an avoidable double-bind that artificially polarised loyalties by obliging lower clergy to decide whether they were priests or 'patriots' first. Under agonising pressure from parishioners, local politicians and colleagues, a narrow majority accepted the Civil Constitution, but not in the north-east, north-west and south-west. In those parts *curés* were inspired by the recalcitrance of bishops who, with the exception of only four of their number (including Brienne and Talleyrand), preferred deprivation to stifling their conscience. In April 1791 Pius VI unambiguously condemned the Civil Constitution, and the non-juring clergy prepared to resist the revolutionary authorities who had, by this single measure, destroyed much goodwill for the Revolution and allowed the refractory clergy and their Church to emerge as an alternative focus for popular loyalties.

They did not blame Louis XVI for promulgating the Civil Constitution in November 1790. Faced with papal tardiness in responding to the proposal, conflicting ministerial advice, and impatient politicians in the Assembly, the king's room for manoeuvre was confined. Louis deprecated the religious schism that had become apparent in the first few months of 1791, and distanced himself from the official Constitutional Church he had allowed to be established. He like other members of the royal family began to contemplate the good sense of quitting France (as Artois had done a full two years earlier) and making an appeal to moderate opinion to rally around him from the safety of foreign soil. The comte de Provence left France on 20 June, his aunts Sophie and Louise about the same time and successfully reached Rome and their friend, Cardinal Bernis, despite some risky encounters with officials en route. Louis's relations were departing at much the same time as many thousands of others. This was the real beginning of the 'Emigration', made up of men and women who had welcomed the political transformation of 1789 but, two years on, had come to feel that the Revolutionary impetus had turned into an instrument of division rather than reconciliation.

However, it was probably less the departure of his kinsfolk than the king's inability to receive untainted Easter communion from a nonjuring priest that brought home to him the extent of his personal constraint. Thereafter he put himself in the hands of advisers, who had for months urged him to flee to the frontiers and rally moderate forces around the monarchy. There followed the abortive flight to Varennes in June 1791 and the ignominious escorted return to the capital. Louis actually made contact with the forward cavalry of the marquis de Bouillé, but as in July 1789, his refusal to risk bloodshed (perhaps indicative of a lingering distrust about the rightness of his actions) undermined the whole point of the expedition. After Varennes, Louis's popularity, which had survived largely intact, plummeted in the main urban centres.

The fact was, it was impossible to offer any justification of the king's flight without impugning the Revolution. The politicians tried. They needed the king's imagined consent to the constitution, and there were signs that his departure had precipitated awareness of how much he had been driven into a corner, and the threat to property that might lurk in a popular republic. Nevertheless, rather than risk an Orleanist monarchy Lafayette and La Rochefoucauld even toyed with starting an American-style republic. Paradoxically, Varennes precipitated a rediscovery of the centre ground with a view to settling the Revolution once and for all.[16] There are signs of a moderate reaction in the summer of 1791, aptly symbolised by the split in the Jacobin Club. Monarchists broke away to form their own *Feuillant* Society, led by two aristocrats, the Lameth brothers and a lawyer from the Dauphiné, Barnave, and Adrien Duport, a founder member of the Society of Thirty. This new axis (soon referred to as the Triumvirate even though, like the three musketeers, there were four of them!) looked to another famous veteran of the American War, Lafayette, to use the National Guard to crush radicals. He did not hesitate: crowds petitioning for a republic were fired on by National Guards in the Champs de Mars, Paris, in July 1791. There were other indications that the centre was reasserting its control of the Revolution: thus the Le Chapelier law was passed to outlaw trade associations and local authorities were encouraged to adopt a more lenient attitude towards non-juring clergy. In the background, although never part of the government, the 'Triumvirs' worked energetically to win the trust of the king and what was left of the royal family. There was a general amnesty in September 1791 when, to mark the completion of the constitution, both those accused of complicity in the king's flight and those arrested after the Champs de Mars massacre were absolved. A constitutional monarchy was always a deeply popular option in the political nation in 1789–91, and the flight to Varennes did little to reduce this preference. The problem was always Louis's double reluctance either to embrace the role wholeheartedly or, because of his fatherly regard for his only surviving son after June 1789 and his rights of succession, abdicate in favour of his brother Provence or despised cousin, Orléans.

Seen from elsewhere in Europe, the moderate reaction in France was harder to discern, whereas Louis XVI's humiliating return from Varennes was an obvious insult to monarchist dignity. *Émigrés* pressed the German princes to intervene, but the response was tentative. Admittedly, in

August 1791 the Emperor Leopold and Frederick William II met at Pillnitz, and declared their concern at developments in France, but with Louis on the point of consenting to the new Constitution, expectation that they would have to turn words into action was low. This suited both powers. The expense of the recent war with Ottoman Turkey made the prospect of another in the West distinctly unappealing, and the eyes of both were on Poland and the need to contain Russian aggrandisement. Of the other powers, Spain remained formally bound by Bourbon Family Compact to France, and Pitt the Younger's government saw Britain as the gainer on the international stage from France's internal commotions.

The monarchs of Europe might have been reluctant to fight revolutionary France, but the politicians in and beyond the new Legislative Assembly soon displayed the extent of their bellicosity. Expectations that an established constitutional framework would give France the stability that had been absent for nearly five years proved elusive. The Assembly turned 'patriotically' against non-juring priests and *émigrés*, but the punitive decrees it proposed were both vetoed by the king in a rare display of tenacity that emphasised the continuing scope for royal power. Ambitious and frustrated men began to look outside France. War appeared the decisive instrument to confirm their personal supremacy, dislodge their opponents, and either halt the Revolution entirely or deflect it into new courses. It ended the distinctive pacific phase of the Revolution, seen most forcibly as recently as the summer of 1790 when Charles IV of Spain asked the National Assembly for military assistance against Britain over her fishing grounds off Vancouver in the summer of 1790. Instead, in the winter of 1791–2, revolutionary rhetoric reinvented France's external enemies – the Habsburgs (ironically led by the pacific Leopold II) and their German and *émigré* allies – and used a populist idiom designed to provoke, inspire and shock. Specific military objectives mattered far less than stirring references to France's 'natural frontiers' on the Rhine, the Alps and the Pyrenees. The revolutionary elite expected to benefit personally from removing conflict from the domestic sphere. Heroes of the American War like Charles de Lameth, Lafayette and the war minister, the comte de Narbonne (the illegitimate son of Louis XV), looked forward to repeating their triumphs and gaining personal ascendancy over those left at home; the journalist turned orator from Chartres, Brissot de Warville, hoped victory on the battlefield would enable him to dominate the government just as he had the Legislative Assembly. And the royal family saw their reprieve in war, whether it was the renewal of Bourbon power under Habsburg protection, or a patriotic rallying to the throne in the event of France's forces planting their flag on the Rhine. A renewal of kingly power was the nightmare of the republican minority in the Assembly, whose fears were most eloquently voiced by Robespierre in his oratorical contest for supremacy against Brissot waged in the Jacobin Club. But when war was declared on the new emperor, Francis II, in April 1792, only six deputies were prepared to vote against it. France's military preparedness was completely at odds with the compelling blend of revolutionary and nationalistic sentiment and, as her armies retreated back across the frontiers in the early summer, the price for precipitating external conflict was apparent: an intensification rather than an end to domestic political crisis, the abolition of the monarchy, and the nullification of the 1791 Constitution which perpetuated that royal power within 12 months of its inauguration.

Crown and Legislative Assembly fell together in August 1792. Wrangling between Louis and deputies over refractory clergy, *émigré* nobles, and the appointment of Brissot and his allies to government continued up to the last moment, with the king making his views clearer than perhaps at any previous point in his reign. But this Indian summer for royal power was only a form of in-fighting which was peripheral to the developments that counted: military setbacks, the threat of invasion, and the popular response to crisis. A Brissotin ministry was no more effective in directing affairs than its *Feuillant* predecessor, and they, together with the royal family, were held directly responsible by revolutionary agitators for the crumbling front line in Flanders. The urban crowds moved in to fill the vacuum left by the ineffectual authority of the elite. They passed through the Tuileries palace on 20 June 1792 hunting for traitors, the war criminals who were subverting the war effort. They denounced 'aristocrats' and priests, but their target was really the government and the legislature. Both could only await their fate with as much composure as they could muster, and it was appropriate that when the Tuileries was finally stormed in August, Louis XVI and his immediate family had taken refuge with the politicians in the Legislative Assembly. Within two days, the Assembly was dissolved and the monarchy suspended. The concept of authority in revolutionary France had finally been separated from a crowned, hereditary head of state. There followed a republican hiatus of 12 years before the old pattern resumed – with a different dynasty.

# Chapter 2: The Convention, 1792–1795

## The Convention Established

The forcible overthrow of the monarchy in August 1792 imposed a republic on France irrespective of popular wishes. With Louis XVI suspended from his functions, the only potential alternative king was his cousin, Philippe, duc d'Orléans, and he had no wish to compromise his patriotic credentials by launching a bid for the throne. The road to the inauguration of the Republic had been prepared by widespread recourse to the treasury of republican values and vocabulary that had been around in monarchical France throughout the eighteenth century, found in the Parisian salons and the Masonic lodges and to be encountered in the works of the abbé Mably (1709–1785) among contemporary authors; they could alternatively be gleaned from the classic Renaissance texts of Machiavelli or the commonwealth republicanism of English authors such as James Harrington writing in the 1650s and, more recently, Lord Bolingbroke. This refined, even abstract republicanism with its pronounced moral emphasis was adapted and popularised for contemporary political usage by factional leaders after the flight to Varennes, hard though it was to earth republicanism as the natural preference of the average citizen: even most of the provincial Jacobin clubs remained monarchist until well into 1792 before the Brissotins asserted their grasp.[1]

Put at its crudest, republicans spoke the language of patriotism at a time of national danger, monarchists that of treason. With overt, often impassioned commitment to the well-being of the commonwealth through the subordination of private advantage and well-being to the public good, republicans deployed rhetorical resonances with echoes of the heroic days of Greece and Rome in antiquity (by definition, anti-monarchical times) that sounded entirely appropriate as the armies of Prussia and Austria approached the French frontier. In the eyes of the revolutionary activists who engineered the 'Second Revolution' of August 1792, the Bourbon dynasty had destroyed what little remained of its patriotic credibility and credentials by intriguing with these foreign enemies of *la patrie*, and it had surrendered its legitimacy. With the Bourbons went the unhappy experiment of a limited monarchy that, lacking adequate domestic precedents, had drawn largely upon a British model that gratified the tastes of few outside a small circle of political activists. Crucially, it had never generated the constitutional vocabulary needed to ground it in public perceptions as a distinctive political option in its own right. In 1792 the natural supporters of monarchy on the Right still conceived of monarchy primarily in terms of undivided sovereignty with Saint-Louis or Henri IV as its principal, patriarchal exemplars.

The politicians in the Legislative Assembly and what remained of royal government had demonstrably lost control of events and were reduced to a spectatorial role as chaos descended on the capital and the regime collapsed in the late summer. The imprisonment of the royal family was followed by blood-letting in the prisons of Paris as the crowds hunted out the 'aristocratic traitors' who were widely blamed for national failure on the battlefields. Condemnation of these atrocities was impossible for those who wanted a future in the post-Bourbon order: they were obliged to make an immediate transition from a monarchist past to a republican future and comply in the closure of the Legislative Assembly as the corollary of the collapse of the 1791 Constitution. The Assembly was replaced by the National Convention, elected speedily on what was technically a wide franchise in September 1792.[2] It remained in existence for the next three years, becoming, in French Revolutionary terms, an organ of no little permanence as well as importance. However much arguments raged in the executive committees or the political clubs, it was the Convention that was acknowledged by all sides as the centre of public life in republican France, all sides that is except the royalists (if passively defined, still probably the majority of the population) who were disenfranchised, their clubs having been closed and their newspapers shut after the August 1792 uprising. The Convention's importance lay in its embodiment of national and popular sovereignty and its absorption of the governmental powers latterly exercised by the Crown. The

Convention was thus a combination of legislature and executive without parallel in any other revolutionary arrangement of the 1790s: its creation was a sign that the decentralising phase of the Revolution was over; its continued existence afforded France some degree of stability during the upheavals to come in 1792–5. As an institution, though susceptible to gerrymandering and manipulation at times of maximum rivalry between the factions, as in the days leading up to the overthrow of the Brissotins at the end of May 1793 and Robespierre and his allies (the Mountain) 14 months later, the Convention's place at the heart of the republican state was incontestable. It was often argued that the Convention as a constituent power rather than a constituted power had been granted unlimited authority until it had finished its task. According to one orator, 'the assembled Convention is the sovereign will'.[3] Power could descend from the Convention to the agencies that it had created, the representatives on mission, for instance, or the Committee of Public Safety, but this was devolution rather than derogation or transfer. Even at the height of his authority in the spring of 1794, Robespierre never ignored the need to explain his policies to deputies and formally extract their consent. Significantly his absence from the Convention on grounds of ill-health was vital in corroding his authority.

Like its two immediate predecessors, the Convention was organised on a unicameral basis. Given the urgency of reconstructing public authority in the wake of the collapsed 1791 Constitution, there was no possibility of doing otherwise. Membership reflected a preponderance of professional, propertied men with some of those who had been in the National Assembly returning to serve the state. Factional divisions, sometimes fluid, occasionally chaotic, were nevertheless more sharply defined than in the previous legislatures. The friends and followers of Brissot such as Clavière, Roland and Servan (who had formed the ministry of March–June 1792) were present in large numbers and emerged as a distinct faction even before deputies settled down to their work and naturally gravitated towards previous friends, allies and connections. Brissot's journalism and pre-revolutionary activities made him an obvious focal point for alliances, with many in his circle having more Parisian links than has generally been recognised. It was friendship rather than ideology that initially separated the Brissotins from the Montagnards in the Convention and, in due course, these varying patterns of sociability sharpened the political disagreements.[4] The Brissotins had polled well in the provinces, appealing to an electorate whose belief in confirming the material gains of the Revolution (their *own* material gains) was a more pressing concern than whether France was a monarchy or a republic. The endorsement of Brissotin candidates in the constituencies did not increase their moral authority sufficiently to stifle populist republicanism in the capital. The experience of the elections to the Convention had turned the Brissotins against Paris and the term 'Montagnard' came to be associated in the first instance with the deputies from Paris (where the elections were dominated by Robespierre and Danton), even though there were numerous Montagnards elected in other *départements*. They and their supporters swept the board and took the *Enragés* in the clubs and sections under their protection, vociferous allies who buttressed their numerical inferiority in the Convention. It should be emphasised that most deputies were not part of any faction. These men of the middle ground – known as the *marais* (the marsh) – held the key to political control of the Convention. For the most part they were responsive to whichever faction was dominant, and while they reluctantly acquiesced in the expulsion of the Brissotins on 31 May 1793, their willingness to abandon support of Robespierre and St-Just the following summer was vital to the success of the Thermidorians' coup overthrowing the Mountain.

Almost the first task of the Convention was to sit in judgment on Louis XVI, a show trial that projected the character of republican virtue to the French nation and those watching (mainly in horror) elsewhere in Europe. The end to the imminent prospect of Prussian invasion steeled and encouraged deputies to arraign 'Louis Capet'. The eventual decision to decapitate him confirmed the new Republic through subjecting the formerly sacred body of the king to the indignity of public execution, which he offset by conducting himself with immense personal dignity at the scene of his death. His going was tersely summed up by the abbé Villard:

> Louis XVI had the courage of a sage or a saint rather than that of a king. His misfortune was to have come to the throne without any experience of government, to have had the *menu peuple* consigned to rule, and to be born into a century in which a fund of new ideas took possession of most heads.[5]

The king's death on 21 January 1793 compromised revolutionary France irretrievably in the sight of her shocked European neighbours and the vast majority of their inhabitants. With monarchs commonly accepted as essential to social and political cohesion in eighteenth-century Europe, there could be no stronger confirmation to outsiders that France had descended into a state of anarchy. France declared war on Britain and Holland on 1 February, and Louis's execution on the scaffold had confirmed the appetite of most Britons for war. Incredulity mingled with outrage and affected most sections of the population. One paper reported:

> At the Haymarket Theatre the indignant virtue of the people broke forth at the sight of the *French Banner*.... They hissed from the stage the ensign of a country polluted by sacrilegious fury and regal massacre. They likewise prevented the announcing of a Play, for this evening, and would not permit the farce to be performed. The intelligence of the French king's fate had this effect upon the house in general.[6]

Regicide boosted the creation of a crusading counter-revolutionary zeal that well matched the French republicans' own rallying cry of 'death to all monarchs in the name of the sovereign people'. In fact the debate on Louis's fate had dragged on for the last three months of 1792, with deputies much divided, as might be expected from a body over half of whom could best be described as tepid republicans. The real zealots were outside in the clubs and sections of Paris and other urban centres, while in the Convention it fell to the Mountain to make an eloquent case for the king's capital punishment, not on account of his personal failings but because of what he represented: no longer the father of his people by dint of his hereditary descent but a tyrant oppressor. Louis himself, skilfully represented in Court by his former minister, the minor *philosophe*, Malesherbes, presented a dignified front throughout his ordeal. It won him a degree of admiration bordering on sympathy. Almost half the Assembly, while declaring him guilty on technical grounds, was ready to commute the death sentence and lost the final vote by the smallest of margins, thanks to the former members of the National Assembly in the Convention, those who had seen his dislike of the Revolution close up, who voted overwhelmingly for his death.[7] The republicans thus ensured their state was baptised in royal blood, but at a high cost of exacerbating existing factional divisions. Girondins had wanted a plebiscite on whether the king be executed. The request was spurned by the Mountain despite Brissot taunting them as 'ambitious imbeciles' who would violate the sovereignty of the people. There is little evidence the bulk of the French population wanted their king put to death, and the comments made furtively to one British prisoner of war sound an authentic note:

> This very day a Frenchman whispered in my ear, 'His death (the king's) in spite of the veil which the convention threw over the real sentiments of the people, struck the hearts of the majority of Frenchmen with amazement and horror'.[8]

## The Destruction of the Brissotins, 1793

The challenge facing ministers was to face down their status as uncivilised pariahs in the sight of the outside world by waging a patriotic war that would both silence their foreign detractors and give a Brissotin-led republic a reputation for winning military laurels that had largely eluded the monarchy in its last decades. When Louis was executed, this still seemed an attainable goal; then came a dramatic reverse of fortunes: the Austrians drove Dumouriez out of Belgium after victory at Neerwinden (18 March), the duke of Brunswick's army recovered the Rhineland, and the naval war with Britain brought a naval blockade of French ports likely to starve the nation faster than the allies could defeat it on land. For Brissot and his colleagues, the escalation of the foreign threat to the state was almost jauntily accepted, acting as a validator of their patriotic credentials for the many doubters inside the Convention.

But it would only hold good so long as France contained the armies of Brunswick, Coburg and York. There was no question on any side of a negotiated peace in the spring of 1793: the Republic's fate hung on battlefield results, thereby making the politicians frighteningly dependent for their survival on picking the right generals. To date, their choices had let them down: Lafayette deserted his army on 20 August 1792 from personal pique and a mistaken sense that France was on the brink of defeat, Custine was executed for losing the Rhineland, and Dumouriez defected to the Austrians rather than suffer the same indignity. The first priority was for more men, and here patriotic fervour (and sheer weight of numbers) would have to make up for what was lacking in training. On 24 February a *levée en masse* was decreed by the Convention to raise 300,000 men. The entire country, whether adjacent to the war zones or not, was required to contribute. This was not a calculated assessment, but it was anticipated that where exhortation failed, intimidation would ensure that quotas were met. In fact the response to external crisis precipitated an internal one. Large tracts of north-west France erupted into rebellion against the Republic rather than fight on its behalf. For the inhabitants of the deeply Catholic, loyally monarchist Vendée, the killing of their king following on so soon from the loss of their Church was intolerable. The Republic and its servants had shown themselves to be the antichrist who must be overthrown in what, for yet another group in 1790s Europe, appeared to be authentically apocalyptic times. The rebels expeditiously formed a 'Royal and Catholic army', drove back the regular forces sent out to repress them and were in control of sizeable towns like Cholet, Parthenay and Fontenay by the end of May.

This formidable combination of internal insurgency and foreign armies marching on France's pre-war frontiers was presented by the Brissotins as an intolerable challenge to the authority of the Convention, and thereby the nation. Yet, if the Convention was going to be preserved, it could not rely on rhetorical declamation to do the trick. Government would have to work effectively but the crisis of spring 1793 had disclosed yet again its chronic inadequacies. Executive authority had imploded several years earlier (July 1788, when the Estates-General was summoned, is a persuasive juncture) and ministers might thereafter huff and puff and enjoy their status without possessing the resources to enforce it. Such government as there had been in 1789–91 really belonged to the executive committees of the National Assembly as part of the exercise of constitution building. The Revolution had been a revolt against centralisation and illegitimate authority and that is why, as late as 1793, the Convention was accorded such respect. It was more than the fast and furious power game played out on its floor; it functioned as a symbol of national unity (at least for non-monarchists) that was not tainted from being part of the apparatus of government.

The emergency of spring 1793 put an end to such innocence. Government had to be reinvented almost overnight if republican France had any prospect of lasting longer than a few months, and the factional survival of the Brissotins depended on the expedients they produced. A Committee of General Defence (CGD) had already been established on 1 January 1793 to help manage the war effort, with the despatch of political commissars to the field armies (in the Convention's name) to overawe the general in charge as virtually its first action. Events gave the CGD a major significance. It was reorganised with a change of personnel on 25 March and renamed the Committee of Public Safety (CPS). It was a recognition that with the enemy at the gates (or inside them in the case of the Vendéen rebels), power would have to be exercised in the

Convention's name from *outside* the legislature, and revolutionary politicians would have to overcome their cultural distrust of the firm hand of centralised government. The new apparatus also offered a major layer of patronage opportunities, an arena in which factions could reward their friends and weaken their adversaries. Looking to ensure loyalty to themselves as well as to preserve the Republic, the Brissotins attempted to link up the Convention more closely with the provinces (and their own allies in particular). Their preferred means was the post of representative on mission, officials empowered in the first instance to supervise the recruiting of men for the army at departmental level, who then tended to stay on to guarantee that local republicans stayed dutiful and obedient to the Convention and the committees. Other representatives were despatched to the front line, to monitor the generals and remind them that their political masters were watching and would not tolerate failure. Eighty-two such proconsular figures were in the field by July 1793.

Command and control politics, which circumstances made easy to justify, were also designed to head off Jacobin criticism that Brissot and his colleagues were simply incapable of acting decisively. In March 1793 a revolutionary tribunal was inaugurated to try what were loosely termed counter-revolutionary offences. Not to be proactive in the cause of the revolutionary state was becoming sufficient to propel any individual into that category. Press freedom was curtailed and the uses of the death penalty defined so that it could be applied to more or less any 'counter-revolutionary' indicators, including asking for the dissolution of the Convention or advocating peace negotiations. Ready recourse to the language of natural rights was discouraged. A journeyman gunsmith arrested at Versailles supported his claim to a fair hearing with an appeal to the Rights of Man. The police commissioner thought it just disguise for anarchy: 'He talks continuously of liberty and the rights of man, which shows clearly enough that he is bent on sedition.' In 1793 Pierre Daunou, the future *Idéologue*, published his *Essai sur la Constitution* in which he called the 1789 Declaration of the Rights of Man dangerous and equivocal. Its incoherence, ambiguity and imprecision had led to feeble laws, constant humiliation and 'our long calamities'. This was quite a volte-face from 1789 when he had endorsed the Revolution on the basis of natural rights.

The fatal problem for the Brissotins was that these draconian and, to some limited degree, effective policy initiatives did not deliver results quickly enough to save either their careers or their heads. And they were enacted against the background of a deadly, unrelenting factional rivalry with the Jacobins and other leftists both in the Convention and in the Paris *commune*. Jacobin deputies cultivated the street politicians among the *enragés* and in the Cordeliers Club as a means of making allies of those outside the Convention whose involvement could make the difference between success and failure in any revolutionary *journée*. One, stillborn, was ventured on 9–10 March when Brissotin printing presses were smashed up. It simply postponed the climax of the contest, one which the Brissotins had not abandoned hope of winning. They took comfort from having a genuinely national power base; what they crucially lacked were friends in the 48 *sections* of Paris. A counter-attack in the form of an attempted impeachment of Marat collapsed in April 1793. On 18 May the Girondins founded the 'Committee of Twelve' to investigate possible subversion by the *commune* and thereby reaffirm the ultimate authority of the Convention. With many of Brissot's key supporters either out *en mission* in the provinces or one of the investigative 'Twelve', he had imperilled his parliamentary management of the Convention and perhaps underestimated the degree to which most deputies were intimidated (intimidation, once again, played its part) into letting the Jacobins into power. But his most fatal omission was to have no counterbalance to the pro-Jacobin sympathies of the Parisian National Guard. On 28–29 May the *enragés* set up an insurrectionary committee, the prelude to the *journée* of the 31st with its demands that the Brissotins be excluded from the Convention and cancelled the 'Commission of Twelve'. Initially repulsed, a second *journée* on 2 June brought in – decisively – Hanriot and the National Guard with an artillery train. The majority of the Convention gracefully accepted the *putsch*. Most of them could at least keep their seats, unlike the 29 Brissotin deputies arrested. Brissot and his ministers Clavière and Lebrun were also taken into custody and promptly sent to the guillotine, lustily singing the Marseillaise as they ascended its steps.

The coup glaringly displayed the extent to which the Convention, officially the inviolable focus and fulcrum of the Constitution, could be intimidated and suborned by the very politicians who subscribed to its legal supremacy. It was a salutary reminder of what an impact revolutionary activists operating in the name of the people, believing themselves to be the people, could have on events. The lesson was not lost on the Jacobin elite: before 2 June 1793 the Jacobins had been ready to acclaim 'the people' as the voice of the nation; afterwards, having benefited from popular intervention, they backtracked and identified themselves as exclusively able to articulate the general will which legitimated all political action. It led to 'The Jacobins are the Convention! The Convention is the people!'

This, at least, was how Robespierre and his allies came to rationalise their grip on power. The demise of the Brissotins had not sown unanimity among the centre-left politicians who had engineered their overthrow; it merely gave them scope to intensify their own latent rivalries in a deadly power struggle that mimicked the real conflict taking place in the Vendée and on the frontiers. There may have been a festival of the Unity and Indivisibility of the Republic on 19 August (celebrating the fall of the monarchy), but it was a formalised travesty of the in-fighting going on for dominance of the principal institutions – the Convention, the CPS, the *commune* and the clubs. The assassination of Marat in his bath by Charlotte Corday on 13 July conveniently (for other radicals) removed a publicist and activist whose influence over the Parisian *sections* was hard for the *conventionnels* to control; his glorious funeral masterminded by artist turned Jacobin, Jacques-Louis David, hinted at the comfort felt by former colleagues that Marat had been translated from, when alive, a resourceful and dangerous activist to, dead, a martyred iconic presence whose popularity could pay posthumous dividends. Le Havre was even renamed 'Havre Marat' in mid-1793.

Policy differences and personality clashes still produced uncompromising and acrimonious exchanges both in the Convention and the CPS. Danton, the darling of the Parisian public, carried much weight (in every sense) when, as the leader of a loose alliance called the *Indulgents*, at the close of 1793 he attacked both dechristianisers and the ultra-revolutionaries. For Robespierre and Saint-Just, though they shared Danton's qualms about dechristianisation, the *Indulgents* were the new corrupt, conspiratorial enemy on the Right; on the Left were the demagogues, the men of the Cordeliers, such as Hébert, the talented editor of the *Père Duchèsne* (perhaps the nearest equivalent to tabloid journalism in the French Revolution), who were interested in social justice and price controls and, as Marat earlier, not susceptible to manipulation by the CPS. Hébert and his followers were judicially executed first, in March 1794, after a show trial,[9] and they were followed a fortnight later by the *Indulgents*, including both Danton and Desmoulins. Thus the Revolution devoured its children in a manner that frightened rather than inspired the mass of *conventionnels*.

Fear was, of course, intrinsic to the Reign of Terror that characterised French high and low politics in 1793–4. Its primary purpose was for Paris to reassert control over the provinces and eliminate any show of political activity that would challenge Jacobin hegemony. The removal of the

Brissotins had ignited a Federalist revolt in Bordeuax, Lyon and Marseille that had republican grievances quite different to the real counter-revolutionaries of the Vendée. The Jacobins, however, needed little incentive to conflate the two challenges to their control and, by late 1793, after some desperate struggles, had reimposed their military authority across the country. Rebels could expect no quarter from the revolutionary armies that were primary agents of the Terror in the provinces. In early 1794 the 'infernal columns' of General Turreau massacred, pillaged and burnt as they traversed the length and breadth of the Vendée. Lyon became 'Ville-Affranchie' after it surrendered in October 1793; other cities contaminated by treachery like Marseille and Toulon (briefly occupied by British forces under the command of Admiral Lord Hood) suffered the same purgation.[10] The prisons of every town and city filled with suspected traitors and public enemies, whether noblemen or women, proscibed politicians, ne'er-do-wells, or priests. In a political culture where plots and conspiracies had become the norm, circumstantial evidence of 'guilt' could bring about a conviction after the Law of Suspects was passed on 17 September and citizens were encouraged to watch each other as part of their patriotic duty to root out 'traitors'. Trial procedures in the Revolutionary Tribunal were correspondingly speeded up in October to cope with the ever-increasing number of cases. The Terror entered its final stage – what would become known as the 'Great Terror' – on 15 June 1794 with the passing of the law of Prairial. It reformed the Revolutionary Tribunal yet again to have it produce still more convictions. Paranoia was thus progressively translated into public policy, a reflection of the insecurities that beset the Republic, which no amount of patriotic braggadocio could wholly mask.

That law of Prairial is, of course, inextricably linked with the personal ascendancy of Maximilian Robespierre, a figure whose persuasion of his own moral (and, by association, political) rectitude made him assume that the survival of the Jacobin Republic depended on his own unassailable supremacy.[11] This conceit proved in time to be his undoing. Robespierre was an unclubbable man lacking humour, who was admired for his efficiency and feared for his icy, self-proclaimed probity of a standard other politicians, compromised by character or career, could not hope to match. Robespierre's regard for the supremacy of the National Convention was nominal, and his ruthlessness towards those who challenged him could readily be justified after implementation of the 1793 Constitution (a proto-democratic settlement based on impeccable Enlightenment principles, the fruit of many years of reflection by Condorcet) was indefinitely postponed and the CPS advised that the government of France should be revolutionary for the duration of the wartime emergency. The key to Robespierre's control was the CPS (he was voted a member of it on 27 July 1793). He there showed himself capable of rebutting opponents to both Left and Right and, usually, building majority opinion around himself. Power was further centralised on the CPS under the law of Frimaire (December 1793). This quickly led to the bureaucratisation of the Terror over the next few months and the reduced possibility of popular pressure having any purchase on the decision-making processes of the revolutionary elite. In April 1794 the CPS (significantly, not the *commune*) imposed its own nominee, Fleuriot-Lescot, as mayor of Paris, and also imposed restrictions on the sectional assemblies in the capital thus effectively nullifying their last remaining powers. That same month Billaud-Varenne declared that the days of spontaneous popular movements were over, everything would henceforth go forward according to a plan, a 'system'. The revolutionary state had become a 'machine'.[12]

Robespierre was, by such measures, unwittingly stripping himself of potential allies among the *sans-culottes* and confirming a reputation for dictatorship that historical tradition has tended, rather misleadingly, to endorse.[13] Deputies were, between April and July 1794, intimidated by this victor of the factional battles of the previous winter, even as the number of talented 'patriots' on whom the 'tyrant' could rely was plummeting.[14] His unanimous election as president of the Convention on 4 June 1794 formally recognised his supreme leadership in national life, but it lasted only a matter of weeks. Other politicians, less principled but resourceful tacticians, turned out to have a capacity for survival that eclipsed Robespierre's. Most *conventionnels* found his great festival of the Supreme Being (8 June) impossible to take seriously, but they were too frightened to stay away from the somewhat bizarre ceremonies. The gathering actually assisted the plans of those plotting against him and they further benefited by his protracted absence from the Convention because of illness. Informed rumour suggested that Robespierre was assembling yet another list of the proscribed and it became a question of who would show their hand first: he or the thermidorian plotters. On 26 July Robespierre attacked his enemies in the Convention as 'les fripons et les dupes', hinting that he intended to curtail parliamentary immunity and send elected deputies before the Tribunal. It was a tactical error because in failing to give specifics everyone hearing him felt threatened; during the next 24 hours his many enemies marshalled by Fouché and

Tallien took advantage of the collective anxiety in the legislature over its future as pretext for his arrest along with Couthon and Saint-Just on 27 July 1794, the *journée* of 9 Thermidor. Execution followed for Robespierre and 82 other Jacobin leaders.

The Thermidorian conspirators have repeatedly fallen foul of a French historiographical tradition that represents the Jacobin ascendancy of 1793–4 as the purest, most complete form of revolutionary expression. That is not how most contemporaries saw it. Rather, the engrossment of power by the CPS and its auxilaries had derailed republican politics and moved them covertly away from that public arena – the National Convention – to which they properly belonged. Certainly, the 'tyrant's' overthrow had been achieved through an alliance of convenience among politicians who themselves wanted a stake in policy making and were not going to either have it or resume it while Robespierre lived. But while the latter's demise would benefit the Thermidorians personally, a constructive purpose to their successful coup should not be ruled out, that of returning meaningful power to the floor of the Convention, thereby stabilising the Revolution by ending the Terror. Recent military successes, such as Fleurus (26 June) and the safe arrival of the grain convoy at Brest (despite a naval defeat at the 'Glorious First of June') had collapsed any objective justification for its perpetuation.

But first the Thermidorians had scores to settle. The vanquished Jacobins had reason for considering that the 'Terror' had not so much ended as been turned against them. In the weeks after Robespierre and St-Just were despatched to the guillotine, some of their most loyal followers met the same fate, while a Commission was set up in December to scrutinise the conduct of four who had escaped the block and even been involved in preparing the coup: Billaud-Varenne, Collot d'Herbois, Vadier and Barère (sentenced to deportation, April 1795). The risk that another Robespierre might step forward could not be contemplated. This sanguinary work was done with little fuss and on a moderate scale: those who had acted as a chorus for the Jacobin Terror out of self-preservation rather than ideological ferocity were generally spared, the new leaders of the Convention reckoning that mercy and magnanimity would get the new regime off to a more settled start, with state execution a last resort rather than the rule. Thus on 19 December 1794 a motion that all former terrorists should be deported was defeated in the Convention. This conspicuous moderation also reflected Thermidorian uncertainty that they had become the controlling power in the Republic, and they correctly calculated that proceeding at a moderate pace acceptable to moderate opinion was the surest way of confirming their acceptability.

The Parisian coup of Thermidor was replicated in most other French cities as local elites emerged from hiding and, backed by the National Guard, asserted their right to govern in the name of the Convention. The representatives on mission, their authority limited to just three months after 13 August 1794, were now deployed to purge local administrative bodies of ex-terrorists and Jacobins. They would not always go easily, knowing the fate likely to await them. Having often been intruded into natural Girondin centres like Bordeaux and Lyon, it was their turn to seek safe havens and plead for their lives when denounced by fellow citizens who had scores to settle. Hundreds of terrorists or suspected terrorists never came before the judges. The French provinces (especially the Rhône valley) witnessed a multitude of revenge killings, lynchings and woundings that occurred outside any judicial process, the so-called 'White Terror' of 1794–5. Jacobins were loathed and laughed at in equal measure, and though their politics ceased to have any validity for some time after late July, they still posed a threat, evidenced on 6 October 1794 when they made an attempt to overthrow the Thermidorian administration at Marseille. Such desperate tactics help explain the security system of the new regime: the law of Prairial was repealed on 1 August, the Paris Jacobin Club was shut on 14 November 1794, and the Revolutionary Tribunal was abolished outright on 31 May the following year. Activists had four alternatives in 1794–5: fight back against the odds; dissimulate and distance themselves from Robespierre and his despised 'dictatorship'; go underground and plot a come-back; or stay silent and retire – for the time being – into private life. Most, unsurprisingly, opted for the last.

In the classic Marxist tradition of French historiography which predominated until the late 1970s, Thermidor was a defining moment of closure, one in which the Revolution, properly considered, ended. It had been an heroic attempt to create a new form of political society that both inspired and anticipated the efforts of later generations of revolutionaries but, for all that, it had failed in its own day. This heroic failure was openly regretted as a reassertion of bourgeois control and a denial of the sovereignty of the people. The recognition that Thermidor was a decisive turning point was taken by Marxists from an earlier historian of the Revolution, Michelet, and this insistence has outlived Marxism. It has been very recently argued by Gueniffey that the death of Robespierre marks the end of the revolution 'in its period of incandescence'. Hopes of a total refoundation of political life in the state, alongside the absolute moral regeneration of its citizens, were over.[15] Such grandiloquent conceptualisation both underestimates the extent to which violence persisted for months after Thermidor on a scarcely diminished if unofficially authorised scale. It much exaggerates the interest of the average citizen in the regenerative aspects of the Revolution, and barely registers the real mid-1790s context of fear, suspicion, terror and bitter personal rivalries that the Thermidorians decided, for a variety of reasons, could not continue. Robespierre's replacements in 1794–5 had ambition and appetite aplenty, but they accurately grasped that the Jacobins had turned into a narrow, elite caucus incapable of admitting the validity of anyone else's perspectives on or opinions about the Revolution. They had no respect for majority opinion in the Convention, while their claims to embody the 'general will' of the nation were a sham that validated their monopoly on power and labelled those who disagreed with them as 'traitors'. The true interests of public safety demanded their overthrow and an end to the Terror. The French public endorsed this perspective judging by the number of petitions which poured into the Convention in the months after the coup, denouncing Robespierre, St-Just and their cronies in the most vituperative, even scabrous language and thanking the *conventionnels* for overthrowing these enemies of France. The Jacobin leaders were vilified as bloodthirsty tyrants whose sins were far worse than those of any Bourbon.

Thermidor was many things other than the physical destruction of Robespierre. Far from ending the Revolution, it attempted to restore its breadth of appeal, returning power to those moderate republicans who had lauded and engineered its best achievements before they were, cadre by cadre, displaced by the events of 1792–4. Thus, a general amnesty was issued to all 'federalists' on 22 Germinal/11 April 1795. As events would show, their constitutional creativity had not been exhausted and the relative tolerance of the political climate $c.1794$–7 put a much wider range of talents at the service of France than had been the case since the start of the Revolution. This broad band of republicans, tactically united by their enmity to extremists (especially of the Jacobin kind) and restored to national leadership in 1794–5, were well aware of what they stood to lose to their opponents on both the left and right if their working alliance fragmented. On this reading, Thermidor can be represented as merely the latest in a hectic series of realignments within republican circles. The coup cannot be labelled a victory for decentralisation, a reassertion of provincial power against the centre: in July–August 1794 the French regions followed the lead of Paris and the Jacobin power brokers at local level found survival was impossible when their masters at the centre had been swept away.

Where Thermidor did mark a break with revolutionary experience was in its negation of the scope for direct popular action. Crowds of militants deployed in favour of one faction or another would no longer be permitted to determine the outcome of the struggle for control of the Convention. Virtually all the deputies could agree on so much, as was made plain when the small-scale *sans-culottte* rising in Paris of 20–24 May 1795 and the royalist one of 5–6 October 1795 were resisted. French Marxists may have deprecated the defence of the Convention as repressive and illegitimate, but it is pure myth making to suggest that the mobs involved were in any sense representative of the French population as a whole. As the petitions showed, most men and women yearned for stability and safety of the kind only a moderate, relatively non-partisan regime was likely to deliver them, one founded uncompromisingly on the final authority of the Convention, not the Parisian *sections* or the *clubbistes*, not the CPS (which survived with much diminished status after powers were returned to the Legislation Committee in the Convention) as the embodiment of popular sovereignty. The Convention remained the one institution whose final supremacy was respected more or less universally throughout these years by a broad swathe of republican opinion; as one political dispensation succeeded another in 1792–4 no one dared to advocate an alternative focus of power. Its recovery of sovereignty in 1794–5 recreated a moderate regime based on order and the restitution of some of the freedoms held out in 1791. Its members were hard headed enough to have learned lessons in abundance about the fragility of constitutional authority in a revolutionary polity, and they would be embodied in the new settlement of the Year III (adopted 22 August/ 5 Fructidor). The underlying point was that none of this would be coerced or done at the point of a sword, and the legitimacy of the Directory at its inception was due in large measure to the transfer of supreme power from the Convention when it finally disbanded on 26 October 1795 through lawful, authorised channels.

# Chapter 3: An Attempt at Moderation: the Directory and the Consulate, 1795–1804

## The Directory, 1795–1799

The Constitution of the Year III (1795) that established the Directory was a creative and inspired construction, one that may have used the language of classical antiquity but was rooted in the experience of the immediate past. In sanctioning a new governing order at the centre (that the local government reorganisation of 1790 stayed intact – it worked – was a measure of the new pragmatism), the *conventionnels* signalled the completion of their drive to stabilise the state from extremists, doctrinaires and popular agitators of all descriptions, and that there was more to achieving stability than closing down the clubs and the popular societies (23 August 1795) and suppressing the Parisian sectional assemblies (8 October 1795). In seeking to ensure a smooth transition to this new order, deputies decided that the infant Constitution would need protection from the malign and the excluded and that the protectors in the first instance should be themselves. They produced the notorious 'Law of Two-Thirds' concurrently with the Constitution of the Year III on 22 August 1795, under which two-thirds of the new legislature were to be drawn from the existing membership of the Convention. It gave what would be the Directorial regime at its outset the impression of being self-perpetuating and self-serving, little more than the decorative relaunch of the Thermidorians and their cronies, one which may have been unfair at the time but which later events appeared to confirm.[1] It also reflected a sense of precariousness behind the official rhetoric, one which, given the rapid turnover of regimes since 1789, was hardly surprising. The propertied public registered its distaste for the two-thirds law by largely boycotting the plebiscite in September on the Constitution of 1795; the turnout was a derisory 16 per cent. Those who felt particularly aggrieved were in part responsible for the Vendémiaire *journée*, Year IV (5 October 1795), which was presented as a monarchist rising but also registered bourgeois concern that the Constitution was both too oligarchic and too populist.

The Constitution of the Year III was a substantial document of 408 articles that had taken the so-called *Commission des Onze* five months to produce. Checks and balances to safeguard its smooth operation could be found at every level. The legislature would be bicameral, a startling innovation posthumously vindicating the minority that had argued unpersuasively for one in August 1789: a *Conseil des Cinq-cents* of 500 members that initiated legislation and a 250 member *Conseil des Anciens* that approved or rejected it. Age and marital status was built into the system, to cancel out the perceived destabilising predominance of young people in the Revolution to-date: a member of the 500 had to be at least 25 years old (30 from the Year VII), an 'Ancient' to be either married or widowed and aged 40 and upwards. The legislature's mandate would last for three years with a third of the deputies retiring annually on rotation. Sovereignty in 1795 was invested in the last analysis with propertied citizens, men with some stake in making the Republic work.

There were two electoral stages. The franchise was allotted to about 5 million males who paid direct taxes or who had fought in the army; they elected a college of about 30,000 male property owners. The latter operated at departmental level using the secret ballot, another notable innovation that gave a flavour of the Constitution makers' good intentions. So did creating what was in effect a collective headship of the Republic in the Directory of five members. There would be no more Robespierres that way. He would anyway have been ruled out by the stipulation that a Director had to be a minimum of 40 years old. The Five Hundred drew up a list of ten candidates for each place on the Directory, the Ancients made their choice from this list on the basis of a secret ballot. No director could stay in office more than five years, but while in power collectively with his colleagues commanded the army, was responsible for the security of the Republic, and appointed the ministers and the generals. In other words, they possessed a huge share of patronage. How it was to be portioned out among the five was to be crucial, one of the few points to escape the notice of the 1795 Constitution makers.

Whatever the illusions of monarchists, the incoming regime was solidly republican. Indeed, the *Commission des Onze* intended it to be an amalgam of the best republican practices of ancient and modern times, the better to endow it with the durability they prized. The hope was that, despite the ordered prescriptiveness of their arrangements (the moderate revolutionaries could not have any confidence that the politicians of the 1790s would respect political conventions – even if there had been any in place to guide them), liberty would not be a casualty. Thus the Declaration of the Rights of Man and the Citizen headed the new constitutional arrangements. A cursory glance, however, revealed that this 1795 document was a far cry from the heady libertarianism of 1789, lacking in any reference to men as being 'born and remain free and equal in rights' for fear that it would condone a demand for universal suffrage. This Declaration placed as much emphasis on the 'Duties of Man' (the phrase was actually built into the formal title) as it did on rights: from August 1795 Frenchmen were required to defend and serve society; to live under society's laws; to respect its agents, and to undertake military service. Individual rights such as equality before the law and freedom from arbitrary arrest were certainly mentioned, but the impression was given that the Constitution had other priorities. It looked for stable government, for the subordination of private advantage to public service, and, though the distinction between passive and active citizens was not reactivated, the marginalisation of the unpropertied, the repression of a Jacobin political underclass, and the continued exclusion from citizenship of refractory clergy, *émigrés* and their relatives. After the ideological excesses of 1792–4, moderate republicans were anxious to move the emphasis away from natural rights and discouraged well-disposed citizens from thinking too strenuously about the theoretical foundations of the Republic.

In many respects, the Constitution of the Year III was a bold, pragmatic, and important revolutionary achievement. It was also excessively ingenious, over-complicated and fussy in its details. At least, this was the charge made by the opponents of the Revolution, including the former minister, Calonne, who tellingly asked: 'How can a machine so complicated in its whole, so incoherent in all its parts, so fettered in all its movements, clogged with so many wheels, subject to a continual collision, continue its regular movements without soon breaking to pieces?'[2] It was a point well made (one that experience would bear out), but there was another side to it. This elaborate construction was at least partially a response to the sense of the politicians of 1795 that the main requirement of the overwhelming majority of citizens was not to end the Revolution but to consolidate it, to admit that some very bloody mistakes had been made in six hectic years and to guard against their recurrence. To that end, they borrowed from the contemporary world to a degree seldom appreciated. Thus, the principle of the separation of powers incorporated into the 1795 instrument owed far less to Montesquieu than it did to the influence of the new United States constitution. If the *Commission des Onze* was ultimately unsuccessful in fashioning a polity that would last, their efforts merit a little more recognition than historians (of Right, Left and Centre) have been disposed to give them. Until Martyn Lyons produced his mould breaking *France under the Directory* (Cambridge, 1975), it was hard to find any historian with a good word to be said for Directorial France. According to the received wisdom, the heroic days of the Revolution were liquidated in favour of a corrupt, militaristic regime in which blatant ambition displaced ideological engagement and a genuine commitment to popular sovereignty. Echoes of that view still persist, not least with the majority of books on the French Revolution opting to bring it to a premature end in 1795 with the assumption of office by the first Directors on 3 November.

Such a view, as Professor Lyons's survey showed, is neither fair nor appropriate, and scholars now queue up to acclaim most aspects of the 1795 settlement, James Livesey, for instance, has recently argued attempting to make the Republic work in effect created the future European model of democracy.[3] This beguiling revisionism with its nod to teleology is an invaluable corrective but it tends to overlook the ruthless power politics of the Directory and its contemporary reception by a jaded citizenry. To outward appearance, the creation of the Directorial order was a tangible token of revolutionary consolidation, paralleled as it was by the annexation of Belgium as part of metropolitan France in October 1795. The Directory was an indicator that France was not going to collapse into internal chaos, however much over-optimistic politicians like Pitt professed to expect it. Britain never succeeded in shipping out enough arms and powder to the rebels in the west to threaten mortally the Republic's survival, though the regime was fortunate George III's cabinet in the mid-1790s was divided on strategic priorities. As the destruction of the three *journées* of 1795 and the *émigré* defeat at Quiberon Bay indicated, Jacobins and royalists were on their knees, giving the incoming Directors the chance to build up a national consensus based upon a moderate republicanism and a national patrimony whose boundaries extended beyond anything previously achieved by Louis XIV. The French Republic reinvented itself in 1795, having shown beyond dispute its capacity for grinding down all its internal and external enemies, while offering the well-disposed (or the cowed) the chance to get on with their lives and serve the state at the same time. It can thus be considered the apotheosis of the political moderatism of the early Revolution, a return to the values of the 1791 Constitution, suitably modified in the light of experience and shorn of the unworkable constitutional monarchy. The *conventionnels* saw the desirability of dignifying the organs of the state, making republicanism stately as befitted a formidable military power in Europe. The Directors adopted a flamboyant costume, they worked and received visitors in a palace – the Luxembourg – and something resembling a Courtly protocol emerged. Unfortunately for the regime, putting state officials into uniforms coincided with the desperate revival of frivolity in metropolitan society and made the Directors ridiculous rather than resplendent to the gilded youths of Parisian society – and to many others besides. Neither could Court dress make the Directorial order respectable, for the new dispensation still had royal blood on its hands and was still waging war in Europe. It was a regicide Republic, an outcast and an anomaly in 1790s Europe, one whose existence gave great offence, and the first job of the incoming Directors would be to show the world that it would, per force, have to respect the order France had just given herself rather than presume to dismantle it and impose their own.

Those who served as Directors were, on the whole, gifted politicians, whose career paths since 1789 had marked them out as survivors, men able to shift allegiances quietly as circumstances changed without jettisoning commitment to revolutionary values. Hence the longevity of most of them in high office between 1795 and 1799. Paul Barras (1755–1829), the former army officer and nobleman, served as a Director from the beginning of the regime until its end, thus giving him a continuity in office holding at the highest level unmatched by any other revolutionary politician. Endowed with an acute judgment of day-to-day politics, he had no compunction about bringing down fellow directors when their activities threatened his own pre-eminence, as his organisation and execution of the Fructidor 1797 coup showed. If Barras was corrupt, he was too powerful as senior Director for his adversaries lightly to hazard laying charges against him. His colleagues, Louis-Marie de La Révellière-Lépeaux (1753–1824) and Jean François Reubell (1747–1807) served almost as long, until June and May 1799 respectively. La Révellière-Lépeaux was a former botany teacher turned Girondin, one of the

*Commission des Onze* who had created the regime in which he held office. Imitating Barras, he aligned himself against the revival of the right in the Fructidor coup; unlike Barras he was more interested in ethical religious cults than in monitoring military policy. Reubell, an Alsatian lawyer, had somehow managed to avoid miring himself in faction politics before 1795 and, as a Director, specialised in foreign affairs and French frontier expansion, especially on the Rhine. Of the other men who served, Lazare Carnot's reputation as the 'architect of victory' in the Year II might have been expected to have made him Barras's main challenger for executive supremacy. The reality was different. Carnot was distrusted as a one-time Jacobin who had worked with Robespierre on the Committee of Public Safety and his surprise emergence as a champion of the moderate Right in 1796 did nothing to reassure his colleagues. Barras had Carnot bundled out of office and into exile at Fructidor 1797. It is important to remember that much of the daily business of government during these years was in the hands of ministers (who did not make up a cabinet) rather than the Directors and that some of these men, by dint of personality or office, were powerful figures in their own right. Talleyrand, Minister for Foreign Affairs between July 1797 and July 1799, is an obvious case in point or François de Neufchâteau, Minister of the Interior for two years from July 1797, an energetic, experienced administrator and a moderniser in both education and technology. Efficient service as a minister sometimes led to election as a director. This was the career path of Merlin de Douai (1754–1838), who had spells in office as Minister of Justice and Minister of Police during the first two years of the Directorial regime. His work with Barras and La Révellière-Lépeaux in preparing the coup of Fructidor made him an obvious choice as a fellow Director and he served alongside them from Fructidor 1797 until June 1799.

In policy matters, the Directors were never short of business. The first priority was inevitably ensuring success in the war. The regime was blessed with a bevy of outstanding generals who not only confirmed revolutionary France's reputation as an expansionist power, but did it on the cheap by levying taxation on the conquered provinces of Italy and Germany. It was just as well that the war paid for itself as the Directory was no more successful in managing public finance or maintaining public solvency than any of its predecessors. They started intelligently by ending the issue of *assignats* in February 1796, merely to replace them four weeks later with another paper currency, the *mandats territoriaux*, which collapsed almost at once. It was revived intermittently later in the year but the experience was that it only held its face value when set against tangible assets, such as the sale of lands. Exactly a year after its introduction this hated latest version of paper money was withdrawn from circulation to be replaced by metallic currency. Other attempts to give the state a fresh fiscal start included proclaiming the freedom of the grain trade in June 1797 and levying a tax on land the same month and on movable wealth the following August. These were essentially palliatives. After the Fructidor coup one of the first policy initiatives of the 'Triumvirs' – Barras, Reubell, La Révellière-Lépeaux – was to use their newly consolidated authority to start afresh with the 'bankruptcy of the Two-Thirds' (30 September 1797) when the state repudiated two-thirds of the national debt (at a stroke reduced from 250 to 83 million livres), soon followed by all its other financial commitments. Along with new indirect taxes on doors, windows and tobacco, the regime received the illusion of stability for another 12–18 months before the shortage of revenue became acute once more and it fell back on the time-honoured expedient of a forced loan in mid-1799. If the four-year balance sheet was unexceptionable – the curtailing of the annual deficit stands out – it still merits consideration under something other than the stale heading of 'corruption'. The three finance ministers were technicians, not incompetents, who had access to considerable expertise within their increasingly bureaucratic offices. But none of them had the power to create that climate for financial stability and growth which only peace and established institutional procedures were likely to achieve. Inflationary pressures had assisted in stoking up a flourishing 'black economy' that, in its way, encouraged an entrepreneurial revival in the late 1790s without any thanks to the Directory. There was money around in the country, and plenty of signs of conspicuous consumption on a scale unseen since 1789. But wealth creators were spending rather than saving and investing, and events like the 'bankruptcy of the Two-Thirds' only reinforced the impression among taxpayers and businessmen alike that the state was their enemy, not their ally.

Directorial policies towards French citizens in religion were no less erratic. In principle, the regime was committed to religious neutrality though not, significantly, religious freedom. So long as their politics were not deemed to subvert the state (under the law of 25 September 1795 all those leading public worship were obliged to swear an oath of loyalty to the Republic), religious groupings could meet without hindrance. Republicans had learnt from the grim experience of trying to enforce the Civil Constitution of the Clergy as part of a seamless state settlement and nothing was said in the Constitution of the Year III about a national Church. This gave those who had remained loyal to the ideals of the Constitutional Church the opportunity to reorganise as they did, brilliantly, guided by Grégoire, culminating in the holding of their first national council in August 1797. These 'Gallicans' had no difficulty in living under a republic; refractories did, and they received few concessions throughout 1795–9. Conditions gradually eased for nonjuring clergy immediately before the Fructidor coup in 1797, with the way opened for their return to active ministry in France without having to submit to the 'Liberty–Equality' oath. The exiling of Carnot and Bathélemy scotched any such hopes and the last two years of the Directory were marked by what amounted to a 'second reign of Terror' for the nonjurors. As in the first Terror, intimidation and discouragement of Christian practice (more priests were deported in 1797 than in any other year of the Revolution), went hand in hand with a renewed attempt to commend observances unsuccessfully attempted in 1793–4. Back came the legal stipulation to observe the *décadi* and the rites and national festivals associated with it. There was one interesting innovation founded by Chemin, a Parisian bookseller, and sponsored by La Révellière-Lépeaux; this was the cult of Theophilanthropy, whose adherents met for the first time in January 1797. This nebulous, undogmatic deism was more an expression of ethics than religious belief. Its followers – tiny in number outside Paris – assembled in churches (often shared with Catholic congregations so mockery and petty vandalism were frequent on both sides) to hear readings from sages like Aristotle, Socrates and Rousseau, and mutually acclaim their insights into right conduct for humanity. This emphasis was paralleled by the philosophers favoured by the regime, Cabanis (1757–1808), Destutt de Tracy (1754–1836), Garat (1749–1833) and Volney (1757–1820), those making up the Auteuil circle of 'Ideologues' who commended natural laws rather than Christianity as a foundation for public morality.

The Directory had, implausibly, lent its support to state-sponsored moralising. As early as April 1795 the Committee of Instruction in the Convention ordered that 3000 copies of Condorcet's *Esquisse d'un tableau historique des progrès de l'esprit humain* (an outline sketch for a history of mankind in which all the major events are intellectual ones and progress leads ineluctably to a bright future) be circulated throughout France. In October that year, a National Institute of Arts and Sciences was founded. It became the working centre of 'Ideology', men committed to systematising and correlating knowledge to serve as a guide to social reform, men 'infatuated with utility'.[4] For the 'Ideologues', there was no viable alternative to the Directory and they supported it on an unconditional basis as prime recipients of its patronage. Typically, Cabanis simply rationalised the electoral outrages perpetrated by Fructidor: 'the government has saved the republic....The Constitution has not been violated an instant, except in order to conserve it'.[5] Such refined, self-serving ethicism was remote from the outlook of the average citizen (male or female) who, for the most part, was more preoccupied in opening their parish church (and keeping it open) and having a priest to minister to their community. The continuing religious tensions after 1797 were a major cause of the Directory's instability and are important in explaining the readiness of the public to acquiesce in its liquidation.

Neither did the prescriptions of the 'Ideologues' do anything to reduce the acute problems constantly confronting the regime – and its citizens – from the collapse of law and order in the provinces. For a variety of reasons – reviving royalism, revenge killings, the unstable currency, antipathy to conscription – criminality flourished under the Directory to the extent that it has tainted the regime as a whole. The trend was especially marked in the south-east, with approximately 800 homicide victims recorded in the *départements* around Lyon and Marseille between 1795 and 1800. Concealed in the forests and the hills, bandits and counter-revolutionary gangs (the groupings could be interchangeable) preyed viciously on travellers and residents alike. The latter could not expect much relief from the government. Extra troops were stationed in the Midi and though a few arrests were made, the military constituted a token rather than a useful presence.[6] Efforts by the authorities to rationalise the violence as politically motivated White Terrorism was an excuse for inaction and was scorned by the rural population. It was not until 18 January 1798 that the legislative councils decreed that the death penalty should be mandatory for criminal offences such as highway robbery and larceny committed by two or more persons. This belated decree was unlikely to deter hardened criminals. The fact was that the Ministry of the Interior had a pitifully small presence in the provinces and, with the removal of the *représentants en mission*, controls on thugs, thieves and vengeful political dissidents also vanished. For the Directors, both before and after Fructidor, the priority was always to keep troops stationed on the front line, and they resented having to tie down even a small proportion of them in police duties on French soil. Instead, the Directory relied much on its *commissaires* in the provinces. The costs of this policy bias, in terms of the denial of public goodwill, were incalculable. If the Directory could not secure the conditions in which people could carry out the duties of everyday life, then the citizens of the Republic would look for a regime that could, whether royalist or Jacobin.

To survive and prosper, the Directory needed all the friends it could get and its failure to build up a national constituency of supporters ultimately proved fatal to its continuance. At its inception the Constitution of the Year III appeared to offer political moderation and a commitment to pluralism that would allow for the resumption of civil life relatively untrammelled by the requirements of the state. However, one of the side-effects of this relaxation of state control was the creation of a political vacuum rapidly occupied by those forces that yearned for a restoration – either of extreme Jacobinism or one of several varieties of royalism on offer. In March 1796 Babeuf set up his Insurrectionary Committee for his 'Conspiracy of Equals' and Carnot arrested Babeuf and Buonarotti two months later, only just before they could bring their *énragé* conspiracy to fruition. Their idelogical appeal had even spread to the army, as the abortive *babouviste* Grenelle Camp rising of 9–10 September disclosed. No fewer than 32 death sentences were handed out by the military commission afterwards and the Directory in the winter of 1796–7 was ready to look more kindly on the Right for possible allies as the elections of the Year V approached. It seemed just about safe to do so, especially after a law was passed on 20 March 1797 obliging all members of the electoral assemblies to swear an oath affirming their hatred of both anarchy and monarchy. Despite this filter, official candidates still underperformed. Only 13 out of 216 ex-*conventionnels* were elected, giving the Right a major victory. In 1797, for the first time in the Revolution, the men in power were beaten with the Councils briefly presided over by 2 royalists, Pichegru and Barbé-Marbois. Openly royalist organisations – the *cercles constitutionnels* – were founded in Paris and the provinces in the spring of 1797 giving a majority of the Directors and the army an uncomfortable sense that the regime would be dismantled not by another *journée*, but by the success of the royalists at the ballot box and the treachery of two colleagues, Carnot and Barthélemy.

Once again, the regime via the three other Directors (Barras, La Révellière-Lépeaux and Reubell) launched a pre-emptive strike against its enemies with the *journée* of 18 Fructidor 1797. Troops moved into Paris, the minority Directors were arrested, elections were annulled in 49 *départements*, 177 deputies were removed, and 65 individuals were deported. New laws were rushed through the Councils closing down the right-wing press, reopening (left-wing) political clubs, requiring electors and jurors to swear another oath of hatred of royalty and anarchy, and giving the Directors emergency powers to dismiss officials. Even the Protestant lawyer Boissy d'Anglas, the major architect of the Year III Constitution, was stigmatised as a royalist Clichyen, and obliged to go into exile in England after the coup. Fructidor was an admission that the Directory had proved incapable of occupying the middle ground that the framers of the Constitution in 1795 had singled out as an essential fulcrum on which the whole edifice depended. The regime had not done enough to tempt voters to abandon long-held loyalties. It embarrassingly suggested that after eight years of revolution, the French public were looking again (many had never ceased to do so) to a monarchy to provide the bedrock stability successive republican settlements had proved incapable of delivering.

Fructidor also showed the complicity of the executive in subverting those elements of the Constitution inimical to itself. If elections failed to produce the result desired by the 'Triumvirs' of Fructidor, they would intervene to cancel it. This was gerrymandering on a massive scale, a token not of moderate politics but of contempt for the sovereignty of the electorate. For the last two years of the regime therefore, the electoral process was a dead-letter, not a means of determining the preferences of a propertied, responsible college, but a device to confer a spurious legitimacy on a stumbling executive. If the triumvirs could cancel one lot of elections, there was nothing to stop them cancelling another lot, as they duly did in 1798. The months after Fructidor per force made the left respectable again as the Directors geared up to produce the 'right' result in the elections of the Year VI (spring 1798). They even permitted the creation of 'schismatic' electoral assemblies thereby giving themselves a choice of candidates. The tactic had only a limited success and was not enough to stop the next *journée*, 22 Floreal (11 May 1798). Numerous left-wing candidates had their election as deputies annulled in favour of those voted by 'schismatic' electoral assemblies. At least the Directors were correct in seeing the public preference for right-wingers in 1797 and left-wingers in 1798 as being in the first instance a vote against the complacent status quo, and the trend was repeated in the spring elections of the Year VII when, despite efforts to keep out declared opponents, the councils were refreshed by a 'third' which was basically Jacobin.

It was the final occasion on which the directors coerced the legislature. Press controls could not disguise the unpopularity of the regime, blamed for leaving Bonaparte and his army stranded in Egypt after Nelson's smashing victory at Aboukir Bay on 1 August 1798, and tired of the mutual recriminations of the Directors among themselves. During the winter of 1798–9, the legislative bodies began to register this disquiet. Justified by France's developing foreign policy crisis of 1799 (virtually the whole of Italy was lost), the councils at last found the resolve to not be intimidated, confident that the military men were, at last, on their side. In what turned out to be the last months of the Year III Constitution, the Councils sat in permanent session from June 1799, and launched their own coup on the 18th of that month, 'the *journée* of the councils': with Treilhard's election already voided, they expelled both Merlin de Douai and La Révellière-Lépeaux as Directors in favour of two little-known men – Roger Ducos (1747–1816), a client of Barras's, an ex-Jacobin who had presided over the Ancients during the Fructidor coup, and Louis-Jérome Gohier (1746–1830), a very moderate Jacobin and lawyer. After four years of intimidation and coercion, the checks and balances that the constitution makers had built into the system were finally coming into play. On the eve, as it transpired, of its dissolution, the parliamentary regime intended to be at the heart of the Year III arrangements was finally emerging, using the wartime emergency of 1799 as the launch pad for overcoming executive hostility to allowing it to function as such. It would not be easy. Parliamentarianism was not a style the new Directors relished and, as news from the front became gloomier, they began to cast around for a powerful deliverer. After June 1799, only Barras and Moulin among the five Directors were still committed to its continuance; Sieyes (he had replaced Reubell as a Director on 9 May), Ducos and Gohier were open to offers.

The Constitution of the Year III had neither delivered the normalisation of French politics its founders had intended, nor yet established a republic as the indisputable basic model for any post-revolutionary polity. The Directory had neither operated the constitutional machinery impartially enough for the whole political nation to feel 'represented', nor yet tried to act as a conciliator and reconciler. It was also vexing for many of the deputies who survived the purges of 1797 and 1798, those who were not primarily parliamentarians but technocrats keen to implement specific reform projects and frustrated by the way the machinery of the Year III made that hard for them.[7] Yet, as historians like Malcolm Crook and James Livesey have recently pointed out, the regime of 1795–9 operated an electoral system which, with its broad franchise, allowed for a greater degree of public involvement and discussion than anything seen since the Republic was created back in 1792. It was part of those continuing efforts to revive civic society after the depredations of the Terror, reaching their height in the twelve months before Fructidor stifled so many voices.[8] That the Directory thrice nullified and constructed its own set of results was, without question, a blatantly illegitimate, not to say illegal, act of *force majeure* against public opinion and yet the executive did not then proceed to close down the whole electoral process. They sought to control rather than suppress, though those republican and royalist activists condemned to the 'dry guillotine' in Guyana might have contended that it amounted to much the same. On this evidence, it might be argued not that the Constitution was essentially unworkable, but that the most senior politicians of the later 1790s thought they knew better than the sovereign electorate. At least in that unconscious sentiment, they were turning out to be consistent with every other post-1789 regime. This is not to deny the creativity and originality of the 1795 Constitution, but it turned out that the checks and balances built into it were much less effective than had been intended. The ongoing Revolutionary War also worked against success: trying to make a major political experiment function effectively during hostilities was asking too much. It was winning that war rather than preserving the (latest) constitution that finally mattered most for the French.

If the Directory was better at inspiring enmity than loyalty, at least the Constitution under which it operated was in operation for a full four years, longer than any regime since 1789. Designed to appeal to moderates by its Thermidorian architects, they both exaggerated the size of that constituency and underestimated the appeal of more extreme political creeds based on loyalty and blood. The centre could not hold, at least not on the flimsy basis of loyalty to the Directory, not exactly the kind of regime calculated to inspire citizens to hazard either their lives or their livelihoods. Its lack of emotional rationale was always an embarrassing omission and finally fatal to its perpetuation: the God of the Theophilanthropists or the natural rights theories of the Ideologues were hardly adequate enough to prompt heroics of self-sacrifice. Where those sacrifices were made during these years of incessant warfare, men died for France, for the 'grande nation' (the ringing phrase was current from *c*.1797), for their generals and, above all, for their comrades rather than the likes of Barras, La Révellière-Lépeaux and their cronies back in Paris. The regime was strangely disconnected from the emotional lives of the French and it would take a new constitutional settlement under a charismatic young leader to put it back again.

## The Coming of the Consulate, 1799

After four years of erratic policies and election rigging, it was clear to most observers that the Directorial regime was not delivering the stability that the Constitution of the Year III had promised. Its wayward actions interested the politically engaged but annoyed everyone else. In the winter of 1798–9 the regime even sponsored a programme of democratic-republicanism with classic components: persecution of the clergy, republican festivals and a fresh emphasis on the calendar. That was the limit of its political impetus. By early 1799, the Directors had stopped driving the state; the coup of 30 Prairial appeared to show, for the first time, the initiative passing to the Councils and the possibility of the Directory becoming a genuine parliamentary regime. The question remained – would the senior politicians sanction this development and, more importantly, would the generals? Propelled by the neo-Jacobin Left, many of them veterans of the Year II, political life in the summer of 1799 was still turbulent and unpredictable: press freedom (re-established on 1 August) lasted just five weeks, a Law of Hostages voted by the 500 allowed the relatives of *émigrés* to be gaoled; a progressive income tax alarmed financiers and the newly propertied; all classes of conscripts were called up to defend the frontiers against the armies of the Second Coalition, and there were royalist uprisings in the Haute-Garonne, Anjou and Brittany. With the war situation less favourable than at any time since early 1794, Sieyes, Ducos and Gohier viewed constitutional evolution in domestic politics as untimely, tending only to encourage destabilisation. And so five and a half years after the overthrow of the Jacobin Republic, there was a reversion to conspiratorial politics in the Thermidorian mode with leading politicians agreeing that there needed to be a new Constitution which invested primary authority in one individual rather than five. Those who shared this perspective, such as Daunou, Roederer and Talleyrand, began to gravitate towards Sieyes, the veteran political survivor. Meanwhile, Barras was treating with Bourbon emissaries in the spring of 1799 with a view to saving himself.[9]

The consensus was that Republican France stood in need of a saviour, but who? None of the politicians who had dominated public affairs since 1795 were obvious candidates and all those who had served as Directors were to a man discredited by self-interest and lack of achievement. But in 1799 two powerful figures had re-emerged into the top flight of politics, Sieyes and Fouché (the latter appointed Minister of Police on 20 July). Both men were formidably talented and notoriously ambitious. After having been briefly in Italy as ambassador to the new Cisalpine Republic, Fouché was propelled into high office by his patron and was soon using his powers indiscriminately against the enemies of the state, whether on the Right or the Left. His links with the fading star of Barras actually hobbled him as a constitutional conspirator in 1799 and allowed Sieyes to make all the running as a plotter. The ex-cleric was planning to build a completely overhauled constitution around the figurehead of a successful military man who would be, in practice, dependent on himself. This arrangement he hoped would create a regime which acknowledged the centrality of the army in French public affairs and put an end to Directorial-style wariness in dealing with senior officers who were more popular with the public than the politicians. Caution amounting at times to suspicion had denied Directors and ministers securing credit either for themselves or their Constitution from foreign victories or the scaling down of the civil war.

The increasingly sordid contrast between the likes of Barras and Reubell with the kudos of generals such as Hoche, Moreau and Bonaparte had done nothing to predispose the Directory to the citizens of the *Grande nation*. As all knew, France only merited that epithet because of their achievements on the field, like Bonaparte's stunning victories against the Austrians in Italy in 1796–7 or his occupation of Egypt in 1798. The Directors had always needed the generals; the converse did not apply. After the Prairial coup in 1799 there was a frantic bid to reverse the trend when the reliable but unexciting Moulin (1752–1810), commander of the Army of England since January that year, accepted appointment as successor to La Révellière-Lépeaux as Director. Thus it was politically expedient as well as militarily desirable to keep the best commanders out of metropolitan France, to prevent the Directory being too much in thrall to the army top-brass. In the run-up to Fructidor 1797, the Directors had been terrified that Hoche (recalled from command of the Army of the Sambre-and-Meuse to intimidate the right-wing Councils), having refused the post of Minister of War, would establish his own military autocracy. His death almost immediately afterwards removed that possibility, but still left them to face General Napoleon Bonaparte (1769–1821), the charismatic commander of Italy and hero of Egypt. He had already made one dazzling entry into Paris in December 1797 to recognise his part in signing the Peace of Campo Formio, and there had followed a series of public banquets in which his heroic stature was fêted. News that he had landed at Fréjus in October 1799 caused consternation in Paris as the politicians jockeyed for position, knowing that Bonaparte would be central to any constitutional settlement.

After intially registering surprise at the General's escape from Egypt, Sieyes was privately gratified for, with Bonaparte's return, he perceived that, at last, his most competent stalking horse had arrived. It was Talleyrand who brought Sieyes and Bonaparte together after the latter reached Paris on 16 October. Bonaparte seemed the best instrument available for the task. General Joubert's mortal wound leading the Army of Italy against the Austrians and Russians at the Battle of Novi on 15 August 1799 had ended his flirtation with the conspirators while, of other generals, Moreau, had a royalist past and would not become involved and Bernadotte was an associate of the Jacobins. It was assumed that Bonaparte would be the most compliant because he had left his army stranded in Egypt.

It took less than a month between the arrival of Bonaparte in Paris and the termination of the Directory. The key to the manoeuvrings was having Napoleon's brother, Lucien, elected as president of the Council of the 500 on 23 October, since he was able to prepare the ground from within the legislature by persuading deputies that an insurrection was being planned in Paris (a phoney one as opposed to the real Bonapartist one) and that they had best move to Saint-Cloud. Indeed without Lucien's steady nerve, the two-day coup of 18–19 Brumaire (9–10 November 1799) may never have succeeded. Napoleon brought troops down to the councils as arranged, but his hectoring speechifying for a time jeopardised the whole operation of what was intended to be an essentially legal transfer of power. Nevertheless, by the evening, a provisional Consular Commission was in existence with two of its three members, Sieyes and Ducos, as ex-Directors, providing a fig-leaf of continuity. Bonaparte, naturally enough, was the third. However, when the Consuls were actually named on 13 December 1799, only Bonaparte's name still figured (Cambacérès, a member of the 500 and Lebrun, savant, ex-*Monarchien*, and member of the Ancients, were the other two).[10] What had happened in the interim?

The simple answer is that Sieyes lost control of events. As was succinctly said in the 1950s by one of Napoleon's most distinguished English biographers:

> Brumaire really consisted of two distinct coup d'états – first the day of Saint Cloud, which was planned primarily by Sieyes, and the second, in which Napoleon disposed of Sieyes.[11]

Whereas Sieyes had envisaged the Consulate as a scaled-down Directory, Bonaparte saw in it a vehicle for the satisfaction of political ambitions that Sieyes had underestimated even more than the general's administrative competence. He wanted a complete break with the discredited order of 1795–9, and was not prepared to wait for the protracted business of constitutional overhaul to be worked through. The pace of external events made that impossible. Thus, in Bonaparte's hands, Brumaire became much more of a thoroughgoing military *coup d'état* than most of his supporters and sponsors had ever imagined. He exploited his huge advantage as France's most successful living field commander ruthlessly. Knowing he had the army behind him, Bonaparte was master of the field, and could create a political order in the Republic that reflected his priorities and preferences, not Sieyes's. A secret meeting which hammered out the Constitution saw Sieyes worsted and Bonaparte taking control from the other conspirators without resorting to the use of force. The plan for a weak Grand Elector and two co-equal Consuls was rejected, and Sieyes was compensated with the presidency of the new Senate, with power to nominate the members.[12] What Bonaparte unashamedly demanded from his colleagues in government was loyalty to himself as First Consul rather than mutual co-operation, and Sieyes could not provide it. There was therefore no place for him in the new polity. The ex-regicide, Cambarcérès, and the ex-monarchist, Lebrun, were ready to accept Bonaparte's supremacy which was why they were acceptable as Second and Third Consuls respectively, a numerical subordination which accurately mirrored their political status in 1799–1804.

Just as Bonaparte dominated the executive, so he planned to deny significant independent life to the legislature. The government itself chose deputies to the new Legislative Body, Tribunate, and Senate from a list of candidates again elected on the basis of universal male suffrage, and there were no elections to them anyway before 1801. Bonaparte respected earlier republican conventions when he submitted his Constitution (and it was to all intents and purposes his creation and property) to a plebiscite, which was remarkable both for the public's apathy and Lucien Bonaparte's determination to deny it (he actually doubled the number of voters who turned out). Ten years into the Revolution, the public were disillusioned with politics and desperate for a return to stability that no set of politicians had so far proved able to give them. As for the electoral process, the reluctance of politicians to respect results and the instability caused by annual elections and the stand-offs between executive and legislature that often followed made many voters see it as a dubious trophy, one which they would be content to put aside.

In 1799 France was groping towards an awkward, immature liberalism, but that process was killed off by internal and external crises and the necessity of having a general as the supreme authority in the Republic, albeit one acceptable to the electorate if only because he seemed likely to end the intolerably erratic way in which government power had been exercised since at least 1795, arguably for longer than that. But why should Bonaparte succeed where all the civilians had failed before him? In as much as it can be deduced, the expectation at New Year 1800 was that the Consulate would be lucky to endure for any greater length of time than the piecemeal regimes that had preceded it. But the public had not reckoned on the drive and the ruthlessness of Napoleon Bonaparte, or his immense talent for getting the business of government done more efficiently than any previous revolutionary. As has been well said: 'Perhaps the most remarkable part of Napoleon's career was the utterly unsuspected talents he suddenly displayed when handed office by a clique of experienced, astute politicians after the success of the coup of Brumaire'.[13] He undoubtedly benefited from the absence of any sense of public loss at the demise of the Directory and from his own glamorous image, that helped the nation come to terms with the Brumaire coup: By early 1800, said the duchesse d'Abrantès writing in 1813:

> Confidence returned; everyone saw General Bonaparte with the same eyes and at that time those eyes looked on him with love.... Yes, he was loved, he was loved everywhere, and even when there was no love there was admiration and confidence in his character.[14]

## Success and Stability: the Consulate, 1799–1804

Between 1799 and 1804 the Consulate delivered to France the political stability no regime within living memory had managed. It was essentially one man's achievement. Bonaparte soon put behind him the hesitation exhibited at Brumaire 1799 which so nearly forestalled his rule before it had begun, and proceeded to astonish the European world with a series of daring achievements in government much as he had the military establishments a few years previously. Central to his purpose was the creation of strong government responsible to himself, and served by the best-qualified officials irrespective of their past. His only demand was these men have an unquestioning loyalty to the Consulate. The dream of decentralisation with him was finally over. The *départements* would stay as the primary units of local administration, but to each one would be attached a new officer created under the law of 28 Pluviôse Year VIII

(17 February 1800), the Prefect, whose task was to act as the indispensable link between the centre and the periphery. There were superficial resemblances to the *représentant en mission*. However, the prefects were not revolutionary ideologues, existed independently of the army and, crucially, reported directly to the Consuls rather than the legislative bodies. They would work primarily with the local mayors who, in towns larger than 5600 people, would be named by the Consuls, and in the smaller ones, would be the appointees of the Prefect himself. Bonaparte significantly denied the French capital its own mayor: Paris would be his own personal fiefdom. He also manipulated the docile senate, whose procedure of *senatus-consultum* effectively allowed him to govern by decree.

Bonaparte correctly sensed that the citizenry of France were ready to accept restrictions on liberty if the prize was efficient administration. Such a preference also suited his inclination towards control. So back came moderate press censorship in June 1800 and various restrictions on personal freedoms.[15] What successive regimes had dubbed 'brigandage' would not be tolerated, and the Consulate conferred additional sweeping powers on the police and army stationed in the provinces.[16] Once again, Bonaparte felt assured that the public would back him. Napoleon's inexperience could come across as evidence of incapacity (as in his near-fatal failure of nerve before the Council of 500 on 19 Brumaire) making *Monarchiens* such as Montlosier wonder if he would survive very long. But he brilliantly secured the middle ground the intransigent royalists had failed to occupy.

His stabilisation of public finances proved both popular and vital in establishing his grip on power. He relied heavily on the expertise of Martin Gaudin, who had earlier served the Bourbons and the revolutionary governments, and acted as Finance Minister throughout the Consulate, with unchallengeable oversight of tax collection and receivers. Gaudin refused to issue paper money, basing the monetary system on a metallic currency: the *franc de Germinal* was eventually created on 28 March 1803 giving France a currency whose real and face values matched. The monopoly on issuing bank notes was awarded to the new state bank, the Bank of France, created in February 1800, privately owned, with an initial capital of 30 million francs. The Sinking Fund of November 1800 (another feature of state finance copied from Britain) was critical as a means of keeping interest rates low rather than ever being used to pay off the public debt. And the Consul's restoration of general European peace in 1801–2 also eased the financial strains France had endured for the previous decade.

The Consul had no interest in pluralist politics. With his coming to power, as he saw it, both Jacobin and royalist models for France's future had been authoritatively ruled out. The future belonged to him and those who served him in the state, the Churches and the army. Any initial hopes monarchists had nurtured that Bonaparte would be the means to secure the return to rule of Louis XVIII were spectacularly dashed in 1800 when the Consul told the exiled *de jure* sovereign to accept that his future lay permanently in private life. This rude dismissal of royalism certainly played its part in inducing many leading royalists (including the *Monarchiens* Malouet and Mounier) to offer their services to the Corsican usurper, and Bonaparte made use of them where he could safely and conveniently do so. But where he suspected royalists plotting against him, Bonaparte was uncompromisingly ruthless, witness his abduction and execution of the Bourbon prince, the duc d'Enghien, on 21 March 1804. Not that he had any penchant for the revolutionary die-hards: for Jacobins whose precepts and past politics he judged antithetical to everything he was trying to accomplish, he reserved his particular venom. Typically, when royalists tried to blow him up with a bomb on wheels in December 1800 – the famous 'infernal machine' – Bonaparte chose to blame the Jacobins for the outrage, and punishments were meted out accordingly. Where Jacobins genuinely renounced their past, Bonaparte was ready to entrust them with high office, none more so than Joseph Fouché, his ruthlessly efficient Minister of Police.

Fouché was one of the many Consulate officials who had grave doubts as to the desirability of Bonaparte's determination to reach a political settlement with the Roman Catholic Church. But for the Consul, nothing mattered more if his regime was going to last. He saw that he could never construct a broad coalition of support for his authority on the basis of the revolutionary cults patronised by republicans in the 1790s, and still fitfully kept going into the new century by a few enthusiasts. Ignoring the reservations of conservative republicans, Bonaparte took advantage of the election of a new pope, Pius VII, in 1800 to initiate discussions towards making his peace with the papacy. The prize for both men was massive. For Bonaparte, papal endorsement of a new Church settlement would cut the cable linking Catholicism with royalism, and end the still smouldering insurrection going on in western France; he rightly judged that thus ending the antipathy towards the republic of both clergy and laity would do more to underpin his new order than virtually any other policy. For Pius VII, a deal with Bonaparte promised the increase of papal power over the Gallican Church and, more importantly, created the kind of conditions in which Catholicism could begin to rebuild its cultural and pastoral influence after the disastrous depredations and divisions of the 1790s.

Reaching an agreement with Rome in 1800–1 was fraught. Bonaparte was bent on securing his terms, not just because compromise never came easily to him but also to reassure his republican supporters (he could not afford to push them too far when his regime was barely a year old) that he was not about to abandon the deep-rooted anticlericalism that was a fundamental part of the Revolution's cultural heritage. After much brinkmanship, subterfuge and tensions within the extended Bonaparte family (the Consul's wife, Josephine, was a supporter of Grégoire and the Constitutional clergy) and diplomatic tantrums on both sides – it was desperately difficult to induce the refractory bishops to resign their posts to the pope in the expectation of receiving the equivalent post back again: of 93 surviving refractory bishops, only 55 eventually obeyed – a Concordat was signed in July 1801 and proclaimed on Easter Sunday 1802. At Bonaparte's insistence, it amalgamated the refractory and Constitutional Churches although favouring the former. Catholicism was declared to be 'the religion of the majority' rather than the official religion of the state; the minority rights of Protestants and Jews to worship were upheld. Church lands confiscated and sold since 1790 were not restored; neither were the canons and monks of the old First Estate. The parish clergy would be paid a state stipend on condition that they took an oath of loyalty to the Republic; bishops would do the same, owing their preferment in the first instance to the Consuls just as their pre-1790 predecessors had done to the kings of France. Here as elsewhere in the Consular regime, the electoral principle retained by the Directory was abandoned. What Pius VII had not reckoned on when signing the Concordat was Bonaparte following it up in 1802 with a set of Organic Articles that articulated a Gallicanism far more extreme than any of its Jansenist proponents would have dreamed of achieving half a century earlier. For instance, the bishops and clergy could not meet in councils or synods without prior permission from the state or receive communications from Rome: all would be monitored by the Ministry for Ecclesiastical Affairs whose creation signalled the end of the Church–State separation inaugurated in 1795. The pope was powerless to prevent the imposition of the Articles on the Church by an all-powerful Consul bent, by 1802, on ensuring that any institutional independency of himself in the French state was impossible. Another unmistakeable sign of that trend was Bonaparte on 2 April 1802 having himself declared First

Consul for life, along with the right to nominate his successor; he openly rejected the Senate's recommendation that the consulate should be extended by ten years only. The Consul's domestic authority had been guaranteed by international achievements. A hard-fought but essential victory at Marengo in 1800 was followed by the Peace of Lunéville with Austria in February 1801 and the Peace of Amiens with Britain in 1802. Up to the Battle of Marengo, opponents in the Tribunate talked of imposing Carnot, Moreau, or Orléans should Bonaparte fail; after Marengo they fell silent.

*Conclusion*

Two years later the Consulate itself was replaced in favour of an Empire with Bonaparte proclaiming himself Napoleon I, Emperor of the French, with the state remaining a republic in name only. By 1804, very little in public affairs gave much sense of France as a distinctive revolutionary polity, a trend Bonaparte had set in motion soon after assuming power in late 1799. Whereas, ramshackle, discordant and awkward to control though the Constitution of the Year III was, it was nevertheless incontestably a continuation of the Revolution with its calendar and the much derided *décadi*, its distinctive public festivals, its anticlericalism, and its hostility to the *émigrés*. As late as the summer of 1799, after the legislative coup of Prairial, it afforded resurgent Jacobins the chance to renact the patriotic *ralliement* of 1792–3 as the Second Coalition pressed French armies back towards her frontiers. This all ceased in the five years after Brumaire, and very rapidly after Bonaparte assumed the consulship for life. He may have been the product of the Revolution, but his style of government owed more to Louis XIV than any revolutionary leader. Though republicanism in a low-key lingered during the consulate (and Bonaparte's followers had justified the original coup in terms of sacrificing the Directory to save the Republic), even that character was becoming an implausible fiction after 1802. The public rhetoric of the consulate evolved from invoking classic republican tropes into a celebration of the nation-in-arms in the safe hands of its young First Consul, sanctioned by the Church (as his coronation in Notre-Dame cathedral visually displayed) and backed by the army. As the proclamation of a life consulateship had foreshadowed, the hereditary principle had reappeared in French public life, now constructed around the Bonapartes rather than the Bourbons. And the corollary of heredity as the principal criterion for a head of state was monarchy. Bonaparte closed down the Revolutionary Republic in favour of something less precarious and more prestigious – an Empire. The paradox was, as his propaganda presented it, that safeguarding the Republic necessitated his becoming 'Emperor of the French Republic'. He was asked to do so officially by the Senate in May 1804, but it says much that Bonaparte waited until his political supremacy was unassailable before taking this step. It was an acceptable and fair exchange for citizens now turned back into subjects again. After five years of stability and safety, they were ready to see these blessings perpetuated even at the price of an imperial order underpinned by a personality cult far more formidable than anything any single revolutionary had managed. Liberty had come at too high a price in blood; the nation wanted a glorious future and that was best guaranteed by entrusting unfettered power to its most successful commander. The Consulate had worked well, no less was expected of Empire.

*PART II*

*The Creation of a New Political Culture*

# Chapter 4: The Language and Signs of Revolution and Counter-Revolution

*Introduction*

The author of the standard 1960s work on the Enlightenment, Peter Gay, famously observed that 'history is very much a study of perceptions'[1] and in line with that dictum, some of the most creative recent scholarship on the Revolution looks less at the events of the era than at what contemporaries spoke and wrote about that was happening to them and to their world. Could it be that the most significant aspect of the revolutionary dynamic was linguistic and cultural, giving rise not to one event after another (significant though they might be), but to new forms of public life in which the participants saw their experiences differently and spoke about them in a novel manner? If the French Revolution was the midwife of modernity, how should we properly identify its hallmarks? It is along such lines that discussion of the 1790s proceeded in the 1980s and 1990s so that the bicentenary of the Revolution commemorated in 1989 coincided not just with overdue acceptance – thanks to François Furet and Denis Richet – of the revisionist, usually Anglo-American insights into the nature of eighteenth-century France, but, paradoxically and perhaps incompatibly, with viewing the Revolution as the product of definitions and discourses, essentially a 'linguistic event' in which primacy is accorded to speech acts. This became the distinctive hallmark of 'post-revisionist' Revolutionary historians, whose writing, while containing much penetrating scholarship, has not made the subject easy to grasp by non-specialists[2].

The purpose of this chapter is to consider afresh the public culture of France in the 1790s and the claims for novelty made about it as a vehicle both expressive of profound sociopolitical change and a means of achieving transformation in the first instance. In so doing, it raises the question of why the Revolution needed to be 'invented' and its processes represented, and why '1789' gave psychological satisfaction for revolutionaries seeking a new beginning, just as it has for so many historians studying this period in the last two centuries. It has suited both to set up a series of polarities between the so-called '*Ancien Régime*' of pre-1789 and the new order that followed it. The result has been a misleading misapprehension of the range of links between what are less two distinct eras than is commonly inferred. The early modern does not suddenly end in 1789, the modern just as suddenly begin. If cultural history is one of the most energetic areas of current historical practice, much fine scholarship on the French Revolution has helped create its reputation as a valuable tool with which to unlock and understand the meaning of social practice in past societies. The work of historians like Lynne Hunt, Mona Ozouf, and Michel Vovelle has been central to establishing these insights into the reshaping of discourse and display, particularly in the way the new public authorities used language and symbolism to underpin their legitimacy and extract loyalty from the population. Their findings have been received enthusiastically, other historians only disputing the primacy of event in relation to language.[3] This chapter, however, sounds a cautionary note in considering their insights. It argues that while this recent scholarship has told us much about what was new in the 1790s, it has not been adequately counterbalanced by treatment of what remained unchanged after 1789. Continuities can be at least as striking as ruptures, cultural changes appear as superficial by comparison with what remained unchanged. Where the Revolution did impinge on the lives of the individual, it was often unsought, a disruptive influence rather than one for the better, intruding its way into areas like the spiritual and the private, and contributing to the sum of human misery as the great Richard Cobb's *Death in Paris* (Oxford, 1978) graphically demonstrated in a study of suicides. The political ambition of many of the new participants in public life was running out of control, and that, combined with their inexperience, could be lethal for many of their fellow men and women.

Before 1794, many of the revolutionaries self-consciously conceived of themselves as constructing a new society, one based on revolutionary norms rather than those of the old society. That was a possibility within a large urban setting and as far as the middling and the upper ranks of the lower social orders were concerned. However, the revolutionaries' estimate of their capacity for changing the attitudes and outlooks of France's rural masses, in short turning them into proactive supporters of the revolutionary project, was much exaggerated. In the countryside, harsh seasonal experiences limited the extent to which smallholders and their families could be in charge of their own destinies, as ardent revolutionaries liked to insist; such a notion would not get the average *métayer* very far when the harvest failed as it famously did in the summer of 1788 after ferocious thunder and hailstorms in many parts of France caused catastrophic damage to crops. At Raincy one gardener found hail as large as lumps of ice had sliced through tree branches and killed 'hares, partridges and many other things'.[4] That poor harvest was followed by the third worst winter of the century, one of unrelenting frosts when charitable resources were stretched to the limit and thousands starved or froze to death. These depredations actually served to increase the hopes of most countrymen for the kind of changes from the Estates-General that would increase their conditions of tenure and, perhaps, their material comforts so that when the National Assembly failed to act promptly, across large swathes of rural France the peasantry purposively forced the pace in destroying feudal anachronisms. But those ends accomplished and ratified by the legislature after the night of 4 August, the Revolution had relatively little to offer of much comfort to a rural peasant just getting by on his income (and nothing for his wife and children) and, where change did occur it was usually resented: the sale of *biens nationaux* to the highest bidder, the creation of the Constitutional Church, and the abolition of the monarchy are cases in point.

*Language, Ideologies and Revolution*

Despite the gap between the rhetoric and the reality, the Revolution was predicated upon the notion of popular sovereignty, and it is this area where the search for the new linguistic 'turn' should begin. Any search for the origin of revolutionary language must start with the political writings of the *philosophes*, particularly Montesquieu and Rousseau, acknowledging Norman Hampson's important assessment of their varying influence on the revolutionary generation. Hampson even went on to contend that the revolutionaries themselves could be conveniently divided into two approximate categories: the Montesquians and the Rousseauians, corresponding to the moderates and the centre left. Yet these distinctive linguistic influences did not suddenly create a new political epistemology with a vocabulary to match in 1789 or even in 1793. The range and associations of political language in eighteenth century France was vast and sophisticated, drawing on antiquity as it did on modern writers, constantly feeding and enriching itself, and being utilised by politicians to their own ends. What one sees after 1789 is the extension and coarsening of the terminology but even that process had been going on throughout the century thanks to the 'Grub Street' popularisation of *philosophe* writings. At every level, the public was reclaiming its right to the ownership of language, challenging the claims of the Church and the Crown to exclusive rhetorical power, and stirring up what David Bell has memorably called the 'bubbling ideological stew' of the pre-revolutionary era.[5]

Every one of Montesquieu's writings was mined by politicians for insights into their own world. It made abundant sense to do so: Montesquieu was a *parlementaire* himself, one who could draw on the politics of aristocratic constitutionalism popularised by Fénelon's circle in the 1700s and extend, enrich and universalise these perceptions in a masterpiece, his *Esprit des lois* (1748). Finding their role as intermediary bodies reconceptualised and updated, the *parlementaires* couched their remonstrances to the Crown thereafter with justifications inspired directly by Montesquieu. One could not talk the language of constitutionalism without reference back to him and that remained the case for 1789–91 when Norman Hampson's 'Montesquians' thought that their moment had come, only for them to see pet schemes like a bicameral legislature and an absolute royal veto dismissed in favour of more radical, alternative models. Thereafter, Montesquieu's essentially historical perspective on social models was replaced by one much less in awe of tradition, and it would not be until the Thermidorians took power that his recommendation of a balanced constitutionalism and the separation of powers found some favour again with a revolutionary elite.

Influential though he was, Montesquieu never had anything like the vast sway on the revolutionary generation of Jean-Jacques Rousseau. That owed less to Rousseau's political writings than to the public's identification with Rousseau the man. All his readers thought they knew him at first hand and could find in their own lives echoes of the muddle and the embarrassment he had scandalously pointed up in his *Autobiography* (published 1782) or the pangs of unrequited but dutiful love in his *Nouvel Eloïse*. The French public's identification with Rousseau began in the 1750s and it just went on and on, his death in 1778 serving only to intensify it. He taught his own and the next two generations the exquisite raptures of sensibility while also urging the moral reconstruction of society in a way which would end the errors and evils of the existing one. Incapable of resisting melodramatic utterance, Rousseau envisaged moral and political reform. Denying the Biblical insistence on a corrupted order *ab initio*, he found that men had corrupted the world of their own free will but that it lay in the power of humanity to cleanse it again. Rousseau's appeal was that he 'described the people with love';[6] the world that properly belonged to ordinary men had been appropriated but, aroused and led by those alert to their historical (although essentially moral) predicament, that pristine world could be recovered. Rousseau thus established his own Messianic vision of how things might be and it was taken up by all sorts of readers turned revolutionaries between 1792 and 1794, most notably, of course, by Robespierre.[7] His reading of Rousseau led him to collapse personal and public meanings in the expectation of regenerating the future world through ruthlessness in the present. Jacobin messianism and Christian apocalypse thus became convergent explanations for what was going on in the traumatic revolutionary decade.

When Revolution came, its votaries largely interpreted it according to Rousseau's vision of moral transformation; its opponents saw it as inflicted on their society through the deliberate conspiracy of malign men like the king's cousin, the regicide duc d'Orléans, 'Philippe-Egalité'; the majority of the population could only have recourse to what the Church had always taught about the imminence of apocalypse and saw in the revolutionary upheavals a sure sign that the Antichrist's return would not be long delayed, an anticipation strengthened by its coinciding with the century's impending end and the impact of dechristianisation. Commentators at home and abroad could only make sense of the events they had lived through by consulting scripture and finding every sign that the Antichrist was abroad. As one Oxford academic had it:

> we have seen the Revolution in France, which is universally allowed to be in its origin, its principles, and its consequences, unparalleled in the history of the world, to be the work of the *Infidel Antichrist*, and the accurate accomplishment of Prophecy, while it baffles explanation upon any principles derived from experience, or any other source of human knowledge.[8]

This theme of the Revolution as apocalypse is not one that has much interested historians,[9] so that its Messianic aspects (both of language and symbol) are ripe for further recovery, and this would in turn fit its undoubted utopian strands into a fresh perspective.[10] The Enlightenment had done nothing to dampen fascination with the end of history as foretold in the Book of Revelation and other scriptural texts. Quite the contrary. A high proportion of the lower clergy and their rural parishioners looked to the return of Christ in glory as ending the pretensions of proud moderns to knowledge that uniquely belonged to the divinity, while the progressive minded – variously taking their inspiration from a medley of French rationalists, Rousseau, and the English Unitarian, chemist and honorary French citizen, Joseph Priestley[11] – persuaded themselves that the reconciliation of reason and revelation would help to usher in a new era, the immediate prelude to the coming of God's kingdom. This was particularly the case in 1791–2 for the leaders of the new Constitutional Church, notably Bishops Adrien Lamourette and Claude Fauchet, men who tended to end up in the Girondin camp. Their heady blend of Enlightenment optimism, Messianic expectation and revolutionary commitment has too easily been forgotten. The strong millenarian streak in the Constitutional Church was typical of other religious currents tracking across Europe in the 1790s. Fauchet, bishop of the Calvados *département*, was adamant that recent events in France were linked with Biblical apocalypse and the building of the New Jerusalem, that the times were coming when would befall 'the great evils foretold by the Prophets which would precede the total conversion of the nations and the reign of Jesus Christ on earth'. Prophecy was pressed into the service of the Revolution. The Carthusian monk, Dom Gerle, claimed in July 1790 that the Civil Constitution could be authenticated as truly the work of God, since a poor girl inspired by Heaven had foretold it 11 years earlier. He had in mind the Périgourdine prophetess, Suzette Laboussée.

If scripture provided the key to making sense of the events of the Revolution, the religious origins of revolutionary language should also not be neglected. Take the key word in any revolutionary's vocabulary, the 'nation'. As the late Adrian Hastings acutely observed, 'nationhood was not created by the Revolution but existed prior to 1789, even if it needed the Revolution fully to actualise itself.'[12] For centuries, it was the Roman Catholic Church in France that had most need of the concept, for Gallicans defined themselves according to their membership of the French nation, prided themselves on exclusive ecclesiastical liberties and a working independence of the papacy. The Jansenist disputes of the pre-revolutionary era had sharpened the Church's sense of national identity, with Jansenists unsuccessfully insistent on summoning a national council of the French Church in order to resolve their quarrel with the majority. A sense of nationhood with its origins in Christian teaching was not unique to Catholics. The Reformed Church in France (technically illegal until the Edict of 1787) had constant recourse during its time of persecution – the years in the Desert as they were called – to Old Testament idioms of nationhood and belonging/exclusion, with themselves cast as the Israelites in the wilderness, desperately seeking tribal admission into full French nationhood. It was no coincidence that so many of the Revolutionaries had Protestant backgrounds and were as familiar with the Bible as any of their contemporaries.

The Bourbon monarchy also worked hard in the pre-revolutionary decades to align itself with the rekindled sense of nationhood and the French kingdom as *la patrie* to which the so-called 'Second Hundred Years War' with Britain had given rise. Linda Colley famously claimed in *Britons* (London, 1992) that the Protestant British defined themselves against French 'otherness' and, accepting that point for the sake of argument, it might be said that the process was really two-directional. Soldiers from all over provincial France served globally in a manner that brought their common Frenchness to the fore; the challenge to the late Bourbon sovereigns was to ensure that 'nationhood' and 'monarchy' were two sides of the same coin. They were only partially successful. When Louis XV in 1766 told the *parlement* that 'the rights and interest of the Nation,...are necessarily joined with mine and rest only in my hands', he was actually forcing policies on the reluctant magistrates calculated to do exactly the reverse. The imposition of the Maupeou coup between 1771 and 1774 widened the semantic gap between Crown and nation, and it was never entirely closed in the reign of his grandson Louis XVI, although progressive ministers, Necker for instance, saw an imperative need to establish 'nationhood' and 'monarchy' in a necessary relationship. By the 1780s, the various idioms of 'patriotism' were the constant recourse of those out of favour with the king and his ministers, and they never failed to conjure up connotations of a coalition of interested parties working for the national good, transcending social divisions. The rhetoric may have been far from the reality, but the important thing was to lay claim to it, to use it plausibly to brand one's opponents as 'unpatriotic' and claim the moral high ground that, after 1789, would also coincide with the political high ground. In an important sense, everyone was talking the same language when the Revolution started: they just meant different things.

The language of 'patriotism' and 'republicanism' were always closely aligned. Few in pre-1789 were eccentric enough to regard a republic as a viable political option for the state; where they did see republicanism as relevant was through its classic values of good citizenship and disinterested service in the state, values which could be inculcated in Louis XVI's subjects to the benefit of all. Despite doubters like Moreau, the government had reached the same conclusion by 1780, with the minister in charge of public works, the comte d'Angivilliers, commissioning Jacques-Louis David's 'Oath of the Horatii', exhibited at the Salon of 1785, and noticeable for its uncompromisingly republican allusions. Yet the regime did not see this painting, or the many others with comparable values exhibited at the annual Salons in the 1780s, as incompatible with a monarchist constitution, or a neo-absolutist polity. Generations of the French elite had been educated on classical texts such as Plutarch and Tacitus and they had not turned into militant enemies of the state. Paradoxically, republican values were widely disseminated during the later Enlightenment in France because they were thought on every side to be the finest training for contemporary citizenship and those civic virtues that, as Montesquieu had reminded his readers, were so desirable in any civilised state. Louis XVI, in his own muted way an Enlightened monarch, could not disagree, and so presided over the invigoration of republican idioms over which the monarchy and it supporters had lost control by 1791. Thus if the Republic was new in 1792, the language its supporters used was not.

The monarchy's interest in patronising artists sympathetic to d'Angerviller's preferences also revealed its desperate attempts to control and limit public debate about the nature, values and organisation of the state. Notoriously, although there was no free press in France until the Revolution, controls were only haphazardly effective. Thus the 25 established journals available in 1760 had grown to 60 in 1785.[13] When restrictions were enforced, this only gave ammunition to those who wanted to allege the despotic character of the monarchy.[14] Meanwhile, ministers such as Vergennes in the 1780s were not beyond using journalists to plant articles in the semi-official *Gazette de Leyde* and thereby undermine his rivals, making a nonsense of official policy and confidentiality inside the royal council. Before the 1780s, the press worked mainly underground or from just outside France's frontiers, the Austrian Netherlands, Britain and Switzerland. After 1789 the legal restraints were for a time relaxed and the press and journalists of every persuasion worked hard catering to every conceivable political taste, and helped give the nation a greater sense of itself: by 1792 perhaps 3 million people, or about half the adult male population, were exposed to the power of newspapers. Reading about the events going on around them became a passion even for passive citizens. As one English visitor just back from Paris reported in late 1791:

> as to modern politics, and the principles of the constitution, one would think that half the people in Paris had no other employment than to study and talk about them. I have seen a fishwoman reading the journal of the National assembly to her neighbour who appeared to listen with all the avidity of Shakespeare's blacksmith.[15]

If the Revolution was perceived in the first instance as a textual act it was down to this press prominence, a fluid world of petty jealousies among journalists, but one which gave Jacobins such as Fabre d'Eglantine, Fréron and Marat the opportunity to win public attention and develop a distinctive voice for themselves and against each other. Brissot admitted the reach of the printed word, by which 'one can teach the same truth at the same moment to millions of men; through the press, they can discuss it without tumult, decide calmly and give their opinion'.[16] On every count, Brissot was too optimistic, unless one reads his comments solely in terms of the provincial press that had a vast exponential, almost overnight, growth. Parisian journalists soon showed they had a capacity to stir up tumultuous opinion between 1789 and 1791, not surprisingly when as many as 400 newspapers were on sale in the capital. The future *enragé*, Jacques Hébert, began his archetypal populist paper, the *Père Duchesne*, in 1790. Hyperbole, abuse and scandalous rumours became his stock-in-trade and made him a dangerous enemy for the respectable politicians of the First Republic. He turned his paper into a brilliant rabble-rouser, with a proven capacity for getting his *sans-culottes* allies out on to the streets and keeping the pressure on the Paris *commune* and the Convention. On the whole, the press was less a forum for national debate than a means of pressurising politicians to act in a way favoured by printers and writers, and using the evidence of sales and letters from readers (often fictitious ones) as another means to that end. If Popkin's claim that the press scripted the Revolution, creating a nexus of tensions and anticipations, is correct,[17] then no wonder that republican politicians by 1792–3 were so anxious to close down what they could not command. Journalists had the formidable power of opinion formation that politicians envied. Counter-revolutionary scribes lay open to intimidation in proportion to their effectiveness, none more so than Mallet du Pan. On 15 November 1790, 'patriots' called for his dismissal and a mob chanted the pun coined by Desmoulins, 'Mallet pendu'.

*The Revolution and the Arts*

The preference of revolutionary zealots was more for depicting the Revolution than writing about it: the Revolution and its values would prevail fastest by pleasing the eye and creating a republican symbolism that would entirely displace the familiar iconography of a Christian monarchy. This cultural transformation was enacted at a hectic pace during 1790s in a bid to win the Revolution a mass following and lend some credibility to its claim to rest on popular endorsement. The most enduring changes came early on during the era of constitutional monarchy, notably the cockade of red, white and blue worn on a hat (even Louis XVI sported it on 17 July 1789 for his visit to Paris) and a new *tricouleur* flag, the banner of the nation from October 1790 in preference to the fleur-de-lys of the Bourbon family. It was typical of the hybrid nature of French public life between 1789 and 1792 that the two standards were often flown together, signs of the uneasy marriage between old and new that soon collapsed. At the great festival of the Federation held on 14 July 1790 a Mass was celebrated and the royal family attended a huge thanksgiving for the Revolution. It was an uneasy combination of symbols. It had minimal connection with the ceremonies of the old order and the weather was atrocious; the king and queen viewed what Fersen called its 'orgies and bacchanalia' with contempt.[18] After the proclamation of the Republic every token of the old order became an embarrassment to the new one, its replacement a priority, starting with the coinage.

Central to the pre-1792 order had been the Catholic Church and its distinctive images were less acceptable to Jacobin republicans than royal ones, a constant reminder of a value system adjudged incompatible with the Revolution. It was this conviction which lay behind the frenzy of vandalism inflicted on sacred Christian sites in 1793–4: churches were closed and stripped of their fittings in an outbreak of destruction hardly any parish escaped (see Chapter 8 below). Dechristianisation had strong ideological roots in pre-revolutionary disenchantment with the material standing of the Gallican Church, but it was also a tactical manoeuvre which gambled on winning hearts and minds at an unrealistically rapid pace given France's emphatically Catholic character down to 1789 (however much it was contested). It scarcely helped the cause of the dechristianisers that in the cultural war waged by the Revolutionaries against the Church, they abolished the Christian festivals (saints' days often had royalist connotations) which were a welcome part of annual life for most men and women, days when they relaxed as well as worshipped. As an alternative, the Convention and the civic authorities introduced a range of republican festivals to act as a focus for loyalties to themselves. Accordingly, Paris staged a 'Festival of Liberty' in November 1793 with Notre-Dame cathedral converted into a 'Temple of Reason' for the occasion, and other towns followed suit. The commemoration of Christian saints was replaced by remembering the 'martyrs of liberty' like Marat, Lepeletier de Saint-Fargeau and Chalier, and the most important and potent female symbol of the Catholic faith – the Blessed Virgin Mary – gave way to her republican successor, Marianne.

Most provincial centres participated enthusiastically. In Tours, Athanase Veau, a *conventionnel*, recited several paens on the inauguration of the cult of reason in the Year II. His 'Hymne aux Grands Hommes' suggests that in place of the saints of the old order, a new group be raised up for veneration, including Voltaire, Rousseau and Mably. These dechristianising cults lauding reason were not to the taste of every revolutionary. Robespierre famously denounced them as 'aristocratic' and immoral on 21 November 1793 and at the height of his power in the spring of 1794 moved the emphasis to his preferred cult of the Supreme Being, celebrated as part of a package of decadal festivals which included themes such as 'Hatred of Tyrants and Traitors', 'Frugality', 'Conjugal Love' and 'Happiness'. Many of these survived his own overthrow and the Directory made periodic efforts to reinvent festivals as an integral and indispensable part of the republican order, especially in 1798–9. There was a move to giving celebrations an increasingly militaristic character even before Brumaire. Once the Bonapartist era began, this theme was carefully choreographed, and popular festivals lost their last shreds of spontaneity in favour of solemn, martial programmes.

Once the novelty value of the new festivals had worn off, the authorities found it a struggle to involve the average urban family in the celebrations and keep them interested in the spectacle; the day off work might have been welcomed, but most would much sooner have had their Sundays back along with the familiar ways of community life in preference to this aggressive politicisation of leisure and the uprooting of the familiar. As in other regards, the French Revolution won over the young rather than the middle-aged and the elderly, precisely that age group whose adult experience of the pre-1789 order had been minimal. Dancing around the tree of liberty in a *bonnet rouge* at any rate offered them opportunities for meeting members of the opposite sex, however tasteless or embarrassing their parents viewed it. Revolutionary cults and public imagery fired up their devotees, but they were just too abstract to mean much to most men and women over 30. They found in them – and this was particularly the case for women in the provinces – nothing to celebrate and much to deplore. Yet these discovered that retreating into family life (such a feature of the 1790s) was no guarantee of escaping the state's intrusiveness, extending even into what was in an individual's wardrobe or on their dressing-table, and whether they had a penchant for expensive, 'aristocratic' food. Powdering one's hair or tying it into a queue was a prima facie sign of republican disaffection among men, in the mid-1790s while their wives found from September 1793 that wearing the revolutionary cockade had become obligatory for women.[19] In one sense, such stipulations marked a return to the medieval sumptuary laws that had become impossible to enforce long before the end of the *ancien régime*. And the rapid coming and going of revolutionary governments could soon make the dress codes associated with each one personally compromising. During the Terror, as citizens were encouraged to detain and denounce the enemies of the state, wearing a costume that too closely resembled what the well-dressed *sans-culotte* was supposed to be wearing could have lethal consequences for a man who was just trying to look like a good patriot.

In one sense, dress triggered the most violent phase of the Counter-Revolution. In February 1793 the Republic ordered the immediate enlistment of 300,000 men to meet the external threat, recruits who would be required to wear the blue uniform that had replaced the white of the former royalist line army. Coming only a month after Louis XVI's execution, thousands of young men in the west of France preferred open rebellion to putting on the colours of a regicide republic. Quite soon thereafter, the Vendée revolt was often referred to as a conflict between the *Bleus*, the republican forces, and the *Blancs*, their royalist adversaries. In fact, the counter-revolutionary irregulars of western France seldom had uniforms of any distinctive colour, but they still had access to the huge treasury of royal and religious symbols available to all men and women who shared their convictions. Most favoured was the Sacred Heart of Jesus, a medallion worn around the neck signifying unerringly the individual's attachment to the Catholic Church and, by extension, the monarchy. Battlefields would be littered with these badges after an engagement between *Bleus* and *Blancs*.[20]

These medallions showed counter-revolutionary iconography at its most basic. There were many other ways of representing this cause. The execution of Louis XVI on 21 January 1793 and the events leading up to the regicide, the monarch on trial, and his taking leave of his family, all appealed to the artistic imagination and generated a massive print culture with access to markets across Europe. Painters who had never been to France, let alone been witnesses to the events they depicted, found in the excesses of the Revolution an endless source of creative inspiration and market opportunity. Thus Johan Zoffany, a German-born artist living in England, produced in about 1794 two extraordinary imaginative works – 'Plundering the King's Cellar at Paris, August 10, 1792', and 'Celebrating over the Bodies of the Swiss Soldiers' – to show the British public that violence and debauchery were right at the heart of the Revolution.[21] Zoffany's imagery was impassioned, Burkean in its intensity, putting aside accuracy in the interests of rousing opinion in Britain and elsewhere to present the Revolution as an intrinsically brutal and destructive force. On the other side of the political divide, the revolutionaries were equally determined to deploy the arts in their service. The Académie Royale was abolished in 1793 and replaced by the Institut de France two years later as the main organ of state patronage. The Convention, too, encouraged the arts by holding a competition in 1794 on the theme of its historic session of 10 August 1792, won by François Gérard (1770–1837). The 1790s continued and intensified the neo-classical art forms favoured in the last two decades of monarchical rule and these were given supreme expression in the paintings of Jacques-Louis David (1748–1825) and the pupils of his studio, such as Gérard. During Robespierre's ascendancy, David's artistic dominance was underpinned by his political acceptability (he had voted for the execution of the king and produced superb paintings of revolutionary martyrs such as Marat and Joseph Bara) and he was given responsibility for organising the programme for the Festival of the Supreme Being. As has been recently noted, 'the more coercive and conformist the political moment, the more abstractly beatific [his] images had to be'.[22] After surviving the fall of the Jacobins, David produced his 'Intervention of the Sabine women' (1799), a painting at once more primitive and Grecian in style than some of his earlier masterpieces, with revolutionary reconciliation as its theme.[23] David found his greatest patron in Napoleon (he was appointed *Premier Peintre* immediately after the coronation), producing inimitable images like 'Napoleon Crossing the St Bernard Pass' (1801) to commemorate the Battle of Marengo and the Consul's fresh conquest of Italy. The First Consul recognised the artist's flair for memorialising events in a way that was fresh and accessible to a vast range of sensibilities. As his biographer points out:

> For with David French painting had become a vehicle capable of expressing great emotion with the simplest possible means. This astonishing simplicity, together with his immensely sensitive response to historical change, ensures that his subjects seem as surprising today as when they were painted.[24]

The mature commercial art market of the 1790s ensured the widespread reproduction in the form of prints and lithographs of defining Revolutionary images such as those produced by David and other artists. Memorabilia could be found in the most unlikely places, even on tea services! The same themes of patriotism, republicanism and the national good also recurred incessantly in all forms of literature, including the verse of André Chénier (1762–94), arguably the greatest poet of eighteenth-century France. Originally committed to the Revolution – as his *Le Serment du Jeu de Paume* made plain – Chénier was imprisoned during the Jacobin ascendancy and executed two days before the fall of Robespierre. His posthumously published satirical *Iambes* arraigned the *Montagnards* for talking grandly about human liberty while denying its citizens their natural rights of justice and freedom. Of all literary forms, it was, however, drama which both paralleled and inspired the events of 1789–1804. Theatre flourished in revolutionary Paris: twice as many plays were written and enacted between 1789 and 1799 as in the previous 250 years. By spring 1791 there were 45 theatres in the capital attracting a widened audience. It was hard to keep political overtones out of drama even if it has been shown that blatantly political plays were not the most successful ones.[25] The poet's younger brother, Marie-Joseph Chénier (1767–1811), in bringing out a play called *Charles IX* (the Valois king) in 1789, struck contemporary echoes with themes about the integrity of the people in comparison with the corruption of the Court. There were some unsubtle pointers for Louis XVI when Chénier gave the first Bourbon sovereign, Henri IV, these words: 'Instead of servants subject to my orders, I saw around me equals, friends.' New works showed additional attention to the merits of the lower orders, lovers put love of country before love of each other. Sylvain Maréchal's *Le jugement dernier des rois* (1793) even brought the people on to the stage to confront deposed European monarchs and the pope, dragged there in ignomy. Its combination of burlesque, pantomine and farce encouraged audiences to enjoy themselves as well as find moral uplift from a suitably republican theme for wartime. This kind of production troubled many *conventionnels*: they saw the stage as an agency of moral uplift in the first instance, and decreed that a range of patriotic plays would be produced regularly and staged gratis. Despite the incentive of free seats, the auditorium was hard to fill. Soon, doubts about the political content of much in the repertoire, a respect for Rousseau's claim that the theatre stimulated vice and sanctioned inequality through unequal pricing, and the sensitiveness of Jacobin leaders to criticism led to the reinstatement of censorship on 2 Floréal, Year II (21 April 1794). Claude-François Payan, a member of the Commission on Public Instruction, declared: 'The theatres are still encumbered with the rubbish of the old Order, feeble copies of the masters.... We must sweep this chaotic mass out of our theatres...'.[26] Thereafter, the revolutionaries were careful to control the stage, fearing the damage that dramatic subversion could inflict on their standing and therefore on their survival.

Song could be quite as threatening. At one level, the Revolution produced stirring, inspirational martial music (much of it performed in the theatres), and there could be no one in the country who did not know the words and tune of the 'Ça ira', even if it was only to parody it as the counter-revolutionaries readily did. However, a good song with the wrong words – from the angle of the authorities – could be devastating and no regime had ever stopped the average French man from singing. The summoning of the Estates-General in 1789 had given rise to a huge range of melodies with matching words celebrating popular gladness at this defining moment in the life of the nation and it continued thus. People literally sang the Revolution. They also sang against it. Opera was particularly problematic for the authorities given its association with the high culture of the unreformed monarchy, and it maintained a conventional repertoire until autumn 1792. It had been the singing of a celebrated chorus from the opera *Richard Coeur de Lion* (1784) by Grétry – 'Richard, O Mon Roi, l'univers t'abandonne' – that had intensified popular Parisian suspicions of the counter-revolutionary circle around the king in July 1789. Immediately after the King signed the Constitution of

1791, there was a royalist revival in miniature and on 19 September 'Richard' was given at the *Italiens* theatre to a full house. On that occasion the song 'was not interrupted until the excessive applause of the Aristocrats provoked it, and the piece was heard throughout'. Yet there was still enough clamouring before the audience dispersed to require a magistrate to come on the stage and ask for silence in the name of the law.[27] During the Terror, as revolutionary rhetoric became focused on groups rather than individual performers, so the chorus became more considerable.[28] Composers adapted quickly. When the remains of Voltaire were moved in 1791, there was music specially composed by Gossec and lyrics by Marie-Joseph Chénier were chanted. The hymn became the format of choice for the nation's music in a time of revolution.[29]

As well as making a cult of itself, the Revolution wanted to monumentalise itself, to develop a public architecture appropriate to a country which had discarded its 'corrupt' recent past in favour of a republican road to greatness. It was an Enlightenment commonplace that ideology could be inculcated through powerful imagery.[30] Architects were encouraged to submit projects to the Convention and to think on a grand scale, to work around the concept of public spaces that would actually be filled with citizens in the way that republican Athens and Rome had been, and to create the buildings in which a renewed state might explore and express itself. These heroic aspirations may have caught the imagination; the problem was that before 1795 regimes (and the values associated with them) had such a high rate of turnover that, funding problems aside, commissioning projects with any realistic hope of completion was minimal. The leading neo-classical architect, Etienne-Louis Boullé (1728–99), came up with megalomanic proposals including a 5oo-ft-high sphereical monument to Newton and a Cenotaph for a warrior in the shape of a sarcophagus about 250 ft high, grand, abstract, geometrically satisfying, but impractical in the climate of an unstable political order. Boullé's major competitor and contemporary, Claude-Nicolas Ledoux (1736–1806), had even proposed a bordello in the shape of an erect phallus before the Revolution. Such an *architecture parlante* was favoured by the revolutionaries, a literalism proclaiming its functions. Ledoux had executed some remarkable neo-classical buildings before the Revolution, but his suspect monarchist politics confined him to prison for most of the 1790s. His intention was to reform society through the buildings that he proposed: yet he remained a monarchist throughout his life. 'His attitude was monitory, hortatory. His buildings were sermons in stone.'[31] After 1795, stability encouraged a modest surge of public building, for instance a simple semicircular amphitheatre by Gisors and Lecointe for the Council of the 500 in the Palais Bourbon (1797). Bonaparte, as First Consul, also gave much work in Paris to his favourite architects, Fontaine and Percier; the creators of the Empire style. Their construction of the Rue de Rivoli in 1801 was the first of many designs successfully completed. Yet, on the whole, the architectural remains of the French Revolution before Napoleon are few and fragmentary, either adaptations of existing buildings or low-key such as the unfluted Tuscan columns (for which there were pre-revolutionary precedents) used by Poyet along the Rue des Colonnes in Paris in 1798 rather than the grand designs which fired the exponents of civic republicanism. Stylistically, the break with pre-1789 neo-classicism was hard to detect, and the continuity of design in buildings executed in the 1790s with those erected a decade or so previously is striking: for all their rhetorical aspirations, the Revolutionaries conspicuously failed to deliver a new architectural idiom. That would be the product of more settled times under the emperor Napoleon.

## The French Revolution and Antiquity

It suited the most ardent revolutionaries – as it has some several historians subsequently – to present their era as one which marked a new start for humanity, one which discarded the dead hand of history as any guide to recasting society in a new, regenerated mould. Everything before 1789 belonged to the 'Old Order'; 1789–92 became a transition period, and 1792 became the Year I in the new calendar. Time had been stopped and restarted again on 22 September 1792. A new, rational system of weights and measures created a fresh framework for daily lives. The unit of the metre linked the revolution to the globe itself, as it represented one ten-millionth of a line between the North Pole and the Equator. Two astronomer-*savants*, Jean-Baptiste-Joseph Delambre and Pierre-François-André Méchain spent seven years measuring the section of the meridian line that lay north from Paris to Dunkirk and south to Barcelona. They 'triangulated' every inch of the way, and it all culminated in the horrific discovery by Méchain that his sums didn't add up![32]

It suited the zealots to deny the continuities between old and new, to make any concession to the possibility that their new order was not as new as they preferred to think. The French past, denoted by princes and priests, was damned as having nothing to offer except object lessons in oppression, leaving the opinion makers of the 1790s to seek inspiration elsewhere in reconstructing the public sphere. As is well known, many Jacobins, including Robespierre, having found in Rousseau their diagnosis of what was wrong with France, sought in his writings the inspiration to put it right. But it was less the past *per se* which the Revolutionaries disowned, than the *Christian* past. Since the Renaissance, the culture of the classical world had comfortably coexisted within the Christian world, but the revolutionary leaders of 1792–4 (and many afterwards) were determined to break that connection. Where were contemporary republicans to find the emblems and exemplars to construct the purified public order they sought? They looked in the first instance to the regimes of the ancient world before they were replaced by royal despots such as Alexander the Great or Augustus Caesar, and to pagan polytheism before it lost out to Christianity. It was the primitive past that had to be recovered and restored, but that was no longer to be seen through anything resembling a Christian or a monarchical prism. They turned back to the republican polities of the pre-Christian Mediterranean world. In creating the Constitutions of the Year III (Directory) and the Year VIII (Consulate) the terminology and the balancing of powers drew directly on classical precedents.

This veneration of the ancient world – and selected politicians and philosophers – may have been a hallmark of revolutionary authenticity; it was also not a cultural trend that was abruptly given life in 1789. Throughout the eighteenth century, as had happened since at least the Renaissance, the French elite had read their Cicero and scanned their Plutarch, and been directed by their tutors to look on such men as role models for living a life of probity in which the good of the state counted for much. The fact that they would live out their public lives in the monarchies of Louis XV and Louis XVI might have been incongruous but it did not invalidate the educational prescription. Witness Archbishop Fénelon's decision to offer Louis XIV's grandson and heir presumptive, the teenage duke of Burgundy, guidance in government in his *Télèmarque* (1699) not through a Christian hero, but via the Virgilian character of Mentor. French culture in the pre-revolutionary decades was saturated in classical influences and classical styles and we cannot read revolution through as if this prism was original to it. What happens after 1792 is that the classical heritage officially displaced the Christian past that, down to the Revolution, had coexisted with it and, arguably, remained the dominant partner. That remained the case well into the Consulate until Bonaparte, for reasons of political convenience, attempted their partial reintegration, the fruits of which were dramatically on display at his coronation in 1804. Some enthusiasts took the vogue for classicism to extreme lengths. Maurice Quai and Paulin Duqueylar, young acolytes of David, walked about Paris in *chitons* copied from Greek vases and let their beards grow, sufficiently eccentric even in revolutionary times to have them dubbed 'les barbus'. Quai, who liked to be addressed as Agamemnon, was a fluent and persuasive speaker, and pinned his faith on nature and the Antique.

A recurrent problem in republican Rome had been to stabilise relations between plebians and patricians; the revolutionaries hoped to avoid that difficulty. This insight helps to explain a key difference between the obsession with antiquity before and after 1789. Before the Revolution there was no attempt to popularise the classical heritage; afterwards it became a propaganda weapon in the associated causes of republicanism and dechristianisation. And since the hold of Christian and monarchical values and symbols was most tenacious among the ordinary men and women of rural France, they would be one of the major target audiences in this seismic shift in the public culture. The French populace encountered basic changes in their everyday lives. The streets on which they lived lost the names of kings and emperors, bishops and saints in favour of republicans – living and deceased – in the process called *débaptisation*. Time was measured differently. The Gregorian calendar was abandoned from October 1793 in favour of Fabre d'Eglantine's alternative, one which abandoned weeks in favour of *décades* and found no place for Sundays. Coins lost the king's head and were adorned instead with classical symbols. Modes of address that connoted deference were officially abandoned in favour of the neutral 'citizen' and 'citizenness', terminology deemed apt in a republic of free and virtuous citizens, much as the *tutoiement* encouraged by the Committee of Public Safety from November 1793.

The revolutionary festivals were another striking visual sign of this bid to inculcate the new values up and down provincial France, and they were kept going until the last days of the Directory. Festivals and funerals often went together for republicans needed their own martyrology to wean popular opinion away from commemorating those who had died for their Christian faith. When the illustrious dead – Lepeletier, Marat, Bara, Chalier – were buried, they had their own cult and commemorations to keep their memory alive. A hopeless task it might be supposed in the light of the parish clergy's experience over more than a century in commending only officially recognised saints, but the revolutionaries were as hurried here as they were in formulating policy everywhere. Today's heroes could be tomorrow's traitors. Thus all those who were buried or reburied in the Panthéon (the Parisian church of Sainte-Geneviève was made into a monument for the great men of the fatherland as early as April 1791) were liable to have their bodies flung out when the politics of the living moved on.[33] Urban citizens, many of whom were members of the clubs, could have strong views on these matters but it is unlikely that they found much to inspire them in the neo-classical idioms that all the revolutionary regimes favoured. Its avoidance of the sensuous and its reference to abstract ideals made it suitable for conveying transcendent revolutionary truths (this was the foundation of its appeal to moralising Jacobins such as Robespierre and Saint-Just), but its very abstraction limited its popular impact. The Jacobins never grasped that allegory was too allusive, too recondite for popular taste, and therefore an unsatisfactory medium to entrench themselves in power.

Politicians varied in their choice of favoured republican dead. Different figures from antiquity were pushed into prominence and then removed as politicians came and went, but if there was one figure to whom revolutionaries kept returning it was Brutus, the celebrated consul who loved the Roman republic so much that he was prepared to see his two sons condemned to death for plotting against it. David exhibited a painting of him at the Salon in 1789; Voltaire's play of the same name dating from 1730 was revived 60 years later and played to packed houses; and Brutus's marble bust was set in a conspicuous place in the assembly hall of the convention, an inspiration and a warning to speakers.[34] The revolutionaries read the Roman historian Livy to recast Brutus in their own image, but there were perils. By 1793 (when it was being performed free in 9 Paris theatres), Voltaire's plea for balance in Brutus had become uncomfortably prominent and it was condemned as counter-revolutionary. Sparta was another model regime for these scores of thousands who had read their Rousseau although the absence of written sources for its history both limited its iconic value and increased the moralising use to which Spartan models of republicanism could be put, though these fell out of favour after 9 Thermidor. French revolutionaries hoped that recourse to the images of previous republican polities would guard against the dissolution of their own. But theirs, too, shared the fate of republican Rome. Despite the perpetuation of republican trappings and rhetoric during the Consulship, all likewise ended in the triumph of a general, once Napoleon Bonaparte, just as Julius Caesar before him, came home from Egypt.[35]

## Napoleon and the Signs and Symbols of Revolutionary France

The official imagery of the Directory had superimposed a modified set of classical republican values on the symbols of 1792–5 without their ever winning the public's imagination and offsetting the rather tawdry feel the regime possessed by the late 1790s. A year into his position as First Consul, and with the Battle of Marengo behind him, Bonaparte was ready to temper the republican iconography inherited from the Directory with his own personality cult. His policies had, by 1801–2, restored general peace to Europe with the treaties of Lunéville and Amiens and apparently settled the religious question through the signing of the Concordat and the imposition of the Organic Articles. These successes ensured that having himself awarded the First Consulship for life was popularly regarded as a service to the state rather than a reinvention of autocracy far more formidable than anything attempted by Robespierre. Bonaparte was ready to use an eclectic range of images that would both stabilise and popularise his regime. For instance, he had the remains of the great seventeenth-century general, Turenne, translated to the Invalides on 23 September 1800, which Montlosier, writing in the *Courrier de Londres* (5 January 1802) believed symbolised 'the making of peace between the century of Bonaparte and the century of Louis XIV' and 'brought to an end the unnatural war of the new France against the former France, the war of children against their fathers'.[36] It was very much 'his' regime by 1802. Artists and propagandists (the two categories often merged) variously depicted him as a successful general, a dedicated servant of the republic and a glamorous princeling. As late as 1803, Bonaparte was not quite ready to dispense with the official paraphinalia of the Republic: the revolutionary calendar continued, Frenchmen still addressed each other formally as 'citizen' (though 'monsieur' and 'madame' and the use of 'vous' over and against 'tu' were heard everywhere), and, above all, they identified with the most successful and enduring piece of revolutionary imagery, the tricolour. Nevertheless, a return to pre-republican manners, modes and symbols was becoming everywhere apparent. The Consul from that year commenced using his Christian name only to coincide with the striking of a new medal in March carrying the old royal motto 'God defend France'. It became customary to address Napoleon as 'Your Highness', his elegant wife Josephine presided over gala occasions at Court (for there was again a Court with real aristocrats in attendance which lacked only the name of royal or imperial), and foreign diplomats were presented to her after they had first had their official audience with him. Believing that it was by baubles that men are led, Napoleon established the *Légion d'Honeur*, giving France an honours system again. As the Prussian minister to France reported: 'Everything around the First Consul is resuming the general character and etiquette of Versailles. Ostentatious luxury, fine carriages, liveries, crowds of servants are seen on every side'.[37]

Bonaparte sensed that although initially indispensable to his success, republican cultural trappings were an uncomfortable reminder of national divisions, and not the emblems around which the *Grande nation* could unite. Napoleon's personality cult was one way of giving all but the most die-hard republicans and monarchists a token of the national leader and modern hero who would heal divisions and restore national pride. And he would do it through the army and a cult of glory. The army had, by the early 1800s, turned out to be far more powerful in French society than the republican state that had originally called it into life ten years previously. The ultimate expression of Consular France was not a Roman toga, the unconvincing official endorsement of the 1792 Calendar, or the courtly dress Bonaparte fostered among his officials and ministers at the Tuileries palace, but a military uniform. The army and everything connected with it moved centre stage during the Consulate and it would remain there so long as Napoleon was head of state, either as consul or emperor. It made his government glamorous, it guaranteed his rule, and it had kept at bay all that the monarchies of Europe could do to dislodge him. No other institution better symbolised French greatness than the army. Bonaparte gloried in his association with it and lost no opportunity of showing himself to the public surrounded by his soldiers. In 1804 he talked of the army as representative of the real people of France because its ranks were full of men from all parts of the country.

Between 1799 and 1804 the militarisation of French national life proceeded apace with regimental flags and eagles coming to embody the greatness of the state in a way that the original signs and symbols of the revolution no longer managed to do. They also afforded a rallying point for national pride that nothing else quite managed for those millions who rejoiced in French achievement on the battlefield, who loved to hear tales of heroism and sacrifice, and who had a personal stake in the army through the conscription of their sons, brothers and husbands. These things stirred the blood in a way that the stilted rhetoric of republicanism no longer did, though it remained the language of officialdom. Bonaparte persisted with it for the time being precisely because it calmed the fears of the ex-Jacobins (Fouché was the most prominent) in his government that the regime was heading back to a monarchy. While he needed their support, the supreme prize was always building a national consensus around the state over which he presided and Bonaparte, in maturity the supreme political realist, never underestimated the hold of traditional symbolism on the French people, those symbols of Church and monarchy which went back many centuries and which at the beginning of the nineteenth century had to underpin his state rather than threaten it. This was particularly the case with Catholicism, for most of the 1790s the great engine of the counter-revolution. Through his Concordat with Pius VII, Napoleon intended to harness its cultural power to that of his regime through such means as prayers at Mass for the Consul and then the Emperor, as well as imposing on the Gallican Church such officially approved cults as that of his legendary ancestor, 'St Napoléon', who had his annual feast day on 15 August at the expense of the Assumption of the Virgin Mary. The supreme expression of ecclesiastical support for Napoleon was, of course, his coronation by Pius VII in Notre-Dame cathedral on 4 December 1804. It was a full-blooded state occasion, more spectacular than any *sacre* for centuries, and inaugurated the empire so uncompromisingly that it seemed both unnatural and ungrateful for either Jacobins or monarchists to complain – had either dared. It also embodied the adaptability and eclecticism of the Napoleonic regime, involving state, Church, and army, in a colourful ceremonial with one man at the centre of the celebrations who would draw on any symbolic sources so long as they served one purpose: confirming and strengthening his own dominance.

*Conclusion*

Napoleon tried to adapt the language and signs of revolution and counter-revolution to his own purposes, but the fall of his empire in 1814/15 unscrambled them again and showed how deeply divisive the 1790s had been for the entire French nation. So many of the quarrels and disputes of the next 150 years had their origins in the revolutionary decade, and the ancestral loyalties and attachment to symbols originating then constantly resurfaced from generation to generation. Having a neutral attitude to the revolution and its culture was next to impossible because of the upheaval and violence its proponents and opponents had inflicted on each other with all the accompanying bitterness. Every symbol became heavy with accumulated layers of significance, such as the Sacred Heart of Jesus for monarchists, the dear trophy of the Vendéen rebels in the 1790s and carried into battle again by royalist officers and their troops on several occasions, notably during the Franco–Prussian War of 1870–1. Even the tricolour flag was divisive after its rejection by the restored Bourbons. Notoriously, the unwillingness of the comte de Chambord, their claimant to the throne after Napoleon III abdicated, to abandon the fleur-de-lys wrecked his hopes of returning to Paris as 'King Henry V' in the early 1870s. The Revolution had transformed the manner in which French people spoke about politics and depicted them; it had irrevocably altered existing conceptualisations of action in the public sphere and in so doing had a major creative impact, but at a massive cost in stable state building or of creating a nation at ease with itself. It created rival political identities with their own languages, rituals and symbols dating back to the Revolution (or before in the case of legitimist monarchists) who could not easily coexist and who had ancestral scores to settle. Had Napoleon genuinely proved capable of ending the Revolution as he wished to do during the Consulate then French history after 1815 would have been very different. As it was, Bonapartism just became another, complicating part of the symbolic heritage of the French Revolution.

# Chapter 5: The Transformation of Institutions

*Introduction*

The Revolution brought public life in France to a rapid, even a forced maturity, it did not create public life from nothing. Modern scholarship is in no doubt about the emergence of 'public opinion' in the middle decades of the century, and the way it acted as a legitimising force capable of operating independently of the monarchy. Before 1789 the institutional fabric of the state had a vigour and a variety which few of the revolutionaries – and many historians after them – would admit, but institutions like the *parlements* or the other sovereign courts adapted and evolved in changing circumstances rather than suffering outright displacement. Innovation in government was rare and usually disguised as renovation, justified by a return to an older and more authentic past within the life of the kingdom: even the summoning of the Estates-General of 1789 was sanctioned by early seventeenth-century precedents, and it took a great deal of petitioning from the Third Estate to persuade ministers to jettison the exact compositional arrangements of 1614.

The coming of the Revolution swept away a concern for custom and unleashed a surge of instant institutional creativity as part of the process of modernising and overhauling the French state. The revolutionaries prided themselves on their commitment to innovation as a sign of the vitality and impeccable moral standing of their state. The old order would be replaced by political arrangements designed for the future, inspired by republican antiquity, and constructed according to scientific models. Some scholars explain this new trajectory as having its basis in what they have called the 'desacralisation' of institutions, notably the monarchy. This controversial proposition has not commanded universal assent, but one can say that the classic Enlightenment emphasis on what worked (utility, in other words) was more apparent in France at the close of the eighteenth century than in any other European state. This amounted to a profound cultural shift, the discarding of organicist notions of the public sphere in favour of the creationist and the purposeful. It cannot be denied that the sometimes frantic tempo of change was inspired by politicians desperate to disassociate themselves from the institutions operated by their disgraced opponents, for instance the speedy dismantling of the Directorial state apparatus almost straight after Brumaire 1799. After 1791 the hope that the revolution would achieve consensus was in practice abandoned so that institutional alterations within (from 1792) an overarching republican framework became the norm down to the Consulate and beyond. Monarchists were necessarily excluded from involvement in this new France and even their national identity was declared forfeit because of this 'treason'. At least as significantly, the political creations of the Revolution were designed to reflect popular rather than royal sovereignty. Elites (republican rather than royalist) may have continued to dominate political life but they officially did so in the name of French citizens, reflected either in votes or in direct action on the revolutionary *journées*. In the spring of 1789 the monarchy had called out Frenchmen to cast a vote in the elections to the Estates-General and to produce a list of grievances and recommendations for their deputies to take with them to Versailles, the *Cahiers*. Forty thousand lists of demands were produced, with taxation emerging as the main grievance and the empowerment of national and provincial estates the main demand.[1] The participatory ideal of 1789 remained a constant inspiration thereafter that politicians forgot at their peril, though the exigencies of war and counter-revolution afforded excuses enough, as in the failure to implement the democratic constitution of the Year I (1793). Even Bonaparte was careful to respect the spirit of popular sovereignty by holding plebiscites on the constitutional alterations of 1799 and 1802, and a poor turn out was never an adequate reason for dispensing with them altogether.

In 1790-1 hopes were high that the Revolution could achieve a balance between authority and political liberty. Though the constitutional arrangements of both Britain and the infant United States had both been consciously rejected, the monarchical settlement of September 1791 set a premium on freedom under the law and obtaining a measure of liberty previously unknown in France.[2] Those observing the modernisation of the kingdom sensed that it might make France more of an international force to be reckoned with:

> If the National Assembly, in the mean time, continue to preserve this laudable spirit of unanimity, they may soon have to boast of a constitution equal, if not superior to any in Europe; while a proper application of their native resources will effect the speedy removal of their present incumbrances, ... [so that] France will become so truly formidable that the utmost vigilance and exertion of the neighbouring powers will be required, to keep her wonted ambition within due bounds.[3]

This new dispensation was stillborn because of the king's profound hesitation in operating within it (as the Flight to Varennes in June 1791 had already made public), and the concomitant growth of republicanism only led to rooting the legitimacy of subsequent regimes four square in public validation. Ironically, this trend came at exactly the moment when attitudes towards the Revolution were fracturing and majority opinion was perhaps even turning against it. Still, the pretence had to be kept up by the revolutionaries – as they unfailingly did between 1792 and 1804 – that their actions were sanctioned not just by majority opinion but by popular opinion *tout court*, on the questionable basis that those who disagreed with them were not good citizens and therefore inadmissible components of the public sphere. Good readers of Rousseau as so many of them were, the republicans of 1792–4 found it intellectually unconvincing, as well as politically inconvenient to atomise the idea of a sovereign people, to contemplate let alone deal with the possibility that this sovereignty was reducible to a variety of expressions. The Jacobin elite depicted itself as being uniquely in touch with what the public sought, or would have sought had it known what was in its best interests, meanwhile virtuously articulated by the likes of Robespierre, Saint-Just and Couthon. They would create for the new society the institutions through which it would conform to the ways of righteousness. Meanwhile, the views of the electorate could be disregarded if it was for its own good, to protect it from those 'immoral' demagogues such as Desmoulins, Danton and Hébert whose claims to connect with popular preferences were in reality the negation of that 'general will' (another concept closely associated with Rousseau, and his *Du Contrat social* [1762] in particular) which the Jacobins used as their ultimate justification. The 'general will' had its origins in Enlightenment debates and, until 9 Thermidor taught more pragmatic lessons, was habitually invoked by radical intellectuals and politicians. As Lynn Hunt astutely pointed out, it was the founding paradox of revolutionary France that legislators had always to deny that they acted politically and therefore for particular interests, while they continually sought to speak in the name of the general will.[4]

As long as the Revolution persisted, those in public life never abandoned a political language that disguised or rationalised sectional and personal advantage in the name of the sovereign people. This was the strategy compellingly deployed by Jacques Necker in 1788–9 in a successful bid to combine a ministerial career with a reputation as the saviour of the nation and it was a commonplace of politicians scrambling for survival in the turbulent 1790s. Even in 1804 Bonaparte's supporters in the Senate cited popular acclamation as well as security considerations as a justification for their man turning himself from First Consul into Emperor. Between 1789 and 1795 invoking the sovereign nation in practice meant revolutionary activists in Paris, those whose willingness to take direct action in moments of crisis, could push affairs of state in unpredictable directions. The October Days of 1789, the September Massacres of 1792, the coup of 31 May 1793 which destroyed the Brissotins' power were all the work of an uneasy alliance of street demagogues and members of the revolutionary elite struggling for political supremacy, and it is no coincidence that the relative stability of the Directory between 1795 and 1799 was due to the determination of the executive to use military power to repress the populist challenge in both its Jacobin and royalist format and not tolerate the ready recourse of politicians to urban street agitators as an agency of personal empowerment. The creation of the Year III Constitution therefore has a symbolic importance in the Revolution as the moment when the *conventionnels* decided that it was both legitimate and necessary to look back over the course of the Revolution in the interests of creating enduring constitutional structures. Hence the notorious law of the 'Two-Thirds' which critics (notably Babeuf) denounced as oligarchic self-perpetuation on the part of the Convention, but which can also be seen as a determination to give the Republic a stability it had patently lacked hitherto. Directorial success in keeping the regime going for the next four years of course involved much gerrymandering and vicious internal manouevring but at least the 1795 Constitution just about survived. It looked briefly as if the French revolutionary elite had broken its endemic addiction to theory-driven constitution making that had memorably led Edmund Burke to deride the Abbé Sieyes as being a 'constitution monger', constructing and displaying constitutions as one might an item for sale in a shop. Burke's scorn should not disguise the creativity and often originality that attended institutional remodelling during the 1790s,[5] but such revisions frequently did not allow for controlling the populist forces that might nullify legalised arrangements. Revolutionary politicians were not very successful before the mid-1790s in making regimes endure, a sure sign both of the absence of consensus among them and their inexperience. The ascendancy of one group over another usually involved the creation of a new constitution or major remodelling of the existing order, while those who had lost out were consigned not to legitimate oppositionist roles, but to imprisonment, exile and death.

*Central Government Power and Performance in the French Revolution*

The ending of ministerial absolutism in 1788 meant that royal government at the outbreak of the Revolution was weaker than at any point in living memory and, with the country intent on ensuring that state reform ushered in decentralisation, there was no possibility of its recreation in the 1791 Constitution. Parallel parliamentary committees virtually superseded the power of ministers after 1789. In effect, the National Assembly acted both as legislature and executive between 1789–91 for, while the king retained the old great offices of state down to the abolition of the monarchy, those who held them could not hazard policy initiatives that did not command the backing of the Assembly. Foreign Minister Montmorin discovered as much during the Nootka Sound war scare of 1790 when there were attempts to reactivate the Bourbon Family Compact with Spain. With ministers barred from sitting in both the National and the Legislative Assemblies, the scope for mutual distrust was appreciable, and deputies saw any strengthening of the executive as likely only to benefit those opposed to the Revolution, a sizable proportion of France by 1791–2.

The outbreak of the war and the ending of the monarchy in 1792 ended governmental drift; there was no alternative except to reactivate central administration if the Revolution was going to survive. There followed a resurgence of executive power unknown in France's recent history and with it the advent of bureaucracy. Ministers may have come and gone, but the exponential growth of government in the 1790s gave a fillip to the creation of a modern political civil service, staffed by men who saw themselves less as political activists than as administrators. Bureaucratisation was a marked feature of the Revolution, with the number of officials staffing ministries in 1793 eight times the number of 1789.[6] Under the auspices of the Convention, the 21 committees that would operate 'Revolutionary Government' during the Great Terror were created, headed by the Committee of General Security (CGS) in October 1792 and the Committee of Public Safety (CPS) in April 1793, transmitting and enforcing the will of their members through the Representatives-on-Mission. For about a year these powerful organisations worked alongside ministries that continued the formal exercise of their functions until 1 April 1794 when they were superceded by 12 administrative commissions. The Committees – and the CPS in particular (it had nominated the membership of the CGS from September 1793) – then enjoyed four months of unprecedented power. After 9 Thermidor, the Convention retained but reorganised this framework of emergency government (law of 24 August 1794/7 Fructidor II) and imposed strict limits on the capacity of the Committees for independent operation. The CPS lost out to a resurgent Legislation Committee (in charge of communications with the provincial authorities) and to the CGS that supervised the release of prisoners, disarmed former terrorists, and held sweeping powers of censorship. The exercise of executive power through Committees finally ended under the Year III Constitution. This created a wholly new pattern for the executive, a five-man Directory that appointed ministers who were individually responsible to the directors. The ministerial system survived the Constitution of the Year VIII, though directly dependent on First Consul Bonaparte whatever the legal niceties, as ministers including his brother Lucien (Interior), Talleyrand (Foreign Affairs), and Fouché (Police) were perfectly aware. Government, in Napoleon's hands, was a mechanism for reinforcing his personal control of the public sphere in France.

One of the lasting achievements of the Revolution lay in restoring power to the centre and creating a system of subordinate administrative institutions instead of the confusion of what was now known, pejoratively, as the *ancien régime* (a confusion which actually allowed for the operation of a degree of public liberty rarely acknowledged) which no subsequent authority – whether monarchy, republic, or empire – was inclined in essentials to dismantle. This was not the outcome intended by those fighting for the restoration of provincial rights in 1787–9 yet it proved to be the only way to ensure the security of the new Republic during a period of international warfare when its legitimacy was rejected by perhaps half the population. The creation of 'Revolutionary Government' in 1792–3 was the price of national survival. The powers of the 'great' CPS under the dominant personality of Robespierre made it the real executive force in France, its supervisory reach extending into every area of the Republic's affairs, yet its obtrusiveness and the atmosphere of distrust created by the draconian laws of Frimaire Year II soon impelled the Thermidorians to curtail its supremacy and their comital recasting of 1794–5 prepared the way for the constitutional balancing act that was the Year III Constitution. The Directors possessed sufficient reserve powers to ensure that excessive shows of independence in the legislative bodies and in local government were kept within limits despite the violation of the spirit of the constitutional settlement within which they all operated. By early 1799 these controls were breaking down as external and internal crisis engulfed the regime and the legislative bodies briefly seized the initiative. That moment passed after Brumaire 1799 and within two years Napoleon had accumulated a degree of executive control that he never relinquished so long as his rule lasted. There was a major shift back towards centralisation in the spring of 1800 with the establishment of the prefectoral corps (all chosen by the Consul, not elected[7]) and other appointed officials, and a move away from the widespread use of elections in favour of patronage and plebiscites. There was a consensual veneer to the consulate that persuaded very few, for all avenues of executive power led back to Bonaparte and, in the end, to the army.

The way that the Year VIII Constitution was so loaded in favour of government ascendancy over the legislature was a complete reversal of the Revolution's original objectives a decade earlier. The constitution making of 1789–91 was undertaken by the legislature when, following the traumatic events of June–July 1789, the absolute sovereignty in abeyance following Louis XVI's decision in 1788 to summon the Estates-General passed into its hands. Distrusted by the majority in the Assembly and by the nascent counter-revolutionary groupings, the Neckerite administration of 1789–90 was marginal to the new decision-making processes. The 1791 Constitution was a brave attempt to create a balance of powers between parliamentarians and ministers that was undone by mutual distrust and a controversial resurgence of royal authority after the Flight to Varennes when the king vetoed decrees on *émigrés* and refractory clergy. The establishment of the Republic had as its cornerstone a sovereign National Convention that was a *de facto* legislature and executive combined, where real power lay with its various Committees; the coup of 9 Thermidor can in large measure be interpreted as an attempt to restore the sovereignty of the Convention as a whole. Between 1794 and 1795 the Convention enjoyed the sort of supreme authority comparable to that possessed by the National Assembly had deployed five years previously and relinquished (again the comparison holds) once it had drawn up the Constitution of the Year III – the Directory. Relations between executive and legislature from 1795 and 1799 were exciting and unpredictable; in 1797 (Fructidor) and 1798 (Floréal) the Directory twice intervened to thwart electoral preferences and reshape the legislative councils so that they reflected the Directors' rejection of both royalism and Jacobinism. However, the possibility of parliamentarianism was vividly seen as late as June 1799 when the tables were turned and the legislative councils purged the Directory (Merlin de Douai and Roger Ducos) in the 'Journée of the Councils' (30 *Prairial*). But this distinctive phase of the Revolution had only five months of life before Bonaparte intervened and founded the Consulate. There were, admittedly, the vestiges of a parliamentary regime at its inception. Thus the Senate was designed as a genuine constitutional safeguard, not the agency for rule by decree that it became once Bonaparte was secure in the driving seat and pushing his collaborators into authoritarian policies they may not originally have anticipated or endorsed.

The French Revolution failed to produce a parliamentary polity on British lines that corresponded to the hopes of so many in 1789. Instead, executive authority in 1804 was actually far stronger than it had been fifteen years previously and seemed more likely to offer Frenchmen the stability they desired than a constitutional regime of checks and balances where oppositions tended to think in terms of setting up new political structures rather than just replacing the government in power. But if parliamentarianism was never given a real chance as a revolutionary model its adherents included some of the most creative political talents of their era and they had begun to adumbrate the moderate liberalism that would have its hour in Europe during the next century. Their hopes (classically articulated by the *Monarchiens* around Mounier, Clermont-Tonnerre and Bergasse) were initially on an absolute veto for the monarchy and a bicameral legislature and their early failure to achieve these objectives in September 1789 transferred the initiative to those in the National Assembly who regarded dissent from the revolutionary project as just one step from the treasonable. The parliamentarians of 1789–91 needed the king; Louis XVI was reluctant to confess that he needed them and

Mirabeau's premature death in April 1791 confirmed his refusal to go down this road.

In the course of 1791-2 the apologists for parliamentarianism – Malouet, Mounier, Rivarol and Mallet du Pan prominent among them – for the most part emigrated and merged into the wider counter-revolutionary stream where they had no more friends than they had among the revolutionaries. Parliamentary liberalism was not a serious political option between 1792 and 1795, but it did enjoy a brief flourish under the Directory in 1796-7 and was on the point of converting itself into a serious political movement for the first time before the coup of Fructidor wrecked such hopes. It suited the majority in the Directory to present the Clichiens and their followers as nothing more than counter-revolutionary agitators (and to close down their club on that basis) but some of them had begun to contemplate parliamentary constitutionalism independently of the monarchy, or at least a Bourbon monarchy, for Philippe Egalité's eldest son and successor, Louis-Philippe d'Orléans (1773–1850), was just starting to attract following in the late 1790s.

The Directory briefly patronised the *cercles constitutionnels* in 1797 where young moderates such as the Swiss Benjamin Constant (1767–1830), the gifted protégé of his lover, Necker's daughter, Madame de Staël, took up the challenge of articulating a workable liberalism compatible with republicanism. He wanted a return to the principles of 1789. Government should stop trying to 'improve' men and allow them the order and toleration needed to pursue any gaols they chose.[8] But who would listen? The ruthless and the worldly would have no truck with the compromisers, and intimidation had been a recurrent problem from the outset as those who returned chastened to the provinces after the October days of 1789 testified. Another besetting problem was that parliamentary liberals were much better at defining and refining ideological variants rather than creating an institutional framework in which they could put their creeds to work. Snubbed by the unscrupulous and the expert intriguers, many among them poured their energies into brilliant journalism in tracts written both at home and in exile. The range was immense, from the reflective *Journal des Impartiaux*, February-June 1790 and the more scurrilous and bitingly funny *Actes des Apôtres* to the *Mercure britannique* produced by Mallet du Pan in London between 1798 and 1800.[9] In its retreat from the politics of power to the politics of protest this frantic journalism well reflected the first and decisive failure of liberalism in France.

## The Revolutionary Renewal of Local Government

It was not at the centre but in provincial France that the Revolution in its early manifestations made most impact on the life of the average French man and woman. In the 1780s the belief that the renewal of public life in the monarchy must take in the overhaul of provincial institutions as well as recalling the Estates-General was widely shared. It was expressed particularly in the circle around Jacques Necker who in 1778–81 had founded Provincial Assemblies for the Berry and the Limousin; the experiment, that 'certainly contained the potential to evolve into institutions of a modern, representative character',[10] had so gratified the local elites that it was imitated for the rest of the *pays d'élection* in 1787–8 plus, at a lower level, district and municipal assemblies.[11] However, this initiative was a royal concession and, as such, second-best for those who lived in the *pays d'état*, who wanted their Provincial Estates respected or restored. Political agitation in Brittany, Languedoc, the Dauphiné and Provence in the late 1780s was built around this demand, to which the revolutionary doubling of Third Estate representation was bolted on, often at the cost of splitting the forces working for provincial reform.

The considerable changes in local administration brought in *before* May 1789 were not, however, intended as a general blueprint for reform. They were superimposed on the existing apparatus and the consequences of this (re)creation had not worked themselves out before the Revolution rendered it mostly redundant. The opponents of 'despotism' in the provinces were gratified that the changes checked the authority of the *intendants*, but the *parlements* continued *in situ*. Significantly, Necker chose not to incorporate the provincial assemblies and estates in the consultative and electoral process for the Estates-General opting, daringly, to involve a far wider cross-section of male opinion from outside those loosely definable as 'notables'. From mid-1789 onwards, with everything hinging on what was done inside the National Assembly, the attention of the political nation became riveted on events at the centre. Traditional royal authority collapsed in July that year, and the August decrees that followed insisted on the end of privilege at every level, taking in Estates, municipalities and all inferior agencies. Patriotic sentiment competed against provincial identity as those who had been in the vanguard of regionalism were forced to compromise. As the declaration of the night of 4–5 August stated:

All special privileges of the provinces, principalities, pays, cantons, cities and communities of people, whether pecuniary or of any other kind, are abolished forever, and will remain fused in the common rights of all Frenchmen.[12]

Meanwhile, across provincial France institutions dependent on the Crown both for legitimacy and day-to-day operation either imploded or just stopped working. Most *intendants* fled while, on 3 November, it was decreed that the *parlements* would be on permanent vacation until a new Court system was up and running.

The National Assembly was therefore starting again the process of encouraging and channelling political activity in the provinces and it extracted the co-operation of the local elites who were caught between fear of violence in the countryside and pressure from the centre. After the experience of the Great Fear, the alternative seemed to be anarchy and the propertied were desperate to avoid that fate. Hence the willingness of many such, including both bishops and nobles, to act patriotically as leaders of *ad hoc* authorities in 1789–90 pending the establishment of the National Assembly's regularised reform of local administration throughout France. This proved to be an enduring piece of legislation but which, before and during its passage through the Assembly, witnessed unprecedented lobbying of deputies in Paris by interested parties from most towns in the nation, desperate to ensure that their own locales gained rather than lost out from the process. Much was at stake. The question was not just what was to replace provinces, generalities and other traditional jurisdictions, but where the new local government bodies were to be located and where the boundaries between jurisdictions would run. Municipal government was overhauled first in December 1789 and the same month a law on administrative assemblies established that the new units for the whole country would be departments, districts and municipalities. Over the next two months, the horse trading between the politicians at the centre and from the provinces was at its most intensive, all leading up to a decree published on 26 February 1790. Acting in general accordance with the extensive preparatory work by the *comité de division* under the chairmanship of Thouret (1746–1794, a lawyer from Normandy who had been *procureur-syndic* of its provincial assembly in 1787), the Assembly agreed that France would be divided into 83 *départements* with districts and cantons [there were 44,000 *communes*] as units below them in a hierarchy which would apply equally across the whole nation.

The *départements* were charged with organising such matters as tax collecting, military recruitment and policing in a concession to the decentralising phase of the early Revolution. They would implement the decrees of the Assembly in conjunction with the lower authorities.

It was an immensely significant project based on considerations of enlightened geography where distance, convenience and communications in principle counted for everything rather than tradition or prescription; in practice, some local politicians and power brokers (whose co-operation the Assembly could not easily forego) had done rather better than others.[13] In the Auvergne, for instance, the traditional rivalries of the towns of Riom (seat of a presidial Court) and its neighbour, Clermont-Ferrand (seat of a bishopric), was given a new twist when the Assembly determined that the latter should be the departmental capital of the Puy-de-Dôme. Elsewhere, Saintes wanted primacy over La Rochelle in the Charente-Inférieure, Bazas wanted a *département* of the Bazadais.[14] Such decisions were not easily reversed, despite counter-petitioning going on in some cases into 1793 and 1794, and could determine the shape of urban allegiance for the rest of the Revolution on the crude basis of which faction was most likely to redress the 'wrong'. Nevertheless, the relatively easy creation and operation of a new local government system on the electoral principle in 1790 was a solid achievement that pleased more people than it upset. Compared with much of the Assembly's other work, the potential divisiveness of what it enacted was avoided through a consultative process. The deputies actually asked propertied opinion what they wanted and tried to reach fair solutions. There were, of course, both winners and losers, but at least there had been a two-way process of engagement between the electorate and the elected. Unfortunately for the popularity or the persistence of the Revolution, it was not a model that was otherwise much followed after 1790.

During 1790–1, many prominent revolutionaries cut their political teeth in the new local government bodies and the membership of the Legislative Assembly (1791–2) drew heavily on their numbers. Yet no sooner was the new apparatus in operation than, with the coming of the war in April 1792, the devolutionary moment passed. As early as August 1792, scores of local authorities were 'purged' of those who could not be trusted to uphold the political values and priorities of the republican order, and the same happened again on a large scale after the 'Federalist Crisis' was over in mid-1793. Even these draconian moves had a limited impact on increasing local loyalties to the Convention and its committees.

Jacobin politicians looking to the Parisian clubs and *sections* as their power base could not allow their enemies to use their regional supremacy as a means of challenging the centre: the necessity of putting the resources of the entire state uncompromisingly into the military struggle precluded allowing for the independent operation of the *départements* and the units below them. These bodies were distrusted as agents of delay not to say sedition and the 'Terror' was predicated on restoring centralised controls either through by-passing the 1790 apparatus or galvanising it into directed, sometimes frantic activity. The key figures of control were the Representatives-on-Mission, officers sent out from Paris commissioned by the Convention with an authority that made them far more than just the reinvention of the *intendants*. Some were keen to be responsive to local circumstances, others such as Fouché in the Nièvre experimented with one or other aspect of the Terror (in his case dechristianisation) or, as with Claude Javogues in the Loire, saw counter-revolution as a ubiquitous presence in his fiefdom.[15]

The Representatives needed assistance. Their essential agents in every commune were revolutionary committees who made sure that administrators towed the line and reported back to the central government regularly. Where officials in the vicinity either could not or would not co-operate, they would be re-educated or removed and, as was often the case by early 1794, sent back to Paris to be browbeaten by the CPS. Though the Representatives-on-Mission did not long survive the Thermidorian reaction, the improvement of the international situation in France's favour and the creation of the Directory did not appreciably reduce the desire of politicians in Paris to maintain a decisive amount of control over local government across the country.

In April 1795 the pre-1792 powers of the *départements* may have been restored with extended authority over the districts but *commissaires du pouvoir exécutif* and *commissaires de police* (set up under a decree of 24 August 1794) were attached to the city councils where their job description was officially to ensure the execution of legislation and, unofficially, to guard against Jacobin and royalist infiltrators and, rather secondarily, increase the efficiency of the bodies with which they liaised. These commissioners operated so effectively that they provided a ready model in February 1800 for the prefectoral system that Bonaparte wasted no time in creating. He appreciated that to allow local government genuine independence was to sacrifice a regulatory device that would jeopardise his power and his policies, and elected councils met only infrequently during the Consulate. The institutions of 1790 may have survived the Revolution, but the limited latitude allowed them was at odds with the intention of their creators. Their failure was yet another vivid testimony to the Revolution's inability to deliver political pluralism to France.

## The Machinery of Justice

The achievement of the National Assembly in transforming local government is relatively well known, rather less so its substantial judicial reforms. In this area, too, the collapse of the sovereign and *seigneurial* courts (recognised and sanctioned by the August decrees 1789) gave the Assembly the opportunity to bring in root-and-branch reforms in line with the principles articulated in the Declaration of the Rights of Man. The Committees which worked on the detailed proposals were determined to show their commitment to the rule of law applied universally across the country and to set up institutions which would inspire confidence among the propertied classes. Success owed much to the numerous lawyers sitting as deputies in the National Assembly, including the leading talents of the Parisian bar, Target (1733–1806) and, until the October Days, Bergasse, men who drew on their experience as pleaders and practitioners to ensure that the new blueprint would deliver justice and be administratively manageable.

Enlightenment principles of jurisprudence were powerfully reflected in the new system of criminal justice. As early as October 1789 recommendations on interim changes in criminal law had been made, including extending the rights of defence lawyers, abolishing all forms of torture, and bringing the accused before a judge within 24 hours of arrest. Exactly a year later the Assembly published a law on criminal procedure and decreed the appointment of public prosecutors. In January 1791 it was determined that every *département* should have its own criminal Court, staffed by three judges and with a president elected by active citizens. Finally, in September 1791, another decree on the organisation of criminal justice enshrined the importance within the system of trial by jury. The penal code these courts would operate was enacted the same month. It included a scale of punishments, insisted on the principle of uniform application, and abolished heresy and blasphemy as offences. It maintained capital punishment as well as specifying long prison sentences with hard labour where appropriate.

The civil courts were also thoroughly overhauled by a decree of August 1790 that dovetailed into the three local government levels of *département*, district and canton. English-style elected Justices of the Peace (JPs) presided for cases at cantonal level, bringing cheap dispute resolution and the possibility of mediation for citizens instead of costly formal litigation; above the Justices, in the districts, was a tribunal of five judges whose duties included the hearing of appeals. The same edict also established commercial tribunals and 'family tribunals' (giving women and children more influence), both, again, with elected justices staffing them. Although a Ministry of Justice was created as a clearing-house for the new system, the deputies believed that the separation of powers was an essential condition of making the Constitution of 1791 work satisfactorily and judicial office holders were disqualified from holding office in the state.

This new framework aroused much admiration in France and beyond, but, as part of the 1791 Constitution, most of the judicial changes shared its fate (setting up the new bodies had, in many cases, stretched well into 1792) and were constantly compromised by the exigencies of public affairs. The separation of powers and the principle of judicial independence were early casualties as the executive used the wartime emergency to assume quasi-judicial powers. The Republic arrived in September 1792 at the same time as any judges regarded as unpatriotic were purged; judicial office was also declared open to all citizens, regardless of whether they were legally qualified: purely patriotic credentials were more important for the Brissotin ministry at this juncture. The principle of election just about survived the Jacobin ascendancy though it was considerably curtailed. Thus, whereas the property qualification for membership of juries was abolished in December 1793, it was decided the next month that districts could nominate JPs so long as 'revolutionary government' lasted'. During the Terror, the judicial apparatus had to deal with those who were guilty of political crimes and the system of 1791 was bent constantly to reflect factional priorities, a process facilitated when, in the interests of state security, the Law of Suspects (September 1793) withdrew rights recently conferred such as habeas corpus and trial by jury. At one with this repositioning, *agents nationaux*, answerable to the Minister of the Interior, replaced locally answerable public prosecutors. Their function was to enforce revolutionary laws as the first priority and bring suspects to trial. Achieving the right result had become the principal criterion for assessing judicial competence and judges had to do this or take the consequences – loss of office certainly, loss of life very possibly.

As the showtrials of Fouquier-Tinville and Carrier demonstrated, when it came to disposing of their rivals, the Thermidorians were not prepared to respect judicial impartiality any more than the Jacobins had done. However, with the repeal of the law of 22 *Prairial*, the stranglehold of the executive on the instruments of the law was gradually relaxed, most notably by the curtailment of the Tribunal's authority and then its abolition in May 1795. Just as the framers of the Year III Constitution looked to revive the balances they found in the 1791 document for the legislative sphere, so they hoped to revivify the judiciary on a comparable basis. The hope was not fulfilled.

Minor changes to the machinery of justice were included in the 1795 Constitution and, soon afterwards, the principle of election to office was compromised when the Directory took powers in December 1795 to appoint to vacant judicial posts. The regime was desperate to prevent its numerous opponents gaining the upper hand at any institutional level and the coups of 1797 and 1798 only reinforced this priority, even at the price of abandoning its commitment to the rule of law. In April 1797 there was a major reform of judicial organisation (it had been preceded by removal of the family courts) that reflected the Directors' concern to stand firm against the threat posed to their continuance by provincial anarchy and disloyalty. If civilian courts could not adequately punish criminals, then the army should be brought in, and from late 1797 military tribunals were empowered to deal with a whole range of civil offences and offenders, in 1799 40 per cent of the state was subject to the jurisdiction of senior commanders. It was not a precedent that Bonaparte chose to ignore after he took power; indeed, the widespread use of army officers entrusted with sweeping powers of justice should be considered vital in establishing his rule and, no less crucially, he had extra troops available for domestic policing after peace treaties were signed with Austria (February 1801) and Britain (March 1802). Special Tribunals were inaugurated early in 1801, sitting in public, and staffed by both civilian and military justices. Over 1200 suspected malefactors had been dealt with in their first six months of operation. During the Consulate the principle of electing judges rather than selecting them was officially abandoned. As far as the Consul was concerned, there was no more reason for judges to exist independently of consular patronage than any other official. Bonaparte continued the directorial project of codifying the law. It appealed to him as a useful measure of administrative tidiness, though work was still incomplete when the Consulate became the Empire in 1804.

In 1790–1 France produced a judicial system that had no counterpart in Europe for rational structuring or for the operation of an enlightened jurisprudence. It had elected, salaried judges and standardised procedures that caught the admiring attention of progressive lawyers from Warsaw to London. And yet the new judicial system was as much a casualty of war and 'revolutionary government' as decentralised local government proved to be. The changes were just too daring and too extensive to be permissible to the successive managers of the state during an international war. Revolutionary politicians could not, in practice, bring themselves to accept an independent judiciary or allow the rule of law to have the final word over *force majeure*. The reality was that in republican France, the final source of authority was not respect for the rule of the law but fear of a powerful central state, especially when seconded, as it was after 1795 and fundamentally from 1799, by a vast military arm.

*The Subordination of the Church*

Before 1789, the Gallican Church had maintained its proud formal independence of the monarchy and, much like other institutions in Bourbon France, defended its 'liberties', including such prized privileges as direct tax exemption and holding a quinquennial general assembly. Yet the Church–State dualism was a most unequal partnership for, in any clash of wills, the Crown would invariably get its way. The three-way tussle between Louis XV, the *parlements* and the First Estate in the 1750s and the destruction of the Jesuits in the 1760s were cases in point. The Revolution abolished any pretence at an alliance of equals and turned the Church into just another public agency dependent on the national rather than the divine will for its sanction. In due course, as an essential part of Terror and dechristianisation, the state would turn against the Constitutional Church it had so recently inaugurated.

Once the National Assembly began its work in July 1789, it was obvious that the Gallican Church could no more be exempt from the remodelling of public life than any other institution. The clerical *Cahiers* had shown the lower clergy in particular embracing the widespread desire for moral as well as political regeneration and reform, and even the bishops had in many constituencies signalled their approval in principle to tax changes which would involve the sacrifice of their exemptions. Religion came well down the list of the concerns of the Third Estate with only 10 of its

*Cahiers* demanding the abolition of tithe.[16] What few could have predicted was the pace of change or how quickly the Church would lose control of the reform process following its junction with the other two Orders to form the National Assembly:

> Could a spectator of this august scene have supposed that, in the space of a twelvemonth, the Clergy would be ruined by those very Commons [the Third Estate], and reduced to a worse condition than the hostile nobles themselves?[17]

The decrees of 4–11 August 1789 making a bonfire of 'privileges' including tithes and the *casuel* (the fees on which many unbeneficed priests depended) cleared the way for root-and-branch reform. Continuing as members of the National Assembly brought home to clerical deputies the realisation that the First Estate had gone and that their preferences would not be paramount in the reconstitution of the Gallican Church. In November Church property was taken into state ownership as prelude to selling it off to the highest bidder; most of the religious Orders were suppressed in February 1790; in May, the Assembly began to debate the far-reaching proposals recommended by its Religious Committee, what would become the Civil Constitution of the Clergy. Its provisions included reducing the number of bishops to 83 (the same number as the *départements*), to be elected by all tax-payers irrespective of whether they were Catholics or not, abolishing all non-pastoral offices including cathedral chapters, rationalising parishes and altering their boundaries, and turning the parish clergy into state employees who would swear an oath of loyalty to 'the nation, the law, the king and the constitution' as a condition of assuming office.

Most of the lower clergy were 'good' patriots who wanted, if at all possible, to work with the grain of the Revolution not against it, as their temperate conduct in debate showed. They had welcomed constitutional reform as a process that would help the clergy and the laity together to recreate the ideal of primitive Christianity approximating to the first few centuries of the Christian Church's existence. Pastoral care would become the overwhelming priority of *all* the clergy, a compelling vision whose appeal should not be underestimated. But the Civil Constitution appeared to many among them to propose such a fundamental reordering that it would require not just the approval of the king and the pope (Pius VI) but of the Gallican Church gathered as a national council. This perspective was unacceptable to majority opinion inside the National

Assembly, where the prevailing view was that the Revolution had abolished all corporate rights including the Church's and that nothing could be allowed to compromise the ultimate sovereignty that they exercised on the nation's behalf.

Deputies, with some justification, suspected the growth of counter-revolutionary sentiments inside the Church but would not admit that the Civil Constitution was likely to foster such sentiments on a comprehensive scale. Most of them, to a greater or lesser degree, were influenced by the anticlericalist tone of the French Enlightenment and sought to cut the Church down to size. Opening it up to lay influences through such contentious proposals as the election of bishops would be one way of doing it. The end product would be turning the Church into a genuine part of a *civil* constitution. Typically, few could admit the clergy's plea not to compromise the spiritual authority of the Church, to accept that by definition the Catholic Church was not reducible to another bureaucratic state department with the clergy as salaried civil servants. The pious Louis XVI deplored the legislation, but was constrained into consenting to it on 24 August 1790; meanwhile, the pope stayed aloof, and the Assembly was losing patience. On 27 November 1790 it decreed that all state functionaries (naturally, the clergy fell under this heading) had to take an oath upholding the Civil Constitution. Failure to do so would result in legal deprivation. The result was schism. Just over half the clergy accepted these terms, just under half refused.

Many commentators were stupified at the Assembly's determination to impose its will despite the absence of any consensus. As one foreign journal perceptively noted:

> But how does the exaction of such an oath accord with their pretended system of liberty? By swearing to maintain and observe the particular decree alluded to in the oath, the clergy would bind themselves to approve those violent measures which have deprived them of their lawful possessions – They would kiss the hand that robbed them! – Can a greater exertion of tyranny over the human mind be conceived? – Can a sway more arbitrary and despotic be exercised?[18]

Establishing the machinery of the Constitutional Church (as the Church conforming to the Civil Constitution became known) and putting its personnel in place was both fraught and deeply divisive. Juring and non-juring bishops and clergy traded insults, sometimes physical blows, and the humblest laity were involved in the process, for few things mattered more to the average countryman – and especially countrywoman – than what was going on in their parish church and who was living in the presbytery. In Flanders, the Pyrenees, much of Brittany, and in the Vendée, they disowned the new religious dispensation, a testimony to the successful inculcation of Tridentine values in rural France. As one bishop had noted back in 1782: 'Our countrysides, above all, are inhabited by true believers who serve you [Lord] in the uprightness of their hearts.'[19]

The Civil Constitution gave clergy and citizens a stark choice; accept the new law and be viewed as a good citizen, reject it and be included in the ranks of the counter-revolutionaries. The influence on the clergy of their parishioners in determining their attitude to the oath should not be underestimated. In parish after parish (the Revolution had not changed the basic civil and religious unit in France) relations between the clergy and the laity, neighbours with one another, could be complicated and poisoned by the Civil Constitution with far-reaching consequences for France's future. Minorities in all parts of the country, jurors in Brittany, nonjurors in most of Provence, for instance, were hounded officially and unofficially. On 10 March 1791 Pius VI condemned the Civil Constitution – and, for that matter, the Revolution – unreservedly and thereby bolstered the efforts of nonjuring bishops to keep their clergy loyal by enjoining adherence to his Holiness's wishes, a ploy used by the bishops of Metz, Nancy and Toul when they published a joint *ordonnance* against the Civil Constitution from just over the imperial frontier at Trier.[20]

The Constitutional Church tried to function in 1791–3 across the whole country, though that was something of a legal fantasy. Most of its bishops and clergy were high-minded men who would not relinquish their faith in the compatibility of religion and revolution in France however unpropitious circumstances appeared to be. In prelates like Henri Grégoire, Louis-Alexandre Expilly and Robert-Thomas Lindet (the first to take a wife), it had a leadership cadre of undoubted capacity, who tried to make it a rule (with varying degrees of success) not to allow political involvement to compromise their pastoral concern. They scarcely enjoyed a honeymoon interlude before the public agenda had moved on. After the declaration of the Republic, the state's growing disinclination to respect the Constitutional Church became abundantly apparent. The registration of births, marriages and deaths ceased to be the responsibility of the parish clergy on 20 September 1792 who, the following year, found themselves under pressure both to get married and to renounce their priesthood in public as part of the state-sponsored dechristianisation campaign. Some foreign Protestants misinterpreted these unprecedented events as a chance to evangelise the French. In 1792 the British Methodist leader Thomas Coke impulsively crossed the Channel and travelled to Paris through Normandy. He was met first by apathy and then threats that if he did not leave at once he would hang from the lamp post.[21]

By 1793 the Republic was openly lending state authority to attacks not just on Catholic priests and places of worship, but on Christianity itself as a rival source of loyalty to the state. In effect, the Republic was repudiating its Church that was forced, as its refractory rival before it had been, to go underground. It only gradually re-emerged after 9 Thermidor. Not that the Directory was bent on identifying itself with Grégoire's followers. Instead, it upheld the formal separation of Church and State decreed by the law of 21 February 1795/3 Ventôse Year III under which freedom was proclaimed for all religions; in practice, many of the Directors still nurtured dechristianising sympathies and were determined to offer minimal concessions to Catholics in France, particularly the refractories, as the civic oath imposed after Fructidor requiring 'hatred of royalty and anarchy' made plain.

Subordination of the Church to the state had therefore given way to outright separation. In these unprecedented circumstances, there was a sufficient degree of public liberty for the survivors of the Constitutional Church to regroup and, under the energising genius of Grégoire, undergo a quiet revival in the later 1790s unfettered by any ties with the Republic. Preferring to call itself the 'Gallican Church' under the 'United Bishops', this Church saw itself as embodying the historic principles of Gallicanism, however much the nonjurors might mock its pretensions. Accordingly, it held national councils in Paris in 1797 and 1801. At these innovatory venues, its episcopal leaders pushed through a series of creative organisational reforms, such as endorsing the wide-ranging powers of clergy known as archpriests, those who could supervise the conduct of the parish clergy and make sure that the Presbyterian currents in the Church were not tolerated.

The last national council met when First Consul Bonaparte's negotiations with the Vatican about the terms of a general religious settlement were almost completed. He had taken up a policy the Directory had toyed with in mid-1796 when Pius VI had even produced a draft circular – the *Pastoralis sollicitudo* – that counselled clerical submission to the regime only to have the government hastily turn its face against a deal that might compromise its republican credentials. Though Bonaparte was surrounded with ministers and generals who were unbending anticlericalists, by mid-1800 he had his own distinctive religious priority: one bent on negotiating a Concordat with the papacy intending to detach the refractory clergy and bishops from the counter-revolutionary cause in the interests of entrenching his own power. He was well aware that the separation of Church and State since 1795 had worked against the consolidation of the Republic and he made it a priority to restore the two agencies into a secure dependent relationship. A partnership was impossible, but Bonaparte offered the Church official recognition and freedom from persecution that he judged, correctly, its leaders would find hard to resist. Certainly, that applied to the new pope, Pius VII, who, with a realism arising out of witnessing at first hand the vulnerability of the Church to military might in the new republics of Italy, accepted that there could be no return to the *status quo ante*. Under the 1801 Concordat, there would be no restoration of Church lands, no revival of the tithe, and no corporate status that in any sense recalled pre-1789 days. Other confessions would be granted recognition so that Catholicism would be referred to simply as the 'religion of the majority'. And when the Consul unilaterally imposed the Organic Articles on the Church in 1802 with their extreme Gallican character – for instance, any communications with Rome required prior approval – any doubts about the extent to which the state planned to keep the Church in an unparalleled grip were laid to rest. As in other areas of consular policy, Bonaparte was making clear that he would not tolerate any disrespect to the authority of his regime. To all intents and purposes, Pius VII had ended up allowing Bonaparte to treat the Church as just another state agency with bishops and clergy required to take an oath to the regime. Despite a ten-year struggle, the refractories had accepted a disguised version of the Civil Constitution, the main difference in 1801 compared to 1791 was that the Consul and the pope were agreed on a settlement, in 1791 the Assembly and the pope were not. Napoleon had allowed for a degree of religious toleration, but never at the price of disobedience to himself and the administrative controls were in place to ensure that state power was exercised over the Church more comprehensively than under the monarchy, the Ministry for Ecclesiastical Affairs intervening in diocesan and parochial affairs whenever policy required.

# Chapter 6: Changing Patterns of Political Participation

*The Political Nation Defined*

Defining the political nation before 1789 made limited legal sense since sovereignty was vested in the Crown and there was no national legislature comparable to the British Parliament in which the opinion of the king's leading subjects could be gauged. Some of the Paris *parlementaires* posed as spokesmen for the nation in the absence of the Estates-General during the constitutional crises of 1771–4 and 1787–9. However, their claims to this privilege were contestable and still left a gap between 'patriotic' rhetoric and the absence of institutions in which it could be legitimately rehearsed. Ministers such as Necker in Louis XVI's reign were conscious that the absence of modern consultative mechanisms were doing the cause of strong monarchy no favours. To the Anglophile Necker, ever conscious of the power of public opinion, a readjustment in that direction was overdue, in the interests of both the king and his leading subjects. It remained suspect to other ministers such as Maurepas, Miromesnil and Vergennes. They saw sovereignty as indivisible and opposition to the wishes of the royal government not far short of the treasonable. There could be no scope in France for an 'opposition' on the British model. Hence their approval for the customary royal practice of exiling fallen ministers and recalcitrant magistrates, a tactic that Louis XVI had blunderingly employed against his own cousin, the duc d'Orléans, in the Paris *parlement* in November 1787.

The outbreak of the Revolution just over a year later forced the king to concede both that there was a (political) nation and that sovereignty had passed to its representatives in the National Assembly. The question of defining that nation in more precise terms was a pressing matter and, as early as autumn 1789, the concept of 'active' and 'passive' citizens had been coined, with the latter having the rights granted in the Declaration of the Rights of Man but not the right to vote granted to the former. There was, in effect, a two-tier element to nation. The higher one's level of official involvement the more disposable wealth and land one required. It has been estimated that the stipulation of 22 December 1789 that deputies must own land and pay taxes equivalent to the *marc d'argent* (worth about 50 *livres*) would have disqualified all but half a million Frenchmen. This determination to restrict membership of the political nation, not to dilute it into a democracy, can be seen at most stages of the Revolution, certainly in 1789–91. The Revolution had to make the world safe for responsible property owners and guard against the threat of anarchy posed by crowds trying to influence events by direct action – except when it suited politicians in the ascendancy to let them.

Despite the Declaration of the Rights of Man and the Citizen (with its explicit enshrining of the general principle of religious liberty) and the wholesale abolition of 'privilege' in August 1789, it was not a foregone conclusion that unqualified civic rights would be allowed to every minority group in the kingdom. To belong to the nation, a person had in the first instance to be considered a French national. There were few problems in that sense with the Huguenots, members of the Protestant Reformed Church, who had already been granted limited recognition in 1787 under the Edict on non-Catholics. On 24 December 1789 the Assembly voted to end every legal distinction between Protestants and Catholics, and further concessions followed in 1790 when the descendants of families who had either fled abroad to preserve their faith or had lost property in the 105 years since the Edict of Nantes had been repealed were awarded compensation by the state under Laws of 10 July and 10 December. The Jewish inhabitants of France found the Assembly much less receptive to incorporating them fully into the life of the nation.[1] Antisemitism was rampant in eastern France, the residence of the Yiddish-speaking Ashkenazim who initially sought protection rather than assimilation, and it could also be heard within the Assembly itself. Thus La Fare, bishop of Nancy, opposed Clermont-Tonnerre's motion of 23 December 1789 for their admittance into full citizenship by warning the Assembly that any such concession could ignite to 'a huge blaze' in Lorraine where 'the people have a horror of them'; Maury, the uncompromising clerical champion of the Right, insisted to his colleagues that the Jews were not Frenchmen, but foreigners living in France, to be left out of the nation.[2] Predictably, it was the wealthier, more Frenchified Sephardim of the Bordelais and Avignon (just 4000 individuals) who benefited from the first emancipation decree of 28 January 1790. The Assembly continued to discriminate against their Ashkenazim co-religionists, specifically excluding them in September 1790 from new laws admitting non-Catholics to judicial office and from the law of naturalisation, and it took another year, right on the eve of the Assembly's closure, for all Jewish communities to receive full equality as citizens. Ominously, the Assembly concurrently ordered a report on loans owed to Jews, a strategy intended to play on popular hatred of Jewish moneylenders, and was interpreted by hard-up peasants as releasing them from outstanding debts. And, even if the Jews were not second-class citizens, progressive opinion nurtured suspicions that they would be no friends to the continuing work of reform under the Constitution of 1791. Despite the establishment of these minority rights, the Alsace-Lorraine area constantly defied the Assembly's decrees.

For all the reluctance to acknowledge its Jewish inhabitants as Frenchmen in 1789–91, the nation as it was defined under the constitutional monarchy was a strikingly inclusive model without any contemporary European parallel. Its generous provisions therefore made the failure to incorporate half the adult population – women – into any category of citizenship or indeed offer them any new legal rights at all, the more startling. Even female influence in high society, exerted by courtiers and courtesans, *salonnières* and actresses was deemed inadmissible by a generation of male politicians who had read their Rousseau and who, while not underestimating the positive role of women in the formation of the next generation of disinterested and virtuous (male) citizens, wanted it confined to the home, to the private sphere. Essentially membership of the political nation after 1789, whether an individual was categorised as an active or a passive citizen, was gendered: women, irrespective of their social rank, properly belonged to neither category. Women were by definition the ultimate expression of passive citizenship, doomed by biology and culture to the domestic sphere. The old regime was excoriated for its domination by women: the revolutionaries did not plan to repeat that mistake again. The rationale behind the sort of sarcastic comment found in pamphlets like that produced by 'la pauvre Javotte' in 1790 is therefore understandable:

We were hoping that the nation's representatives... would concern themselves for a moment about our fate, but until now, they have been able to think only about the Jews and the actors.[3]

A sizeable proportion of women refused to submit passively to the prevailing male consensus that their claims to political rights were inadmissible. In rural France, many women wanted their say in the new structures of local politics. In urban centres they organised, often using their primary importance within the family as a moral justification, and demonstrated in favour of price controls on food and the condign punishment of grain hoarders and speculators. It was this grievance that regularly brought the market women of Paris out on to the streets in the autumn of 1789 and led nearly 3000 of them to march to Versailles on 5–6 October, where they occupied both the palace and the National Assembly, and intimidated deputies and royal family alike. The role reversal amounted to a physical threat not just a harmless charivari, a confirmation of Rousseauian-style theorising about the disruption likely to ensue should women turn themselves unsought into *de facto* 'active' citizens. The revolutionaries found it hard to eliminate the desire of an influential minority of women in urban areas to participate in politics: women could hardly be immune to the emphasis on civic rights as a universal entitlement or wonder why such emphatic language nevertheless apparently excluded them. Women read the newspapers and pamphlets that poured from the press, and were capable of writing their own. Olympe de Gouge's *Declaration of the Rights of Women* (1791) is the classic manifesto of excluded, submerged women who sympathised with the ideals of the Revolution, but were aghast at their marginalisation by its architects. Gouges was uncompromising: all 'public dignities, offices and employments should be open to women', part of her battle to end legal distinctions between men and women. It was a contention often heard in the clubs and debating societies that women set up to shadow the concerns being raised by their male counterparts. At Dijon the women's Jacobin club developed in part to take over social tasks from excluded Catholic religious orders. Many attended the meetings of the men's clubs such as the Feuillants, the Jacobins and the Cordeliers, and applauded and hissed as they saw fit. However, the usual lot of women present at Jacobin celebrations was to serve food and clean up afterwards. Even Jacobin clubs with mixed membership confined women to a segregated area of the hall. As a rule they could neither vote nor pass motions.

There were a few occasions when it suited one faction or another to make use of indirect female assistance. Thus, during the *journée* of 31 May–2 June 1793 which overthrew the Girondins, members of the Society of Republican Revolutionary Citizennesses (which had strong *enragés* links) tried to gather arms to protect the Republic against the 'internal enemies' of the Republic, a useful ploy at the time for the Jacobins who benefited from their intervention. Two of its most prominent members, Theoroigne de Méricourt and Claire Lacombe (a chocolate maker and an agitator for the right of women to bear arms) had both spoken at the Jacobin Club in spring 1793. But the perils of female activism had been vividly highlighted by Charlotte Corday's assassination of Marat in his bath. Thus the *Répertoire du tribunal révolutionnaire*, characterising Corday in July 1793, scorned female politicians, berating her as a type for affecting 'pretensions to knowledge... strength of character and to the politics of nations'.[4] Evidence of women lobbying at the time the 1793 Constitution was produced was unsettling. After the plebiscite was over and the constitution approved, the women of Lévignac, 'dressed in blue, carrying the tricolour flag' were admitted as a special favour to the cantonal assembly, but still insisted:

> Although we are the weaker sex, we have no less courage when it comes to giving proof of our Patriotism... and we all cry together, long live the Republic and death to the tyrants....[5]

Such assertiveness made the Convention take no chances. On 30 October 1793 it declared all women's clubs dissolved as part of a wider turn against the militant followers of Hébert. Jacobin rhetoric throughout 1793–4 repeatedly emphasised the primary importance of gender difference in determining the rules for participation in the life of the republic and neither the Directory nor the Consulate did anything to suggest that the public sphere was an arena in which women could have any role. In May 1795 females were barred from the galleries of the Convention, and divorce for women became more difficult to obtain.

One of the reasons why successive revolutionary regimes did nothing to improve women's status was because most women remained unsympathetic to the policies of the revolutionaries. Few bothered to attend their clubs even in Paris or the other great centres, any campaign to grant them the vote appeared eccentric rather than a serious political proposition, and the move towards equality before the law in social and familial life, for instance civil divorce, made activism seem pointless. Above all, most women simply did not want change on the scale proposed in 1790–4. They did not want their churches closed, their priests imprisoned or executed, and their sons conscripted into military service and death on a far-away battlefield. These upheavals turned the majority of French countrywomen into natural counter-revolutionaries and, as such, potential agents of sedition, who had to be watched by their fathers and their husbands as well as local office holders. The imposition of patriarchy was therefore a policing necessity as much as a deliberate social policy. Besides, monitoring women was notoriously difficult: the same levels of force could not be employed against them as women well knew and exploited to their own advantage when defying officialdom.

It was not that women were anti-republican after 1792 from principle, but only became so when the policies of various regimes loomed as a threat to village life as it had evolved over time, including horizons beyond the hearth that activities centred on the parish church offered them. Women were in the front line against the official anticlericalism of 1790–1, resourcefully using every form of antisocial tactic against the intrusion of an unwanted Constitutional clergyman whose sacraments they knew had none of the efficacy his extruded predecessor had possessed. When the nonjuring Church went underground after 1792, scores of thousands of women from every social background across France put their lives at risk by sheltering refractory priests, hiding precious relics once housed in the church in their own homes, or refusing to recant their faith. With dechristianisation came the denigration of past beliefs that republicans deliberately associated with stupid and ignorant women incapable of telling true from false. This idea of the woman subject to the false domination of priests was repeated endlessly in Jacobin speeches and served to confirm women in their opposition to religious change, for instance in the Haute-Loire and Velay.[6] In 1795 they inundated the authorities with petitions demanding the reopening of their churches, and their militant commitment to the Catholic faith rather than the Revolution was a primary reason for Napoleon negotiating the Concordat with Rome. In these various ways, and whether overtly counter-revolutionary or not, women found that resisting the Revolution offered them far more potential for direct involvement in public affairs (even if only at communal level) than passively accepting the official denial that the citizenness had any public role.

*The Power of Opinion*

The possibility of women influencing public affairs before 1789 through their inclusion in the new force of public opinion is widely admitted by historians. Equally, there is a consensus that the Revolution, if only through loosening the grip of the nobility on affairs of state, took away the opportunity for female hostesses to play politics and use their drawing rooms and salons to influence outcomes in palaces and cabinet rooms. As Arthur Young noted on 10 January 1790, having just dined with a large party at the duc de la Rochefoucauld's, 'another effect of this revolution,... is, that of lessening, or rather reducing to nothing, the enormous influence of the sex: they mixed themselves before in everything, in order to govern everything:'[7]. Only the most determined hostesses, such as the formidable Mme Roland (1754–93), an undoubted influence on Girondin politics not least as advisor to her husband (Minister of the Interior from March 1792), could briefly maintain a profile in the early 1790s. Whether women are included in the category of public opinion, assessing this 'indefinable composite' (as Mercier called it in his *Tableau de Paris*) remains as difficult for twenty-first century scholars as it was for eighteenth-century contemporaries.[8] It was certainly not a proto-democratic movement, for there was consensus that the 'public' only extended as far as the propertied. This constituted a clear cut-off point: thus the *philosophe* Condorcet in 1776 compared popular opinion unfavourably with enlightened public opinion.

What can be confidently said is that before 1789, the public wanted to talk and read about affairs of state and that ministers were finding it almost impossible to deny this voice of what Jacques Necker dubbed 'the opinion of the world'. It could be heard, at different social levels in clubs, taverns, Masonic lodges, provincial academies, vestry meetings and universities, a voice that wanted to be heard, wanted to be legitimised, and then taken into account by the ministers of state. The work of Dale Van Kley has shown how the Jansenist constitutional wrangling of the 1750s and 1760s injected the power of public opinion with an importance it never thereafter lost, even if many conservative jurists and advisers were in denial about its existence. The challenge for the more progressive ministers of Louis XVI's reign such as Turgot, Montmorin and Necker was how best to give this new force an opportunity to express itself formally, and this desire was at the heart of reform initiatives designed to update France's constitution so that it rested on the consent of the governed rather than the fiat of the government. Pretending that politics did not exist by the 1770s was fast becoming an exercise in escapism that could hazard a career. In fact, most ministers were appealing to public opinion to strengthen their own positions. Calonne, for instance, issuing an *Avertissement* in April 1787, in effect appealing over the heads of the assembled Notables when his reform programme had stalled; and Necker publishing a *Compte rendu* or budget account in 1781, notoriously suggesting that state funds were still in surplus despite French participation in the American War of Independence. Between those two dates, the partisans on both sides were busily conducting a pamphlet war each arguing that their minister's interpretation of the kingdom's financial plight was the correct one.

Some caveats are, nevertheless, appropriate when considering the sway of this new 'force' in French life, at least down to 1787. First of all, it was evanescent. It tended to be most apparent in times of sustained political tension, as in the controversy over the Maupeou coup against the *parlements* in 1771–4. Interestingly, the public's outrage at the Crown's autocratic initiative was tailing off well before the collapse of the triumvirate after Louis XV's death in 1774. It was also not a monolith possessed of one voice. Debate was at the heart of opinion formation and evolution, and ministers charged with policy making could look to public opinion for guidance without being much the wiser as, for example, on the issue of free trade as opposed to the retention of some tariffs. These opposed points of view reflected the variety of interests competing for the ear of ministers and hoping public preferences one way or the other would confer an advantage. Not that the king's servants were necessarily disposed to register these suppliant voices. When the Eden trade Treaty was being negotiated at Versailles between Britain and France in 1786 the silk merchants of Lyon were not consulted over the final proposals despite the damage the terms were likely to inflict on the city's primary industry. There was also an internationalist dimension to opinion. Events in France were widely reported in foreign journals and papers to which well-heeled French men and women had easier access than may have suited the French government. And the latter could not afford to ignore opinion makers beyond her borders since it was tied up with the willingness of the financial markets in Amsterdam and Geneva to keep on lending money to service the deficit. Their refusal to do so in August 1788 compelled the king to recall the public's – and the bankers' – favourite, Necker, as first minister.

Historians also tend to assume that public opinion was necessarily a progressive force. On the contrary, most Frenchmen with any political stake in the *ancien régime* worried that it was the monarchy's policies which were, at worst, destabilising because innovatory, at best likely to lead to more taxation. It also remained the case that it was still competition within Court and ministerial circles that was decisive in explaining the success and failure of individual politicians rather than any appeal to outdoor opinion. Thus in May 1787 Loménie de Brienne, archbishop of Toulouse, became chief minister not because he was overwhelmingly the public's favourite (he was relatively little known outside Languedoc), but thanks to the intrigues on his behalf of the Abbé Vermond, Marie-Antoinette's confessor, with the queen. The latter thereupon prevailed on her husband to accede to their wishes and the king, fast losing such limited interest he ever had in politics, gave in.

Summoning the Estates-General for 1789 necessarily enhanced the importance of public opinion, which would be expressed in the first instance through an electoral process. It was in contrast to the procedure for bringing the Notables together in February 1787; they had been selected not elected. However, over the next 12 months, what remained of absolutist power in France collapsed spectacularly, coterminally with the descent into national bankruptcy in August 1788. It was inconceivable that the Crown could rebuild from this nadir without constructing (or reconvening as some royal apologists tried to present it) those institutions which incorporated and reflected the opinion of the public and would enable royal finances to be stabilised in a manner corresponding to that successfully adopted by the British a century previously. Quite suddenly, though in another sense the outgrowth of events since at least the mid-century, public opinion rather than the Crown had come to be seen as the supreme arbiter by 1789. It was this change of direction in government policy – in denial for so long about the significance of this new force – that opened the door for the pamphlet wars of the winter of 1788–9 and the innovatory award of half the seats at the Estates-General to the Third Estate.

Necker and his administration in 1788–9 were not themselves proposing policies for the Estates-General. Instead, they (partly from political expediency and self-interest) asked the electors of the three Estates due to convene at Versailles in May 1789 to furnish their chosen delegates with a list of instructions, recommendations and grievances which could form the basis for a whole series of legislative initiatives. This remarkable consultative exercise, which resulted in the *Cahiers de doléances*, was unprecedented anywhere in eighteenth-century Europe and particularly startling in originating in France, a state where power had, until a few months earlier, been formally vested indivisibly in the Crown. However, the fact that Necker opted to consult the public also discloses the confidence ministers had in the maturity of the electorate. It could also be seen as an adaptation of the petitioning process, one used habitually by individuals and corporations throughout the century when making representations to the king about controversial aspects of policy. Though it has been estimated that as many as half the adult males in the kingdom took part in some part of the process, there were also safeguards built into the mechanisms to ensure that 'democratic' sentiment was given little opportunity for articulation. *Cahiers* were put together at each stage of the electoral process in towns and villages, but the general *Cahier*, the one delegates would actually take with them, was a digest of the demands of these many thousands of preliminary *Cahiers*. To give an example based on Paris: there were 11,706 voters in the Parisian primary assemblies out of a total population of approximately 500,000. They chose the 407 electors who would edit the general *Cahiers* and elect the 20 deputies from the inner city (Paris *intra-muros*).

Unsurprisingly, opinion in the documents of all three Orders displays a commitment to the moderate reformist sentiments so evident across the nation for much of the king's reign. The Estates-General was to be a permanent part of a constitutional settlement; the Provincial Estates and Assemblies no less so as part of a package resting uncompromisingly on the representative principle; *lettres de cachet* were to be abolished as part of a renewed emphasis on the rule of law; juries and Justices of the Peace would come in and there would be a reformed, equitable system of taxation. Such demands were common to all three Orders. Those of the First Estate, the clergy, sought a fairer deal for the lower clergy both in terms of pay and career progression. They were at best lukewarm on conceding anything more by way of religious toleration (the edict of 1787 was a step too far for many voters) or freedom of the press, and hoped that political reconstruction would go hand in hand with the moral renewal of the nation. The hugely variegated Third Estate, energised and emboldened by the government's concession of 50 per cent of the seats to their delegates, wanted taxation to be based only on consent, the last vestiges of *seigneurial* dues ('feudalism') scrapped, bread prices stabilised, and the opening up of public life to men with property.

In seeking local views on matters of national concern, ministers had activated a circuit of exchange between government and governed that looked like a model for the future. Yet the sounding out of the public along the lines of the exercise that produced the *Cahiers* was not repeated. Ministers had turned to the three Estates not from conviction that power resided outside the monarchy, but from a sense that executive initiatives had become discredited and that it was now up to the deputies going to Versailles to make proposals. If these brand-new legislators were disappointed on 5 May that Necker's speech to them was lacking in substance (one deputy told his wife that it was 'very mediocre, and very much beneath what one might have expected from a man who enjoys such a great reputation'[9]), it should not be forgotten that as far as he was concerned, deputies were already individually aware of what their electorates wanted and further intervention from the Crown at that late stage might look like illegitimate interference. Considering the hard work that had gone into producing them, the *Cahiers* were quickly forgotten. The metamorphosis of the Estates-General into the National Assembly was taken to cancel out the mandatory powers originally extended by the electorate to their representatives and the Constitution finally erected in 1791 was done with minimal reference back to the voters of France.[10] In many of its contents, including the wholesale abolition of privilege and the dismantling of monasticism, it far exceeded anything specified in the vast majority of *Cahiers*. This disconnection of the revolutionaries with opinion in the country remained the case for the rest of the Revolution. There were elections (especially during the Directory) and there were plebiscites in 1799 and 1802, but there was no extended consultation by successive regimes of the electorate. Public opinion in the 1770s and 1780s was always an elusive entity; it had its moment of recognition in 1789 and then faded away, blending with many other comparable terms.

As a term, along with 'the general will', it became even less clear than before the Revolution opened. And with political life now much widened, belief in the rationality of the (extended) public's opinion faltered once it appeared to have incorporated popular opinion. A wide cross-section of politicians, whose careers depended on it, habitually rhapsodised the virtues of 'le bon peuple' and the sense of their political instincts. The people were always good although easily misled (usually by the enemies of whoever was making such a claim). Those who were indifferent to or opposed to the Revolution resisted this identification, and continued to associate popular opinion with the unvirtuous, unstable and violent emotions of the *canaille* or the rabble, the sweepings of the streets whose instincts were fitful and misguided. Revolutionary leaders were on the whole suspicious of attempts to encourage the population at large to do more than respond positively to the politicians' initiatives. The Republic conceived of its legitimacy in terms of revolutionary opinion or the 'general will', neither concept readily compatible with pre-1789 public opinion. There was what has been dubbed 'wilful amnesia' from representatives towards their own constituents which amounted to a disparagement of the people at large;[11] the only opinions most of them cared to countenance were those vociferously expressed at first hand by petitioners, noisy spectators and the clubs. For those on the Left, taking Parisian opinion as proof of public opinion seemed appropriate. As early as late 1789 the *Révolutions de Paris*, in tune with militant sectional opinion, insisted that 'the will of the representatives can be in contradiction with the will of the nation'.[12] Danton may have flattered his key supporters in saying that Paris was 'the advance sentinel of the Republic' but he, like most revolutionaries, did not stoop to invite extensive and extended consideration of policy proposals. This exclusivist approach was justified on the basis that the revolutionary elite, as virtuous men, knew what its citizens wanted better than they did and that, in a time of 'revolutionary government', consultation was constrained because of the perceived threat to public order from a range of counter-revolutionary malcontents. There was also a very practical side to this reluctance, such as the likely paralysis of the Convention, one reason why François Chabot's proposal of September 1792 in the Jacobin Club that citizens should meet every Sunday in towns and villages to discuss the legislature's work and vote on all laws was lost. However, the extent of the determination to ignore manifestations of majority preferences which did not accord with the first item on the agendas of this revolutionary generation – to retain power at any cost once it had fallen into their hands – cannot in the end be glossed over. Revolutionaries were of course aware that their enterprise risked being discarded by the very people in whose name it was undertaken. In the immortal words of R. R. Palmer, the Jacobin suspicion of elections came down to this: 'the ruling group knew that in a free election it would not be supported'.[13]

*The Patterns of Participatory Politics in the 1790s*

It was hard for doctrinaire Jacobins to explain the possibility that the sovereign people might be disunited on any other basis apart from their falling victim to the machinations of the malign and the self-seeking who were to be flushed out of the nation's life. Between 1792 and 1795 such high-mindedness set the tone for discussion in many revolutionary bodies from the Convention downwards; it was an orthodoxy from which few dared to dissent in public and yet patterns of participatory politics were too varied and complicated to fit this rhetorical prism. The first law of political survival in the 1790s was, as ever, adaptability and outflanking your opponent, which explains why men such as Barras and Fouché rode the waves while Robespierre and Saint-Just did not. Survival meant using popular politics to personal advantage, resorting to manipulation or even repression where they worked against it. These were the tactics dictated in the dynamic, but unpredictable political culture during the years of the Director, until Bonaparte lost patience with these variables and used his stable power base in the army to impose discipline on the nation.

But for most of the decade down to 1799 Revolutionary politics were played out in a range of institutions, great and small, all of them new and unknown quantities, which were constantly evading the control of politicians and, paradoxically, existed despite the recurrent refrain at the top about consensus and indivisibility in the polity. In 1789–91, with almost two-thirds of males over 25 apparently active citizens in both urban and rural areas,

> The National Assembly, basing the electorate on taxes rather than property and freeing it of any religious affiliation, brought into being one of the most participatory and democratic national communities in the world.[14]

Though the right to vote was supposed to end separation between men, a form of social integration underlining a person's oneness with the nation,[15] yet the generous franchise arrangements militated against harmony by inviting involvement; the only check on the lower orders dictating outcomes being the rules for indirect elections where eligibility for membership of electoral colleges at departmental level was more restricted than in the primary assemblies. This proviso could not stop the creation and operation of a dynamic electoral culture for much of the 1790s, however limited its direct impact on the major political players. Such was particularly the case after the decree of 11 August 1792 discarded the distinction between active and passive citizens; electors to the Convention merely needed to be male, 21 or over, domiciled for a minimum of a year, possessed of an income and not a servant (the last still a serious disqualifier for millions).

The Constitution of the Year I (24 June 1793) went further still towards creating male universal suffrage by abolishing the provisos (*supra*) and even conceding voting rights to foreigners who had lived in France for a year or more. It was never given a trial because of the wartime emergency and the Year III Constitution was much less generous to plebians. It confirmed that democracy was suspect to the vast majority of politicians throughout the Revolution and that, as before 1789, property ownership remained the key to participatory rights. Indeed, those who had purchased *biens nationaux* in 1789–90 were keenest on ending the flirtations with a wide franchise that threatened their new importance as 'Notables'. It was precisely this extended elite that the Constitution makers of 1795 needed to enlist if their instrument was to have much hope of enduring. And so back came the property franchise. Even so, at primary assembly level, about 5 million voters could still participate, the main criterion being either status as a taxpayer or an army veteran. The winnowing process operated forcefully in the electoral assemblies. Here, an individual was only eligible if he owned or tenanted a property valued at between 100 and 200 days' work depending on the locality. This stipulation brought a mere 30,000 men within its ambit.

Another innovation was that of the plebiscite or referendum, inviting the post-operative consent of the electorate to new constitutional arrangements. It was a device generally only deployed by politicians when they expected to win and gain enhanced personal importance from the explicit endorsement of the governed. There were plebiscites for the Constitutions of Years I, III and VIII. That of the Year I (perhaps because of the novelty value) elicited genuine debate, leading Malcolm Crook to conclude that it produced the decade's highest participatory level of them all: about 30 per cent voting as opposed to the 15 per cent in the 1792 elections to the Convention.[16] Voters might be forgiven for responding cynically thereafter when their preferences counted for nothing with the Jacobin administration.

Bonaparte found the plebiscite could be a handy consultative convenience. As is now known, the plebiscite of the Year VII was blatantly fraudulent when only half the official number of voters claimed actually turned out,[17] but he employed it again in May 1802 to secure national approval for his decision to become First Consul for life. The number of those voting 'yes' on that occasion was about 50 per cent of the electorate, twice the figure of 1800, and that was achieved with far less intimidation and gerrymandering. It amounted to unprecedented legitimation for Bonaparte's personal rule and he subsequently obtained plebiscitory approval for the conversion of the Consulate into the Empire. The use of plebiscites was another indicator of the exceptional political creativity of France during the revolutionary years.[18]

The elections of March 1789 were surprisingly well-ordered within the reinvented categories of *bailliages* and *sénéchaussées*, signs that what would soon be referred to as the 'old order' was capable of creative improvisation within a historical context that corresponded to contemporary political requirements. There was, interestingly, no government interference in the process nor even government candidates. Necker had decided that neutrality was in his best interests, though it also reflected the absence of any apparatus linking the government with the power brokers in the provinces. An electoral culture had yet to be created. It was initially hard for the electorate to visualise itself as having the decisive voice.

Thus throughout 1789 and 1790 communications from the electorate to the National Assembly often referred to deputies as 'Our Lords and Masters'. Nevertheless, active citizens would soon forget the novelty of performing their civic duty by turning out to vote at different levels and using the secret ballot, often with not much idea about either candidate or his policies: though the franchise was cast more widely than across the Channel, there was no French equivalent to the canvassing of votes that went on in contemporary British elections. Yet enthusiasm for electoral participation faltered as early as 1791. Attendance at the cantonal primary assemblies of June 1791 to elect a new legislature ran at just 23 per cent of what it had been the previous year,[19] and absenteeism became the norm from 1791. The trend still awaits satisfactory explanation. Admittedly, the electoral process dragged on for several days. It could be impractical for a citizen living at some remove from the cantonal seat to get across there to vote for unfamiliar candidates.

However, it is not coincidence that absenteeism commences suddenly at the moment when the Assembly had imposed the oath to the Civil Constitution and introduced a hotly contested religious policy, despite the provision in the legislation for lay involvement in the election of parish priests and bishops. The response was abstention rather than voting for candidates opposed to the policy.

During the Terror voting counted for little and the practice was not reinvigorated until the Year III Constitution emphasised the importance of a mature, propertied electorate. Unfortunately for political stability, the framers of that Constitution had assumed that voters would opt for candidates acceptable to the Directory. When they failed to do so in 1797 and 1798, the Directors refused to accept the verdict and intervened to manipulate and doctor the results in the interests of personal survival. They cancelled the central role accorded to suffrage under the Constitution, ignored the genuine expression of majority wishes, and in effect privileged the Republic against the Constitution. What would have happened had Fructidor not happened? Peace with Britain almost certainly, a constitutional monarchy quite likely, and no Napoleon. Even the great Marxist historian Georges Lefebvre accepted that the vote genuinely expressed majority wishes.[20] The experiment in electoral politics found no favour with the Bonapartist framers of the Year VIII Constitution and it was countermanded without the Consulate suffering any perceptible loss of popularity among bourgeois voters. If the ballot box could not deliver the stability they so much craved by 1799–1800, then its sacrifice at the behest of a benevolent autocracy was admissible.

Elections and referenda were official events in the life of the state open to all who were legally qualified, irrespective of their interest in politics. Those who were passionate in their commitment to one or other brand of political allegiance found an outlet for their energies in the vibrant club life of the 1790s in Paris and other cities. There were huge varieties. Moderate royalists in 1789–91 had their *Club des Impartiaux*, the more counter-revolutionary of their persuasion belonged instead with Clermont-Tonnerre and Malouet to the *Club des Amis de la Constitution monarchique*. In terms of ideological creativity none excelled the *Cercle Sociale* in the early stages of the Revolution. It functioned as a publishing house and a meeting place for many future Girondins, including Brissot, Condorcet, Fauchet and Roland, but did not survive their demise in mid-1793. Club membership steadily widened as noble and clerical participation collapsed in 1791–2. By 1794 there were over 6000 political clubs, with at least one in every departmental capital and other major towns. Many were incorporated into correspondence networks both with Paris and equivalent entities abroad, such as the London Corresponding Society. The Jacobins' strength as a major political grouping owed everything to their early organisational emergence in 1789 and reputation for vigorous, hard-hitting debates in which reputations were won and lost. Five years later, their provincial outreach was extraordinary: with as many as 2000 branches and a membership of

100,000 their clubs provided, in Sir Colin Lucas's useful phrase, whole 'reservoirs of patriots'. The Jacobin leadership increasingly saw in club members the source of republican legitimacy rather than its lying with the vast mass of the nation who did not belong. The former had a vital role in undermining the provincial power base of their Brissotin enemies in early 1793. The Parisian Jacobins met four times weekly, just as did the Cordeliers, from its inception in 1790–1 a Left-leaning club. Cheap subscription rates (2 *sous*) gave its membership exceptional social breadth (the club recruited well from working-class men living in cramped housing on the Left-Bank of the Seine and they often brought their wives along to meetings), and it was well-placed to act as the vanguard of a democratic, republican nexus after the king returned ignominiously from Varennes in June 1791.

Although popular societies were shut on 23 August 1795 as a security risk, private clubs (the difference between them and the societies was often vague) had an appreciable public impact even after 9 Thermidor, arguably an enhanced one. Without the *Club de Salm*, a pro-government salon caucus meeting in Paris from June 1797, with their influential newspaper, *L'Eclair*, the Directory would have been in a much weaker position to implement or even instigate the Fructidor coup. The 'Salm-igondis' also helped launch the *cercles constitutionnels* in the provinces, the (fragile) basis of Directorial opinion in the major centres of population between 1797 and 1799. Just as the Directors sponsored their own supporters, so they were nervous about clubs inimical to their interests. One of these was the 'Philanthropic Institute', which, despite its innocuous name, was a royalist secret society with members in as many as 70 departments. They were careful not to compromise themselves by mentioning the monarchy in public at the same time as they backed royalist candidates in local and national elections. Barras eventually smoked them out, but it was the fissiparous Club des Clichyens on the Right which was the most spectacular casualty of Fructidor; at the other edge of the spectrum, the Directory shut down the Panthéon Club on 26 February 1797 when its *babouviste* tendencies became too blatant, and did the same to the Club du Manège in August 1799, a late-flowering of Jacobin opinion born after Floréal which lasted just five weeks but which Fouché as Police Minister judged too dangerous to survive. This was an involuntary tribute to the political potency of the clubs during the Revolution. Without them the exceptional degree of politicisation France attained in the 1790s would have been unthinkable. Clubs waxed and waned year by year as the landscape of public politics changed, the phenomenon itself persisted, in their competition and realignments providing further evidence that the notion of a united general will was just fictional. As pressure groups for radical action governments could not readily ignore them short of outright closure and dispersal, a recourse that became habitual after 9 Thermidor. The clubs were vital in the formation of a dynamic political culture but their mutual competition and enmities were destabilising. Their members kept the political temperature at boiling point, so that it is no wonder there was no place for them in Bonapartist France.

For the most part, the clubs were dominated by professional men and property owners. At a slightly lower social level were the urban shopkeepers, printers, journeymen and clerks who provided the leadership of the *sans-culottes* between 1790 and 1795. They were neither the urban proletariat which generations of Marxist historians claimed nor the depraved *canaille* beloved of the counter-revolutionaries, the unpropertied riff-raff of the streets, (though the latter were frequently involved in their enterprises). Richard Mowery Andrews has shown that the *sans-culottes* activists were socially indistinguishable from the Jacobin leadership, while Michael Sonenscher, in stressing the diverse experience of working life in the old order, has compellingly suggested that the image of the *sans-culottes* functioned as a rhetorical meeting ground for artisans and activists: 'It was, and remained, a term [of art] used by Jacobins to denote a popular, and artisanal, constituency.'[21] These men were committed revolutionaries who demanded a deciding role, one which the national politicians were willing to concede whenever they thought it would be to their own personal benefit. Without the *sans-culottes* there would have been no revolutionary *journées* and therefore no Revolution in the form we know it. Their dominance of the *sections* and their presence in the Paris *commune* gave them a platform and a political force that was as hard to control as it could be decisive – as the overthrow of the Girondins in May–June 1793 once again disclosed.

Their price for backing the Jacobins in the Convention was not unconditional: they wanted price controls, dechristianisation, public assistance, democratic involvement and the implementation of Terrorist policies against internal and external enemies. This was not the Robespierrist programme, yet until the latter were in full control of the Committees they could not afford to ignore it. Robespierre had just about succeeded in reducing the popular movement to tractability after the elimination of the Hébertistes in spring 1794, unluckily for him as it turned out making it impossible for them to rescue him from the Thermidorians a few months later.

The *sans-culottes* were not simply a Parisian phenomenon, although their political affiliations in the provincial cities were more variable. Before mid-1793 the 'popular movements' in centres like Bordeaux, Caen, Strasbourg and Lyon were more moderate in their policy preferences though no less committed to direct involvement in the political process than the Parisian *sans-culottes*. From June 1793, Jacobin attempts to impose their power in the country at large depended on giving their urban followers an importance never previously possessed via the patronage of the *répresentants-en-mission* and the *clubbistes*. Another of the ironies of pre-Thermidorian politics is that the Robespierristes' efforts to build up popular support for themselves outside the capital coincided with efforts to dismantle the *sans-culottes* in Paris. From July 1794, the Convention was uncompromising in its determination to keep *sans-culottes* (in as much as there was a role for them at all) exclusively within electoral politics and the Directors did likewise. The *successful* revolutionary coups of 1795–9 were instigated from the top in the interests of the grandees in the Luxembourg palace not by the *sans-culottes* of the streets around the site of the Bastille.

Urban militancy declined dramatically from the end of 1795 and was instrumental in giving the Directory a life of four years, an unprecedented length of time for any revolutionary regime hitherto. It was achieved only after the failure of no less than three more attempted *journées* in 1795. Why did these attempted coups fail? 12–13 Germinal (1–2 April) was a neo-Jacobin demonstration in the Convention hall demanding the activation of the Year I Constitution and protectionist economic measures, neither of which the *conventionnels* had any intention of doing. They bought time for themselves by promising a review of the 1793 constitution and, crucially, declaring a state of siege. Once the crisis was over, the thermidorians simply intensified their anti-Jacobin repression. This tactic still failed to eliminate the popular movement's capacity for direct action. Montagnards and their fellow travellers were back in the Convention on 1 Prairial (20 May 1795) demanding bread and the 1793 Constitution and were evicted with much difficulty. This time the thermidorians had learnt their lesson: the army must be a front-line defence against the revolutionary activists. The Parisian *sections* were purged (they were suppressed completely on 8 October), armed troops guarded the streets of the capital, and military commissions dealt ruthlessly with suspected troublemakers. Threats from the Right were no less comprehensively seen off with the use of artillery in the royalist *journée* of 13 Vendémiaire (5 October 1795) – ostensibly a protest directed at the planned 'Law of Two-thirds', in reality an intended putsch in the interval between electoral ratification of the Year III Constitution (23 September) and the Directory's assumption of office (3 November).

Direct action on the streets only had any hope of success so long as the authorities could not or chose not to rely on the army to protect themselves. And using the military before 1795 in defence of themselves had not been a serious option. Troops could not be relied on to obey orders. The events leading up to the fall of the Bastille on 14 July 1789 had literally disarmed the Crown and made any hope of a coup against the National Assembly an impossible option. After the outbreak of war in 1792 leading politicians, with some justification, looked on the military men as a threat to their domestic ascendancy rather than a support, with the militants in the revolutionary armies best kept at a safe distance on the frontiers or engaging counter-revolutionary rebels in the west, not forging alliances with the *sans-culottes* in Paris. What had changed by 1794–5? First, the patriotic education of the new corps of officers and non-commissioned officers was complete and their acceptance of the sovereign authority of the Convention was its bedrock. Therefore any appeal to protect the Convention against subversion was likely to succeed. Second, the national and international prestige of the army was such that its commanders had every incentive to prop up the regimes in whose name they fought. There was far more glory to be acquired through victory on foreign battlefields than in sanctioning a squalid coup in Paris. Finally, the army had become the emblem of disinterested patriotic virtue by the mid-1790s, whereas factional politicians looking to the crowds to propel them into power could be plausibly depicted as using the preservation of the Republic as an unconvincing pretext to conceal ambition or personal survival.

Under the Directory the crowd was demoted from being the essential patriotic preservative of the Revolution back into the *canaille*, vicious malefactors who deserved to be hauled before the nearest military tribunal. With the Jacobin clubs shut down and ruthless action taken against Babeuf, the legitimacy of direct action was largely discredited and the right to insurrection denied. The one safe and acceptable means of allowing the *vox populi* to be heard was off-stage, as at Brumaire 1799. Then Bonaparte and his fellow conspirators took care to act in the name of the people without having any of them present to obstruct the outcome he sought and secured.

## The Limits to Revolutionary Involvement

The Revolution utterly transformed the patterns of public life in France, indeed it created it as a legitimate form of participatory activity for hundreds of thousands of men on a scale unprecedented in eighteenth-century Europe. For much of the 1790s, the franchise was wide, there were representative bodies in the localities and at the centre, the clubs and the political societies ceased to be socially exclusive, newspapers and pamphlets were everywhere printed and read, and the opportunities existed for large-scale democratic involvement. Millions of young men (always the main constituency and catalyst of revolutionary action) found a comradeship and source of adventure as part of the army that gave them a sense of pride in the Republic and its public values as soldier–citizens. Revolutionary political culture was dynamic and creative and yet the fact remains that a majority of the population of France remained aloof from it. Most people chose not to become involved, or withdrew after having found the experience uncongenial, turning the Revolution into the preference of the minority. How can this abstention be explained?

The destruction of the national consensus in 1790–1 is crucial in this respect. France had a tenacious religious culture which long predated its political one, but the revolutionaries were intent on its subjection and, as their Catholic enemies saw it, its subjugation when they imposed the Civil Constitution of the Clergy and turned every parish into a battleground of competing, incompatible loyalties. Since the revolutionaries controlled the levers of power and identified their chosen policies (however divisive) with the 'general will' there was no realistic hope for dissenters of influencing them through those channels. The disillusioned or the dismayed had two alternatives: either withdrawal into private life as much as possible, keeping out of trouble and shamming support for whichever set of politicians was in control, or setting up their own unofficial networks to rival those sanctioned by the state, usually in defiance of the state. Historians remain too liable to present majority non-involvement as passive endorsement of the Revolution, but this seems wishful thinking. Admittedly, when confronted with unpopular policies, most contemporaries probably chose the line of least resistance and stayed indoors when intimidation and death were the price paid by political losers. Those who tried to mobilise against the policy makers created a genuinely populist counter-culture. This was not, however, necessarily counter-revolutionary and pro-monarchist but rather, to use a term which has found favour with historians recently, 'anti-revolutionary', that is demanding the consolidation of the Revolution, an end to its manipulation by pretended patriots and some signs of increased willingness by politicians at the centre to take notice of moderate opinion in the localities.[22] It was such moderate opinion that the Constitution of the Year III was intended at its inception to court and, more successfully, was won round to Bonapartism after 1799.

Yet millions of men and women who lost faith with the Revolution in the early 1790s did turn into counter-revolutionaries and, in so doing, gave the *émigré* nobles and the refractory clergy a popular power base. At least as much as the Revolution, the Counter-Revolution, in all its various manifestations, attracted a mass following, primarily because of its uncompromising stand on religion. The point should not be overstated. In rural areas, counter-revolutionary guerilla companies could be very intimidating and often found local people, even if ill-disposed ordinarily to the Republic, reluctant to lend active assistance to the cause.[23] But, so long as the Republic was persecuting refractories and keeping the churches shut, so long too would the Counter-Revolution recruit – and women as well as men. Because of their predilection for orthodox Catholicism, females were natural counter-revolutionaries, offering nursing to their troops in the fields, hiding refractory clergy in their lofts and outbuildings, relaying messages and, on occasion, murdering republican troops and officials. The Revolution offered most women nothing except relegation to the private sphere; the counter-revolutionaries, by contrast, used their services gratefully, though this reality is scarcely reflected in the current historiography where utterly disproportionate attention is paid to the tiny minority of pro-revolutionary female activists. The Counter-Revolution was not a monolith any more than the Revolution was but, taken as a whole, the strength of the former was that it was spontaneous, uncoerced and reflected rural opinion in a way the revolutionaries never quite managed after 1789 was over. As has been pointed out:

> We should think of the Counter-Revolutionaries in terms of alliances. On their marches into battle, the soldiers followed their parish, combat groups met up with their brothers, friends and neighbours.[24]

But these strengths could not disguise organisational weakness and ideological variations that its opponents exploited. Counter-revolutionaries may have quarrelled among themselves, had inadequate command structures, and been a prey to the military professionalism of the republicans from 1794–5, but they existed and they recruited, in differing strengths and in different places, despite everything that the Revolutionaries could do to dislodge them before the Consulate admitted the problem and neutralised it to a degree no other regime had done.

## PART III
## The Revolution and its Social Impact

# Chapter 7: The Militarisation of France: the Nation in Arms

*The Army, Autocracy and Ending the Revolution*

Soon after being sworn in as First Consul in November 1799, General Napoleon Bonaparte began to talk about ending the Revolution. It was a daring admission, although one that corresponded to a deep-seated longing across the nation as Bonaparte, with his finely tuned sense of France, was aware. Such articulation was neither unprecedented nor by definition treasonable. The Convention had prohibited lower authorities from using the word *révolutionnaire* on 12 June 1795 when republican became the name of choice (the decree was rescinded after 1797). Bonaparte also knew that as the army's most prominent and best-known (though not necessarily the most popular) field officer, he had at his disposal the only instrument capable of switching off the frenzied political cross-currents of the last decade. The unresolved question in the winter of 1799–1800, however, was would the army lend itself to such an act of closure? Bonaparte's self-confidence (always more measured and less brash than appearances suggested) as a natural leader gave him grounds for thinking that his troops would follow where he commanded whether that was on the streets of Paris or on an Italian battlefield. The army was the indispensable foundation of his personal authority, therefore it also became that of public authority in France after Brumaire. If there were any doubts about loyalties to him personally, his hard won victory at Marengo over the Austrians under General Mélas on 14 June 1800 ended them. He had saved France, shattered the forces of the Second Coalition, and made it possible for France to enter negotiations with both the Imperialists and the British from a position of strength.

Once again, Bonaparte had fulfilled his part as national saviour quite brilliantly and hopes that he could do the same in the domestic sphere redoubled. Where the army and its gallant general led, so the middle ground of opinion would gladly follow. His position was essentially straightforward: to be anti-revolutionary was to be pro-republican and he emphasised that the public good required the disinterested service to the state of all Frenchmen, irrespective of their previous loyalties (or disloyalties). On that basis, Jacobins and royalists were equally enemies of the nation and disturbers of the peace and, wherever necessary during the Consulate, troops were used to flush them out and military courts set up to try them following the precedents of the 'Second' Directory (1797–9). Bonaparte strove to demonstrate a ruthless efficiency in which civilians and soldiers complemented each other, but all parties knew that so long as the Consul's following in the army was unassailable, his personal supremacy in French public life was incontestable.

Of course, Bonaparte's abundant gifts as a politician (on show repeatedly between 1799 and 1804) might lull his fellow citizens into imagining that, beneath the republican forms of the Consulate, France had not become a military autocracy. Yet this was the real price for ending the experimental anarchy of the 1790s. Bonaparte presented himself as the soldier, as political supremo, the one man capable of curtailing chaos and restoring order and unity under the tricolour flag, and the nation would have to take its chances that their young Achilles would not abuse the authority he had taken upon himself.[1] Napoleon Bonaparte was the Caesar predicted by Burke as long ago as 1790 in his *Reflections on the Revolution in France*:

> In the weakness of one kind of authority, and in the fluctuation of all, the officers of an army will remain for some time mutinous and full of faction, until some popular general, who understands the art of conciliating the soldiery, and who possesses the true spirit of command, shall draw the eyes of all men upon himself. Armies will obey him on his personal account. There is no other way of securing military obedience in this state of things. But the moment in which that event shall happen, the person who really commands the army is your master;... the master of your whole republic.[2]

This 'popular general' took office only a few months after the death of another contemporary head of state, George Washington, the first

President of the United States of America. The contrasts between the two men, however, were pronounced. At no point in his career had Washington usurped supreme civil authority on the basis of his prominence as victorious Commander-in-Chief of the Continental Army during the American War of Independence against Britain (1775–83). Some of Washington's fellow generals were anxious to push him into a coup in the early 1780s;[3] he would have none of it and retired to his farm in Virginia, from which he was recalled with acclamation by a grateful nation to stand for the presidency in 1789 after the Philadelphia Convention had established the federal constitution. When he had served two presidential terms, Washington in 1796 stood down. The American republic was greater than him and he was a public servant not a prince.[4] Bonaparte was a successful war leader who had no intention of waiting for the Directory to call him into high, but subordinate office. His military power base was his indispensable springboard into controlling the entire French state without any prior electoral process. Bonaparte was a shameless dynast whose family had helped make Brumaire succeed and they were at the centre of the Court he quickly inaugurated at the Tuileries. His authority was martial rather than civil, his god his own glory and he had no intrinsic respect for constitutional forms for their own sake. Bonaparte was always the master of the state not its servant and was not interested in being an impartial pacifier. By contrast the President's international reputation for impartiality stood so high that in July 1794 one American commentator recommended that 'our venerable President' should create an armed confederation of states leagued for the general purpose of restoring peace to Europe:

> What in effect could be more honourable, what could more gloriously terminate his fortunate career than an arbitration which would confer the blessings of repose upon so large a portion of the globe, which would give thus early to America the rank which she is destined to hold amongst nations, and which would add a civic wreath than which none could be more justly earned, to the laurels which have been so laudably acquired in the field.[5]

Napoleon was by no means the only first general officer with unquenchable political ambitions. Throughout its entire course, the Revolution was recurrently hovering on the brink of closure by means of a military coup. It was just a matter of time before someone tried it, and succeeded. The hero of the American War of Independence, the marquis de Lafayette, was one of the first to fit that frame, one who was 'incapable of attachment to any party, where the prospect of celebrity does not allure him with perpetual gratifications of his vanity, or his ambition, which are without bounds'.[6] As a central power broker (commander of the National Guard until October 1791 and having close connections with the Paris *Comité de Recherches* set up to track political crime under the municipal council, an institution called by Simon Schama 'the first organ of a revolutionary police state'), it has been lately argued that in attempting to suppress extremists on both sides, he had all the hallmarks of a genuine liberal.[7] It was not a phase that lasted long. By mid-1792 he was in command of the Army of the Centre, the war was not going well, and the one sure way of vindicating what mattered most to Lafayette – his reputation – was to halt the Revolution. He was so disgusted by the violence of 20 June 1792 that he left his post on the front line, went to Paris, and tried to rally the Legislative Assembly against the Jacobins' clubs. He also offered to take Louis XVI and the royal family to Compiègne. The queen advised against as it would leave them all obligated to the revolutionary general, and she could not overcome her personal loathing of the marquis for his calculated inertia during the October Days. Lafayette did not force the issue. As a crescendo of 'patriotic' orators thundered anathema against him (at Tulle he was declared by one Jacobin to be Cromwell, Marius and Sulla all rolled into one), in some despair after the fall of the monarchy he deserted to the Austrians, with 16 officers, Alexandre de Lameth, and the military treasure chest. His army remained loyal to the Revolution, whereas Lafayette was imprisoned until September 1797.

Many other commanders nurtured Caesarist ambitions. In March 1793, General Dumouriez (who despised Lafayette) was treasonably talking with the Austrians about a cease-fire in which he would march on Paris, proclaim Louis XVII perhaps with the duc de Chartres (the son and heir of Philippe Egalité) as regent, and disperse the Convention in favour of a constitutional monarchy. Dumouriez was aware of the importance of the army in restoring Charles II to the English throne in 1660 and it was openly reported that he fancied himself as another General Monck.[8] Sure enough, on 1 April 1793 Dumouriez issued a proclamation to his troops announcing his intention of restoring order and the 1791 constitution:

> It is time that the army makes known its will, purges France of assassins and agitators and returns to our unfortunate country the repose it has lost through the crimes of its representatives.[9]

Disappointed in the support he received, Dumouriez abandoned his army and passed over to the enemy, and he was by no means the last senior officer to desert. Distrust of the generals fuelled Jacobin paranoia about internal traitors and, once Dumouriez had gone, suspicion turned to another liberal aristocrat entrusted with control of a republican army, the comte de Custine, a career soldier. If anyone was a candidate for being the 'next Caesar', true Jacobins considered it was Custine, and decided to take pre-emptive action. In July–August 1793, following a series of defeats, the general was arrested and subsequently executed. Jacobins remained fixated on the dangers of military power, convinced that the renegade generals, along with the vanquished Feuillants, Brissotins and Orléanists, backed by foreign agents and subsidies, were out to strangle the Revolution. The removal of all former nobles from military functions in September 1793 was their way of dealing with the perceived threat. It coincided with a concerted effort to instil patriotic, Montagnard values into the officer corps, and it worked to the extent that there was some support for the move against the *Indulgents* to guard the proclaimed sovereignty of the Convention. Just as they had moved into a position of controlling the *sans-culottes* so the Jacobin leadership was bent on moulding the army into a loyalty to the CPS.[10]

After Fleurus and the removal of the Jacobins, the relationship between the senior military men and the politicians became somewhat more stable. The latter expected that tighter control of both the National Guard and the regular army would ensure that successful *journées* would be a thing of the past, while most officers remained reluctant to take sides in public affairs.[11] On the other hand, even if the officer corps was willing to use troops against civilian malcontents, it still left them the option of using military power on their *own* behalf. Commentators were convinced that, given the sheer size of the army, it was only a matter of time before a coup was successfully staged. Writing in 1795, Lord Auckland argued that a large standing army was incompatible with a constitution founded on 'principles of mixed democracy and aristocracy'.

> It was the established army which destroyed the monarchy; it has since been employed to overawe the democracy, and, perhaps, will at last prove fatal to the whole visionary speculation of an indivisible republic of thirty millions of inhabitants,....[12]

Generals were always susceptible to intriguers offering bribes, as the British secret service appreciated. Thus Kellerman (the hero of Valmy) was suborned in 1795. He was willing to turn a blind eye as head of the Army of the Alps to the Austrians occupying Lyon and turning it into the royalist capital of France. Vendémiare killed the scheme. Pichegru was also in their pay in 1795–6, but if he and other generals flirted with treachery they lacked the political skills to make it pay for them personally.[13]

Victories in the Revolutionary Wars had given the generals a glamour and a popularity that few of the civilian politicians of the 1790s could match and, by 1797, the Directors were, to put it mildly, becoming anxious, concocting *ad hoc* alliances with the generals to guard their backs. They also used the aftermath of Fructidor to cashier no fewer than 38 generals suspected of royalist sympathies, many of them holding interior garrison commands that heightened the latent threat. Such strong-arm demonstrations strengthened loyalty to the Republic in the short term and despatching generals to fronts far distant from Paris also eased nerves; that was a major consideration for the Directory when it encouraged Bonaparte to sail for Egypt in 1798. Despite his great success at the head of the Army of Italy, at that date he only just occupied pole position in the cadre of young generals who had captured the French public's imagination. The greatest of them had been Lazare Hoche (1768–97), the victor of Quiberon Bay, ally of Wolfe Tone in planning an invasion of Ireland in conjunction with the United Irishmen, and a worryingly (for Bonaparte) charismatic commander of the Army of the Sambre-and-Meuse in 1797 whom the Directory feared was planning to lead his troops to Paris at the time of the Fructidor coup. Fortunately for the Directors – and for Bonaparte – he died suddenly that year before any attempt at forming a military autocracy. Another politically ambitious general was Moreau (1763–1813), the gifted commander of the Army of the Rhine-and-Moselle in 1796. Compromised by his alliance with the closet royalist Pichegru in 1797, he was rehabilitated and served in the Army of Italy and would not connive in undermining the Directory. Thus, with one rival dead and the other frightened off, the spotlight fell exclusively on Bonaparte who had, ominously for the Directors, already begun to take major foreign policy decisions independently of them, as in his erection of the Cisalpine Republic (July 1797) and his negotiation of the terms of the Treaty of Campo-Formio with Francis II of Austria (18 October 1797).

## The Unmartial Opening of the Revolution, 1789-92

The course of the French Revolution cannot be understood except in relation to the European war beginning in 1792, and its vast repercussions on most areas of national life. French society was thereafter militarised to a degree that still awaits comprehensive coverage and explanation and the army became the fastest road to patriotic prominence for gifted commanders, especially those who tried – publicly at least – to avoid explicit identification with any one set of politicians. Glory on the field of honour spoke for itself, factional manouevering by contrast tarnished reputations, with the corollary (not lost on Bonaparte) that the only way to remain above politics was to abolish the possibility of their meaningful practice, which he duly proceeded to do.

Back in 1790, the possibility that the French army could be the vehicle for either victory in war or a major career in high office, would have sounded incredible. No wonder that Burke's prediction or prophecy that the Revolution would be terminated by a military man appeared preposterous, even to those of his first readers who otherwise accepted his forebodings about the likely course of the Revolution in the light of its first year. This early stage of the Revolution had been marked by a pacific rhetoric that intimated that, in the new constitutional dispensation, the Assembly had renounced war as an instrument of policy. Like the clergy, soldiers in the royal army were to consider themselves as citizens first and foremost, with front-line service a last recourse in a time of international emergency that, so the politicians in the Assembly hoped, France would never precipitate herself. That this was the express policy preference of deputies became apparent during debates denying support to the foreign minister, Montmorin, in the spring of 1790, when he was contemplating sending assistance to France's ally, Spain, who was embroiled in the Nootka Sound (Vancouver Island) affair with Britain. April 1790 had seen 14 ships-of-the-line fitted out for immediate service in French dockyards; the Assembly refused to sanction their use when on 22 May it formally renounced offensive war.

The debate disclosed a commitment to pacific conflict-resolution that owed much to Enlightenment influences, and these sentiments were greeted warmly, both officially and unofficially in Britain who was, of course, the strategic gainer by them. As the *Morning Herald* reported on 31 May 1790, the decree of 22nd was, the very essence of true philosophy! a death's wound to despotism, arbitrary power, and false prerogative of ambitious, cruel, bloodthirsty tyrants... and the total extirpation of that radical disease of the French Cabinet aspiring to universal dominion!... [it] may be said to form a new epoch in the annals of the world, tending to spread universal amity... [the fruit of] this great and beatific revolution![14]

Behind the rhetoric, lay the stark reality of French military disorganisation.

Though French contingents had distinguished themselves in the American War, numbers were reduced appreciably after 1783 as an economy measure, and 1788 was the lowest point in military expenditure for France for any year since 1712.[15] Morale was correspondingly affected. Soldiers had little prospect of recognition from the monarchy immediately before the Revolution, and were correspondingly not disposed to buttress royal authority in the crisis of 1789. Crucially, on 12 July 1789, the *Gardes-françaises*, under the command of the duc de Broglie – 'a pious geriatric'[16] – had refused to fire on Parisian demonstrators and chose instead to fraternise with them, subsequently taking part themselves in the storming of the Bastille. This patriotic involvement raised their morale in a way royal policy between 1783 and 1789 had signally failed to do. The irony was that the National Assembly had even less use for the line army than the monarchy had, as its decree of 22 May (*supra*) made plain. As France lost interest in playing a proactive part in European politics, the size of the army continued to fall in 1790–1, for there was no 'enemy' for it to prepare against. As its size withered, so did the state of efficiency of those who were left in the ranks.

Military inadequacy could also be explained through the emigration of an appreciable part of the officer corps and the dubious loyalties of those who, for the moment, remained behind. Before the Revolution, legal devices such as the Ségur Ordinance (1781) had been designed to prohibit non-nobles from advancing beyond the rank of captain in most branches of the service. Thus, when 1789 came, army officers, as with other members of the Second Estate, either joined Artois in the first wave of exiles (very much a minority option) or resolved to stay only so long as the king was ostensibly committed to the creation of a Constitution. In that manner they could remain faithful to the oath of personal loyalty they had taken to the sovereign and, a poor second, to the Revolution. The flight to Varennes was regarded by many as an unequivocal token that Louis's disillusionment with the process of change had reached breaking point and most quitted the kingdom in the months following, 2160 down to December 1791.[17] Louis XVI had been trying to reach the 'loyal' regiments of the marquis de Bouillé at Montmédy, a citadel occupying a vital strategic position on France's eastern frontier. Even these forces had experienced some of the mutinous pressures within their command structures that jeopardised any pretence at military efficiency. The Châteauvieux Regiment had been in open dispute with its officers in the summer of 1790 before the mutiny had been quelled by Bouillé that August, with the approval of the National Assembly. He also had the backing of Lafayette, one of those senior aristocratic officers who stayed on to serve and command French armies in 1792–3, men whose loyalty to the Revolution was underpinned by, and whose principles were seconded by, having unexpected promotion chances come their way precisely because many former colleagues had gone. Though he refused the title when offered it in late 1789, Lafayette was in effect a medieval-style 'Constable of France' with a force of troops whose intervention one way or the other could determine the course of events.[18] Thus, in April 1791, his National Guard prevented the royal family leaving the Tuileries to take Easter communion at St-Cloud; in August 1791 it fired on pro-republican demonstrators at the Massacre of the Champs de Mars.[19]

Most urban centres had their own National Guard detachments and they were not just an invention of necessity by the propertied middle orders to guard against anarchy in Paris and throughout the provinces. Militias had always been the preference of progressive, classically educated opinion. Citizen–soldiers had a vested interest in protecting any constitutional regime upholding the rule of law, whereas professional troops led by ambitious generals were a threat to the polity. This was received opinion before 1789 and it was still much to the fore over the next two years. The National Assembly was scarcely less enthusiastic for the demilitarisation of French society than it was on decentralisation. In the months after its demise on 30 September 1791 bellicosity would return with a vengeance, as the politicians overcame their distrust of the generals and committed the nation to conflict.

## The Nation Goes to War

For all its original pacific pretensions, revolutionary France went to war with Austria and Prussia in the spring of 1792. After years of inanition, the country suddenly needed an offensive army, precisely at the moment when it had lost three-quarters of its officer corps. It was, therefore, a remarkably risky strategy that courted not just defeat on the battlefield but the complete dismantling of the troubled revolutionary polity. The presence of a large number of *émigrés* immediately east of the Rhine urging the German princes to act was a constant irritant to deputies in the Legislative Assembly, despite the slim encouragement given initially to their hare-brained plans for conquering France by either Leopold II or Frederick William II. These two sovereigns had their eyes firmly fixed on events to the east where another realm, Poland, had provocatively given itself a constitution in 1791. In the aftermath of Varennes, however, Leopold's concern for the fate of his brother-in-law grew stronger. On 6 July he issued the Padua Circular. It asked other European monarchs to take action that would restore the liberty of the royal family. It was a vague document without a substantive threat. Much the same could be said of the Declaration promulgated after he had met the king of Prussia at Pillnitz in August 1791, expressing concern at events in France and inviting other powers to jointly re-establish order there. It was still a long way from intervention, but lent itself to interpretation as a threat to national sovereignty.

French politicians squared up for combat once the brief honeymoon between Crown and politicians over the acceptance of the Constitution was over. There was much talk of treachery in high places, usually centred on Marie-Antoinette, the head of the putative 'Austrian committee', ready to betray the Revolution and her adopted country and welcome the imperial armies of her brother, Leopold. The fact that neither Leopold nor her other brother, his predecessor Joseph II (died April 1790), had shown any sign of interfering in France's internal affairs was interpreted merely as evidence of the 'Committee's' exceptional malignity and subterfuge. Declaiming against the Habsburgs and their counter-revolutionary stooges was a way for ministers and deputies in the winter of 1791–2 to demonstrate their patriotic credentials, fixate for once on an identifiable foreign enemy, play up the unvarying unpopularity of the monarchy's 1756 alliance with the Habsburgs, and though the Assembly insisted it had no quarrel with the other peoples of Europe, tone down the universalism of 1790 in favour of scarcely disguised chauvinist declamations. Brissot spoke shrilly in December of liberating the peoples of Europe from tyranny, imposing the Revolution by force in a truly popular cause. He was well aware that if the armies conquered, it could make his political dominance unassailable; defeat would doom him along with all the revolutionaries. Like other Girondins, his war fever reflected a sense of insecurity: the Revolution would never be safe until it had spread through much of Europe.

To near universal acclamation at home, France declared war on the new Habsburg ruler, the yet to be crowned Francis II (the Legislative Assembly chose to recognise him only as the 'king of Hungary and Bohemia', thereby using international convention to deliver an undoubted snub) on 20 April 1792 and her armies crossed the frontiers full of revolutionary ardour and confident of quick, crushing victory. It all turned sour within a matter of weeks on most of the fronts and precipitated the internal crisis of August–September 1792 which established a Republic and discarded both the monarchy and the Legislative Assembly. Meanwhile, the road to Paris had been closed to the Prussians when the artillery at the battle of Valmy vindicated the pre-revolutionary investment made in this area by turning back the advance of the duke of Brunswick's army and, at Jemappes (6 November 1792) in the Austrian Netherlands, Imperial forces were also checked, and opened the way to Brussels and the first major conquest of the war. Majority opinion was stupified: the survival of revolutionary France seemed inexplicable. Karl Friedrich, Elector of Mainz (in which city the Brunswick Manifesto had been issued) had been so confident of the power of the princely armies on the road to Valmy that he told a well-wisher that the march into France was only 'a promenade'. Typical was one battle-hardened Scottish general who had been convinced Dumouriez's army 'must submit the moment the Prussians thought proper to attack them' at Valmy. Rather than admit the technical competence of the French, James Grant could 'only account for it by the disaffection of the [Prussian] Troops,...'.[20] A correspondent of William Eden (1st Lord Auckland), someone acquainted at first hand with pre-Revolutionary France, sounded a very glum note after Valmy:

> I am most lamentably disappointed & I now see no prospect of any speedy settlement of French affairs. The miscreants at Paris incouraged by an appearance of success will be active to extend their mischiefs & My apprehensions are now by no means quiet with respect to our own affairs. Our ministers will deserve the execrations of all the world if

they do not exert themselves to crush a barbarous spirit which is likely to pervade all Europe if not very speedily prevented ... the conduct of the Prussian army & the neglects of the Austrian quite unhinges all my former notions of things[21]

New Year 1793 brought a breathing space in which the Republic could with all speed hasten the creation and organisation of its most pressing need: the men, materials, and command and administrative structures required for waging offensive war. A new officer corps was quite easily created by giving commissions to the sergeants and corporals of the old line army while it was made plain that the only future determinant of promotion would be talent and ability not wealth or birth. Literally millions of young men were required to resist the invader and carry a war of liberation into his territory. This was to be considered an indispensable duty of citizenship. In March 1793 recruitment quotas were set for all local communities and in August, with all unmarried adults between 18 and 60 mobilised, the Jacobin government instituted the *levée en masse*, a ballot-based scheme of selection for military service for men aged 18 to 25 imposed on every *commune* and unbendingly enforced. These vast numbers had to be fed so army contractors were frequently conceded rights of bulk purchase however little that left for civilians in the vicinity; entire regions were turned into supply zones for foodstuffs of all kinds. Ancillary industries also became a state priority: uniforms had to be provided and that entailed supplementing the domestic clothing industry wherever possible, as through the creation of public workshops in the Paris *sections* in 1793–4. Nothing mattered more to an infantryman than his boots and there were not enough of them. For a time, in late 1793, the shoemakers of France were allowed to work only for the army.[22] The armaments industry similarly was primitive with a few state armouries that worked flat out to meet demand. Thus in 1793–4 nearly 7000 new cannons and howitzers were produced. It was still insufficient to satisfy the requisition requests of the commanders, forcing troops to rely on pikes because there were not enough muskets to go round. No wonder that on 18 September 1793 the CPS ordered commanders to find all the food, clothing, arms and equipment they needed, wherever possible, in occupied territories. What the War Office willed was respected, with the power of the CPS and its officials to drive on the recalcitrant. Necessity increased the reach of government in 1793–4, justified the 'Terror' as a precautionary measure in times of national emergency, and stunted further constitutional change. In this way, under the Jacobins the demands of the war overrode all other considerations and drove domestic as well as foreign policy.

In numerical and organisational terms, the army thus quickly became easily the most important force in the Republic, the leviathan that underpinned the existence of revolutionary France. The experience of military life was, for most Frenchmen, one which brought them directly into contact with the machinery and ideology of the revolutionary state in which they would submit to creation as the soldier–citizen. Turn the reluctant conscript into a republican patriot while he was with the colours and, if and when he returned home, he could be expected to live out the same values in civilian life. As the studies of Richard Cobb, Jean-Paul Bertaud and Alan Forrest have all, in their different ways, emphasised, the militarisation of France in the 1790s had the most profound effects on masculine culture, offering millions of young men an allegiance which could lift them beyond their own local *pays* and a camaraderie which rested on subscription to the patriotic desirability of the Republic, trust in their commanders irrespective of their political ambitions, and loyalty to the men of their own rank in their own unit. They gained, too, a sense of a common French identity no institution had quite managed before the 1790s, forming the nation, as it were, through the regional mix of the regiment.

Not all Frenchmen were caught up in this republicanising nexus. There were the deserters who took to the hills and the forests rather than make up the recruiting officer's quota and there were the counter-revolutionaries (and, to a lesser extent, the federalists) whose loyalties were at variance with the state's. Many men deserted on front-line duties, especially when the enemy were winning and there was the opportunity of transferring to forces commanded by *émigrés*, like the organised deserters coming into the duke of York's forces from 'l'armée des régicides' in late 1794 who wished to serve as hussars in the regiment of the duc de Choiseul.[23] Others emigrated before call-up to join the armies of Condé and the other princes; most stayed behind and were, briefly, irregulars in their own localities, harrying the republican forces at every juncture. Their weapons were non-standard, their uniforms could be homespun, their royalist and religious loyalties put them utterly at odds with their 'blue' opponents but they had this in common with them: participation in the wholesale militarisation of France that the Revolution had inaugurated.

## The Wars of the Revolution

Much of the warfare of the 1790s pitted Frenchmen against Frenchmen, such was the profoundly divisive and disruptive impact of the Revolution. It would be an exaggeration to talk of a civil war affecting the whole country, but there were flash points where it was nothing less than that for months or years on end. Parts of western France in particular, were bastions of popular counter-revolutionary sentiments, seething with resentment even before the military levy of 24 February 1793 triggered off a peasant rising centred on the *département* of the Vendée. The conflict fanned out into neighbouring areas as the insurgents were organised by local aristocrats into a 'Royal and Catholic Army'. They had a spate of victories through the summer until the republicans finally turned the tide at the Battle of Luçon on 13 August. For the next two months the outcome was uncertain until the decisive fall of Cholet on 17–18 October, the failure of the rebels to make any connection with the British at Granville on the Normandy coast the next month, and their decisive defeats at Le Mans and Savenay in December 1793. The unrelenting repression of the west lasted for most of 1794 until serious negotiations began between Hoche (appointed *Generalissimo* in the West in September 1794) and the rebels in January 1795. *Chouannerie* dragged on and was not so easily repressed as south of the Loire. The treaties of La Jaunaye with the Vendéens in February and that of La Prevalaye with the Breton peasant insurgents known as *Chouans* in April were not destined to last: the succession of Louis XVIII and British naval support produced a landing at Quiberon Bay in Brittany in the summer. It went disastrously wrong and 748 rebels were executed on the orders of military commissions after they had surrendered. Such strictness was only one aspect of Hoche's astute 'pacification of the west': over 1200 other counter-revolutionaries were actually acquitted and 200 *Chouans* taken received sentences of four months or less in gaol. He had no doubt about the good sense of clemency combined with firmness:

> I have said it twenty times to the Directory: if we do not accept religious tolerance, we must abandon hope of peace in these areas. The last inhabitant, determined to go to heaven, is willing to die defending the man he believes will open the gates for him.... must we shoot men to enlighten them?[24]

The Directory was persuaded and, just six weeks after its inception, combined the three armies in western France into a single Army of the

Ocean Coasts and, under secret instructions issued on 28 December 1795, gave him unprecedented powers over local authorities and civilians. Hoche proved worthy of the trust and, though there was a brief resurgence of counter-revolution in the west after Quiberon as dazed partisans tried to extract revenge for their setback (the so-called 'second *chouannerie*' of 1795-6), armed confrontations in the far west were gradually confined to small-scale skirmishing until counter-revolutionaries more openly took up arms in the summer of 1799. The epicentre this time was in the south, in the Haute-Garonne, where royalist rebels were crushed at Montréjeau on 20 August after having nearly occupied Toulouse, a Jacobin stronghold. As late as October the Bordelais, the Rhône valley, Normandy and large parts of Brittany were all controlled by counter-revolutionary forces, and the British navy was landing arms for Cadoudal with impunity on the Breton coast.

One did not have to be a royalist to take up arms against the republic on the basis of rescuing it from those who had seized power illegitimately. This was certainly the response of a majority of *départements* to the *journées* of 31 May and 2 June 1793. The Jacobins had no mandate outside Paris for their purging of the Convention and it induced moderate republicans to try and reassert the influence of the provinces in what became known as the Federalist movement. It was an approximate label invented by the Jacobins and often quite misleading. In Lyon for instance, where Jacobinism collapsed in early May 1793 a month before it became all-powerful in Paris, its leaders were bourgeois democrats rather than federalists. Like other 'federalists' they armed themselves and acted in defiance of the CPS. Armies were formed in Normandy and Brittany, in Bordeaux and the Midi, and the federalists took control of Lyon, Marseille and Toulon. Hopes rose that the Montagnards would be defeated and a new National Assembly convened. Their opponents, however, could not co-ordinate their actions effectively and, very quickly, the Jacobins brought up armies to starve these cities into surrender and then punished their citizens mercilessly. After the fall first of Marseille and then Lyon on 9 October, only Toulon still held out before it, too, surrendered on 19 December 1793 to the army of Dugommier and Bonaparte. Many of its terrified citizens chose to embark with the departing British warships of Lord Hood's Mediterranean fleet rather than leave themselves to the mercies of their fellow Frenchmen. Federalism was a phenomenon of 1793. That still left vast numbers of the resentful and the disaffected, whose resentment of heavy-handed officials or soldiers blurred ideology with criminality and produced the

White Terror of 1795 in the Midi and the chronic problems of policing experienced by the Directory throughout the later 1790s.

The internal war had a vicious character that would not easily be forgotten. What moved the participants on both sides to inflict such a level of suffering on their fellow countrymen? After explaining the revolt of the Vendée in material terms, historians at the end of the last century once again began to take seriously the emotional convictions of the thousands of peasant irregulars who decided to risk their lives on behalf of their Church and their king. They had been replaced by alien, outside forces to which they owed no allegiance, which had bought up lands to which they might have had prior claim, closed their churches after first intruding a constitutional clergyman, and called on their sons to fight for them.

Set against this balance sheet, death was preferable. For the Vendéen rebels, and for many of the *Chouan* irregulars, revolt was a sacred duty in defence of every value dear to them and they called on their landlords to lead them against the Satanic forces who had gained control of France. Death in this religious war amounted to martyrdom, as indeed the Roman Catholic Church has subsequently recognised, and attempts continue to secure the canonisation of the weaver Cathelineau (1759–93), the *generalissimo* of the 'Royal and Catholic Army', mortally wounded attacking Nantes in July 1793. The *Bleus*, the men of the Revolutionary Armies who came up against his forces, were under orders to enforce the will of the Republic. But from what we know of the composition of these forces and the inculcation of the values of citizenship Jacobin-style by 1793–4, it can be safely assumed that the rebels were, for them, fanatics whose values were those of an old France that must never return, traitors in league with the external enemies of the *patrie*. Given the remoteness of western France, and the distinctiveness of the various dialects and Breton language, it would have been easy for the republican troops to look on the rebels as no less 'foreign' than the foes they confronted off French soil.

In its way, the federalist revolt of 1793 was no less a clash of competing ideologies between different strains of republicanism with 'federalism' to a significant extent itself a polemical invention directed against the Brissotins. The competition between the Jacobins and Brissotins in the Convention and the clubs in the first half of 1793 was taken out into the provinces and on to the battlefields in the second half of that year as the Montagnards attempted to translate their Parisian coup into one that would hold across the nation. These conflicts were campaigns of cultural conquest in which the winning side not only butchered its opponents (and thereby, of course, stoked up the desire for future revenge), but attempted to extirpate every memory of them and their habitations. Hence the decree of the Convention on 12 October 1793 that Lyon was to be known to futurity as 'Ville-Affranchie'; thus not just the mass executions in early 1794 by General Turreau's 'infernal columns', but the destruction of villages, the crop-burning, the animal maiming and the killing in cold-blood of 'innocent' women and children.

The murderous contest in the Vendée was a reminder to all the citizens of the Republic that they could not opt out of the Revolution. Its values would prevail so long as the central government willed their imposition and that resistance to the regime (or *lèse-nation* as it was termed) would result in death, either by summary execution or through due process of the laws. Turreau's columns were just another manifestation of the missionary zeal that inflamed the officers commanding the Revolutionary Armies between 1792 and 1795 and, to a considerable degree, the soldiers under them. They were neither fighting a war of conquest for the sake of it (that would come after 1795) or defending the *patrie*, but were taking revolutionary principles to other European states where the initial assumption was that subject peoples were eagerly awaiting their liberators. The Declaration of Fraternity (September 1792) talked grandly about 'fraternity and assistance' to all peoples who wished to regain their liberties.

This naive expectation was rapidly dispelled. Most of France's neighbours fought back to protect their frontiers against the incursion of barbarians who came from Europe's pariah state, bringing with them the unwanted principles of subversion, regicide and dechristianisation. It was much harder for the powers making up the First Coalition (1792–5) to decide what they were fighting *for* apart from motives of self-defence.

There was a serious chance of a general European peace in 1796–7 as negotiations began with both the Austrians and the British. These were dashed thanks to Fructidor and, thereafter, the Directory could bang the drum of revolutionary republicanism when it suited, if only to keep in tune with its generals and their troops whose commitment to principle actually made it easier for them to justify looting conquered lands. It was hard to pretend (if it ever had been) that the Revolutionary War was about much more than conquest by the late 1790s: France had pushed out her 'natural frontiers' well beyond their 1789 limits to surpass anything achieved by Louis XIV a century earlier. Savoy and Nice had been annexed; the Austrian Netherlands had been portioned out into a series of *départements* within metropolitan France and, the greatest strategic prize of all, France had annexed vital lands in the Rhineland, including the cities of Frankfurt and Mainz, by the Treaty of Basle with Prussia in April 1795 (formed into four *départements* in November 1798). And her indirect powers of control extended further still after satellite republics were created in what had been the United Provinces (the Batavian Republic, 1795), Italy and Switzerland (the Helvetian Republic, 1798).

T. C. W. Blanning has influentially argued that the foreign policy of the revolutionaries in the early 1790s was more pragmatic than has been presumed and that the continuities with late *ancien régime* priorities are quite striking. It is a useful corrective but one that slightly too readily dismisses the ideological distinctiveness of this war by comparison with anything Europe had known. In this area at least, bellicosity was being redefined not only because of the numbers involved after France brought in a national conscription system in 1793, but thanks to the unprecedented interest of the average soldier in his cause. Certainly, he was fighting for his regiment, his platoon, for his own life, perhaps even for his general, but he was also committed to a value system in which kings and priests counted for little and the revolutionary principles of popular sovereignty and the nation-in-arms for a great deal. These principles were there in 1793, they were still there in 1803 when peace in Europe ended again, and Bonaparte for one never doubted their usefulness in motivating his forces. They were represented in the tricolour flag under which men fought, in the names of the warships in which the navy put to sea from Brest and Toulon. There was, for instance, the *Droits de l'homme*, an early casualty of 1793, and *Le vengeur du peuple*, which fought on until it sank in the 'Glorious First of June', 1794, and thereby made defeat in that engagement less unpalatable.

The Revolutionary Wars of 1792–1801 took Frenchmen all over the world in unprecedented numbers. In Europe, the Flanders battlefront stabilised after Fleurus and opened the way for the annexation of Belgium. The Basle Treaty (*supra*) settled the question of the Rhineland and allowed the French to concentrate their efforts on Italy for the second half of the 1790s. It led to the occupation of Rome in February 1798 and the establishment of a Roman Republic following the displacement of the papacy, and the (shortlived) creation of the Parthenopean Republic in Naples early the following year by forces under Championnet (Commander of the Army of Rome), deliberately disregarding the orders of the Directory. French troops poured into the West Indies throughout the 1790s in a desperate and largely unsuccessful battle to hang on to Martinique and San Domingo in the face of slave revolts and British attacks (see Chapter 11). It did not prevent them looking to establish new imperial conquests. Bonaparte revived the old Bourbon scheme for an empire in the orient and sailed to Egypt in May 1798, capturing Malta en route and entering Cairo on 23 July after crushing the Mamelukes at the Battle of the Pyrenees. French ambitions also extended to Ireland. Thanks to the backing of General Hoche, the leader of the United Irishmen, Wolf Tone, was made a colonel in the French army and both men sailed for Ireland in mid-1797 with an army of 15,000 men. Had they been able to land, their capacity for disrupting British control of their Irish kingdom would have been incalculable. It was the weather gauge that prevented them disembarking their troops in Bantry Bay not the Royal Navy. Their success suggests that the professionalism of the republicans at sea has been too easily underestimated by historians, a mistake not made by Pitt or his First Lord of the Admiralty, Earl Spencer.[25] There was nothing pre-ordained about British naval supremacy, as those who recalled the setbacks of the American War of Independence knew too well. A flag officer of genius, like Horatio Nelson, could make all the difference with an overwhelming victory such as his destruction of Napoleon's Egyptian fleet at the Battle of Aboukir Bay (1 August 1798). But this triumph could not disguise the fact that Britain's fleet was over-committed and that the French navy could make up its own shortfall in numbers through using the vessels of its Spanish and Dutch allies. Such considerations informed the British decision to disarm the Danish fleet in a pre-emptive strike in 1801 at Copenhagen, and made the threat of invasion of southern England in the late 1790s and early 1800s a distinct possibility.

*The Consequences of Incessant Warfare*

It has been argued by Alan Forrest that 'The War took much of the idealism out of the Revolution'.[26] By contrast, this book would claim that the army remained one of the last bastions of early revolutionary values right down into the era of the Consulate and incessant fighting bore witness to a distinctive Jacobin fighting spirit. It had become a disciplined, professional force with battle honours aplenty, but its zeal for what can only be described as neo-Jacobin ideals – dechristianisation, republicanism, revolutionary cults and festivals – persisted. They may have been subordinated to its obedience to orders from above, but these were ideals that no ambitious commander could ever assume had fragmented. Bonaparte assuredly never did so, having originally made his name as a Jacobin general. The Jacobins had used the army as a focus of political indoctrination, 'une école du jacobinisme', to quote Jean-Paul Bertaud,[27] and after 1794 it still kept the fire of the Revolution ablaze on a scale no civilian organisation could match. It also necessitated the creation of state apparatus on an unprecedented scale to organise and support it. Without the army, there would have been no need for the reinvention of centralisation after 1792 or the bureaucracy that went with it. Military needs and conscription, in the last analysis, created what historians know as the revolutionary state. Take the army out of the equation and it would be unrecognisable. Paying for the army imposed another burden on French citizens in the 1790s that wrecked the currency, stoked up inflation and left the majority materially worse off than they were before 1789, until Bonaparte completely overhauled public finances in the early nineteenth century. The Revolutionary Wars terminated the moves towards free trade that had been a feature of government policy in the 1780s and led the state back to protectionism and extensive economic controls.[28] Self-sufficiency was the order of the day for the civilian population for, in times of dearth and shortage like the appalling winters of 1794–5 and 1800–1, the needs of the troops would always come first.

The cost of the army was more than a mere cash calculation for the French peasantry. It took their sons away from their own locality and frequently their farm animals and carts too. Though requisitioning could look like legalised looting, all were required to put private interest aside in the service of the Revolution in the ultimate test of citizenship. Millions refused to do so in acts of collective defiance amounting to civil war (as in the Vendée) or individual disobedience, such as taking to the forests or hills rather than be conscripted. For the revolutionary state did not simply require obedience, it expected Frenchmen to hazard their lives in its defence and for its greater glory. A patriotic contribution was expected from all. As the *levée en masse* of 23 August 1793 expressed it:

> Young men shall go into battle. Married men shall forge weapons and transport food supplies; women shall make tents and uniforms and serve in hospitals; children shall tear up rags for bandages; old men shall betake themselves to the public squares to excite the courage of

the warriors and to preach the hatred of kings and the unity of the Republic.

The Revolution had moved the military ineluctably to the centre of national life long before its most celebrated general took supreme command of the state. It also became a habitual presence in local life, including those cantons well away from the frontier regions that served as garrison towns or centres for the military tribunals which took over the administration of justice when civilian courts were deemed to have lost control. And nowhere was off-limits for the recruiting sergeants when they arrived to collect their quota of men. The military men had achieved a prominence that eclipsed the politicians and ended by containing them. Bonaparte's coup in that sense reflected a change in patterns of decision making and authority from which no area of national life was exempt.

Incessant warfare offered the politicians entrusted with organising the state for war in the 1790s considerable potential career benefits – just so long as the fighting went France's way. It could also save their lives at moments of regime change. Lazare Carnot (1753–1823), a former captain of engineers, made a name for himself in the Legislative Assembly as an authority on military matters and this became his specialist area after he had been elected to the CPS in August 1793. He organised the first conscript army of 1793 into an efficient fighting force, improved medical facilities, and put an end to the experiment of electing officers. Carnot had an exceptional eye for talented young patriotic generals, including Bonaparte, Hoche and Moreau, and they repaid his confidence by delivering success. It was Carnot who initiated the policy of systematically plundering conquered lands in order to relieve pressure on the domestic economy. Widely credited as the 'organiser of victory' in the Year II, he was nevertheless compromised by his familiarity with Robespierre and it took him a year after Thermidor to rebuild his political fortunes. At the formation of the Directory, he was an obvious 'name' for the new dispensation to appropriate as one of the first five Directors, and his heyday lasted until Fructidor obliged him to quit France. Another individual whose skills in turning the war around in 1793–4 kept him off the proscription lists at Thermidor was Prieur de la Côte-d'Or (1763–1832). He became a member of the CPS concurrently with Carnot and was regularly away from Paris over the following year on missions to forces in the field. He made major changes to the armaments industry, including the introduction of an Arms and Powder Commission in February 1794.

It was empowered to requisition premises and recruit workers as they were needed to manufacture the muskets, artillery and gunpowder essential to the war effort. In naval matters the CPS looked to the ex-Protestant pastor, Jeanbon Saint-André (1749–1813) to inspire it. He took up post on it straight after the expulsion of the Girondins in June 1793 and spent much of his time resident in Brest organising the dockyard and the Channel fleet. Though he restored command structures in the navy, it still endured chronic shortages of construction materials, money and sailors: its main threat lay in the fact that it existed and might act in conjunction with Spanish or Dutch vessels. In a state where naval expertise was in short supply, Saint-André even managed to remain in public life throughout 1794, being despatched by the Convention to the coastal *départements* of the south to advise the authorities. Only when the Thermidorians felt strong enough to dispense with his talents was he arrested as a terrorist in the spring of 1795. He was amnestied, served as Consul in Algiers and Smyrna in the later 1790s, and Napoleon would employ him as a prefect.

If organising the war propelled individuals from obscurity into national celebrity, it also required the structures of administration to display a degree of unprecedented efficiency, co-ordination and professionalism. Typical of the scale and urgency with which problems were addressed was the three-man National Food Commission [*Commission des subsistances*] created by Robert Lindet on 22 October 1793 with some 500 civil servants carrying out its orders. It had authority under the Law of the Maximum to requisition, buy, import and transport food as necessary and to establish prices and priorities for its distribution. No eighteenth-century state had ever had such large numbers of men in the field to feed as well as equip. Lindet rose to the challenge. Without the Commission's often dictatorial efforts, the military effectiveness of France's armies would have been wrecked by food shortages. Scientific research was put into the service of national defence, and formed an important tier of the military bureaucracy. Lindet's colleague on the CPS, Prieur de la Côte-d'Or, brought in experts to ensure that the Republic's troops were not let down by their weapons on the battlefield. He seconded the mathematician turned ex-navy minister of 1792–3 Gaspard Monge (1746–1818) and had the chemists Jean-Henri Hassenfratz (1755–1827) (director of Lavoisier's chemistry laboratory in the 1780s) and Louis-Bernard Guyton de Morveau (1737–1816) to advise him. They tested cannons and firearms on the training ground at Meudon and deployed a hydrogen balloon for military purposes for the first time at the battle of

Fleurus.[29] Naval technology was not neglected. France may have spurned the offer of an American inventor to construct an underwater submersible for use against British vessels, but her dockyards built frigates that were bigger and faster than their counterparts in the Royal Navy and were admired by British captains. The revolutionary state set store by having scientists and savants of all kinds in its pay. Significantly, Bonaparte took Monge in his train to Egypt in 1798, while Hassenfratz and Morveau had posts at the *Ecole polytechnique* under the Directory.

These developments are all compelling evidence of the militarisation of France in the 1790s and, competing to overthrow or at least contain her, much of the rest of Europe. France became something approaching an armed camp. Most Frenchmen under 35 were wearing uniform by 1799, as were most revolutionaries. Their presence in the ranks kept the Jacobin spirit of 1794 alive throughout the Directory and Consulate and made the army an unpredictable force as well as an indispensable one in the life of the Republic. None of the Directorial politicians secured enough respect from the army to keep that regime in existence; officers wanted one of their own to lead the *Grande nation* that their own exertions had created. It had become symbolically appropriate as well as militarily and politically expedient that the state should have a general turned consul turned emperor at its head, one who in his own person combined pride in the nation with pride in the Revolution's best achievements.

# Chapter 8: Violence, Vandalism and Coercion

> The French Republic was 'suckled with blood, and in its cradle was delighted with no sound but the voice of murder'.
>
> Thomas Hardy, Regius Professor of History at Edinburgh University and Moderator of the General Assembly of the Church of Scotland in 1793,
> *The Patriot* (Edinburgh, 1793), 48.

*Violence*

Contemporary historians of the French Revolution are returning with compelling insistency to the theme of violence. How essential, how intrinsic was it to the character of that Revolution? This was not a topic that much interested the Marxist class warriors who protected the progressive reputation of the Revolution into the 1970s and beyond. It eventually resurfaced in 1989, embarrassingly for President François Mitterand and a tepidly Socialist government in the Fifth Republic, who were determined all the emphasis in the bicentennial anniversary of the Revolution would be on the Rights of Man and the rule of law, not the violence Frenchmen inflicted on fellow Frenchmen because of the Revolution. The official bicentenary apparently stopped at 1789 as if aware that it would be inappropriate, for present-day purposes, to draw attention to what happened after that year, only to find that the books which received maximum press attention were those which argued that political violence was as much part of revolutionary activity in 1789 as it was during the 'Great Terror'. Historians as celebrated as Simon Schama and François Furet argued that terror was 'inherent' in the ideologies of 1789, setting up a debate that has rumbled on for more than a decade and drawn in historians of all shades of opinion. Schama is quite uncompromising: 'violence was what made the Revolution revolutionary'.[1] Both Marxist and clericalist scholars always had their martyrologies, but revisionists argue that body counts are central to the Revolution not an aspect of it: the blood-soaked images of the 'Marseillaise' sung by the *fédérés* in 1792 (now the national anthem of France) give us an accurate indication that patriotism and violence were inextricably bound up together. Recent participants in the discussion include Patrice Gueniffey and J. Arno Meyer. Gueniffey, in his *La politique de la Terreur: Essai sur la violence révolutionnaire, 1789–1794* (Paris, 2000) insists that the Terror was the logical conclusion of the revolutionary political process, 'consubstantial' with the idea of revolution itself. Such a view is compelling in its way, but tends to skate over the prior formation and implementation of a liberal ideology based on the rule of law.

There is a sharp sense in which the years 1789–91 were not like the Terror at all, or anticipated the 'skid' of 1793.[2] The American historian of early twentieth-century Russia, J. Arno Meyer, sets up in *The Furies* a direct comparison between some of the most violent episodes of the French Revolution and the Russian Revolution of 1917–22, noting that violence was inherent in, and central to, both sides of each conflict. Meyer has been followed by Antoine de Baecque and his *Glory and Terror: Seven Deaths under the French Revolution* (London, 2001, first published in Paris, 1997).[3] De Baecque, a cultural historian, is less concerned to set up comparisons with past or future outbreaks of violence than to ponder the significance of dead bodies in the Revolution (not always those who met a violent end), including Voltaire, the princesse de Lamballe and Louis XVI himself, and the obsession with viscerality which is so often present. The debate has reached the stage where no study of the Revolution is complete without engaging with this theme, as this chapter attempts to do. It examines the strength of the revisionists' case as to whether the Revolution was for most French people, 'a cruel experience' as René Sedillot has put it, one in which violence was justified by the state and interpersonal violence could achieve moral acceptability by being inflicted for the public good. It does so by looking at particular crises.

Considering the nationwide excitement generated from mid-1788 after elections to the Estates-General were announced, outbreaks of violence attributable exclusively to political wrangling were few. Language could be heated for the stakes were high but, overall, pleasure in the king's apparent submission to the nation's wishes diffused hotheadedness. It was rather the combination of anticipated political transformation coinciding with a failed harvest (1788) that increased urban tensions and expectations. The Réveillon riots in the Faubourg Saint-Antoine *quartier* of Paris during April were one expression of those symptoms.[4] After 4 May, violence became a product of uncertainty, an expression of unease. In Paris, fear of a royalist coup against the National Assembly and the presence of hussars in the Tuileries Gardens drove the urban populace to attack the Bastille, not so much because it was a hated symbol of royal despotism as a place where they could find small arms to defend themselves against professional soldiers. When set against a comparable act of defiance against royal authority, the Fronde of the *parlementaires* in 1648–9 for instance, the number of deaths involved in the fall of the Bastille was unexceptionable. Over 100 individuals had been killed by those defending the fortress and there was no blood-bath after it surrendered, apart from the unfortunate de Launey, its governor, who was felt to have violated his word. As a sanguinary episode, it engaged European attention and it reinforced the impression that there was a price in blood to be paid for overthrowing France's ancient constitution. As a correspondent of the Anglican archbishop of Cashel put it: 'There is a great ferocity & Atrocity in the proceedings of that seemingly good humoured & generous people [the French]'.[5] For other onlookers, the overriding feeling on the fall of the Bastille was that the violent phase of the Revolution was almost over and France could begin to recover her liberty. As one poem expressed it:

> Sunk with the fate of these devoted walls,
> The ancient, boasted pride of Bourbon falls,
> And the long splendours of its sovereign name
> Lost in the brighter blaze of patriot fame.[6]

The episode which most drove home a sense of unprecedented violence occurring in France was the 'October Days' when a royal palace was invaded, the queen's private apartments violated, her guards cut down and the entire royal family coerced into leaving for Paris. The National Assembly suffered the same fate with Parisian women inflicting indignities on deputies they associated with 'aristocratic' sympathies, including its episcopal president, La Luzerne, bishop of Langres. It was this combination of violence with intimidation, this inversion of the customary order of society that compelled the attention of the European elites – led by Burke in his *Reflections* – and gave them an indelible sense that the Revolution depended on force for its effectiveness. Beneath the language of fraternity a brutal reality lurked. In the October Days, 'a crowd of men came by Mounier's house at night threatening to cut off his head'.[7] Disgusted by the lawlessness of the October Days and the Assembly's paralysis in the face of it, Mounier resigned his offices on 8 October and left for Switzerland in May 1790. Other moderate deputies joined him and refused to move with the Assembly from Versailles to Paris.

In much of the countryside, the uncertainties that ignited the 'Great Fear' of July–August 1789 resulted in violence that was inflicted less on people than on property. Though the harvest of 1789 looked very promising, the granaries were empty until the yield could be brought in and bread prices were at their highest. Panic ignited a rural *jacquerie* that was fuelled by rural resentment at agricultural 'improvements' that had not benefited smallholders, and a *seigneurial* reaction generated by recent purchasers as well as established landowners (and their lawyers) that had become intolerable. There had been minor peasant insurrections in Flanders and Provence during the spring, but the later troubles were much more extensive.

In the Quercy, Périgord and other areas of south-western France rural communities justified, as a means of self-defence, disruptive and sometimes armed attacks on property, although demolishing weathervanes and burning church pews was more accurately ascribable to a detestation of 'feudal' symbols.[8] The unrest spread to other regions including Normandy, the Franche-Comté and Provence. Landlords and stewards were occasionally assaulted, and the scale of the violence alarmed monied men that social anarchy was impending. Reports by local officials commonly exaggerated, and they overlooked one obvious explanation – that the 'Great Fear' was a sign of communal solidarity in uncertain times – but when these events were set alongside the 'October Days', it lent credence to those opinion formers in France and beyond who were convinced that anarchy stalked the kingdom and that it would only become worse.

1790 is no longer seen as 'the quiet year' of the Revolution: it was marginally less disturbed than 1789. There was terrible unrest in Nîmes when the Revolution reignited the two-centuries-old sectarian rivalry between the Protestant majority (under-privileged before the Revolution, then one of its earliest legal beneficiaries) and the Catholic minority in the 'Bagarre' of Nîmes (13–14 June). It was a hideous rerun in miniature of the sixteenth-century Wars of Religion, which is precisely how most Catholics saw the Revolution, a Protestant takeover. The presence of confessional rivals in that city explains the clash; elsewhere, *ad hoc* local authorities and the new National Guard managed to keep the peace for the most part, a rather unsung achievement. The revolutionaries in the National Assembly, meanwhile, did their best to create the impression that the values of the new France constituted no threat to anyone by renouncing wars of conquest in a motion of 22 May (*supra*, Chapter 6). State occasions like the *fête de la Féderation*, celebrated on the first anniversary of the fall of the Bastille, were also designed to give the impression of a nation at ease with itself and there is a good case for arguing, as Michael Fitzsimmons has done on the basis of the petitions coming in to the Assembly from across the country, that majority opinion still saw the new constitutional order as an improvement on the unreconstructed monarchy.[9]

But the absence of violence on the grand scale in 1790 did not mean that revolutionary sentiments could be presumed in the population. Even before the Civil Constitution of the Clergy polarised opinion, there were signs that dissonant voices would be silenced. The Assembly may have made its pacific intent clear to France's neighbours, at home those who doubted the desirability of key revolutionary projects were under pressure to conform. Coercion and intimidation were commonplace in 1789–91 and they operated right in the midst of the National Assembly. The public galleries were filled with those who hooted and jeered at deputies who dared to voice opposition to projects sponsored by 'progressive' opinion, particularly clerical-deputies defending Catholicism and hopeful that it would be declared the state religion (as the Right proposed with Dom Gerle's motion of 13 April 1790). The pressures were more than catcalls and obscenities. Deputies on the Right frequently had to leave the Assembly through a rear entrance or in disguise to escape the politicised thugs waiting to assault them outside. Opposing the Revolution took courage by late 1790. Those of weaker nerve who had experienced intimidation the previous year had often headed for home in disgust, as Mounier and many *Monarchiens* had done in October 1789. It suited left-leaning deputies that the crowds should be active on their behalf setting up the cry of 'à la lanterne!' whenever an aristocrat or a cleric appeared too conspicuously in public. If these tactics served to confirm the ascendancy of the moderate Left in the Assembly by persuading constitutional moderates that considerations of personal safety should induce them to vacate their places, so much the better. The strategy employed by ruthless progressives within the legislature of using the crowds on their behalf began, on this limited scale, very early in the Revolution and persisted down to at least 1795.

The pretence that the Revolution in France was essentially non-violent ended in 1791–2 when the revolutionaries turned on their critics at home and abroad. Implementing the Civil Constitution in the parishes, evicting the refractory bishops from their palaces and the priests from their presbyteries, and then intruding their replacements, was a deeply divisive process that could often only be implemented with the assistance of the local National Guard. The rivals on both sides denounced and excommunicated each other. Their supporters did not stop there. Violent protests at the presence of a juring priest in a parish were often initiated by women and could take place even during services, for a Mass celebrated by such a one was not, as his adversaries viewed it, a Eucharist at all. But 'patriots' were determined to have their Civil Constitution one way or the other, rationalising this imposition in the name of the 'general will' and justifying state-sanctioned action against protesters on the same basis: the first massacre of counter-revolutionaries occurred at Avignon in August 1791.

They also wanted their foreign war by the winter of 1791–2, speaking the language of hatred and denuciation against the non-revolutionary 'other' as it manifested itself in the established monarchies of Europe. The Revolution must be taken out of France irrespective of whether its values commended themselves to foreigners, or not. The universalist language of the Enlightenment was the one deployed by most deputies in the Legislative Assembly and it was hard for them to imagine that the values dear to them would not have irresistible force to everyone else in Europe. Tyrants must fall, just as nonjuring clergy must leave France. There were innumerable incendiary speeches from the Brissotins about the war, and these were ruthless and unsentimental in their denunciation of their foreign opponents (and the *émigré* communities clustered together for comfort on the east bank of the Rhine with their nonjuring 'allies'). Verbal violence was on display well before its battlefield equivalent, an irrefutable sign of how quickly the Revolution in 1790–1 had brutalised its proponents and generated a degree of intolerance at odds with its original values. Violence had become the necessary means of ensuring the acceptability of the Revolution wherever its supporters went.

Once war broke out, the target became the Austrian and Prussian monarchies, their armed forces and the traitors that deputies claimed to have identified insidiously at work around their own king and queen. The initial failure of French troops to stem the allied advance generated panic on the frontier and made the Paris politicians desperate as they came to terms with the possibility that the Revolution might soon be forcibly ended and their own lives be forfeited. Indeed, the Manifesto issued on 25 July by the duke of Brunswick, the commander of the Prussian army, talked of the exemplary vengeance that would be visited on Paris should the king be harmed. The long and vengeful screed in his name was embarrassingly counter-productive and, on the very point of its disintegration, 'united and armed a whole nation...'.[10] French radicals therefore had nothing to lose by inciting troops and civilians alike into an aggressive frenzy rather than passively wait for the Prussians or the Austrians to arrive. First, came the attack on the Tuileries palace on 10 August 1792 when 600 of the king's Swiss Guards were executed after they had surrendered and almost the same number of Parisians had died in the initial firefight. One Scotsman long resident in Paris, Thomas Blaikie, saw five unarmed Swiss Guards massacred near his door. 'Many of those anthrophages passed in the Street and stopt to show us parts of the Suisses they had massacred', he wrote. Anyone unlucky enough to be caught on the streets whom the crowds recognised and suspected of 'treachery' were fair game and Feuillants, royalists and moderates who were originally sympathetic to the Revolution died in this frightful way, among them La Rochefoucauld-Liancourt, Clermont-Tonnerre, Montmorin. Their corpses were usually mutilated and their heads sometimes carried aloft on pikes. This happened, notoriously, to the queen's lady-in-waiting, the princesse de Lamballe, whose decapitated head was taken to the Temple prison so that Marie-Antoinette could see it. Blaikie personally knew some of the killers:

> Every one seemed to glory in what he had done and to Show even their fury upon the dead body by cutting them or even tearing their clothes as monuments of triumph, so that this seemed as if the people were struck with a sort of Madness.[11]

Frenchmen living abroad were incredulous that such events could possibly take place on French soil. Cardinal Bernis, long resident in Rome, wrote, on receiving the news:

> The ferocity of the populace and the imbecilic terror of honest citizens cannot be compared to anything that's happened in our history. May God spare humanity from still greater crimes.[12]

That was not to be. The monarchy was terminated that same month, but the proclamation of a Republic only increased the stakes for the revolutionaries after news that Longwy had fallen. Marat and others in the Cordeliers club inspired the Paris *commune* and its allies on the streets to attack the city's prisons and butcher anyone suspected of being either an aristocrat or a priest. In a form of blood-letting that had the look of anarchy (the attacks were actually co-ordinated[13]), between 1100 and 1400 'innocent' men and women, including 200 clerics and a greater number of common criminals, were barbarously put to death after appearing before *ad hoc* tribunals in a manner which horrified polite opinion across the continent and removed any doubts about the French Revolution's murderous propensities. What happened in Paris must be seen as part of a trend engulfing the whole state. Political violence was endemic between July and October 1792, and the Parisian prison massacres were imitated on a smaller scale elsewhere in the Île-de-France including Versailles and Meaux.[14] It drew in ordinary men and women who could never once have contemplated participating in killing, but who were complicit in a brutalised collective mentality created and justified by Revolutionary fervour. Moderates at the time were aghast at what had happened, but one needs to remember how much the cult of violence had penetrated many aspects of popular culture, down to children's playthings: a mechanised toy made in 1793 had two blacksmiths hammering at the severed head of an aristocrat while another stoked the forge fire with a motto that read, 'Here we forge new heads of families'.[15] All this went with a willingness to rationalise or excuse what was going on. Even Henri Grégoire, the preferred revolutionary role model of the early twenty-first century and, as such, recently 'pantheonised', used 'an exculpating cultural context inherited from the Old Regime' about the September Massacres. He explained some months later they were 'the fruit of a government without morality, and the depravity of a court that had raised its scandalous triumphs on the debris of morality'. [16]

## The Great Terror

### 1 OBJECTIVES

The state-sponsored violence of the Terror pursued by the Republic confirmed the sense of profound horror at France's apparent descent into chaos. The Terror lasted until the second half of 1794, and it claimed victims throughout France and across every section of society until the political elite finally decided that its destructive momentum must be halted. Its objective was purgative, the physical elimination of those identified by a given regime as its enemies who were, accordingly, demonised. That was straightforward enough on the military frontline where the armies were fighting to destroy the foreign opponents of the Revolution, but at home it was an endlessly elastic concept because the state could be far less confident about knowing who supported it and who did not. Thus citizens had to be coerced into obedience, and imprisoned or executed where there were any doubts. The external threat provided the nearest equivalent of an objective justification that the Jacobins could manage and yet the Terror entered its most murderous phase at exactly the time when the foreign threat had receded after the success of the French army at Fleurus. Historians are therefore with much justification choosing to look elsewhere in order to grasp the logic of the Terror. As Patrice Gueniffey has argued, 'the Terror was the product of the revolutionary dynamic, and perhaps of every revolutionary dynamic'.[17] It may have ended as a cardinal policy of the CPS, but its origins in often complex local struggles are clear.[18] In essence, it is reducible to a chronic sign of insecurity, an acknowledgement that the regime could extract obedience on no other basis than that of terrorising its own citizenry. Yet the arch exponents of Terror allied with Robespierre genuinely believed that a new republic must be peopled with a virtuous populace and that it could be born through eliminating the unworthy. The guillotine would be the inculcator of a revolutionary fundamentalism that would permit no dissent. If paranoia and desperation were the side-products of this drive for cultural conformity then that was by-the-bye.

2 MACHINERY

The machinery of the Terror was contained and directed from within the newly centralised apparatus of government in existence by early 1793. After it had taken power in June 1793, the Jacobin elite, genuinely committed to Terror as an imperative of state construction and control, at last had the levers to pull which would achieve the results it wanted: victory in the war, a republican and dechristianised France, and the overthrow of those at odds with their ambitions. The means to those ends were already in place: the Revolutionary Tribunal set up on 10 March and the CPS on 6 April, to which the 'Twelve who ruled' added the Law of Suspects in September 1793. Any pretence that judicial power could be exercised independently of executive preferences disappeared during the Terror. Under the aegis of the principal public prosecutor, Fouquier-Tinville (1747–95), the state dispensed unflinching summary justice. As he understood it, the judges were in post to enforce patriotic policies and the good of the state was always to be preferred to the survival of the falsely arraigned, and not to proceed on this basis would only result in a judge joining the list of traitors. There was a progressive withdrawal of civil rights, a development culminating in the law of 22 Prairial Year II (10 June 1794) that left death as the only punishment for guilt and prohibited an accused party from calling witnesses without the consent of the court. Thus for the rule of law, so vaunted by the revolutionaries of 1789–91, was substituted terroristic force and coercion.

3 IMPLEMENTATION

The state was still not equipped to act as a directed, remorseless killing-machine in 1793. The number of those who were guillotined amounted to approximately 16,500; another 30,000 or so died in prison or while awaiting trial.[19] These figures, however, disclose only the official aspect of the Terror. To them must be added the blood-letting that occurred as part of repressing the Counter-Revolution in the west and in mopping up the Federalist remnants. In Lyon, over 1800 death sentences were carried out in April 1794 alone.[20] Homicidal violence often attended the arrival of the *Armées révolutionnaires* in a town or village of proven or Suspected disloyalty. Some areas escaped completely: in 7 *départements*, the Aube, Basses-Alpes, Hautes-Alpes, Haute-Saône, Seine-et-Marne, and the two Corsican *départements*, no one was tried and executed; in 31 others there were fewer than ten deaths.[21] The incidence of the Terror really depended so much on the efficiency with which it was implemented, the priorities of local Jacobin loyalists and the means available to them. Different Representatives-on-Mission had different preoccupations. They could pour all their energies into eliminating the enemies of the Jacobin state, whoever they were, as Joseph Le Bon did in the Nord,[22] or opt to hunt down particular types of enemy, for instance 'fanatical' clergy, whether engaged in counter-revolutionary activity or not. The 'enemy' could also be recent political losers. Factional struggles within the Jacobin elite usually resulted in the death penalty for those losers, notoriously Robespierre's elimination of the Hébertistes in March 1793, followed by Danton, Desmoulins and the *indulgents*.

For those potentially on the receiving end of state Terror – and with just one-third of the Terror's official victims classifiable as nobles, clergy or wealthy commoners, these were more often than not working men and women, not the socially advantaged – the uncertainty that the threat of implementation alone created was a terrible burden that could never be relinquished until well after the 'tyrant' had fallen. This pscyhological damage implicit in the unfolding of the 'Terror' should not easily be overlooked. It afflicted the uncommitted as much as the enemies of the Revolution, those who could be deemed guilty simply from inanition or rank or suspicion.

These last categories covered virtually the entire population in the west of France and spontaneous and ordered violence was habitual to day-to-day life in the area between 1793 and 1795. Both sides practised it; both sides refined it. No quarter was given or expected on the battlefield or in its aftermath, and incidents like the refusal of the royalist leadership to consent to the killing of republican prisoners on the retreat from Granville had few counterparts. The so-called 'Pacification of the Vendée' after the military collapse of the rebels in the winter of 1793–4 following defeat at Savenay (17 December 1793) involved terrorising the inhabitants of every village suspected of harbouring counter-revolutionary sympathisers in the 6 *départements* of the west. Most never came before the special tribunals established in Nantes and Rochefort, but were delivered up to summary justice or just executed on the spot after their property had been destroyed and their fields made unsuitable for growing crops. The bitterness of the insurgency and counter-insurgency measures led to the disregard of the decree of the Convention dated 1 August declaring 'total war':

> Forests are to be felled, the hideouts of the bandits destroyed, crops cut down and carried away on the backs of the army, livestock seized. Men, women and children shall be carried to the interior, their subsistence and security being provided for with all the respect due to humanity.[23]

Those that were brought before the revolutionary tribunal in Nantes found the Montagnard representative J.-B. Carrier and his entourage eager to drown them in the Loire estuary rather than shoot them: it was more cost and time efficient. Shooting prisoners in numbers of between 150 and 200 a day was too slow in clearing the gaols or making room for newcomers. His efforts pleased the CPS. As the *Bulletin du Tribunal révolutionnaire* reported him: 'I informed the Convention that we were shooting the brigands in their hundreds; they praised me for that and gave orders for my letter to be reproduced in the *Bulletin*.' To speed up despatching the condemned (Carrier opined that 'all the ills that plague the human race derive from the throne and the altar'), they were placed in boats with portholes bored in their timbers which sank in mid-stream, the so-called *noyades*. Probably about 3500 men, women and children met their end this way so that fish could no longer be sold in Nantes, the river Loire having been contaminated by corpses.

This was an area of France execrated by republican leaders and their paramilitary forces under General Turreau, massacred pillaged, and raped accordingly. The Vendée functioned as the leading laboratory of the Terror in the provinces.[24] They had orders to turn it into a desert and any republicans were instructed to leave the area. Hoche took command of the Army of the West later in 1794 and decided that pacification based on a limited degree of magnanimity in victory was more likely to achieve results rather than just prolonging the cycle of violence, and increasing the number of partisans who saw they had nothing to lose by enlisting under the command of Charette in the coastal area (the Marais), Stofflet in the interior (the Mauges) or Sapinaud in the Bocage. In a proclamation of 15 September 1794, Hoche recalled that he, too, had suffered from the Terror and that it had now come to an end. There was, in the region, a sense that violence was just feeding on itself. Before the CPS issued a declaration on 16 August 1794 prohibiting looting and the quartering of troops in the villages of the Vendée, a conservative assessment would put the number of those massacred by republican forces at about 120,000, in other words a scale of killing that returned to haunt the Fifth Republic in the commemorations of 1989, as the descendants of those who died in the *Vendée militaire* forcefully reminded the Mitterand government and the Vovelle committee charged with leading the state celebrations that it was for them an occasion for mourning rather than celebrating. It was only three years after the publication of Reynald Secher's *Le Génocide franco-français: La Vendée vengée* (Paris, 1986),[25] which had highlighted the sheer scale of violence in the west, accused the French people of having invented genocide and put the death-toll in the Vendée as high as 300,000, counting both sides. Secher's figures have been doubted by scholars (something under a quarter of a million is nearer the mark),[26] but his book reminded his fellow countrymen that violence and intimidation were central to the experience of the Revolution for millions of ordinary men and women in the west. His talk of 'extermination' and a 'crime against humanity' continue to resonate in the literature on the repression of the Vendée. Thus Alain Gerard, writing in 2000, ascribes the destruction of the Vendée, triggered by minor disturbances in just three villages, to revolutionary discourse and dynamics. He somewhat rhetorically observes, 'The regeneration of humanity licensed the use in all righteousness of extraordinary violence'.[27] Thus, two centuries since its pacification, the subject of the counter-revolution in the west remains deeply divisive for scholars. Secher did much to make the subject topical and controversial in the late 1980s but his ready recourse to the language of genocide does not, in the end, make his case for its presence in the 1790s more persuasive.

Of course, the violence in the west was not all in one direction. On their march north from Saint-Florent-le-Vieil through Laval to Granville in October–November 1793, the disorganised Vendéens, reeling after their defeat at Cholet (17 October), showed no mercy on any republican soldiery they encountered. Their religious faith seldom acted as a barrier to bloodthirsty outrages. The *Chouans* practised killing on a smaller scale which could be no less gruesome for that.[28] They marked down local revolutionary leaders and supporters for assassination (Constitutional priests were a favourite), and relied on their familiarity with the local terrain to carry out small-scale offensive operations and then evade their pursuers. As countrymen used to shooting game and vermin, they were an appreciable menace to the authorities once they turned their muskets on the *Bleus*; they also imperilled fellow citizens since their killings often generated a tit-for-tat degree of homicide. *Chouan* ruthlessness was never in doubt. During negotiations for an armistice in early 1795, many *Chouans* redoubled their activities, 'They are killing almost every night', one report from Avranches complained.[29] Their activities lasted ten years, and were almost impossible to suppress. Reinforcements in the form of draft dodgers or deserters replaced those captured or killed by the *Bleus*, and thefts from arms dumps and public depots were rife. Though, as a movement, it lacked workable leadership structures or chains of command, *Chouannerie* was, in the last analysis, ideologically motivated by royalism (republicans certainly considered them all in that light) rather than driven by revenge and that distinguished it from the thugs operating elsewhere, like the cut-throat gangs (*égorgeurs*) who murdered thousands of Jacobin and *sans-culottes* sympathisers in the White Terror of 1794–5. Some of these, including the Company of Jesus in Lyon and the Companies of the Sun in Provence, operated on a crudely systematic basis, others just used the confusion and probable absence of detection to make violence a first resort in their criminal activities.

*Terrorism and Lawlessness after 1795*

Where did criminality end and counter-revolution begin? It was usually impossible to tell. However, the number of assassinations and the level of clandestine activities in the Puy-de-Dôme and its borders and towards the Lyonnais made some deputies in January 1796 try to alert the government by talking of the 'theatre of a new Vendée'.[30] It was a forgivable overstatement given the incidence of homicides in south-eastern France, occurring on an almost daily basis between 1794 and 1799, especially in Lyon and Marseille. Things were so bad in the summer of 1795 that Jacobins talked frantically of 'a Provencal Vendée', a counter-terror along the length of the Rhône valley from Lyon to Arles. Many of the fatalities in those cities and their hinterlands were indeed marked men because of their involvement – or suspected involvement – in the Jacobin Terror which had been inflicted on them after the 'Federalist' risings had been suppressed. Vengeance could not always wait for the judicial process to be completed. There were prison massacres in both those cities on 2 February and 4 May 1795, but it was only the number of the dead that distinguished these killings from the rest. The authorities made little attempt to distinguish between homicides according to whether the perpetrators were politically or just criminally motivated. Thus, when the prison at Lyon had been fired by masked marauders on 4 May, the National Guard had done nothing to intervene. Generally, they made arrests where they could, but the suspicion persists that the Thermidorians were initially relieved that the White Terrorists were eliminating the common opponents of both moderate republicans and royalists. In the Lyonnais area, the killers found it straightforward to gain access to the gaols and the death squads were thereby encouraged to increase their daring. The incidence of non-homicidal violence also soared in these years and was often associated with highway robbery. Mail coaches were often held up and shots exchanged between guards, passengers and footpads that resulted in serious injury. Hunger in the terrible winter of 1794–5 also played its part in driving men and women to crime in a desperate bid to find food. Since they were going to die if they did nothing, perpetrating a theft seemed only a minor matter. In 1799 politically motivated anarchic violence broke out again across the south. On the eve of the counter-revolutionary rising there in August 1799, the commissary of the *département* of the Haute-Garonne complained to the minister of police on 22 July 1799 of:

> Several republicans assassinated, the properties of a greater number burned or destroyed, Liberty Trees chopped down and uprooted in more than forty communes, republican institutions neglected or held in contempt in several cantons.[31]

The local authorities seldom had the forces at their disposal that could make any inroads against the networks of their foes.

The persistent law and order problems of the 1795–9 era makes it technically inaccurate to call the Directory a more peaceful period than the 'Great Terror'. The criminal activities of the murder gangs diminished only slightly after the end of the 'White Terror' and the introduction of a system of military tribunals (*supra*) was not enough to reassure the average citizen that he or she was safe in the street, the fields, or even their own house. Despite the efforts of the army in 1798–9, there were still large tracts of southern France where the Republic's writ did not in practice extend, making up a *de facto* internal frontier where the bandits ran things. It was against this background that state-sponsored violence was gradually ratcheted up again after the initial dismantling of the apparatus of the Terror: restrictions had been imposed on the powers of the vigilance committees in autumn 1794, to be followed by the final abolition of the Tribunal itself on 31 May 1795. The Directory even had its own Terror in the aftermath of Fructidor when it hounded the forces of the Right, particularly those clergy for whom the relative religious toleration of 1795–7 had been a false dawn. About 1400 recalcitrants were sent to the islands of Ré and Oléron in the west; of these about 230 eventually reached French Guiana in South America, or the 'dry guillotine' as it was euphemistically known because of its inhospitable climate. The anti-*émigrés* laws were also reactivated. Those who had returned in the spring of 1797 were given a fortnight in which to leave the country or face the death penalty. About 160 lost their lives under this legislation during the following months. It is therefore not exactly surprising that the Directorial record left the regime's record open to condemnation, castigating '...the foul designs of the Directorial Despots, who in the space of a few years,...have shed more blood, have spent more treasure, have violated more obligations of humanity and of justice, than the old Despotism of Versailles did, in the course of ages,...'.[32]

The French Revolution was enacted in the shadow of death. Of course, as William Doyle has pointed out, its violence must be set in perspective: 20,000 people died in one day in Warsaw after it was captured by Russian troops on 4 November 1794.[33] The figure patently dwarfs the numbers who died in the *noyades* or in the Parisian Terror, although it is not much higher than those who died in the French West Indies after the revolt of the slaves (see below). For an entire decade, the Revolution had such potency both as a symbol and a political reality that millions of human beings were prepared to die in its defence or to secure its overthrow. While it lasted, the chances of anyone living to a natural term of life were mightily diminished. Its insistent ideologies divided families, set neighbour against neighbour, and often men against women. Those who were lucky enough to hold on to their lives came up against other manifestations of the Revolutionary spirit (or the counter-revolutionary response it had engendered). Intimidation, street violence, assaults on women all soared in the 1790s as a consequence of the times, for the Revolution not only militarised France it also brutalised it. The old and female lost out particularly to the men aged between 15 and 40 for whom the Revolution was distinctively 'their' event. All this was the price of political progress. No wonder, then, that all sides of opinion were relieved that with Napoleon consolidating his power between 1799 and 1804, violence could be more wholly externalised than any previous regime had managed. He was able to do so because of his absolute control of the army and his ability to incorporate it within the internal life of the French state as a punitive force that, more than any other, was *the* symbol of national pride. Revolutionary violence was possible because the Crown lost control of the armed forces; that violence was curtailed when government restored that control and coupled it with national pride not in the Revolution (from a Bonapartist perspective in the 1800s, that was best overlooked), but in French international hegemony.

*Vandalism*

The destructive force of the French Revolution was formidable. At first it was rather low-key and utility-based as France moved to a new constitution in which there would still be a place of honour for the buildings associated with a (reformed) Church and monarchy. Thus, when the royal family left the palace of Versailles in October 1789, it was simply left empty.

One of the impulses behind the formation of the National Guard was the protection of property, including that lately acquired by purchasers of the *biens nationaux*. Such destruction as there was in 1789 occurred in the wake of the *Grande Peur*. There was considerable damage inflicted on buildings on several large manorial estates; in some instances on the chateau itself, symbol of a hated *seigneurial* regime. The destruction was not usually irreparable and, after August 1789, died away. During the constitutional monarchy, following the sale of ecclesiastical lands and the parochial reorganisation of the Civil Constitution, local administrators disposed of superfluous churches disinterestedly while using the National Guard to protect others still in use against pilferers. Monastic buildings could often be adapted easily to political uses. In Angers, the medieval tombs and monuments in the church of the Augustins were demolished by workmen to enable the *Club de l'Ouest* to meet there.[34] In the cause of social reconstruction, many Jacobin clubs organised the burning of parchment, papal bulls, feudal records and university diplomas. Jacobin artisans like Antoine Chaudet and J. B. Wiscar argued for the wholesale destruction of books and manuscripts confiscated from private or public enemies of the Revolution such as *émigrés* or monks, while in Paris in August 1793 Hanriot publicly declared himself in favour of burning down libraries.

The French past was, for the Jacobins and *sans-culottes* of 1792–4, an embarrassment as well as an encumbrance. Cathedrals, palaces, churches and convents were converted where possible (they made handy barracks or weapons dumps), destroyed or just left to rot. Some of this work was undertaken by the agents of the state for, as they would have conceived them, the highest motives. A new France would not be born if tangible physical reminders of the royal and Catholic past were left in profusion; these would militate against the successful cultural (re)formation of the republic and its citizens. Since the revolutionary leaders of 1793 saw the Church as a rival to their own alternative visions of human regeneration, its edifices a reminder of its recent omnipresence in national life, their removal was an imperative if future generations of the French were not to succumb to a creed that Montagnards believed to be fundamentally at odds with the Revolution. As Saint-Just observed in 1793, a republic was constituted by the 'complete destruction of its opposite'. These emblems had to go.

The signs coming from the CPS, the Representatives-on-Mission and other ministries suggested to the militants in the clubs and in the *sections* that they would not be penalised if they took unilateral action without awaiting official sanction. As they did. The destructive impulse of the crowd was given unbridled rein and orgies of destruction and looting followed, in which fittings and fixtures were thrown onto bonfires, tombs were desecrated, medieval stained glass smashed and cellars looted. The royal abbey of Saint-Denis, a basilica where the Gothic style had originated in the mid-twelfth century and the burial place of the kings of France, was sacked in 1793, and royal bones flung indiscriminately into the Seine. In Burgundy, Cluny, one of the most powerful monastic establishments of the High Middle Ages, was plundered and then demolished, all except for the west towers. Notre-Dame cathedral in Paris was turned into a temple of reason and the statues of kings adorning its west front cast down as hated emblems of royalty. Though most cathedrals suffered some sort of damage, Cambrai, Boulogne and Arras in Flanders and Avranches in Normandy were demolished completely.[35] Destruction was often accompanied by sacriligious parodies of Christian rites and deliberate desecration by *sans-culottes* members of the Revolutionary Army who often travelled appreciable distances to take part in the spree. Sometimes a Representative would choreograph the proceedings. In Moulins, Fouché organised the smashing of religious statues, calvaries and crosses, then 'on the cours de Bercy they made a heap of chasubles, copes and other sacred vestments, and all these things, along with the veils of nuns, were burnt, while the joyful band, led by the former confrère of the Oratory [Fouché], did a ridiculous dance around the burning trappings of superstition'.[36] Churches and the decorative art associated with them were monuments to 'fanaticism' and 'enthusiasm', relics of a France that the revolutionaries believed would never come again. The physical aggression deployed against religious buildings and works of art may be seen as part of a violation of sacred space; its counterpart in civil life was the invasion and looting of palaces and country mansions. There was a certain crude logic about it. If priests and aristocracy were identified by the law as having no status in a dechristianised polity, it was appropriate that their former residences should be razed in what would be a collective republican act that was at once obliteration, purgation and forgetting.

The incidence of destruction varied from region to region. There was not much, for instance, in the southern Île-de-France or eastern Provence, whereas the Nord *département* was badly affected. Nevertheless, it had come to be an embarrassment to the Jacobin administration by late 1793, confirming the reputation of the Revolution for barbarism and led to protests on the floor of the Convention from moderates daring enough to risk the wrath of Robespierre (in fact he shared these misgivings). Bishop Henri Grégoire even coined a new term for the despoliation of churches and the destruction of works of art: 'vandalism'.[37] Not that naming the phenomenon could stop it, although the state began to try.

To counteract the destructive impulse of the Revolution, the mid-1790s saw the elaboration of the concept of 'patrimony', in other words the cultural inheritance of the Republic from both the monarchy and the Church that could be looked at neutrally as cultural relics from an era that was over. The notion of the patrimonial also hinted at a collective ownership that may have been far from the case in reality, but was a useful contradistinction to a monarchical and patriarchal stress on France as a fief belonging to one man and transmitted in hereditary succession from monarch to monarch. And what belonged to the patrimony could be displayed in museums to which the public could obtain access, such as the Louvre, an enterprise particularly dear to Bonaparte. As early as November 1790 the National Assembly had approved a directive on the conservation of manuscripts, charters and paintings, to guard against the destruction of archives and the dispersal and sale of books. A determination to preserve the contents of libraries and museums explains the setting up of the *Commission des arts* in May 1793. Modern museology is often alleged to date from the opening of the Louvre on 10 August 1793, though its founding purpose was more political than conservatorial. Public depositaries for statues and bas-reliefs at Paris, like that of the Petits-Augustins, the basis for the *Musée des monuments français*, opened in September 1795. These displays of cultural heritage testified to national prestige, offered a shred of historical validity to Revolutionary regimes and put aside the embarrassingly destructive activities of 1792–4. It signalled the victory of aesthetic over religious values or, rather, that the latter had been neutralised. Conservation was a form of public usefulness, an expression of 'anti-vandalism'. A great deal of precious objects, of course, had gone beyond recall and the Directory tried to make good the loss by having its military commanders send back to Paris the art treasures of the towns they conquered. As if making a genuine concession, Clerisseau stated that the liberated people of Europe might receive copies of the great works moved to Paris, and on 9 Thermidor Year VI there was a display of art works sent back from Italy by Bonaparte to celebrate the Directory's new policy.[38]

The Revolution was not a uniquely destructive episode in the history of France. It was said early in the twentieth century that 'Revolutionary vandalism was responsible for a much smaller total of destruction and spoliation than the intransigent classicism of Jesuits and canons of the seventeenth and eighteenth centuries'.[39] The comment is only superficially plausible. During the early modern period tastes changed quickly; buildings were altered or replaced at a fast pace, and much was lost. France was no different in that respect to every other European state. There, as elsewhere, old treasures tended to be replaced with new ones; rebuilding work was undertaken constructively and destruction was not inflicted as a programmatic repudiation of a cultural bequest. The Gothic may have been unfashionable, but it was not loathed as a cultural manifestation *tout court*. Whether a building was classical or medieval was of reduced importance to the revolutionaries than whether it had been polluted irretrievably by its ecclesiastical or monarchical connections. In which case it must be either erased or put to a wholly different use. There were some loose resemblances to the sixteenth-century Wars of Religion in which both clergy and church buildings were subjected to attack. Protestants were iconoclasts whose theological schema made the paraphanalia of the average Catholic church redundant on the grounds of its unscripturalness. But at no point were they bent on eliminating France's heritage of religious buildings. Rather they sought their adaptation to Protestant uses where the emphasis would not be on the sacramental but on the plain, the unadorned and the scriptural. The revolutionary vandals were committed to their work as an essential aspect of creating a new public culture shorn of its royalist and Catholic antecedents; the violations were generally targeted. Better no cultural inheritance at all than leaving intact edifices of some antiquity whose endurance and visual representation of an unacceptable elite culture mocked the brazen modernity of the Revolution and its thin roots in the soil of the nation's past. But only so much could be destroyed before the Thermidorians abandoned the vandalism as part of the Terror and attempted to align (without particularly convincing intellectual foundations) the patrimonial legacy within a Revolutionary present more comfortable with the accretions of earlier societies, whose existence could be tolerated because France had now grown into something else. The pretence could be made therefore that these trophies of the past had been emptied of contextuality and could exist neutrally within the space of the museum as art objects that might inspire revolutionary craftsmen and technicians to outdo them.

The material devastation the Revolution inflicted on national culture was the equivalent of violence against the person inflicted for political reasons in the 1790s; it also had its counterpart in the brutalisation of language itself in the same period. Since the 'general will' delegitimised all those who stood outside it, such persons became liable to *ad hominem* abuse of the strongest kind. Polite references were for debased, aristocratic times; difference was inherently treacherous during the 1790s, denuciation almost a patriotic duty, and in the most astringent or obscene terms, often both. 'Aristocrats' were a constant subject of scorn; it was a term capable of innumberable adaptions and angularities, as in the commonplace reference to the clergy as 'black aristocrats'. That was relatively restrained. Fast-selling newspapers in the cities, the Parisian *Père Duchêsne* remains the classic example, used the argot of the streets on the printed page, reflecting the language of the *sans-culottes* readership and inspiring them into fresh bursts of verbal intimidation (which might well shade into the physical) against the enemies of the *patrie*. Thus, in considering the issue of vandalism, historians of the Revolution do well to bear in mind its verbal dimensions. This is particularly the case in the early twenty-first century because of the continuing revisionist attachment to discourse and speech acts. If the Revolution is considered less as event than as a way of perceiving and speaking about those events, then a intimidatory discourse is fundamental to it, one that extends across every section of society, and is ever poised on the brink of conversion to physical violence.

*Conclusion*

Many events in European history over the last two millennia have seen overwhelmingly greater incidents of violence and vandalism than the French Revolution. In comparison with the ideologically driven bloodshed witnessed in the wars and civil upheavals of the twentieth century, it registers only slightly (although the French death rate in the Revolutionary and Napoleonic Wars per head of population was on a level with that obtaining in the First World War). The significance of the Revolution is, as Arnold Meyer has underlined recently, that situated as it is on the cusp of the modern, it established a precedent and a pattern for regime change in which a new governing ideology is imposed regardless of popular consent (although it proceeds on the pretence of an unarticulated approval) and therefore is attended by violence, vandalism and erasure of the recent past in favour of a new start to history.

The Revolution in France was initially grounded in popular approval. Episodes of violence were short-lived if eye-catching and, apart from the earliest counter-revolutionaries and the prescient Edmund Burke, were set against the palpable gains for France and her citizens in creating a new constitutional monarchy. But, perhaps as early as late 1790 onwards, change comes to be widely perceived as no longer gainful, and the price of Revolution as instability tending towards anarchy. Thereafter, the extent of violence and destruction adds up to a formidable argument in favour of the revolutionary consensus of 1789 breaking down at a relatively early stage into a coercive imposition of revolutionary norms on to a wide section of the French population (and their neighbours). Lawmakers disregarded the law when it suited them, and often defended the illegal actions of crowds. Respect for the sanctity of the law was continuously weak during the 1790s, despite the constant claims made for it.

The sheer viciousness of the violence and vandalism is hard to get over both in France and beyond. The West Indies were a theatre of appalling strife and brutalisation. When Guadeloupe was recaptured by the French, orders were issued that the body of Major-General Thomas Dundas, who had died of fever on 3 June 1794, should be dug up 'and given as prey to the birds of the air'. On the spot where this happened the French erected the following memorial:

> This ground, restored to Liberty by the valour
> of the Republicans, was polluted by the body
> of Thomas Dundas, Major General and Governor
> of Guadeloupe for the bloody King George III.[40]

It is still important to acknowledge destruction as inseparable from creativity in any revolutionary balance-sheet. The intellectual commitment of the Girondins and the Jacobins after them into reconstructing their society afresh resulted in an astonishingly creative set of blueprints for a new France which would enable the hopes of the Enlightenment to be enacted on a scale the *philosophes* had never imagined possible; the problem came first in deciding whose proposals should be turned into official policy (this could in itself be a murderous business) and then shoe-horning a reluctant populace into accepting them. The process of coercion that inevitably followed allowed full vent to death and destruction.

The god Moloch was well served by the revolutionaries, and continued to be during the more cynical era of the Directory, and by Bonaparte as he sealed up the internal hurts of the Republic and consigned an entire generation of young Frenchmen to death on some distant battlefield. The ideological commitment of the revolutionaries before 1795 to their task was so overwhelmingly forceful that it engendered a repudiation of the non-revolutionary past that could be ferocious. As the Revolution made a cult of itself that would brook no rivalry from either Christianity or monarchy it gave full rein to that willed determination to put aside history, one which had always been latent in the sequence of events from 1789. The history of France had nothing to teach the revolutionaries except what to avoid. They were starting again in a year zero of unlimited scope and opportunity, another harbinger of future cataclysms over the next two centuries. The past was just an unsupportable burden for the pre-Thermidorian revolutionaries; to emphasise continuity was to misunderstand the nature of what they were trying to achieve and those who did so were enemies of the state to be remorselessly swept aside, and their palaces and temples with them. After 1790, the Revolution had become so intrinsically divisive that differences could not be settled by debate, but by killing or imprisoning one's opponents. To end this cycle of viciousness became an overwhelming imperative from 1794–5. The Directory, in the interests of preserving itself, never managed it and the task was left to Napoleon, who refused to contest the heritage of France by preferring to establish his own personal greatness, subsuming the revolutionary option in the Bonapartist one.

# Chapter 9: The Economy and Society

*Introduction*

After several decades in which economic historians of the French Revolution have found it hard to gain a hearing, the revisionist emphasis on explaining events exclusively through politics and language appears to be faltering. Post-revisionist writings are unashamed at looking once again at the impact of economic change on eighteenth-century France and searching for signs of social change in town and countryside as a precipitant of revolutionary action. No longer are the nobility necessarily synonymous with a lack of interest in estate improvement. Many agriculturalists in northern France were more than ready to adopt intensive farming techniques of the sort once thought exclusive to East Anglia or the Dutch plains; other members of the Second Estate – and more than one prince of the blood – owned and invested in industrial plant. Even the bourgeoisie are enjoying their moment in the sun again at the hands of scholars like Colin Jones, whose emphasis on the vitality of commercial life and the professional classes gives grounds for imagining that a full-scale social interpretation of the Revolution is ripe for revival.[1]

In fact, this kind of scholarship never ceased and, in the hands of immensely learned and readable historians like François Crouzet, was always appreciated by those who sensed that its time would come again. As has turned out to be the case. Crouzet was fascinated by the contrasts and resemblances between Britain and France on the eve of the Revolution, and confronted the abiding question of whether it would have been France rather than Britain which in the nineteenth century would have been the 'workshop of the world' had the French Revolution not intervened and prevented France from enjoying an industrial one until the 1840s. While not overstating the point, Crouzet was insistent that France in the 1780s was not far behind her cross-channel neighbour in terms of investment in industry and had managed to attract British entrepreneurs and patenters to assist her efforts at economic growth. In both the number of cotton businesses (115) and the metres of cloth produced (16 millions) France was actually narrowly ahead of the British competition in the mid-1780s. The buoyancy of the French economy pre-1789 was tested not just by Crouzet but by eminent British economic historians such as Nicholas Crafts and Patrick O'Brien. All confirmed that luxury and semi-luxury goods, the consumption and production of which were stimulated by a large court society, played a more important role in the French industrial sector than in eighteenth-century England. A consumer society was definitely emerging in France, market sensitive and commercially orientated.[2] Crouzet could not deny that the Revolution had a retardatory impact on the French economy; the questions which follow from that are, by how much, and which areas of economic life bucked this trend and why? This is the primary area for discussion in this chapter, together with an assessment of social change fostered by the Revolution. Who were those in French society who benefited from the upheavals?

*Economic Liberalism and the Market Economy*

The political reformers of 1789 thought as much in economic as in constitutional terms. A modern state needed an economy to match in which the social and institutional obstacles to wealth creation had been discarded along with antique monarchist traditions. Unfettered freedom in which to trade and own property was, for the prosperous 'middling sort', one of the advantages of the Revolution. This preference long ante-dated 1789 and was shared by those members of the Second Estate who were wealthy. Turgot's Controller-Generalship of 1774–6 had disclosed the political risks that the removal of price controls could unleash with the so-called 'Pacte de famine', but had not blunted the appetite of prosperous French nobles and professionals to pursue policies based on free trade and the removal of tariff barriers and customs duties which lay in their path. It was a policy preference that was often accompanied by Anglophile political leanings and undermined the conservative corporatism of late *ancien régime* society and such institutions as the trade guilds. When Calonne was in office (1783–7), the monarchy took up one aspect of this agenda – an interest in negotiating free-trade treaties with France's European neighbours – partly out of high policy, to prevent Pitt's government (the young Premier was very sympathetic to Adam Smith's free-trade sentiments) from stealing a march on them, but also out of the genuine intellectual commitment of public servants like the physiocrat Dupont de Nemours (1739–1817), originally Turgot's Inspector General of Trade.[3] A treaty was arranged with Britain in late 1786 (the Eden Treaty) and the marquis de Ségur was sent fruitlessly to St Petersburg to try and achieve a comparable arrangement with Russia soon afterwards.

The National Assembly was even more interested in economic liberalism than Louis XVIs ministers, and the Revolution was seen as giving a boost to the spirit of enterprise and innovation, not constraining it. The nascent pre-revolutionary consumer culture flourished as goods poured onto the market, some sold off by *émigré* nobles, including art works. International collectors like the fabulously wealthy William Beckford snapped up bargains in 'Lucifer's own metropolis' (as he called Paris): 'Happy – aye – thrice happy are those who in this good capital and at this period have plenty of money – their Kingdom is come, their will is done upon Earth, if not in Heaven'.[4] Government was scaled down, corporate privileges abolished and every pre-revolutionary obstacle to the unfettered operation of a market economy eliminated wherever practicably possible. France became a unified customs area in November 1790 after the abolition of the *traites* and all other internal customs barriers. The East Indies trade was open to all in April 1790 as the *Compagnie des Indes* lost its surviving privileges and was abolished outright a year later. However, the retention of the *Exclusif* (the obligation of the colonies to trade only with the mother country) in March 1791 showed that there were one or two token limitations to the *laissez-faire* approach of the Assembly.

Because the Assembly was committed to an open economy in which prices and wages were determined by market rates, it was bent on eliminating every form of trade association or monopoly whether for masters or craftsmen. Guilds were abolished as were the *compagnonnages* to which journeymen and apprentices turned when labour disputes occurred. Unemployment rose steadily into 1791, and in June the National Assembly had no hesitation in closing down the *ateliers de charité* because deputies feared these public workshops (about 31,000 were employed there on subsistence wages) were recruiting grounds for extremists and democrats. Faced with rising militancy by Parisian carpenters and other workers, the

Assembly acted again. Workers' associations and other forms of collective representation were outlawed by the *loi Le Chapelier* passed on 17 June. It made it impossible for groups of artisans to meet, pass resolutions and agitate for improved conditions through strike action without arrest and prosecution. The following month, the act was, significantly, extended to agricultural workers and servants. With the nation in turmoil; after the king's ignominious return from Varennes and demands for a republic growing daily, the deputies were going to take no chances on what was also a public order issue.

The onset of the war and the priorities of political survival modified this doctrinal love affair with individualism. Revolutionaries throughout the 1790s professed their opposition to imposing trade and price controls, but they could not always be avoided, especially after the strengthening of centralised government authority in 1792–4. Both Girondins and Jacobins were in principle united by their commitment to a free-market economy. But the maintenance of this stance unbendingly in the circumstances of 1793–4 came at the price of political oblivion; the Girondins paid it, their rivals did not. Putting to one side an unregulated economy was, for the Jacobin leadership, the economic concomitant of leaving the Constitution of the Year I inoperative. Both would have to wait their turn until the imperatives of revolutionary survival became less demanding. Hence Robespierre's relatively unconstrained support for both the General Maximum and the Ventôse Decrees. This won the CPS vital popular endorsement when it was most needed, a more pressing need than any lingering ideological inclination for a minimally intrusive state. The state could not afford to wait on the market to decide whether or not it wanted to subscribe to an issue of stock. Instead, there was fresh resort to forced loans and the organisation of industry for war in a manner that compromised rights of ownership.

Though the reassertion of the Convention's supreme authority after 9 Thermidor once again permitted a semblance of normality to return to France's internal trading life, it was acutely limited by ministerial manipulation of the new paper currency, the *assignats*. On their initial issue, many merchants simply would not accept them, and at home many continued to demand payment in bullion. They also depressed the value of the currency. On 8 April 1793 the Convention ordered that all government purchases and payments to soldiers be made in *assignats*, and three days later the circulation, sale and purchase of gold and silver was prohibited. In 1793–4 these hovered between 20 and 50 per cent of their face value. After the fall of Robespierre, the position deteriorated again and the over-issue of *assignats* to meet the exceptional expenses of war had stoked up an inflationary pressure that made them worth only 3 per cent of their face value in the summer of 1795 and totally worthless by early 1796.[5] Nothing daunted, the Directory had no other expedient than issuing yet another paper currency, the *mandat territorial*, which was supposed to have an equivalent value in gold. The public was unpersuaded and its end was unlamented. Expert opinion outside France constantly anticipated that unstable public finances and a paper currency would be the undoing of revolutionary France. Thus the former British Treasury minister, Sir Grey Cooper, in late 1794, while accepting 'the very formidable & overpowering force which the Republic exerts, & the unparalleled success which attends her exertions... yet I am still convinced that this external Exhibition is in many parts false & hollow': If the allies persist 'for 18 months longer, The Bubble will burst.' Though amazed that France appeared to be staggering under the weight of unpaid taxes, Cooper was prepared to admit over a year later that he had been wrong. 'My conjectures however upon the fate of that wonderfull public security were, like all the prophetical calculations of Statesmen & Bankers on the subject, visionary & erroneous, I mean with respect to the duration of this Paper Edifice.[6]

After Thermidor the Convention gradually restored freedom of trade and suppressed the Maximum on 24 December 1794. Joint-stock companies (abolished in August 1793) were possible again after November 1795. The Directory was cautiously supportive of capitalism. Thus it restored free trade in grain from June 1797 and was intolerant of trade union agitation. Typical of this was the law of 2 September 1796 by which paper workers were forbidden to leave off their employment without giving 40 days' prior notice.

*The Predominance of Property*

The Revolution collapsed the boundaries between nobles and non-nobles to create an elite of notables where property was the sole key to influence in the constitutional monarchy. Its founding articles referred to the secure ownership of property as a 'sacred and inviolable right'; nothing was said about its distribution. That depended on market forces in which individuals could trade freely on the exclusive basis of their wealth, assisted by laws that encouraged buying and selling. The majority of those within the loose grouping of 'active citizens' had no intention of letting the Revolution slip from their control or allowing theoretical notions of social equality to deflect them from consolidating their holdings or creating more wealth for themselves and their families. They were appalled by the urban disturbances that marked the first year of the Revolution, disquieted by the *Grande Peur*. One answer to instability was concession in the form of the August decrees, the other was the establishment of the National Guard to protect both property and persons. For the sale of Church lands in 1789–90 to the wealthier members of society created a property boom in miniature for the purchasers of the *biens nationaux*, not the nation as a whole. The pattern of purchase predominantly reflected trends of the previous decade when a land-hungry trading elite bought up land in their neighbourhoods as they came on to the market. All that changed in the immediate aftermath of 1789 was the amount of property available for purchase.

What could be considered legitimate property was one of the most contested questions of 1789. Venality was out, so were most forms of *seigneurial* dues. However, those who had hoped for complete abolition in the light of the August decrees were disappointed. Deputies spent much time in deciding which dues could only be discarded after financial compensation. In March 1790, those who paid them were given the first option of buying those that were deemed legitimate. The uptake was disappointing because the high purchase price was out of reach for most peasants. The matter was only finally settled on 17 July 1793 when the Convention suppressed all *seigneurial* dues without compensation.

Not surprisingly, this upwardly mobile bourgeois elite rejoiced in Revolution, at least initially. They wanted the Constitution of 1791 to work and when it quickly faltered, it hazarded their gains. Not that any subsequent regime thought in terms of confiscation or dispossession. Property ownership was consistently accorded full legal protection. What had been bought or exchanged in good faith would not be overturned in order to benefit *émigrés*, the Church or any previous owner or to reward the Left materially for past political favours.

*Economic Egalitarianism*

The market preferences of successive regimes were not to everyone's taste, either in town or countryside: there was a sharp contrast with wage earners who looked to government to uphold fair prices on basic commodities.

As historians have long stressed, the preferences of urban populations for prices based on fairness formed a key constituent of 'the moral economy of the crowd'. The pre-1789 monarchy was all too familiar with the sociopolitical tension that could spill over into street violence when bread prices rose and crowds rioted to find cheap loaves and flush out suspected hoarders. Those pressures had not diminished because of the Revolution, as events in the spring and summer of 1789 demonstrated. If anything the expectations of townsmen and women that the new order would deliver to them an assured supply of staple products at a fair or reduced price had increased. That this aspiration made no allowance for the unpredictability of every harvest or the *laissez-faire* passions of the parliamentarians was beside the point. The revolutionary militants in Paris and the other cities were insistent that the price of their support for a republic and the war was policy concessions that paid more than lip service to the ideal of economic egalitarianism and, on and off during 1792–5, they had their way. Opinion in the Legislative Assembly and the Convention had to be coerced for concessions to be forthcoming. The ideological gulf was well illustrated in March 1792 when Simonneau, the mayor of Étampes, south of Paris, was murdered after he had refused popular demands for fixing the price of bread and, two months later, was accorded a state funeral by deputies to show their support for a man who sacrificed his life for the principle of free trade.

One should not exaggerate the egalitarianism of the *sans-culottes*: they were more concerned at reducing specific inequalities rather than having a blueprint for general equality.[7] They stood to lose much personally from commending any such policy. As craftsmen, traders, printers and shopkeepers, they were not opposed in principle to private property and they did not make up in any sense a kind of proto-Marxist proletariat. But they were anxious to use state power to maintain their own independent standing against the threat of larger emerging capitalist units, and this meant price controls in times of dearth and an unapologetic taxing of the wealthy, especially the hoarders and the speculators. They also found it impossible to discard their preference for collective bargaining. Theirs was a preference little different to their fathers or grandfathers before them; the Revolution afforded them the chance to realise this ideal of limited redistribution to the patriotic and the deserving (the two categories were interchangeable).[8] The first breakthrough occurred in September 1792 when the Legislative Assembly, in one of its last edicts, temporarily suspended free trade in grain and gave civil authorities the right to requisition it. But then, that December, the Convention repealed the enactment, its only concession to those who wanted controls being the prohibition of grain exports.

This was not enough for the *sans-culottes* and the *enragés*. Incited by politicians such as Marat and Jacques-René Hébert who talked their language and were not frightened of making blood-curdling pronouncements against the class-enemies of the Revolution, there were disturbances in Paris during February and March 1793 with wholesalers being targeted for pillaging. Pressure on the Convention for price controls was at its height during that spring, leading deputies – with much reluctance – to declare a grain and fodder price maximum on 4 May and for all other foods and fuel on 29 September. Though a law of 26 July on hoarding laid down the death penalty for offenders and set up commissions to monitor the grain trade, problems of enforcement were insuperable. Nevertheless, the Jacobin regime had to keep trying, partly because of the debt it owed the *sans-culottes* for their assistance in the *journées* of 31 May – 2 June 1793. Prices had risen fast by summer 1793 thanks to inflation (wheat, for instance by 27 per cent, and potatoes 70 per cent), provoking a minor uprising on 4–5 September to which the government response on 11 September was to decree national maximum prices. The highpoint of state regulation of the economy was attained on 29 September 1793 with a general price ceiling in the Law of the General Maximum, and, in October, the establishment of a National Food Commission. In February 1794 there was a further general fixing of price levels that ambitiously extended across the entire nation. The control of food prices was as far as the Jacobins were prepared to go towards achieving a degree of social equality.

As far as the CPS was concerned, such extremist measures could be justified as a response to the exigencies of war rather than any attempt at social justice. None of its members condoned the lobbying of the renegade priest, Jacques Roux (1752–1794), with his talk of declaring open war on the rich. He was a thorn in the side of the Jacobins and was denounced in the Jacobin Club by Robespierre on 6 August. They had him arrested more than once for agitation in September (his paper *Le Publiciste* was scarcely less incendiary than Hébert's *Le Père Duchesne*) and then again in November 1793. But Roux had already achieved his purpose by effecting the *journée* of 5 September 1793 when the *sections* had marched on the Convention and secured most of the economic concessions they wanted. This was the highpoint of the *enragés*' influence. Throughout the next few months, the CPS took every opportunity of presenting them as vicious extremists whose relentless demands were especially culpable in wartime. On 21 September Leclerc, threatened with arrest, was obliged to suspend publication of his radical journal, the *Ami du peuple*. By the close of 1793 the *enragés* were no longer a political force. Roux was imprisoned and killed himself before he could be executed, although his programme remained official policy for the time being and was upheld by the Hébertistes, another faction whose influence was also waning. Unsurprisingly, by summer 1794 the sectional leaders were increasingly critical of the CPS but then found they had few friends among the Thermidorians. The abortive Germinal and Prairial insurrections in the Year III can be interpreted as a last-ditch attempt to have the Convention register their pleas for a control economy and, as discussed above, they were entirely counter-productive. The only concession made in the face of the worst winter of the century was the imposition of bread rationing and, yet again, that could not be enforced. Otherwise, what remained of the Food Commission was abolished that winter, restrictions on grain prices relaxed and the Maximum put on one side.

This return to market discipline at a time when citizens were dying because of food shortages generated the first autonomous workers' movement that Revolutionary Paris had seen. The layoffs beginning in November 1794 led to a wage riot, as food became the priority with inflation unstoppable. The return to market conditions also precipitated the most politically extreme movement in the French Revolution, that of the *babouvistes*, expressive of radical frustration at the absence of political will to apportion *biens nationaux* on the basis of social equity. It was named after Gracchus Babeuf (1760–1796), originally from the Aisne in northern France. He was unrepentant in his advocacy of an egalitarian redistribution of wealth and deplored the failure of the Revolution down to 1796 to have made any effective steps towards a communistic end. After Thermidor, as a journalist and a pamphleteer lobbying for the implementation of the Year I Constitution, he was prominent in the Panthéon Club, the left-wing society founded in November 1795 that had a membership of over 1000 by early 1796 and was regarded as extremist by the Directory. Its closure was ordered on 26 February. Babeuf then took the risky step of planning a coup against the regime and engineering a 'conspiracy of equals' involving ex-Hébertistes such as Varlet and the former Terrorist, Darthé. Babeuf set up an Insurrectionary Committee in March 1796, but it was soon infiltrated by informers and he and his lieutenant, Buonarotti, were arrested on

10 May as part of a major crackdown on those suspected of involvement. *Babouviste* prisoners were moved for their trials from Paris to Vendôme in August to lessen the security risks in the capital and, the following month, a pro-Babeuf rising at Grenelle Camp was unsuccessful.[9] Babeuf was condemned to death by a court that he refused to recognise, deriding it as a 'Punch and Judy show'. The Directors were not distracted by his taunts from doing a thorough job in dismantling the *babouviste* organisation (such as it was) to ensure that Babeuf left no obvious heir, but his immortal words: 'The French Revolution is only the forerunner of a much bigger, much more solemn revolution, which will be the final one',[10] gave comfort and inspiration to many subsequent left-wing agitators around the world.

## The Changing Rural Picture

Babeuf's was not the kind of movement calculated to arouse much interest from the rural population of France, the largest bloc of peasant proprietors in Europe before 1789 that the *philosophes* had commonly identified as an obstacle to progress rather than its catalyst. Divisions within the peasantry were actually appreciable, as in the south-west where wealthy peasants were loathed because they were rent collectors in their own right.[11] Population growth combined with the economic downturn of the 1780s were causing strong pressures towards rural pauperisation in most areas of the kingdom As Peter Jones reports the situation after the harvest failure of 1788 and the appalling winter which followed:

> Tenant farmers defaulted on their leases, plot holders were forced to sell up, whilst the lowest tier of the peasantry consisting of those dependent on agricultural or industrial wages were often driven into vagabondage.[12]

Smallholders and sharecropers were desperate for better times and a regime that could deliver them after the collapse of grain prices in the 1780s. Many were close to destitution and pinned their hopes on the Estates-General moving quickly to reduce the financial burdens they had carried for so long. Peasants and small landowners had played their part in the elections of spring 1789 and the drawing up of the *Cahiers*. Their main demand was for the removal of *seigneurial* dues, not a lowering of their rents or the abolition of the tithe. But the disappearance of what remained of manorial customs in the form of money payments and the performance of labour services could not come soon enough, for they had no associated *quid pro quo* to benefit peasant communities. Peter McPhee has shown how, in the lower Languedoc, peasants in a hill country of small villages and extensive wastelands or *garrigues*, had long-standing grievances against their *seigneurs* that explain why they welcomed the Revolution. So did those in the Franche-Comté, who also had to pay an exceptionally heavy rate of tithe.[13]

What rendered *seigneurial* dues even more of an anomalous exaction was that its beneficiaries were increasingly wealthy bourgeois purchasing land who had no necessary connection with a locality (and their lawyers) enabling them to plough back – quite literally – that outgoing into their own estate. Though many petitioned the National Assembly vigorously over the winter of 1789–90 (disturbances in several provinces including Brittany, Quercy and Lorraine spanned the Christmas and New Year period over the tardy pace of land reform[14]) the initial reluctance of deputies to abolish them outright was a disappointment, a reflection of the absence of any peasant to gain election to Versailles, and a disillusioning experience for peasants warming to their new legal rights as citizens. Rights allegedly grounded in violence and usurpation ended forthwith, not so those which had originated in some form of contractual relationship. The onus lay with the tenant to prove the contrary, thus opening up a legal process beyond the cost of most. Resentment could spill over into violence as successive governments evinced no desire to cancel the arrangements, one reaffirmed in the consolidatory Rural Code of 28 September 1791. Between February and April 1792 there was a wave of violent anti-*seigneurial* disturbances across the Midi, which helped secure the eventual outright abolition of all dues in the autumn. As a prelude to that step, on 18 June the Legislative Assembly abolished adventitious *seigneurial* dues (*droits casuels*) without indemnity, except where the original title deed was still intact.

The discountenancing of the post-1789 order by countrymen should not be overstated. The tendency to minimise the Revolution's uses for the peasantry has been counterbalanced by Peter Jones's work stressing the advantages ensuing from the scaling back of the *seigneurial* regime and manorial jurisdictions, including the outright abolition of mortmain and hunting rights, as well as exclusive rights to own rabbit-warrens and dovecotes. John Markoff is also in no doubt that peasants were critical in the radicalisation of the Revolution through to 1793.[15] He claims that peasants had a nascent sense of themselves as citizens of a national polity, 'some sense of public service, of equity, and of citizenship', and rural participation in the first elections under the post-1790 system produced a higher return than in urban constituencies.[16] Communities were often internally divided about how to respond to the ebb-and-flow of political change in their nearest big town, let alone Paris, and varying systems of land tenure could set apart one neighbouring parish from another, as well as a host of other variables. The Revolution brought an extended land market, from which *some* peasants, proprietors (*laboureurs*) rather than tenants were, in time, able to derive advantage. Nevertheless, the inability of the less prosperous among them such as sharecroppers to make serious bids at auction for the *biens nationaux* was a source of early disillusionment with the possibilities of change in the western parts of Anjou, Upper Brittany and Poitou. It was exacerbated by the sudden presence of a new set of landowners with social tensions caused by the displacement of the old ones.

The Revolution's capitalist ethic was confirmed as a source of peasant grievance. It was not as if the burden of taxation had been reduced. Those who had once lived in the *pays d'état* now found themselves paying more in direct taxation than their previous level of the *taille*. The new *contribution foncière*, a land tax on agricultural revenues and the *contribution mobilière* on movable goods (both dating from 1791) were much resented. For a time, one way round the incapacity of individual peasants to purchase new lands on the open market was for them to pool their funds with their neighbours in the hope of outbidding wealthier outsiders. The tactic had some success until these collective bids from peasant associations were made illegal by the Convention in the name of individual rights on 24 April 1793.

The Republic might not be offering peasants much, but it wanted a lot from them: their grain at controlled prices according to the legal price ceilings fixed in May and September 1793, their horses and asses to go and support the armies, their sons to do likewise. None of this came with any respect for the dominant form of rural culture, and the dechristianising campaigns of 1793–4 made an impact on most lowland settlements, once Catholicism became tainted through association with counter-revolutionary agitation and the representatives and *armées révolutionnaires* got to work. Though as many as one in ten Jacobins was a peasant, the leadership cadre constructed policy from a predominantly urban perspective.[17] However, Jacobins in deeply rural areas had no alternative but to construct alliances of convenience with disgruntled countrymen, as in the Cantal where local Jacobins wooed traditional peasant rebel types and linked the demands of the peasantry to their own political platform.[18] It was symptomatic that Jacobins affecting an interest in their peasant neighbours referred to them as *cultivateurs* rather than *paysans*. Only briefly in 1793–4 was there any sustained attempt to use national lands for social ends, and no regime was interested in land redistribution for its own sake. Most Jacobins detested the very idea of agrarian communitarianism. As Jacques Montbrion said in Marseille:

> Every time that someone says 'you should have half the property of your neighbour': shun that man! He is a veritable enemy of the constitution; he wants you to misinterpret equality so that he can slander the Declaration of the Rights of Man.[19]

Nevertheless, in September 1793 poorer heads of households were given a bond worth 500 *livres* with which they might purchase national lands. No interest was charged and they were allowed to pay in up to 20 instalments. This was as close to a policy of rural equality as the Jacobins got. Other schemes were decreed, but the government made enforcing them a low priority. Thus a law of October 1793 prohibiting landlords from adding on to their leases the value of lost tithes and *seigneurial* dues and one of February–March 1793 ('Laws of Ventôse') making the property of suspects available to the poor were never properly implemented. The Jacobins for a while followed a policy of *partage*, dividing common lands between individual plotholders, on the request of one-third of the inhabitants (law of 10 June 1793). In the least prosperous areas, in much of Auvergne, for instance, where communities could not exist unless they held a large proportion of land in common, take up was patchy. It was nowhere regarded as an adequate means of compensating rural communities for the state regulation of agriculture. This was so deeply scorned that producers fought back by deliberately underproducing. The weather did nothing to increase prosperity during the revolutionary decade. Though the harvests were slightly better than those of the 1780s, the terrible winter of 1794–5 took a heavy toll. Of course, it must constantly be remembered that, in a primarily rural state like France, the implementation and response to rural policies varied remarkably. It was only in a minority of areas where a special combination of circumstances applied – always involving profound religious zeal – that peasant protest led to sustained, large-scale armed resistance to the Republic. Nevertheless, most country people were aware of what had gone on in the Vendée and, while it may have reduced the likelihood of emulation, it did nothing to abate the deep-seated detestation of this regime and especially its servants operating locally, widely regarded as despicable turncoats. The thousands of poor but ambitious men who monitored their own *pays* for the Republic may have gained influence over their neighbours briefly in 1792–4; over the medium term they were outcasts and many would end up as victims of the 'White Terror'.

It was the Directory which evinced most interest in the national potential of rural France, though this perception remained at a fairly academic level because of the extent to which huge swathes of the countryside remained a 'no-go area' for the regime due to their royalist and, less often, Jacobin sympathies. The Directory flirted with a policy of permitting the sale of national lands without auction until September 1796. It also abandoned any pretence of implementing the policy of *partage*. Arguably, it took the needs of rural France more seriously than any previous revolutionary regime. Between 1797 and 1799 the talented economist and Minister of the Interior François de Neufchâteau encouraged the establishment of local agricultural societies, and he issued a great deal of agrarian information and propaganda. This is all the more surprising coming as it did just as the regime had taken a lurch to the left. It was, to some extent, part of a policy of pacification in the countryside that at least ensured France saw no equivalent of the *jacquerie* which swept across Belgium in 1798. Other than that, its impact was slight, and such rural tranquillity as there was owed more to a run of improved harvest yields than public policy.

The upper as well as lower social strata of rural France were both alike affected by the upheavals. To belong to a noble family in the 1790s was in itself compromising. If political survival was, except in rare cases, improbable, maintaining the patrimonial estates was a realisable objective for the majority. The key to so doing was keeping the lowest of local profiles, not challenging the regime of the hour, and avoiding ostentation or anything else that could attract unfavourable notice. This was more attainable for the lesser nobility, whose smaller landholdings were commonly their only source of wealth. It was usually asking too much for their more prosperous counterparts, most of whom had left France in the winter of 1791–2 out of their loyalty to monarchy. Such a move hazarded family landholdings: *émigré* lands were sequestrated by the state in February 1792 and, on 17 July, placed on the market for sale alongside those of the Church. Those who were arrested and executed during the Terror likewise paid this forfeit. Ironically, many of the new owners were smaller noblemen themselves, consolidating their estate ownership and relying on their popularity among locals who were likely to prefer having them for a landlord than a monied man from the town. The only way of avoiding dispossession and sale under the 1792 legislation was to transfer land to another member of the family or to trustees prior to leaving France for exile so that ownership passed outright to a non-*émigré(s)*. It was not a foolproof device, especially where the counter-revolutionary sympathies of a particular clan were too overt to be ignored, but it worked in a majority of cases. Thus many nobles returning home under the Bonapartist amnesty between 1800 and 1802 found their estates intact, and they could resume personal ownership without legal obstacles placed in their path by the Republic. Even those whose estates had been confiscated were not necessarily losers provided their holdings had not been sold off. The land market was very active during the Consulate as noblemen took advantage of uncertainties over title from recent purchasers and often persuaded the latter to sell back to them, sometimes at discounted prices.

## The Impact of the War

The Revolution had a transforming effect on society and the economy, and the war compounded it further. It compelled republican politicians, as discussed above, to set up the nearest equivalent to a 'command economy' that the eighteenth century had yet seen, including, briefly, the price controls that were such anathema to the majority of the Convention. An undoubted motive for the Brissotins' commitment to free trade was the first-hand experience of its benefits many of their supporters living in the Bordeaux region had. The city was one of those west coast ports (Nantes and La Rochelle were the other main two) which were the entrepôts for the West Indies traffic in sugar, slaves and tobacco, as well as a peacetime trade with Britain that had doubled in value during the 1780s. Both the Atlantic and the Channel trade stopped in 1793 once war with Britain erupted and colonial shipping had to run the gauntlet of a naval blockade. The occasional merchant ship sometimes slipped through the net of patrolling warships (there were 'inner' and 'outer' blockades), but not enough to prevent the destruction of the sources of wealth for cities like Bordeaux and Nantes which had prospered so much under the Bourbon monarchy. Destitution and the loss of their political influence became the lot of the Bordelais mercantile elite and the multiple economic benefits conferred on their city (seen, for instance, as recently as the early 1780s with the building of a new theatre in the fashionable neo-classical style) were at an end. Population in the city began to fall so that by 1805 Bordeaux had less than 100,000 citizens again. From these trends followed the impoverishment of society in the major coastal towns and their hinterlands. The French colonists in the Caribbean with whom they traded faced corresponding losses as their markets collapsed and the whole area was set alight by slave revolts (see below) and invasion by British fleets and armies. These were not the only losers. French manufacturers who had relied on unfettered access to raw materials found their markets closed off by the Royal Navy, so conferring on their British rivals a competitive edge they never afterwards lost. The recurrent disruption of the continent by war in the 1790s and 1800s destroyed many traditional French markets in Europe and those merchants who had depended on them, precisely those who had at first welcomed the Revolution's advent as a decisive moment in the collapse of trade barriers.

Towns and villages on the frontier zones in Alsace, Lorraine, Flanders, Roussillon, Foix and Navarre were repeatedly damaged in the fighting and thousands of civilians lost their lives as the war passed through their locality and then often returned as the tide of fortunes shifted. Not everyone suffered from the relentless bellicosity. For some, war on an unparalleled scale was their moment of opportunity. As John Roberts memorably said, 'a last golden age was beginning for those who could make money while governments still had no effective means of taxing income'.[20] As always, the contractors supplying the armies with everything from boots and buttons to muskets and shakos grew fat on the profits to be made. They bought up land, helped revive the consumer market after 1795 and used their 'new money' to establish themselves comfortably within the higher echelons of post-revolutionary society. Speculators in stocks and bonds lived dangerously in the 1790s, making and losing fortunes with equal speed, but most did well out of the war. As did the criminal fraternity. It took the best part of a decade for government to reduce the incidence of crime that had made the Revolution such good news for opportunist thieves, burglars, thugs and murderers. Prostitutes – and their pimps – saw an increase in numbers and profits thanks to the Revolution, the number of 'street women' trafficking in Paris rising well beyond the estimated 40,000 active in the 1780s. With most of the army tied up beyond the frontiers or policing counter-revolutionary zones, and political crimes hard to distinguish from private ones, law infringers had a field day. Petty crooks had an easy opportunity for larceny knowing that houses were unprotected with men away at the war; on the coasts, smugglers confronted a scaled-down excise department and often benefited from British collusion in their operations. The activities of all such merged into a cultural framework in which politicised violence had become a legitimate expression of republican values. For those who were their victims, the damage inflicted on their property and persons by law-breakers was calculated, in many instances, to act as recruiting agency for the Counter-Revolution.

Patterns of consumption changed dramatically. Decreasingly lavish lifestyles within the new elite and the switching off of aristocratic spending drove to the wall those tradesmen who had grown rich catering for the luxury end of the market. Milliners, hairdressers, mercers, glovers, couturiers, perruquiers, all had a hard time of it; some of them followed their former customers into emigration. Female unemployment in the luxury trades was a clear sign of this recession, although such occupations were traditionally if not wholly fairly regarded as a privileged preserve of Parisian prostitutes.[21] Furniture makers and interior decorators found their profit margins squeezed beyond endurance, either forcing them out of business or sending them to foreign capitals like London or Vienna where a wealthy clientèle still needed their services. A few stayed on, including Georges Jacob (1739–1814), who established the distinctive 'Directoire' designs in cabinet making inspired by David's neo-classicism and the fashion for everything 'Greek'. He was able to hand on his factory successfully to his sons in 1796.

Chefs previously working for the nobility in their Paris *hôtels* or rural seats were badly hit. Sometimes their employer had fled abroad, or they were left with one who could no longer afford their services. Some eventually tried to cater for the wider market by opening some of the first public restaurants in Paris in the later 1790s. By that date, (vulgar) displays of wealth were no longer hidden, private patronage was again possible, Parisian salon life was reviving and the new post-Thermidor revolutionary elite wanted to impress their friends with the best food and drink available. These trends should not be exaggerated: the market for luxury goods may have reawakened after 1795, but it was on nothing like the pre-revolutionary scale.

The impact of the Revolution on dress-codes was profound. No longer were clothes with costly ornaments either socially or politically acceptable. As *Le Cabinet des modes* put it, 'luxury went out, but is now within reach of all citizens, since it resides in the comfort, propriety and elegance of forms'.[22] The male social elite had been 'dressing down' even before

1789 by such fashionable accessories as wearing the English frock coat (the *frac*); the revolution accelerated that trend and put the revolutionary leadership (when they were not wearing military uniforms) into twill trousers and working men's coats *à la jolie sans-culotte*, inspiring the counter-revolutionaries to laugh about them as the 'trouser brigade' (*pantalonnades*) and 'Punch and Judy sansculottes'.[23] Only gradually, in the mid-1790s, as taste discarded the drabness of the Jacobins and their addiction to scruffy plainness, did male fashion display its peacock side again and permit a slight increase in employment in the clothes trade. Men affected skin-tight pantaloons from waist to ankle that could be so tight that it was uncomfortable sitting down with the risk of marring the beauty of a creaseless line. Collars rose and cravats came right up on to the cheeks. The dandies were back with a sartorial reaction to mirror the political one. Only the trend for un-powdered hair without a queue survived the style reversion of 9 Thermidor. The dandies had their female counterparts, whose dress sense tended towards a daring and diaphanous simplicity. Corsets and stays were abandoned in favour of a high-waisted dress cut low, clinging in simple folds from neck to ankle. The penchant for mimicking antique statuary was such that fashion leaders often dampened the folds of their gowns so that they clung to the body. The scanty attire of the women after the Jacobins had gone may have offended some sensiblities, but it was impossible to stop as an expression of exuberance and enjoyment.

*Summary*

It would be an exaggeration to claim that France was returning to social and economic stability during the Consulate. Nevertheless, there were reassuring signs that, under the protection of their dynamic head of state, citizens could hope for better times. The establishment of the Bank of France in the spring of 1800 was designed both to reassure investors and establish a public credit system for the nation that would ensure none of the crises that had afflicted the late *ancien-régime* state were repeated. Taxes might be rising to help pay for the costs of war, but at least the public could be confident their contributions would not be mismanaged so flagrantly as the late Bourbons had done. The Consul was anxious to secure the formation of a relatively open society, in which old and new families could feel comfortable and play a part irrespective of their political pasts. All that was asked was loyalty to his regime.

For most French men and women that seemed a small price to pay, particularly if Bonaparte ushered in the return of general peace in Europe. For a brief span, while the Peace of Amiens with Britain lasted between 1802 and 1803, that hope was realised. Visitors poured into Paris from all over the continent, court life achieved a sumptuous splendour unknown since the 1780s, and it became meaningful to talk of high society life in Paris again. The Consulate was developing a distinctive decorative style to reinforce the impression of political solidarity, one that naturally paid tribute to Bonaparte through the craze for all things Egyptian, as fostered by Baron Dominique Vivant de Denon (1747–1825). To no one's particular surprise, this peacetime interval provided a false if tantalising glimmer of normality. Diplomatic wrangling soured Anglo–French relations and Bonaparte's restless spirit found it hard to resist using his army as an instrument of first resort with which to confirm his dominance over his enemies, both foreign and domestic. By the winter of 1803–4, the opening stages of the War of the Third Coalition were in progress. Once again, French traders and manufacturers found themselves shut off from the outside world other than neighbouring satellite states, and the opportunities for wealth creation it offered. At least in social terms, as the country moved from Consulate into Empire and confirmation of its standing as the first military power in Europe, the opportunities for social distraction were more extensive than they had been for a generation.

# PART IV
## The Revolution and the Wider World

# Chapter 10: The Impact on Europe

> I wish, for my own part, that although we enjoy such perfect tranquility as we do at present at home, that this scene of horror and discord, and rage for innovation and for new constitutions, were in a country at a greater distance from our own. It is such a conflagration, that the very sparks which arise from it may chance to light upon our own heads.
> (George Selwyn to Lady Carlisle, 17 Aug. 1789, HMC Carlisle, 663)

Though its initial advent was greeted hopefully in most of Europe, the implications of the Revolution for France's neighbours soon made them wish it away. Its irresistible force was all too readily translated from rhetoric to the battlefield. Boissy d'Anglas talked ecstatically in these terms:

> To set the destinies of the world, you have only to will it. You are the creators of a new world. Say 'let there be light', and light will be.

Such words were not music to the ears of the leaders of Britain, Spain, the United Provinces, the Habsburg Empire and Prussia, for they suggested that France was bent both on conquest and imposing its new values willy-nilly. And thus the coming of the Revolution had major international repercussions: it destroyed the peace of Europe for a generation, ignited an armed ideological struggle, and led to the loss of millions of lives. No European state could affect neutrality on some of the most contentious doctrines of the Revolution; even if not formally at war with France, they had to police their own populations to ensure that the spread of Jacobin principles was not undermining established authorities in Church and State. Most regimes did collapse under the impact of the Revolution, including the papacy (between 1798 and 1800) and the Holy Roman Empire (abolished in 1806). Only Great Britain retained its territorial integrity and, even here, the French republican challenge, the inspiration behind the Irish Rebellion of 1798, impelled Pitt's government to proceed apace with the Act of Union, effective from 1 January 1801.

*An International Dimension*

The principles of the Revolution in its most creative phase between 1789 and 1791, were not intended to have a limited national application: they were for appropriation everywhere by reformers to modernise and renew the life of a state and its citizens/subjects. Such was predictable in the light of Enlightenment cosmopolitanism. Though the decision of the National Assembly to disregard history as a foundation for its own constitutional reformation might have been expected to increase its usefulness as a blueprint for reformers outside France, it actually restricted its appeal. The other 'new' constitution of this era, the short-lived Polish Constitution of 1791, was more historically engineered than its French equivalent, although the mutual inspiration was certainly there and ardent Jacobins liked to think of Poland as 'the France of the North'. Across the Atlantic, the United States had given itself a legal settlement in 1787 that was more pragmatically constructed than its French counterpart. Of course, Enlightenment principles profoundly influenced the 'founding fathers': their obligation to Montesquieu and the principle of the separation of powers separated executive, legislature and judiciary as firmly in the USA as it did in France. The crucial distinction between them was in the American provision of checks and balances. All that mattered in France was the transfer of sovereign authority in the kingdom from the Crown to the National Assembly, leaving the royal government lacking in substantive authority (George Washington had powers of policy initiative and management quite lacking to Louis XVI and his ministries of 1789–92) and the judiciary rationalised and reformed, but without the decisive voice in the interpretation of the 1791 Constitution that fell to the Supreme Court in the United States. Both polities, republican American and monarchical France, took pride in their commitment to the rule of law. However, in France it was the politicians (many of them, admittedly, lawyers) who ultimately decided what was lawful, while in the United States, it was the judges who upheld the constitution and protected it from abuse in the name of political self-interest, invariably rationalised as the public good.

The French constitutionalists of 1789–91 looked on themselves as granting their countrymen public liberties on a scale never previously seen in Europe. They welcomed in a spirit of fraternity and universalism those from other nations who wanted to share their principles and their prospects. It was in this spirit that on 19 June 1790 Baron von Cloots led to the National Assembly a delegation of partially disguised foreigners who were supposed to represent the many but now (courtesy of the Revolution) united nations and races of men. The progressive minded across Europe were quick to send brotherly greetings, like the Dundee Whig Club that, in an address to the National Assembly, spoke of 'the triumph of liberty and reason over despotism, ignorance and superstition'. Honorary French citizenship was offered to foreigners whose career or work was believed to anticipate or echo revolutionary values. Thus in 1791 the German dramatist Schiller was so honoured for his play *Die Rayber* (*The Robbers*) about Karl Moor, a rebel against injustice. The prospects for a new start across the whole of Europe for a time seemed unprecedentedly rosy, not least to many of the leading British sympathisers for the French Revolution. They tended to be 'rational dissenters', ordained ministers who rejected trinitarian Christianity, men such as the Reverand Richard Price, whose sermon on the Revolution inspired Burke to produce his great riposte to the Revolution, the *Reflections*, and Joseph Priestley, polemicist, chemist and millenarian, whose whole life was devoted to those progressive causes he viewed as leading to religious renewal and the emptying from Christianity of those corruptions (trinitarianism and priesthood, for instance) which had hamstrung its progress. As Price wrote to Thomas Jefferson, until very recently American ambassador to the Court of Versailles, it was:

> A Revolution that must astonish Europe; that shakes the foundation of despotic power; and that probably will be the commencement of a general reformation in the governments of the world which hitherto have been little better than usurpations on the rights of mankind, impediments to the progress of human improvement, and contrivances for enabling a few grandees to oppress and enslave the rest of mankind. Glorious patriots![1]

Price and Priestley were both part of the Bowood Circle, a group of cosmopolitan intellectuals who looked to a former Prime Minister, the marquis of Lansdowne (1737–1805), for patronage. Lansdowne was one of the minority of British peers (they also included Pitt's brother-in-law, the third Earl Stanhope, or 'Citizen' Stanhope as he liked to call himself) whose commitment to the Revolution in 1789–92 never wavered. Lansdowne was the focus of an Anglo–French nexus that included Clavière, Dumont, Morellet, Mirabeau, and his internationalist status was detested by counter-revolutionaries led by Burke. Even the marquis was too moderate for other British revolutionaries. Most notable among them was Thomas Paine (1737–1809), whose reply to Burke, the *Rights of Man* (1792), was a best-selling tract that alarmed the British establishment. Scarcely less influential was John Oswald, a member of the Jacobin Club and the Cercle Social, who launched his own paper, the *Universal Patriot*, in May 1790, with a prospectus which talked of the Revolution arousing 'from a state of political delusion the supine Englishmen of the present day... [so that] the French nation will have the glory of giving a Lesson of Liberty to the people whose disciples they have been'.[2] Some of those in the Bowood Circle were Swiss who had sharp memories of the abortive revolution of 1782 in Geneva. The promise of 1789 had inspired uprisings in the early 1790s in both the cantons of Zurich and Bern, while many exiles from the Bern-controlled territory of Vaud formed a Helvetic Club in Paris that planned the transformation of the Swiss confederation and tried to spread notions of liberty.

Just as support for the Revolution in 1789–92 had an international dimension so, too, did opposition. Thousands of *émigré* nobles and clergy fanned out across Europe, most concentrated in the Rhineland in and around Coblentz, others relocating temporarily (as they hoped) everywhere from St Petersburg to London, from Naples to Stockholm. And wherever they went, so did their tales of spoliation and destitution. However, the impact of these exiles on the policy making of their host countries before the outbreak of war in 1792–3 should not be exaggerated. Their numbers were very few until the third year of the Revolution, and their complaints commonly sounded like special pleading to other governments. In the Austrian Empire, Leopold II had to endure the repeated requests of his sister, Marie-Antoinette, for Habsburg intervention, as well as the appeals of those thousands of militant exiles whom he had allowed on to imperial soil. But he had no intention of fighting France when only in September 1791 the war against Turkey was finally halted. The Declaration of Pillnitz might have given the opposite impression, but the emperor intended it as a diplomatic warning to France rather than the immediate prelude to armed conflict. Leopold was a tolerant, pragmatic sovereign whose record as Grand Duke of Tuscany before 1790 displayed reformist credentials. His main task, as he conceived it before his premature death in March 1792, was returning the empire to stability after his brother's tumultuous decade as emperor in the 1780s. This was no less the case in Britain, despite the epic denunciations of Revolution in Burke's *Reflections*. Burke and his son Richard were frequently in *émigré* company in London and although their diagnosis of the Revolution as cultural catastrophe made sense for conservative Whigs like Portland, Fitzwilliam and Windham, Pitt and his right-hand man in cabinet, Henry Dundas, looked on the Revolution primarily for its impact on international relations and rejoiced at French international weakness. It seemed to open the door to peace, budgetary surplus, and the completion of Britain's full international recovery after the disastrous loss of the American colonies in 1781–3.

These harbingers of peace and international harmony were in tatters as early as the spring of 1792 when European opinion turned against the perceived extremism of the Revolution and French politicians sought a conclusive settlement of internal tensions in a foreign war. With Brissot demanding 'a new crusade, a crusade of universal freedom' as early as December 1791, the revolutionaries rediscovered the political possibilities of chauvinism and the public's receptiveness to discarding the despised 1756 alliance with the Habsburgs as a relic of an absolutist past. The occasion for the rupture was the build-up of *émigré* numbers in the Rhineland Electorate of Trier, a visible sign of the Counter-Revolution's emergence as a force to be reckoned with as well as a symbol of a different model of Frenchness with the values to match. In the declaration of war against the 'king of Bohemia and Hungary' on 20 April 1792, the Legislative Assembly was careful to emphasise that France's quarrel was not with the subjects of the Emperor Francis II let alone the peoples of the German states. The declaration talked of 'the just defence of a free people against the unjust aggression of a king' and adopting 'in advance all foreigners who, abjuring the cause of its enemies, range themselves under its banners...'. The phrasing did little to elicit pro-French sympathies east of the Rhine, where most Germans who interested themselves in international politics rekindled a degree of anti-Gallic sentiment for long concealed by more generous

Enlightenment impulses. Bouyed up by unexpected victory against the allied armies at Valmy and Jemappes, the Convention kept up this insistence that the issues in the war transcended national or monarchical rivalries: the decree of fraternity (19 November 1792) offered assistance to the oppressed peoples of Europe who wished to recover their liberties, notoriously declaring that the war was one on palaces not on cottages. In other words, the humble (a group presumed possessed of politically correct impulses once aware of their best interests as disclosed to them by Jacobin emissaries) had nothing to lose and everything to gain by the defeat and overthrow of their kings. The battle, as the revolutionaries of 1792–3 deemed it, was against the political status quo across Europe, an unrelenting confrontation with existing elites in Church and State. On 15 December the Convention further ordered French generals to cancel existing governments and privileges in occupied lands and to have new administrations elected by those citizens who swore to uphold liberty and equality. It was presumed in France that this was an offer the peoples of Europe would not hesitate to accept. In fact, the reverse held true: the Revolution excited a vigorous minority of male urban progressives leaving other sections of populations either inimical or unmoved. After the massacres perpetrated against the Swiss Guards in the Tuileries on 10 August 1792 after they had surrendered, Swiss citizens readily contrasted their traditional liberty with the more dangerous French version and spurned it. The subjects of George III, Carlos IV, Francis II and Frederick William II did not recognise the French armies as somehow disinterested disciples of a new and irresistible ideology, but rather as a vast armed force intent on coercing them into accepting a new order considered to be profoundly at odds with traditions and values that they were less inclined to put aside than the French had done so abruptly in 1789. France 'not satisfied with the possession of her own political creed ... exhibits the fiery impatience of Mahomet, to spread it through the earth by the havoc of the sword'.[3]

The *ancien régime* states of Europe turned out to be more robust in resisting revolutionary values than the proponents of the same had anticipated. The map of Europe was altered appreciably in the 1790s as a result of French victories, particularly through the extension of France's borders in Belgium, the Rhineland, Savoy and on the Pyrenees; but the changes made came about as a result of military success not spontaneous, pro-French agitation *within* states. Such internal pressures as there were tended to be viciously anti-French and anti-revolutionary. It also discloses a good deal about the nature of Revolution in the later

eighteenth century which suggests that there will be no going back to
Jacques Godechot's thesis of an Atlantic Revolution, a notion born in the
heady aftermath of the revolutionary *événements* of May 1968 in Paris
and widely influential over the next generation. Godechot argued that
a progressive, revolutionary impulse was at work in later eighteenth-
century Europe, spectacularly manifesting itself in British North America
and France but also in a host of smaller states, including Ireland, Geneva,
the Dutch United Provinces, Hungary and the Austrian Netherlands.
Godechot was too ready to pass over dissimilarities, ignore the extent to
which established elites were using international crisis to shore up or extend
their own reach and, most importantly, his 'revolutionaries' were often
reacting against the perceived incursions of modernising authorities such
as the British governments of the 1760s in their colonial policy or the
Emperor Joseph II in his bid to centralise and control the Holy
Roman Empire and the privileges and customary rights of his subjects.

France was the odd man out in implementing progressive revolution.
There was no attempt to use history as device to disguise change as
a reversion to earlier models or precedents: revolutionary France was
a new creation with a political culture that marked an undisguised
rupture with pre-1789. As Barère had said: 'We have revolutionised
government, law, habits, manners, customs, commerce and thought
itself'. In that starkness lay the seeds of its unpopularity and the difficulty
of exporting it, for none of the countries where 'revolutions' had
occurred in the two decades before 1789 proved eager to accept the
French Revolutionary Gospel. Why were foreign collaborators so few?
That the French appeared bent on the wholesale destruction of social
order and religion was reason enough, led by those whom Robespierre
memorably called 'armed missionaries', but if one can point to a single
defining event which created a cultural rupture between France and
the rest of Europe it must be the shockwaves created by the trial and
execution of Louis XVI on 21 January 1793. France was a regicidal
republic, a pariah state that had dismembered itself in the person of
the king. It needed no immersion in the tenets of Jacobinism for the
ordinary European to register repugnance for the king-killers and to
feel alarmed by what they might accomplish once in control of someone
else's territory. There appeared a nightmarish aspect to events. William
Stevens, Anglican high churchman, wondered if the tribulations of the
French Revolution and the Jacobins had been sent by God to punish
a Europe that had abandoned religion and his sentiments were not
uncommon.[4]

For three years before the European War commenced, the French Revolution had been interpreted in the light of individual national experiences and it had made a profound impact, as might be expected from the sight of Europe's oldest monarchy and most populous state initiating a major upheaval in its institutional life. Britons had largely welcomed the events of 1789 as a movement that would end with the French granting themselves the equivalent, slightly updated settlement that had been erected after the 'abdication' of James II and the consequent Revolution settlement of 1688–9. Many Whig clubs and societies had only just stopped celebrating the centenary of Britain's (more properly, England's) 'deliverance' of 5 November 1688 and were delighted as news came through from France that the Bastille had fallen, absolutism was at an end, and that the French were going to award themselves a constitutional monarchy along, presumably, British lines, in which the rule of law and public liberties would be upheld. Among British travellers, it was not just Arthur Young who sent back positive reports from France. One army officer noted:

> Upon considering my intended Tour through France a more desirable end could scarcely be wished for, a general spirit for Liberty diffusing itself through that most extensive country which has been so long burthened with an arbitrary government. The *lettres de cachet* [are] already abolished and the Bastille, that formidable Hydra raised to the Ground.[5]

The dissentient voices, those who saw in events in France as *ab initio*, a far more sinister and fundamental upheaval were few, though they did exist. After the French had given liberty to America and had tried to do the same in Holland, Louis XVI, as one English Tory peer argued in July 1789, had 'no reason to be greatly surprised that his own subjects begin to have a little hanckering after Liberty themselves. I believe the scene at Paris at present is horrid to think of. One can not but pity individuals, but as a nation they deserve it'.[6] The numbers of those viewing the scene like Lord Bagot grew steadily after the October *journées* of 1789, the humiliating return of the royal family from Versailles to the Tuileries, and the retirement of the *Monarchiens* to the provinces. Younger people were less willing to take fright easily, and these included the 20-year-old William Wordsworth who walked with his fellow Cambridge undergraduate, Robert Jones, across France to the Alps. They landed in Calais on 13 July 1790 and were there for the Festival of the Federation when France was 'standing on top of golden hours/ And human nature seeming born again'. They walked through

> hamlets, towns,
> Gaudy with relics of that festival,
> Flowers left to wither on triuymphal arcs, and window garlands....
> Unhoused beneath the evening star we saw
> Dances of liberty, and in late hours
> Of darkness, dances in the open air.

After 1790, the unfolding perception that the Revolution might be going well beyond the confines of the 'Glorious Revolution' did not cause British reformers to lose their sense of fraternal identity with what the National Assembly was trying to achieve. Most among them approved of root-and-branch reform and took inspiration from the French lead to advocate a fresh wave of institutional reform in Britain, including a widening of the parliamentary franchise and the elimination of Anglican religious privileges, including the repeal of the Test and Corporation Acts. The Revolution had commanded attention, sometimes awe, and it fed the hopes of those who were elsewhere engaged in the cause of political reform, like William Taylor of Norwich whose father was secretary of the Revolution Society of Norwich. On 9 May 1790 he recorded that he had kissed the earth on the land of liberty on landing at Calais, writing a few days later from Paris:

> I am at length in the neighbourhood of the National Assembly, that well-head of philosophical legislation, whose pure streams are now overflowing the fairest country upon earth and will soon be sluiced off into the other realms of Europe, fertilising all with the living energy of its waters.[7]

Two years later British radicals, growing impatient with the pace of change at home, began to contemplate extra-parliamentary action, the Society of the Friends of the People in Scotland holding its first General Convention in Edinburgh in December 1792. Significantly, they still proclaimed their attachment to 'the established constitution on its genuinely acknowledged principles'. They spoke not of manhood suffrage, but of 'an Equal Representation of the People'.[8]

This was an effort at moderation just as the country prepared for war and put all progressive-minded politicians on the spot. The leader of the opposition in the House of Commons, Charles James Fox, would never disavow the achievements of the Revolution even though it provoked internecine warfare between the Whigs and led to the entire rupture of the 'party' in July 1794 when the majority under the duke of Portland entered into a coalition government with Pitt, leaving Fox, Sheridan, Tierney and Grey to battle on as a vociferous minority in Parliament. Fox saw the Revolution as a fillip to reformers everywhere, even though he conceded the damage inflicted on their cause by the revolutionary extremism of 1792–4. Fox was not a republican but a parliamentary reformer, a supporter of religious liberties rather than the proscription of Christianity, but his generous sympathies and his unguarded language laid him open to merciless criticism. Fox took care in 1789–92 to keep himself aloof from groups that sprang up such as the Corresponding Societies, dedicated to debating and spreading French political ideology and sponsoring comparable changes in Britain. Younger colleagues, Charles Grey (1764–1845) particularly, had no such hesitation in working to form an alliance between the aristocratic knot of Whigs in Parliament and reform opinion 'out of doors', and by 1793 had taken up the reform question for the Society of the Friends of the People. By that date, following on from Louis's execution and the outbreak of war between Britain and France on 1 February, Grey's behaviour was verging on the treasonable.

Irish 'patriots' (generally Protestants in a late eighteenth-century context) also embraced the values of the Revolution in its moderate stage, seeing in them both universal ideals to embrace in the spirit of the Enlightenment and a means of exerting pressure on the government in London to grant further constitutional concessions following the legislative independence already granted in 1782. The United Irishmen, founded simultaneously in Belfast and Dublin in 1791, started out as a debating society recruiting both Catholics and Protestants and rejoiced in the protection of Charles Fox's nephew, Lord Edward Fitzgerald (1763–98), and it was soon led by a Dublin barrister looking to make his name, Wolf Tone (1763–98). They agitated for constitutional reform, along with sister organisations such as the Defenders, a Catholic body more concerned to damage 'Protestant ascendancy' than show disinterested commitment to any universal application of the Rights of Man. The results achieved were impressive. Pitt's government was looking to create an Irish propertied elite where loyalty to the British state was not dependent on confessional membership. In 1792 and 1793, in the teeth of Protestant resentment at the highest levels, it pushed through the Dublin Parliament emancipatory legislation that took off virtually all Catholic disabilities apart from eligibility to stand or sit in the legislature. Here again the Revolution was acting as a catalyst in state (re)formation as a response to a changed international order. It is easy to overlook the tactical successes of Irish politicians inspired by the Revolution before a sizable minority of them changed their objectives to embrace the overthrow of British rule in Ireland with the assistance of revolutionary France. The United Irishmen were identified as potential fifth-columnists in wartime as they moved towards holding out the prospect of citizenship to the 'men of no property'.[9] A Government clampdown in 1792–3 ended optimism, and movements proposing major change went underground in 1795–7.

In the Habsburg Empire Leopold II in the spring of 1790 inherited his own internal revolutions in Hungary and the Netherlands and was keen to defuse them before they were complicated by pressures emanating from France. That threat could not be lightly dismissed when Paris was full of refugees from Belgium anxious for French assistance in launching an anti-Habsburg crusade. Partly because of his own sensitive diplomacy, the emperor delayed that event until after his own death almost two years later, by which time Habsburg authority across the empire had been quietly re-imposed. Leopold worked hard to introduce constitutional controls designed to reassure the enemies of the Emperor Joseph that there would be no resumption of, for instance, the arbitrary activities of Minister of Police, Pergen. For instance, he entrusted command of the police to the latter's principal critic, Sonnenfels. Leopold re-enlisted the help of the governing elite by restoring cancelled privileges and so temporarily drew the sting of French-style reformers in his dominions. Leopold wanted to attract support from among his non-privileged subjects, his son and successor Francis much less so. Ministers who thought in terms of continuing reform were removed from office by the end of 1792 and Francis expressed his satisfaction at having, in his own words, 'cleared out all the black sheep'. There were many Austrian opponents of the war with France, both on grounds of cost as well as Enlightenment ideology. By no means were all prosperous townsmen and Masonic lodge members. In Bohemia the prospect of unremitting labour services and tithe payment aroused peasant discontent. They had set much store by Joseph's agrarian reforms and had a sense of the concessions made to their counterparts in France. By the winter of

1792–3 the new emperor's armed intervention against the French Revolution had achieved nothing, the Austrian Netherlands had been lost, and Francis's only answer to the growing chorus of critics was fresh police repression and the recall of Pergen, a prelude to the anti-Jacobin Terror of 1794–5 in the empire when foreign policy reverses created an atmosphere of panic at the spread of French subversive tenets.

In his handling of policy about the impact of the Revolution in his own territory, Francis betrayed his inexperience by exaggerating the interest of his subjects in the French Revolution. Similar tendencies were on show in Spain. The ministers of Carlos IV sensed their vulnerability to revolutionary currents from the common border they shared with France. Exclusion through the Inquisition and civil agents was deemed the best policy. The government of Floridablanca tried and failed to keep news of the fall of the Bastille from the populace, the arrival of pamphlets and papers from across the Pyrenees making that impossible. On 1 January 1790 a royal order prohibited the introduction, printing or circulation of books, papers, prints, boxes, fans, folders and other objects referring to the Revolution in France and the government's jitters were not eased by a botched assassination attempt against Floridablanca on 18 June 1790 when he was walking alone in the royal palace at Aranjuez by an impecunious Frenchman long resident in Spain. By early 1791 there was a cordon of troops up against the French frontier.

The interest of the educated in the events unfolding in the northern neighbour's lands could not be erased. As Jean-François Bourgoing, French ambassador to Madrid in 1792, admitted, from the start of the Revolution the Spanish 'were very eager to get our papers and procured them in spite of all our prohibitions'.[10] Floridablanca's replacement for domestic reasons by the conde de Aranda in February 1792 ushered in a period of more relaxed controls before the September Massacres obliged the government to revert to a repressive policy in the run up to the outbreak of war between the two states in March 1793. In Italy sympathies for the Revolution in its more moderate phrase were pinched. The annexation of Avignon by the Holy See in September 1791 outraged Pius VI and the blatant anticlericalism of the revolutionaries led to anti-French demonstrations in Rome. Pro-French agitators urging revolt against lawfully ordained authorities tended to receive short shrift.

*An Authoritarian turn in Europe?*

After 1792–3, the generous libertarian spirit the Revolution had originally kindled was snuffed out as war descended on the continent and states battled for survival against a militant and militarised republican France. The titanic contest led to the appreciable growth of state power in most kingdoms through the 1790s and with this came a shift to authoritarianism that partially mirrored events in France. As before, the Revolution was setting the tune to which the rest of Europe was obliged to dance.

It compelled the articulation of competing conservative discourses capable of ready simplification, for the defenders of the status quo saw the desirability of keeping ordinary subjects loyal to the crowned heads of Europe by persuasion as much as coercion. The influence of Edmund Burke was not restricted either to the British Isles or to the English-speaking world. His *Reflections* established him almost overnight as the doyen of counter-revolutionary ideologists, a far-sighted sage or cranky Irishman (Burke was repeatedly caricatured as the Don Quixote of his times) according to choice, and he had almost prophetic status in the last three years before his death in 1797 as the extremism he had foreseen captured public notice. Burke's insights into the character of the Revolution gave him 'a remarkably acute sense of the nightmare quality of revolution, its capacity to take all of social, political and economic life to pieces and taunt a human population with the challenge to put it back together again'.[11] Burke put aside his Whiggish libertarianism in the 1790s in favour of monarchism rooted in Europe's Christian past, and he despaired that governments at war (particularly his own) saw that conflict in contingent terms rather than as a battle royal for the survival of civilisation itself. In the face of taunts from Fox, Sheridan and his other former friends among the Whigs, Burke returned to a version of 'Church and King' Toryism that suddenly gained a fresh currency. A plethora of tracts, journals and pamphlets appeared extolling the virtues of George III and his regime and designed for popular markets never before targeted by polemicists.[12] Energetic women like Hannah More and Sarah Trimmer devoted themselves to writing and producing pamphlets of a Burkite persuasion whose aim was to persuade the working poor that preserving the British constitution from French-style contamination was the highest good of everyone irrespective of social status. The pious publishers, Rivingtons, in 1791 set up *The British Critic*, to promote Anglican loyalism in the wake of Revolution. Even Robert

Burns, so pro-French hitherto, anxious to retain his appointment as an excise collector, turned his hand to an anti-French ballad in 1795, 'The Dumfries Volunteer', to inspire his local militia:

> DOES haughty Gaul invasion threat,
>    Then let the louns beware, Sir,
> There's WOODEN WALLS upon our seas,
>    And VOLUNTEERS on shore, Sir:
> The *Nith* shall run to *Corsincon*,
>    And *Criffell* sink in *Solway*,
> E'er we permit a Foreign Foe
>    On British ground to rally.[13]

Burke urged obedience to lawfully established authorities and acceptance of their divinely established status. This was the starting point for other theoreticians of the Counter-Revolution. In the face of cataclysm, humanity – and the French nation especially – must turn back to God and repent. This emphasis, for instance, was central to the Declaration of Verona, published by Louis XVIII after his succession as *de jure* king of France on the death of his nephew in 1795. It was articulated at great length throughout his lifetime by Joseph de Maistre (1753–1821), another remarkable counter-revolutionary theoretician who saw in strong monarchical government and the restraining power of Catholicism the only hope for fallen man, justly punished by the occurrence of the Revolution.[14] This was a powerful and persuasive voice but it was not the only one found within *émigré* circles in the 1790s and 1800s as recent studies of their journalism suggests. Even at the darkest moments for their cause, former *monarchiens* and other constitutionalists did not lose faith in a model of royal government resting on consensus and pooled sovereignty. The problem for those who shared the aspirations of men like Rivarol and Mallet du Pan was persuading others in exile from France to accept that there was a case for constitutionalism even if they could not accept it. Burke's writings had inspired a crusading mentality among those dispossessed and disempowered by the Revolution and they could not see any place for Whiggish checks and balances in a post-restoration France: Louis XVIII must be accorded an absolutist power more extensive than his executed brother, and the alliance of throne and altar must be adhered to uncompromisingly in a manner which conservative critics felt had not been the case before the outbreak of the Revolution.

The outbreak of the Revolutionary wars in 1792–3 killed off serious interest in state reform across Europe. As William Windham, Burke's loyal lieutenant, strong supporter of the *émigrés*, and Secretary-at-War after July 1794 put it in the Commons, no man would sensibly try to mend his roof while a gale was raging outside.[15] Windham took up office just at the time when the final loss of the Netherlands to Austria confirmed that the French Republic would not be easily defeated and dismantled, and that the threat to the identity and existence of the great powers was very real. The only answer to terror appeared (to the satisfaction of the Burkites) to be counter-terror. The Revolution thus precipitated the consolidation of the organised state through policemen, spies and the cancellation – temporary or permanent – of public liberties. In the Austrian Empire, *agents provocateurs* were used in 1794 to secure numerous arrests among disaffected intellectuals, many of them Masons or Illuminati. Although Francis resisted attempts made to set up an extraordinary tribunal for the trial of treasonable suspects with the power to impose the death penalty, Austrian and Hungarian Jacobins were still rounded up. Nine were executed in 1795 alone. Censorship was enforced and most Masonic lodges shut on the orders of Pergen and Saurau, the efficient head and deputy of the Police Ministry. Although their authoritarianism alienated large swathes of opinion, it was certainly effective. As one visitor to Vienna reported in 1802, 'In all the coffeehouses there reigns such a reverent silence that you might think high mass was being celebrated, where no one dares to breathe'.[16]

In Britain, though historians once referred to Pitt's 'Reign of Terror', the current consensus is that government, while taking up new powers on the basis of state security, were not prepared to compromise the rule of law. In May 1794 secret committees were appointed to investigate radical societies and the Habeas Corpus Act was suspended even though the treason trials at the end of the year acquitted the main suspects. Ministers greatly expanded intelligence networks and paid informers were enlisted at home and abroad including, one recent publication has argued, the disillusioned poet William Wordsworth.[17] Claude Antoine Rey, former lieutenant-general of police at Lyon established the first Anglo-French intelligence service in the French interior. He was a key member of the London *comité français*, officially recognised by government in 1793, as 'an unofficial royalist ministry in exile',[18] making information available to British ministers when required. Four espionage networks were in operation by 1795 working, with varying degrees of effectiveness, with French royalists.[19]

Maintaining public order was the main desire of government rather than policing or censoring opinion. In late 1795 ministers extended the law of treason and prohibited mass meetings unless approved by JPs. In 1799 certain named political societies were prohibited, including the London Corresponding Society and the United Irishmen, organisations identified as being a direct challenge to British security in the wake of the Irish Rebellion the previous year. Progressive opinion formers, provided they did not openly endorse seditious intent, were watched by the authorities but, on the whole, left alone. In Spain after 1791 the governments of Aranda and Godoy were reluctant to endorse the determination of the *Inquisición* to keep revolutionary literature out of the country. After France and Spain agreed peace at the Treaty of Basle in 1795 it was much harder to present anti-French sentiments as tied up with patriotism, and enlightened opinion – the *luces* – enjoyed fresh influence in public life, though often despairing of the commitment of the royal favourite, Godoy, Principe de la Paz as he was titled, to a progressive cause for its own sake rather than as a demonstration of his stranglehold on public business through his affair with Queen María Luisa. Nevertheless, Enlightenment influences survived more markedly in Spain during the 1790s than in any other European state, and were the harbinger of nineteenth-century liberalism.

One of the reasons behind the growth of state power in Spain and elsewhere was because the Revolutionary Wars obliged the enemies of France to increase their armies and navies and raise the capital required to finance this manpower. The diplomacy of forming and maintaining Coalition forces became bound up with hard bargaining over funds. Voluntary contributions to the war effort, such as those solicited from his subjects across the empire by the young Francis II in 1793, stimulated patriotism but they were seldom enough to satiate the appetite of the military machine. Of course, Coalition powers did not have the option open to the armies of the *Grande nation*, of levying taxes on conquered peoples and sequestrating all their best assets for France. Raising tax revenues could be hazardous. In Spain, during 1794–5, interest-bearing government notes called *vales* circulated widely. When combined with the wartime shortage of commodities, they stoked up prices across the kingdom at a rate of between 10 per cent and 20 per cent. Although no *vales* were issued between 1795 and 1799, their exchange rate fell steadily after Spain switched sides in October 1796 and allied with the Directory against Britain. By mid-1800 they were estimated as worth less than 75 per cent of their face value. The possibility of royal solvency was thrown into doubt and increased the ill will felt towards successive governments and an unpopular war against Britain still further. At least Spain did not resort to borrowing abroad between 1793 and 1795. The other power that dropped out of the war in 1795, Prussia, did, borrowing from Britain in 1793 to put a smaller army into the field than Spain did the same year for less. Only Austria fought on after the Peace of Basle and after having extracted a vast amount of additional cash subsidy from Pitt and Grenville.

Britain under Pitt and Addington acted as the financial milch-cow of the First, Second and Third Coalitions against revolutionary and Napoleonic France.[20] That she could bear financial burdens impossible to other states was predictable given the century-long existence of a fiscal-military state, principally the Bank of England, the sinking fund, and a mature tradition of state credit finance. London was the world's capital market in the 1790s and Pitt's administration was locked into City business at many levels. That was just as well given the burden of costs that could fluctuate widely. Thus in 1799, the year in which the Second Coalition was formed, Britain paid out over £3 million in subsidising and paying for Coalition troops engaged in the Low Countries, on the Rhine and in Italy. This was in addition to Britain paying for her own armed forces. The parliamentary grant required for the Royal Navy rose from nearly £2 million annually in the last year of peace (1792) to a steady £13–£14 million annually between 1798 and 1802. The exactions of the French war at times came close to wrecking the British state. Perhaps the most perilous time was the Bank crisis of February 1797 and the temporary suspension of cash payments by the Bank of England. After dealing with the immediate crisis, Pitt brought in a fundamental change in the pattern of direct taxation – an income tax, first proposed in his Finance Bill of November 1797 and enacted the following year.

This came after the failure of peace negotiations at Lille and the much harder-line stance of the Second Directory towards a compromise settlement with Britain. Both nations entrenched themselves for a perpetuation of the bruising struggle and at the close of the 1790s used every device of xenophobic denunciation and derision at their disposal. John Bull stirred in defence of throne and altar and the war of ideas attained new levels of biting humour mixed with vitriol. 1798, 1799 and 1800 were the heyday of the *Anti-Jacobin*, the most brilliant British periodical of its day, staffed by dedicated counter-revolutionaries, whose ridicule of the Directory, its politicians and personalities gained the journal an international readership. Its appearance coincided with a serious invasion threat of the British mainland and a full-scale rebellion in Ireland in 1798 in which about 30,000 perished. The United Irishmen had been suppressed after the extent of its treasonable contacts came to light during the trial of the French agent, the Reverand William Jackson, but they still posed a major security risk to British control of Ireland even when driven underground.[21] Their hope had been that an Irish rising would coincide with a landing of French troops. No less than five French naval expeditions were despatched to Ireland between 1796–8 with many arms, the most serious a force of 15,000 troops under the command of Hoche and Tone which reached Bantry Bay in December 1797 only to find that storm-force conditions made it impossible to disembark the troops.[22] The remnants had returned to France when the 1798 Rebellion started and was ruthlessly suppressed by the British Crown.

By the late 1790s, the French revolutionaries had long discarded their generous fraternal overtures to their European neighbours in the face of hostility and indifference to the regicide republic and its armies. Between 1789 and 1793 the attitude of the revolutionaries towards foreigners had been generous, but it had been constructed on a fundamental misunderstanding: that the average Briton, Spaniard or Italian was keen to have his own version of the Revolution at the earliest opportunity, desperate for liberation. The coming of the war soon gave the lie to that delusion. The decree of fraternity was cancelled only five months after its passing and in September 1793 the Convention decreed that French armies would renounce 'philanthropic' ideas in favour of conquest and exploitation. The nearest friend France had left in a foreign power in 1793 was Poland, where opinion was divided on the September Massacres. Some were indignant that France had fallen into anarchy, others saluted the bravery of the French to cast off a dishonest king and called on their countrymen to do likewise to Stanislas Poniatowski. Mourning was proclaimed at Warsaw on the execution of Louis XVI: each resident Frenchman was required to take the oath of loyalty to his son. However, by the time of the national uprising of March–November 1794 (when the country's survival against Russian expansionism appeared at stake), emissaries were sent to Paris, republican France appeared an ally, and the Marseillaise was chanted in the streets along with a Polish version of the *Ca ira*.[23]

The situation in eastern Europe barely impinged on French domestic policy makers. Under the Law of Suspects (also September 1793) foreigners were deemed prisoners subject to the authority of the mayor and forbidden to leave the *commune* in which they were domiciled. The cosmopolitanism of the revolution in its four years was ending abruptly; 'strangers' could readily be presented as spies and *comités de surveillance* were set up in every *commune* to vet suspects and issue *certificats de civisme*. Robespierre worried about what would happen 'if we pass for imbeciles in Europe', but one deputy (Drouet, in debate on 5 September 1793) thereupon commented, 'What need do we have of a good reputation in Europe?' Among those who died in the Terror were many unwanted foreigners, one-time allies of the Girondins, including Anacharsis Cloots. He could still shout 'Hurrah for the fraternity of nations! Long live the Republic of the world!' on the scaffold on 24 March 1794'.[24] Anti-British bile was uncontainable. One Lille Jacobin wished that wolves could be set loose in Britain once again. Prime Minister Pitt was singled out as the villain behind all manifestations of anti-French statecraft. He was the 'enemy of the human race'. On 29 May 1794 Barère had denounced Britain in the Convention as the Carthage which was the obstacle to France's New Rome and which, like Carthage, must be reformed. 'National hatred must sound forth', he trumpeted, 'Young republicans should suck a hatred of the name Englishman with their mother's milk.' The English were to be exterminated along with their Hanoverian allies and his proposition that no prisoners should be taken alive was adopted without dissent in the Convention on 26 May 1794.[25]

This was a propaganda gift to France's enemies. The coalitions arrayed against France in 1794 and 1799 never lost a chance of playing up the cultural gulf between themselves and the *Grande nation*, though it was too hazardous for most monarchies to encourage the identification of their subjects with any emerging sense of national self-determination. The emphasis was on loyalty to the existing royal order, the social security that the status quo guaranteed, and the need to protect local rights and privileges from French destructiveness. And, it must be said, these were the values which meant the most to the average European in the revolutionary decade. Loyalist addresses and anti-French declamations were the response to the security threat posed across Europe by the French nation-in-arms. The invasion of Franconia by Jourdan's troops in 1796 produced a series of brochures directed against the disasters they brought in their train, aimed at a rural population far from seeing them as liberators from a feudal yoke.

Any man of property felt obliged to wish death to the French and enlist in a militia regiment – or at least encourage his neighbours and tenants to do so. The republicanism of the French was bad enough, it was their irreligion which really outraged the rural populations of the continent, particularly those who had experienced the desecration of churches, the wanton disrespect for sacred objects, and the militant anticlericalism of the Revolutionary Armies, sometimes held in check by their commanding officers but always latent among the troops. The French revolutionary armies crossed the German frontier in 1792–3 with a reputation for blasphemy and iconoclasm which events confirmed. Atrocity stories disgusted local inhabitants and stiffened resistance to this foreign invasion and cultural violation. The Catholic regular clergy were generally in the vanguard of those sounding the alarm. A Franciscan preacher from the Lower Inn valley warned in 1794 that the 'Fatherland', 'our dear Tyrol', was in grave danger from 'the unholy enemies of the state and religion'.[26] This was the country that, after all, had taken over the Papal States, proclaimed the Roman Republic and sent Pius VI packing to die in exile. No one liked having a marauding, conquering foreign army in their vicinity, but when these troops advanced bent on inflicting their values on the populations in their way, then resistance was inevitable, and gave many of the armed clashes of the 1790s between peasant forces and French regulars a savagery which in many ways anticipated that of the Peninsula War after 1808.

*Conclusion*

The impact of the Revolution was almost as momentous outside as inside France. Ideologically, militarily, dynastically, the old Europe was confronted at every level and challenged either to accept the new France (and preferably to ally with her) or to defend every inch of territory against her armed forces and against their Jacobin allies, to be found in virtually every European city acting as apostles and agents of the Republic. At the dawn of the nineteenth century in 1801 the European political order had changed beyond recognition: the map of Italy had been redrawn to include the extinction of the historic Republic of Venice, France had advanced her frontiers north into the Netherlands and east to the Rhine, and the Treaty of Rasdatt in 1798

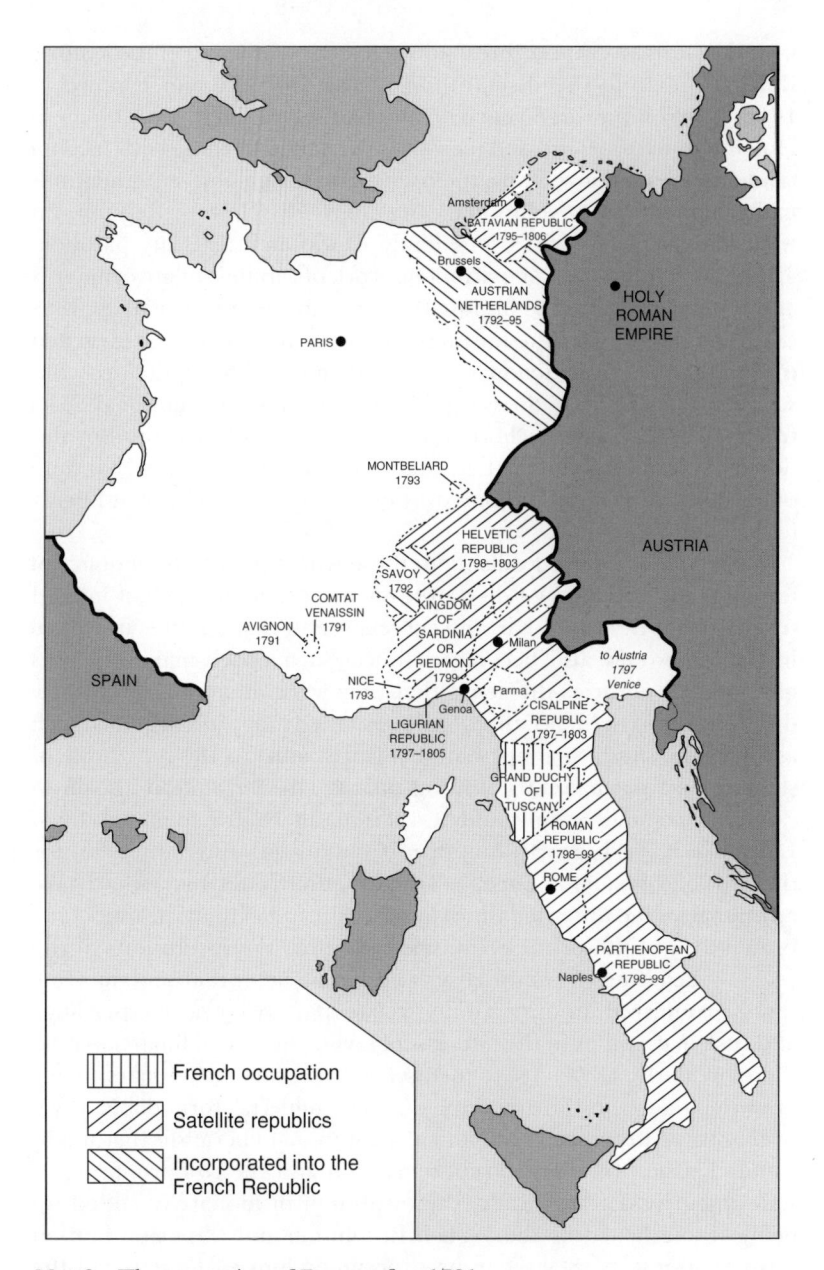

*Map 2* The expansion of France after 1791
*Source*: Adapted from J. F. Bosher, *The French Revolution: A New Interpretation* (London, 1989), 197.

with the German princes foreshadowed the remodelling of the historic Reich to include the dismantling of the Holy Roman Empire in 1806. The conquering French armies had set up satellite republics in Holland, the Rhineland and most of Italy, staffed by those with Jacobin tendencies eager to delude themselves that the subject populations had an appetite for revolutionary freedoms. The Helvetic Republic (in what had been the Swiss Confederation) was an interesting paradox. The French destroyed an existing network of republican governments and instead attempted to impose their own forms and structures, thus causing a debate over the meaning of liberty and freedom. It rescued the population from feudal claims and imposed a republican constitution that the 'free' Swiss rejected in the name of traditional Swiss freedoms. Here, as elsewhere, there was every sign that the Revolutionary Wars had given birth to French cultural imperialism, handing out a superior version of liberty other Europeans were not at liberty to decline.

What comforts were available to those who deplored the politics of their age? When Pius VI died in French captivity in 1799, it looked to many that he would have no successor and that another universal institution would also become defunct. Such epoch-making events gave contemporaries the sense that they were inhabiting an utterly different world to their fathers and persuaded many intellectuals, such as Chateaubriand, to adopt Catholic Christianity as the only hope of stability in a permanently shifting order. The Revolution also indicated that republicanism could be a serious alternative to monarchy in Europe as it was in North America. It was an alarming intimation for the crowned heads of Europe. On the other hand they could take advantage of the unsettled times to shore up and extend the autocratic pretensions of the princely houses; reshaping the institutions of the realm – including the boundaries and the name of that state in some cases – conferred an opportunity to sweep away corporate privilege and customary rights in the interests of saving the state. Monarchs could therefore derive advantage to themselves from the revolutionary threat knowing that, for the majority of their subjects, formidable royal prerogatives were preferable to a constitutional liberalism that might simply be the prelude to French invasion and the compromising of state integrity. Paradoxically, the institution of monarchy ended up being strengthened by the French Revolution and Napoleon himself was to adopt it in 1804 when he proclaimed himself Emperor of the

French. The effect of the Revolution was such that by 1799, around the time of the formation of the Consulate, both conservatives and republicans were looking for authoritarian solutions to the problems of disorder and instability unleashed by the Revolution. Liberty had been tried, its effects stood revealed, and men of property across Europe, whether citizens or subjects, wanted done with it in the interests of a more settled and secure existence.

# Chapter 11: The French Diaspora and the Wider World

*Introduction*

French expansionism between 1792 and 1804 brought her armies into many areas of central and southern Europe, part of those 'magnifications of public space' which historians currently see as triggered by the Revolution.[1] With conquest and control, there naturally came pride in the capacities of the *Grand nation* as well as its distinctive republican culture and rapidly accumulated heritage. In defining themselves against the disintegrating world(s) of the *ancien régime*, the revolutionaries were also defying that world and creating an alternative. By the close of the Consulate, the Revolution had thus completed the task of building a sense of national pride that could operate without any necessary reference back to the distinctive character of the state but, where polity and pride were tied in, created a patriotic momentum of formidable force.

The armies of the Republic between 1792 and 1804 exhibited French international power wherever they appeared, be it in Europe, Egypt or the West Indies. They were not in any sense the only manifestation of Frenchness, for many of those living in France when the Revolution came in 1789 left it year by year, the numbers reaching a peak in 1791–2. This was the emigration, that movement abroad of a small but exceptionally influential section of the population who could not come to terms with the Revolution and the massive changes it had set in chain. Most scholars would set the total number of those leaving at about 130,000, about one per cent of the total population. These people created a large French diaspora in the 1790s that existed as a counter-cultural alternative to what France had so suddenly and notoriously become: a militarised republic that had rejected Catholic Christianity. This other version of Frenchness helped maintain community identity while abroad and, by its presence alone, tended to create sympathy for the refugees. The reason for their presence was not hard to explain and it could be considered a warning of what would happen to elites across the continent and in Britain if the French armies were not stopped. Some had only just managed to leave France in time. Lally-Tollendal had narrowly escaped death in the September Massacres and his nerves, like many other *émigrés*, were shattered. As one of his British friends reported, 'Poor Lally has been here and he seems better than when he left us except being somewhat subject to start when the Door opens...'.[2] Too few in number to be a threat to the dominant cultures of the host states, too many not to constitute an interesting, sometimes exotic and occasionally forceful new presence, the *émigrés* helped define the attitude of other Europeans to the Revolution as much the Revolutionary armies did.[3] Even where there was no French diaspora or military presence, as in the Americas, the Revolution could not be ignored. Individuals were inspired or infuriated by its coming, and found their lives unimaginably changed. The revolutionaries were ready to sacrifice themselves if that sacrifice would help protect and extend what they perceived as its gifts of liberty and equality, while a comparable number perished in defence of older traditions and state systems trying to stem this revolutionary contagion. The blood chilling words of the 'Marseillaise' were anathema to them, an inspiration to those who believed passionately in 'French values' 1790s-style and looked on them as personally liberating, none more so than the slaves of the French West Indian islands who saw the events of 1789 as delivering them from bondage. That was precisely the opposite perspective to those members of the social elite in France who voted with their feet and left.

*A France Beyond the Frontiers: the* Émigrés *and Their Varied Worlds*

Most subjects of Louis XVI kept faith with the Revolution until well into 1791 and they displayed it by remaining on French soil. After the passing of the Civil Constitution and the abortive flight to Varennes, the emigration began in earnest and peaked before the start of war with Austria and Prussia in April 1792. It is one of the great myths of the emigration that the nobility and the clergy made up the majority. They did not.

According to Donald Greer's figures in *The Incidence of the Emigration During the French Revolution* (Cambridge, MA., 1951) – which are still taken to be authoritative – those two categories together made up just 42 per cent of those abandoning France. Initially, the emigration tended to be limited to those noblemen and their families who could afford to quit their estates and still contrive to live comfortably (albeit *less* comfortably than they were used to) in another state. The king's youngest brother Artois, and his kinsmen, Condé, his son Bourbon and his grandson d'Enghien, and the prince de Conti, left after the fall of the Bastille, leaving the rump of the royal family to linger for almost two further years, including Monsieur and his wife and the king's two spinster aunts, Madames Victoire and Adelaide. They went to Brussels and Rome respectively, the latter an early centre for exiles to meet and exchange their hard-luck stories, unsurprisingly so in the light of the papacy's inflexible attitude to the Revolution, a position confirmed in Pius VI's decrees of March and April 1791 condemning the Civil Constitution of the Clergy. The bulk of the noble exodus was in 1790–1, bringing their total number to approximately 16,000 or about 17 per cent of the whole. D'Aligre, first president of the *parlement* of Paris, managed to bring most of his fortune to Richmond, Surrey, with him; Poincaré, first president of the Rouen parlement, arrived in London with virtually nothing in August 1791.[4] As regards the former First Estate, few prelates left France in the year 1789, Grimaldi of Noyon, Juigné of Paris, d'Agoult de Bonneval, among the exceptions. Their very public refusal to take the oath to the Civil Constitution created a major exodus in the spring of 1791, and they were followed (especially after the law of August 1792 ordered all refractory clergy to leave France within a fortnight or face deportation) by thousands of the parish clergy who tended to move to the foreign state nearest their diocese; thus Normans went to England and the Channel Islands, Gascons to Spain, and Provencals to Nice and Savoy. About 24,000 of the *émigrés* belonged to the clergy according to Greer's figures, perhaps a quarter of the total overall. Much is known about the nobles and clergy, far less about the majority of the *émigrés*, those who were categorisable as Third Estate members according to the discarded classification. These were professional men or clerks making up 17 per cent, artisans 14 per cent, small farmers and day labourers 20 per cent. These are remarkable and significant indicators and yet in the half-century since Greer wrote, research on non-elite exiles has been insignificant and it remains one of the most glaring inadequacies in scholarship on the Revolution. The assumption remains that, in most cases, women left France with their husbands. Writing tends to focus on well-born females such as Mme de la Tour du Pin or Necker's daughter, Mme de Staël, rather than humbler female emigrants and we are simply ignorant of the extent to which a decision to emigrate or not created tensions within family circles or led to the head of the household going abroad, while his partner and perhaps his children for a variety of reasons opted not to go. There were also the political undesirables, those who lost out when a regime fell and opted to flee abroad rather than face death or imprisonment inside France. No study exists of this malleable grouping, those who could anticipate one of the loneliest and most fearful of exiles wherever they ended up.

Until these gaps are filled generalisations about the nature of the *émigré* experience are going to be suspect. One point can be insisted on: its sheer variety depended on place and individual. Wherever they resided the *émigrés* had to learn to get on with each other, as propinquity brought together those who might never otherwise have met. In these makeshift communities, it was rare for there to be much like-mindedness. The little *émigré* colony in rural Surrey at Jupiter Hill orbiting around Talleyrand and Mme de Staël was a notable exception. Some of the nobility found compensation by enlisting in Condé's Army of the Princes or competing with each other in intrigues to gain the ear of either Louis XVIII or his younger brother. In Britain, politically committed royalists gravitating towards Burke's circle tried to influence the making of Cabinet policy even where they might not have access to sympathetic ministers like Lord Grenville, the Foreign Secretary, or William Windham, the Secretary-at-War. Archbishop Boisgelin, for instance, bombarded his host, Henry Herbert, 1st earl of Carnarvon, a Portland Whig, with his prescriptions hoping that some of it would percolate down to ministers. The confidence extended to the moderate royalist, the comte de Puisaye, by Pitt's administration in planning the ill-fated Quiberon Bay expedition, was exceptional and was not repeated after 1795. The less ambitious counteracted boredom with writing of every sort, often trying to assess how revolution had befallen France or offering manifestos for a counter-revolutionary settlement. François de Chateaubriand in 1797 produced his *Essai historique, polique et moral sur les Révolutions anciennes et modernes considérés dans leur rapport avec la Révolution française*. It was a remarkably detached book, untypical of its kind, with Chateaubriand half-heartedly leaning towards a kind of constitutional monarchy as the best sort of settlement for which France could hope, and finding himself disowned by other members of his family. Two other major authors, Louis de Bonald and Joseph de Maistre, also wrote extensively in exile, though gravitating towards more uncompromising forms of monarchical and religious authority than anything Chateaubriand had advocated.

Like many *émigrés*, Chateaubriand had taught French to make both money and friends among his English hosts. It was a common resort, one that attracted customers out of the sheer novelty of working with an aristocratic tutor, and an immediately obvious means to hand for impecunious noblemen to have some money to live on. Even the new duc d'Orléans, Louis-Philippe, had a spell as a jobbing English tutor. There were actually far more threadbare priests than aristocrats desperate for ready cash in this way and with the genuine pedagogic skills to attract serious clients, once the latter had overcome any lingering doubts about popish insinuations. It was yet another way of keeping at a distance the unsettling emotions attendant upon exile: boredom, nostalgia and recrimination. So was catching up with one's reading. In London's Soho, *émigré* bookshops did good business. Dulau's, run by a former Benedictine monk on Wardour Street, was a large shop where browsers and loiterers congregated and gossiped. As the improbability of counter-revolutionary success without massive allied assistance sunk in, so the mutual recriminations and dissensions among the excluded mounted as the temptation to blame each other for their plight became irresistible. Quarrelling was common. The political divisions within the elite that had featured before the Revolution were only exacerbated by the destruction of the *ancien régime* and the battles of the 1780s among each other were refought in the 1790s, partly as a means of evolving a policy that would unite the counter-revolutionary movement. Observers were frequently struck by the selfish preoccupation of the exiles with their private interests rather than any disinterested bid to restore Louis XVI. In the autumn of 1791 (just when divisions became apparent within the royal family between the king and his younger brothers who claimed, quite unjustifiably, to be acting in Louis's name) the British *chargé* in Brussels trenchantly asked what had their quitting France actually achieved? He concluded:

> the worst thing for their own cause the French aristocracy ever did, was leaving their own country, and every reflecting person, even amongst themselves, is of the same opinion.[5]

Some of the more realistic among them never imagined that a return to the status quo was going to be straightforward. Bouillé spelt this out bluntly in advice for the princes at Coblenz in spring 1792. In his *Note sur les affaires de France* he observed that with half the country attached to the new constitution: 'If anyone believes they can re-establish the old order of things...they are deceiving themselves.' He had an uncompromising message for the first two Orders that a high proportion of them did not want to hear:

> Sacrifices have become necessary if they wish to recover and conserve not only their distinctive existence, but that of the kingdom.[6]

General Dumouriez, from the safety of exile in Britain, was even more forthright about the *émigrés'* ostrich-like qualities:

> the country is more different from the France of 1788, than from Gaul in Julius Caesar's time; that it even changes every six months; and that, unfortunately, the Jacobins have been more prudential in the gradation of their crimes than the emigrants, who, without giving themselves the trouble to examine the progress of the national genius, build all their schemes on the state of France at the point of time that they left it.[7]

The degree to which Louis XVI's younger brothers could come to terms with this new order of things in a bid to recover the throne remained to be seen. Their leadership qualities were under scrutiny on all sides and the deficiencies were plain. The leading churchman, Archbishop Boisgelin of Aix, told his influential contacts close to the British government that the princes must show themselves in France – Artois to the north, Monsieur to the Midi, possibly Toulon – and set up institutions in which their authority could be displayed. These should include a council of regency in which the different orders would be represented.[8] Nothing much happened as the princes waited on events rather than trying to set an inspiring example and lead the Counter-Revolution. Louis XVIII got as far as commissioning Prince Louis de la Trémoille in early 1797 to go to Paris and set up a royalist council, one that imploded after Fructidor crippled the royalist underground.[9] The once dashing Artois was also a disappointment. Puisaye and some of his London friends tried to goad Monsieur into action by signing an open letter to the prince in December 1797 urging him to put himself at the head of an insurrection. Artois turned down the request on the grounds that it would only lead to further bloodshed. A disillusioned Puisaye soon afterwards abandoned London in disgust and headed for Canada.

After the early hopes of a swift return in 1793–4 faded, most *émigrés* successfully created for themselves the kind of routines which dulled the disappointments and disenchantments the Revolution had brought in its wake including, for many, the necessity of fleeing France to be sure of their lives. The extensive francophone press beyond France variously raised their hopes and fears as regimes came and went in Paris, but it was not until after the amnesties offered from 1799 onwards by the Consulate that any of them were able to return home to a very different France from the one they had left. Even if most *émigrés* had no wish to serve Bonaparte (the possibility that he might be a stalking horse for Louis XVIII took a long time to be dispelled), they could at least retrieve whatever remained of their ancestral patrimony. The minority staying behind tended to have objections in principle to one or more consular policies, notably those bishops who found the terms of the 1801 Concordat an insult to their Gallican principles (especially the stipulation that they resign their see into the hands of the pope) and refused to kow-tow.

There were no serious or sustained attempts during the 1790s at integration with host states whose governments were generally determined to keep the French diaspora at a convenient distance so as to preclude unwanted interference in decisions of state. The one exception was Sweden whose eccentric sovereign, the unstable and ineffective Gustavus III (assassinated 1792), was openly sympathetic to the plight of the French royal family and the royalist exiles. It helped that Marie-Antoinette's lover, Fersen, was a Swede and with ready access to the court in Stockholm. Elsewhere, politically minded exiles could only lobby indirectly, hoping that foreign friends in high places would speak up for them. Nationality, language and religion could both set the *émigrés* apart. Suspicion that apparently counter-revolutionary guests could be double agents or, against their better judgment, continue to be well disposed to French national interests, possibly even to the Revolution itself, were commonplace. Desperately trying to ensure the return to loyalty of the Austrian Netherlands, Joseph II saw the French exiles as making a bad situation worse and had them ejected before his death in early 1790. In order to guard against Jacobin contamination, with the *émigrés* acting as unwitting carriers when they were allowed in at all, most governments coerced or encouraged the exiles to remain together. In Spain, under a royal decree of 20 July 1791, French refugees granted permission to cross the frontier (which in practice meant confinement to the provinces bordering the Pyrenees) were required to swear obedience to the king and laws of Spain and not to talk about political events in France. Governments did not want to hazard lightly the impact of such tidings on their own populace.

In England, security concerns prompted the passing of the Aliens Act 1793, intended to control the movement of foreigners on British soil. It appreciably increased the bureaucratic requirements imposed on the French exiles. Pitt's ministry concentrated most of the *émigré* clergy in Winchester at the King's House. British anxieties about the large refractory clergy presence in the south of England reflected the awkwardness of having numerous Catholic priests living off the charity of a people not normally well disposed to 'popery'. All classes of the population had raised large sums for John Wilmot MP's Emigrants' Relief Committee in 1792–3; but two years into the presence in Britain of a large exile community the strains were beginning to show. No fewer than 31 bishops had come to live in London, often supported by members of their diocesan administration such as vicars general, canons and university professors.[10] Despite repeated injunctions by the unofficial leader of the Gallican clergy in London, Jean-François de la Marche, bishop of St Pol-de-Léon, for all priests to hold themselves apart from the national life of their host country, popular dislike of a foreign Catholic presence threatened to spill over into the kind of public order disturbances that Pitt's government dreaded. It was avoided thanks to constructive mutual co-operation. There were also anxieties in the English Catholic hierarchy that having French clergy on English soil might undo the gradual progress towards Catholic toleration at home (the last Act had been passed as recently as 1791) as well as possibly compromising their own jurisdictional claims. Once again, the bishop of Léon's constructive but insistent commands to French clergy in England and his good working relationship with John Douglass, Vicar Apostolic of the London District, ensured that tensions were kept to a minimum. This was not just a feature of Protestant states.

In Spain, where over 6000 clergymen had crossed the frontier by April 1793, restrictions were marked and carefully monitored. French priests could only live in religious houses, must keep out of Madrid and the provincial capitals, and were banned from preaching and teaching.[11] The relations between elite exiles and their host counterparts were usually aimiable despite political divergences. In Britain, they had the unceasing and energetic support of Edmund Burke, whose efforts were instrumental in establishing a school at Penn in Buckinghamshire to educate and train up to arms the sons of French royalist officers, in the first instance, those who had died in the Quiberon Bay expedition. But by the late 1790s *émigré* aristocratic style was much diminished, few were immune from cash-flow problems and homesickness exacerbated mutual jealousies.

No wonder that so many of them took advantage of the First Consul's amnesty and left so that, by contrast with the 1790s, the 1800s were a decade in which talk of a French counter-revolutionary diaspora exaggerates the numbers involved. For the majority of counter-revolutionaries Bonaparte's capacity for delivering order to France was a blessing that outweighed what remained of any obligations still owed to the Bourbons. Even a figure like the baron de Breteuil, ex-minister of the maison du roi (1783–8), the man to whom Louis XVI had secretly entrusted quasi-royal powers in 1791 in his dealings with the crowned heads of Europe, could not resist the siren call of home in those circumstances, still bitter over the way in which the late king's brothers had refused to acknowledge his status in 1791–3.

For a time after the Civil Constitution and the regicide, the hostility of the exiles to the Revolution and all its works ran very deep. The idea of compromising with it was anathema until at least 1794–5 when the hopes engendered by the fall of Robespierre were offset by the realisation that the defeat of the allies at Fleurus on 25 June had major military repercussions, an insight that Quiberon Bay a year later only served to confirm. As French armies fanned into north-eastern Europe annexing Belgium, occupying Holland, crossing the Rhine and the Alps, the places which had been apparently safe havens in the early 1790s ceased to be so. *Émigrés* were often just one step ahead of the Revolutionary Armies, having to keep on the move while doing their best as they travelled to win over politicians and opinion formers to the justice of their cause.

Having at first welcomed the defeat of French armies in the expectation that it would entail their own fast return, it became morally less acceptable to salute setbacks to French arms. They were caught in a double-bind: a French victory weakened the Counter-Revolution, a French defeat too publicly saluted weakened their cause with the uncommitted because it showed the *Émigrés* in an unpatriotic light. It was one of the contributory causes of terminating the Counter-Revolution in the early 1800s. Napoleon talked about ending the Revolution once he was established in office as First Consul, but he was aware that he must do the same with its opposite and, for a time at least, he succeeded. The *émigrés* packed up and left in their thousands, taking with them the searing and humiliating experience of living involuntarily abroad. It was on individual French men and women that the lasting effects of the diaspora endured, whereas in their host countries their presence was generally forgotten as the great powers tussled with the Napoleonic Empire for dominance of the continent.

## The French Revolution in the Atlantic World

If, for a time in the early 1790s, the Revolution had been an unsettling cultural offering to Europe, that was scarcely less the case in the further flung world. France's colonies, those that had survived in her ownership after the losses incurred in the Seven Years War, could hardly not be affected by events in the mother country. Would the slaves who worked on the plantations in the West Indies be deemed to possess the natural rights enunciated in the Declaration of the Rights of Man, or would they be doomed to continue as excluded beasts of burden? The question was insistent but not clear-cut. Slaves were, after all, legally chattels, the property of their owners, and property was fundamental to the Constitution eventually completed in 1791. Liberty might in principle be as desirable in the French West Indies as anywhere else but was it feasible? Liberty, equality, and fraternity would have less to do with shaping actions than external factors such as slave rebellions and relations with Britain.

In 1789 the French West Indies were packed with 675,000 slaves, generating two-thirds of the nation's trade, and producing approximately half the total of the world's sugar and coffee. The jewel in the crown was San Domingo (the western half of modern Haiti), home to 40,000 Frenchmen (mainly, but not exclusively plantation owners) and approximately the same number of those of mixed race (mulattos) plus half a million blacks, mostly slaves though with an increasing number of those who had secured manumission. The 8000 plantations on Saint Domingue made it perhaps the wealthiest colony in the world. If these slaves were released from bondage because of the Revolution, then the whole economy of the islands would be jeopardised and the wealth of those trading cities on France's Atlantic seaboard that had grown fat on the slave trade – Nantes particularly – would abruptly dry up. This was the argument put to the National Assembly in 1789 by the planters who represented the West Indian sugar islands. Deputies listened sympathetically at the same time as they heard the moral abjurations of the *Société des Amis des Noirs*, a powerful lobbying group set up a few years previously around the influential journalist and future Girondin leader, Brissot de Warville. They argued fervently that slavery was inconsistent with human dignity and each man's moral worth. Brissot in February 1790 attacked the 'commercial spirit' that made slavery an exception to French liberty: 'Liberty for us, chains for others'.[12] Its survival was inconsistent with the first principles of the Revolution and it must go. Interestingly, no Jacobin club corresponded with the *Amis des Noirs* until 1791. Brissot may have been consistently interested in slavery, but other revolutionary leaders such as Marat and Robespierre were publicly unconcerned.[13]

The majority of deputies in the National Assembly were initially ultra cautious and preferred to skate over the subject of slavery or use terms like 'colonial property' and 'colonial trade' as euphemisms:[14] the priority was preserving French West Indian colonies from seizure by the British and keeping the trade routes open with metropolitan France. All it granted in May 1791 was a stipulation that coloured children born of free parents were to have equality with whites (a minute percentage of the non-white, non-slave population), and that concession was in part a panic reaction to an insurrection by mulattos at Port-au-Prince. Between 1789 and 1791 disorder in San Domingo had grown steadily as the slaves lost patience with the Revolution's failure to do much for them while their anxious white owners moved closer to embracing the counter-revolutionary cause. By the summer of 1791 the Constituent Assembly had still not ended slavery outside France and their, perhaps surprising, temperateness in the cause had induced the negroes to give up hope and begin a bloody uprising in August involving 100,000 slaves in San Domingo. The colony was dominated by young men in their twenties, most of them born in Africa. In the 1791 uprising some preferred to wear the royalist white cockade because the tricolour symbolised freedom for whites only.[15] For their part, the planters blamed insurrection on the Revolution. The Legislative Assembly in April 1792 at last conceded citizenship to free blacks and mulattos (those adjudged duly qualified) to the fury of the plantation owners to whom that was a step too far. This was the situation when France went to war in 1793 with Spain and Britain, and the West Indies became a cockpit of bloody and chaotic violence lasting several years and costing scores of thousands of lives in what was both a race war and a civil war. Early that year, planters from San Domingo and the Windward Islands asked the British government to send forces to their islands. Thanks to the backing of Pitt's key lieutenant, Henry Dundas, the Cabinet agreed.

To win round the blacks the Convention granted them full citizenship and turned most of their white slave owners into uncompromising royalists bent on resuming control of their estates and their slaves. Slave emancipation had been unofficially proclaimed by French forces in San Domingo on 29 August 1793 as a means of giving the blacks no incentive to join the British expedition heading for the island. The following year (4 February 1794) the Convention abolished slavery throughout the French colonies. Abolition was approved by the Jacobins for policy reasons and it was celebrated in the Temple of Reason, formerly known as Notre-Dame cathedral.[16] Six months later, British forces under Sir George Grey took Port-au-Prince in time to celebrate George III's birthday. However, the emancipation decree coincided with the emergence of Toussaint l'Ouverture as a powerful and constructive black leader, keen on ending the civil war and restoring order to the island. His alliance of convenience with the Republic combined with an outbreak of yellow fever that devastated the British expedition and weakened its grip on the ex-French islands. As death approached the patient would throw up large quantities of digested blood, the notorious 'black vomit'. Drink offered the only way out for officers and men on these expeditions, and contributed to the high mortality rates. More alarmingly still for London, the West Indian-born Jacobin, Victor Hugues (the 'colonial Robespierre'), sent out agents to foment revolutionary sympathies among slaves in Britain's own colonies. The Maroon War erupted in Jamaica in July 1795, and it was not until the delayed arrival of Sir David Dundas's expedition in 1796 that British control *in her own colonies* was reasserted.[17] San Domingo was divided between black forces under Toussaint L'Ouverture and mulattos under André Rigaud, who was defeated by Toussaint in 1800. The latter ran San Domingo, which remained nominally French, as his personal fiefdom. He even denied access to the main harbours on the island to French vessels. Nevertheless, Jacobin influences were present in Haiti, including revolutionary courts of justice and the redistribution of white property in the name of Liberty, Equality and Fraternity.[18]

This was to change after 1799. Bonaparte envied and admired l'Ouverture's charismatic efficiency at the same time as he determined to overthrow him. The excesses of liberty were as unacceptable to the Consulate in France as they were in the West Indies and once secure of his authority at home, Bonaparte lost no time in attempting to bring down one whose career and capacities bore resemblances to his own. First came some flattering blandishments: Napoleon in March 1801 appointed Toussaint captain-general of the colony, in effect third in command after the Minister of Marine and the First Consul. This was the end of accommodation. Once the undeclared naval war with the United States was over, peace with Britain and Louisiana ceded,

Bonaparte briefly thought in terms of a restored French Empire including the Floridas, Louisiana, French Guiana and the French West Indies – where slavery would be reinstated (the Treaty of Amiens restored all her conquered islands to France except for Trinidad). A French army was despatched in December 1801 in a huge fleet of 32 men-of-war to San Domingo. The French expedition sailed with the blessing of the Addington government in London. It failed to accomplish its mission. Bonaparte's brother-in-law, General Charles Leclerc, was sucked into a costly guerilla war. After one artillery barrage of a fort the black defenders began singing French revolutionary patriotic songs causing the French troops to doubt their own purpose:

> Our soldiers looked at each other questionably; they seemed to say: 'Are you our barbaric enemies? Are now we the only soldiers of the Republic? Have we become servile political instruments?'[19]

Fighting on the island attained a new ferocity and although l'Ouverture was kidnapped and whites returned to reclaim their properties, the French could not enforce their authority, especially after war with Britain was renewed in May 1803. Leclerc's successor, Rochambeau, was bent on killing the blacks rather than disarming them. Thousands of prisoners were deliberately drowned, killer hunting dogs were brought over from Cuba, and most of the coastal towns fell to the French army which, however, had its food supplies cut off by the British fleet. Hemmed in at Le Cap, Rochambeau had to arrange a truce with the British for safe transport of his men to Jamaica.[20] He signed another truce with Toussaint's successor, Jacques Dessalines, and evacuated the island in November 1803. The Haitians destroyed Bonaparte's hopes of a New World empire. It was arguably Napoleon's single greatest humiliation as First Consul. Toussaint may have been returned to France and execution, but Bonaparte could not prevent the year of his Empire's proclamation (1804) being marked by the inauguration of the world's first black republic, that of Haiti on 1 January. In the West Indies at least, the popularity of a (French) republican model remained incontestable. Meanwhile, the Consul had had no moral doubts about reimposing slavery as a legal state on 20 May 1802. In Guadeloupe and Martinique discrimination against freed slaves was once more legitimated, their entry into France was banned, and proscriptions against miscegenation were enacted. It was, in a domestic context, not likely to count against the First Consul. The massacres and savagery of West Indian affairs had left French public opinion in no mood for natural rights rhetoric and the reversal to the pre-revolutionary status quo stirred up little controversy in metropolitan France.

In other colonies, where slavery was not a complicating factor, the French Revolution brought legal changes reflecting events in Paris, but no decolonising initiatives. Colonial tariffs were eased in March 1791 but the *Exclusif* (the requirement of colonies to trade only with France, the French equivalent of the British Navigation Acts) was maintained. The strategic uses of dependent territories were far too important for France's maritime pretensions to be relinquished lightly. They also had more utilitarian, punitive uses. The Directory found it convenient after the coup of Fructidor to use French Guiana on the north-east coast of South America as one large prison camp for housing political prisoners. Many refractory clergy were shipped out to that inhospitable resort with its torrid unhealthy heat. But the economic value of France's colonies collapsed following the Revolution. French exports to the colonies in 1776 had been 61.5 million *livres*, imports 172.2 million; those figures stood at a mere 4 million and 19 million respectively by 1792.

It was strategic considerations that underscored France's drive in the 1790s to consolidate her existing overseas territories and acquire new ones. The Directory and Bonaparte both coveted the kind of imperial presence which British possession of India gave her and decided that an expedition to Egypt in 1798 would unsettle the enemy by absorbing an Ottoman territory that was only loosely tied to Constantinople. Russia and Austria had fed on Turkish lands earlier in the century, so the strategic case for revolutionary France doing so was as compelling as the moral case against it was weak. Bonaparte chose to present himself not as an invader, but as a liberator come to bring to the disempowered Egyptians the rights of self-determination that their Mameluke overlords would not concede.

His victory at the Battle of the Pyramids overthrew the latter but the Egyptians decided that they had exchanged a haphazardly effective autocracy for a military power that had only a nominal interest in conferring any legal rights on them. They were, to all intents and purposes, a conquered people. Nelson's victory at the Nile in 1798 and Abercromby's at the second Battle of the Pyramids (1801) wrecked France's imperial pretensions in Egypt. The local inhabitants were pleased to see them routed. It was symptomatic that the plane trees planted by the French to Gallicise the Egyptian roads had all been uprooted by furious mobs in 1803.[21] France had no more success in India. There the Republic was involved in a proxy sense stirring up the Maratha confederacy of princes to move against the British. Its leader, Tipoo Sahib, had independently begun that initiative in the early 1790s and he was a constant thorn in the side of Pitt's administration for the rest of the decade until his capital of Seringapatam was captured in 1799. Tipoo died in the fighting, the Maratha confederacy battled on into the early 1800s. Such French help as could be proffered was insubstantial and no match for the 'forward' diplomacy of the energetic British Governor-General of Bengal, Marquis Wellesley. It was brother Arthur, the future duke of Wellington, who delivered the *coup de grâce* to the confederacy and the French hopes riding on it at the Battle of Assaye in 1803.

But revolutionary France sought international influence for its values even when colonial acquisition was out of the question. It was partly an ideological drive for its own sake, partly a means of waging worldwide war against Britain and its Empire. One obvious focus was France's sister republic, the United States, which had been legally free of British suzerainty for a mere decade when Louis XVI was executed. American and French politicians trying to construct a new political culture took a keen interest in each other. In both states, there was a sense of untrodden ground (though in France politicians could pretend there were precedents), of politicians making their first extended contact with people from other parts of the country. As in America so in France, 'national politicians behaved like actors on a stage, hungry for the applause of their audience'.[22] With Thomas Jefferson serving as Secretary of State in Washington's first administration, a francophile stance could be predicted in Philadelphia. By the early 1790s the emerging party disputes between Federalists and Republicans partly mirrored those between Girondins and Jacobins. The analogies continued to be striking with the Revolution forcing Federalists and republicans to define their differences in a volatile and disturbing situation. It 'helped to open American politics to wider political participation and debate, but it helped to close American culture to the influences and ideas of the wider world'.[23] Matters came to a head in the United States when the arrival of Edmond Charles Genêt as ambassador from the Girondin Republic in April 1793 prompted the creation of so-called 'democratic societies' sympathetic to French republican ideals. France had declared war on Spain in March that year and was keen to win American assistance in expelling the Spanish from Louisiana and Florida as part of a mission to foment revolution in Spanish America. Genêt's intrigues infuriated the Washington administration that was determined on maintaining a strict neutrality in the European conflict; it held a tantalising appeal for Secretary of State Jefferson who wanted American frontiers to expand. He was particularly keen on acquiring the Floridas for the United States. Genêt's mistake was to threaten on 6 July 1793 to appeal over the heads of the American government with its refusal to abandon neutrality and ask the American people to help outfit French privateers in American ports. Even after his removal, French intrigues continued.

Despite Washington's consternation, the French consuls in Charleston and Savannnah organised an attack on the Floridian capital of St Augustine in April 1794. A declaration of independence was prepared for Florida with a salutation worded 'from the free French to their brothers in Florida'. Nothing came of the plan as the President sent troops to the Georgia–Florida border and a French warship *Las Casas* was pulled back to Charleston harbour. Meanwhile the Jacobins replaced Genêt and issued a proclamation on 6 March that every Frenchman was forbidden to violate the neutrality of the United States. In point of fact, French agents continued to infiltrate anti-Spanish movements in America, and in July 1795 shots were fired under the French flag when the republicans briefly captured the battery of San Nicolás and held Amelia Island for almost a month. The signing of a peace treaty with Spain in August that year ended French interest in encouraging rebellion in Florida.[24]

It did not stop French political intrigues during the Adams presidency of 1797–1801 which worried the administration so much that it passed a series of controversial legislation designed to guard against subversion. The sister republics had fallen out so badly after the immensely controversial Jay Treaty of 1795 between Britain and the United States that by 1797–8 there was something resembling a phoney war going on between them. Both sides recognised that it was in neither of their interests to precipitate matters but even the diplomacy intended to wind down the crisis was attended with controversy. This was the so-called 'XYZ affair' when American envoys to France were informed that the Directors would only begin serious discussions once money had been handed over to them. This was another crisis born of the Directors' eye to the main chance which had to be defused on the very cusp of conflict: President John Adams damaged his standing in the sight of most Federalists when he sent a peace mission to Paris.

In South America, the French showed an early interest in overthrowing Spanish control and encouraging independence movements among the Creoles during the war of 1793–5, just as they did in Florida. They were incited to do so by the Venezuelan Francisco de Miranda, one of the founding fathers of the 'new' South America. Creoles remained cautious, especially after stories of the atrocities in Haiti reached them. In 1795 slaves, led by free coloured leaders who used French revolutionary slogans, ransacked plantations and killed planters before the army could restore control. However, his influence ceased abruptly once the two European neighbours made peace and France lost interest in encouraging anti-Bourbon subversives in that continent for more than a decade. By 1797 Miranda was advising Venezuelen conspirators to imitate the American rather than the French revolutionary example, and the conspiracy of Pedro Gual that year found more Creoles on the side of the Spanish than on that of the conspirators with their cries of liberty and equality.[25]

By the end of the Consulate not much remained of the French overseas Empire. Its economic value was tiny and the costs of defending it were excessively high. Scarred by his Haitian experience, Bonaparte was ready to disencumber himself of most of what remained to the highest bidder. France had received Louisiana in 1800 in return for the cession of Tuscany, in effect all the land known and unknown west of the Mississippi river. It could have been the basis for a vast continental American empire. It did not, however, excite Bonaparte's imagination in the way that an invasion of England did. He told his foreign minister Talleyrand on 11 April 1803:

> I renounce Louisiana. It is not only New Orleans I will cede: it is the whole colony without reserve; I know the price of what I abandon... I renounce it with the greatest regret: to attempt obstinately to retain it would be folly. I direct you to negotiate the affair.[26]

The treaty with the United States was agreed on 4 May and most of the proceeds were spent on preparing his forces for the intended invasion of southern England.

The abandonment of France's last remaining continental American possession came in the same year that Sir Arthur Wellesley's defeat of the Maratha Confederacy at Assaye put paid to Bonaparte's persuasion that he could construct an empire to vie with Britain's in terms of global outreach. In the European theatre, his armies gave him an instrument of command that was a primary and reliable instrument of policy making; elsewhere, the vulnerability of French naval power put at hazard the lines of communication between metropolitan France and the rest of the world. The failure of the relief expedition to San Domingo in 1801–2 had once again demonstrated as much. Napoleon as Consul still toyed with the possibility of succeeding in the Levant where Napoleon the General had failed, his Foreign Minister Talleyrand admitting that 'the acquisition of Egypt was a favourite object of the First Consul'.[27] Arguably, this aim was related more to establishing French supremacy in the Mediterranean than in threatening the overland route to British India. Hence the acquisition of Elba and the occupation of Malta in 1803, despite its being a signal for the abandonment of the Treaty of Amiens and the resumption of war with Britain. It was no longer a clash of ideologies (Napoleon was only a year from proclaiming himself emperor), but a classic great power struggle that would go on for over a decade, and Napoleon could and did draw selectively on revolutionary memories and inspiration to keep the French state behind him. An authoritarian sovereign found that libertarian rhetoric had its uses and could stir hearts and minds as nothing else could. The Revolution might have run its course by 1804 but its memory was compelling, forceful to the extent that even Bonaparte had to reckon with its potency. It had created a revolutionary culture with a life and momentum independent of the imperial French state that would inspire zealots and trouble establishments in a manner that transcended international boundaries and national communities.

# Conclusion

> we live in an age when such extraordinary events arrive, that all reasonable foresight is totally derouted.
> (Colonel William Gardiner to duke of Dorset, 17 May 1792, Centre for Kentish Studies, Sackville MSS U269/C180)

The practice of writing about the French Revolution over the last two centuries has shown historians on the side of the exponents of moderate change in the 1790s keen, even after the collapse of Marxism as a viable project in the 1980s, not to lose faith with the well-intentioned politicians in the Jacobin Republic, and where possible, recover their reputations.[1] Their determination has, if anything, latterly increased, in reaction to the emphasis on the Revolution's essentially violent character as proclaimed by Furet, Schama and Meyer.

If only the Revolution could have ended sooner is the scarcely concealed wish of all sides. As, of course, it might very well have done. There was nothing inevitable about its march down to 1794, 1795, 1799, 1802, 1804 or wherever one prefers the Revolution to have 'ended'. Having once opened Pandora's Box closure was always going to be problematic, with the army, responsive to a charismatic general, the most likely instrument of restoring authority and ending the experiment with liberty, which tended for too many to chaos rather than enhanced personal choices. Successive generals from Broglie in 1789 dithered or declined to do much to any purpose for a decade before ambition and acclamation delivered the republic into Bonaparte's hands and he could, to general relief (and with much wishful thinking), proclaim the revolutionary experiment over and France could get on with being Europe's greatest power again.

One of the attractions of Napoleon to the public was his carefully stage-managed presentation of himself as above politics, patriotically disinterested, repudiating the cynical *sauve qui peut* style of the Directory as well as the inability of most Jacobins to stop thinking of France and its people as a laboratory for the creation of a new society. French republicanism was in terminal decline in 1799, and Bonaparte's 'suspension of politics' was a relief.[2] Napoleon was young, glamorous, talented, with a Court culture that recalled the glory days of the *ancien régime* and an army capable of stirring citizens of all ages and both sexes in a manner that politics could no longer do. When the alternatives to Bonaparte were faceless Jacobins, other generals (before Marengo) or Louis XVIII, the First Consul could follow his star with relative confidence and show himself in touch with the French nation in a manner that no one had really succeeded in doing since the Revolution had begun with such high hopes. No wonder that the ideologically driven, Thomas Paine, for example, author of the best-selling *Rights of Man* back in 1792, felt the dream was over, complaining in 1802: 'This is not a country for an honest man to live in; they do not understand anything at all about the principles of free government... They have conquered all Europe only to make it more miserable than it was before.'[3]

Military adventuring was not part of the Revolution at its inception. Constitutional monarchy was bound up with peace, retrenchment and modernisation that would, *in time*, make France a stronger power, able to avoid damaging diplomatic retreats, such as her humiliation by Prussia and Britain over Holland in 1787. But constitutional monarchy needed a king confident enough in himself to give a lead where appropriate and lend himself unambiguously to the constitutional project. Louis XVI was not such a monarch. He was well-meaning and decent, but inglorious and irresolute. In a monarchy where heredity and divine sanction suddenly mattered far less than popular sanction, he was not the best qualified candidate. He was quite unable to exploit the popularity he had as 'Louis the restorer of French liberty' for a few months in 1789. The Revolution coincided with his own mid-life crisis: a disengagement with politics dating from the mid-1780s, intermittent personal depression aggravated by the death of his eldest son in June 1789, and a retreat into over-drinking and overeating. The Revolution mercilessly exposed previously existing fault lines within the royal family as his younger brothers Provence (at home) and Artois (abroad) intrigued to serve their private ends; too many decisions were left to the queen (who was too keen to make them) and her willingness to carry on Court vendettas against men like Necker, Mirabeau and Lafayette – those who genuinely wanted to make monarchy work – severely weakened the viability of royal constitutionalism. The Crown needed protection from whichever quarter it could come after the October Days in 1789, deeply traumatising for all involved and making more impression on foreign commentators than the fall of the Bastille for (and this comment was typical): 'Perhaps no day so ignominious to the Royal dignity has been beheld, since the elevation of the Capetian Princes to the throne of France.'[4] The queen could not or would not grasp that she had to find this armed support inside France, not from her imperial Habsburg brothers, let alone the tiny battalion of *émigrés* who had left in 1789.

Timothy Tackett has argued that a constitutional monarchy would still have been viable in 1790 if the king and aristocracy had lent their support since the influential 'society of 1789' was, by mid-1790, determined to close down the Revolution. In purely political terms, Tackett's case is compelling; what it leaves out of the equation is the Civil Constitution of the Clergy and the religious issue. The king was determined (especially after he had been intimidated into formally signing the decree imposing the oath to it) not to compromise his faith or co-operate with the new religious establishment, and his inflexibility much decreased his usefulness to those who would otherwise not have sponsored a republic. Louis in 1792 readied himself for a kind of religious martyrdom and thousands of his fellow countrymen and women followed his example and died for their Christian faith. After a brief experiment with the Constitutional Church in 1791–2 the revolutionaries insisted on fighting a cultural war against Catholicism, of setting up the Revolution against revealed religion as two distinct blocs in a way that was at odds with the way the bulk of the population viewed things. Even the officially proclaimed neutrality of the state in religious matters in 1795 scandalised. 'I call it *Atheism by Establishment*', wrote Edmund Burke, 'when any state, as such, shall not acknowledge the existence of God as a moral governor of the world ....'[5] The price paid by revolutionary activists for their militancy against Christianity and the Churches was to turn support for the Revolution into a minority activity for the rest of the 1790s.

Not that any of the major players between 1792 and 1799 could publicly admit as much. They exercised power in the name of the sovereign people and, on the basis of that justification, notions of guilt and innocence became relatively circumstantial as foreign enemies were confronted and 'traitors' exposed and executed in France. Power was blatantly abused, as might have been anticipated by those who could never, in the normal pre-1789 course of things, have expected to exercise it on any scale. Their actions turned the Revolution into a revenger's tragedy, a bloody cycle from which there seemed to be no escape until the advent of Napoleon. Fear became overwhelming, a handy device to keep the populace cowed. As one prisoner of war wrote from Brittany in May 1795: 'of its [fear's] influence in this country I have witnessed astonishing proofs, which demonstrate, beyond volumes of reasoning, the terror inspired by the revolutionary government'.[6]

Whatever meaning the Revolution may have had drained away as a result of the uses to which it was put. Thus Mercier, one-time Girondin and prolific journalist, writing in 1798, had no idea what to make of the Revolution apart from this note of disillusionment: 'They wanted to make entirely new men of us and what they did was to tun us into virtual savages.'

The Revolution may have been civilising in theory; it was commonly brutal in its application, proceeding on the basis of exclusion.[7] Not, for reasons of alternative loyalties, preferences and prejudices, to be uncompromisingly committed to its existence and perpetuation was unacceptable in a citizen, until, that is, Napoleon established a bridge between the revolutionary Republic and the pre-1789 French past. Among the obviously excluded were the vast majority of females, whose precise allegiances still remain inadequately charted. These women were not progressives, the Revolution closed down the religious institutions that were their primary vehicle of sociability outside the family and offered them no compensatory civic involvements. Outsiders were repeatedly struck by the absence of participation by citizens in this brave new political culture. As early as 1790 one Russian traveller observed:

> Do not think... that the entire nation is participating in the tragedy now being played in France. Scarcely a hundreth part is involved. The rest only look on and judge, arguing, crying or laughing, applauding or hissing,...'[8]

The Revolution may have been founded on popular sovereignty, yet its policies were conceived with minimal or highly selective consultation. Neither the Republic, nor the monarchy before it, allowed for the possibility of an 'opposition' on the British model. Yet the merchants, manufacturers and lawyers, those 'new men' who 'steered' the Revolution, needed to imagine, to fantasise properly speaking, that their changes were valid in the eyes of the nation, for, as Lynn Hunt has argued, the Revolution was radically new in creating a politics which envisaged the complete refashioning of society via the political mobilisation of the people.[9] The possibility that 'the people' either might not act, or would be averse to change was one which dared not be admitted. That the result was abuse of power was predictable. As the physiogonomist, Lavater, from the comfortable distance of Zurich, pointed out to a CPS member: 'You tyrannize men ten thousand times more than your tyrants did.'[10] Furet and his followers would argue that democracy was doomed to failure by the inadequacy of the early political conceptualisations. Nevertheless, discussion about the meaning of citizenship took place, much of it – despite the Directory – in 1794–9, an era which gave France the nearest she came in experiencing an apprenticeship of democracy during the revolutionary decade. There were workers' petitions, educational reform and voting, though all of these were closer to constitutional rather than democratic experiments. On that basis alone, the current revival of interest in the later 1790s is thoroughly justified and the habitual practice of historians before the 1980s of 'ending' the Revolution at Thermidor looks embarrassingly ill-considered.

Few doubted in 1789 that change on an unprecedented scale was required to modernise France's precarious political and fiscal structures. It was the scale of change produced by the Revolution that was essentially not wanted, the way it proceeded with such minimal reference to the people directly affected, the disinclination to consider the disruption to lives where the familiar was reassuring rather than threatening. Where individual voices can be heard, these submerged angles of the Revolution can be recovered. In *The Life and Adventures of Peter Porcupine* (Philadelphia, 1796), William Cobbett, a red-faced former sergeant-major, recounted his adventures in 1792 at the village of Tilque near St Omer from March to November 1792, a region of marshes and canals, on the main road from Paris to the Channel ports.

> People may say what they please about the misery of the peasantry under the old regime; I have conversed with thousands of them, not ten of whom did not regret the change. I have not room here to enter an inquiry into the causes that have led these people to become the passive instruments, the slaves of a set of tyrants, such as the world never saw before, but I venture to predict that they will return to that form of government under which they were happy and under which alone they can ever be so again.

Cobbett was wrong to make that assumption, for the war was starting that would carry the principles of the Revolution around the world and give it an enduring fallout, but his report gives a flavour of the disconcerting, disturbing dimension of the Revolution. So many changes occurring in so short a span. As Boissy d'Anglas, the architect of the Year II Constitution told the Convention in 1795:

> We have used up six centuries in six years. If we run over the vast area of our revolution, it's already covered with so many ruins that all it seems to offer us are the traces and ravages of time.[11]

The challenge of how to make sense of it all was always there. The cataclysmic scale of what had befallen France could only be explained for many in cosmic terms and it gave the 1790s a markedly millenarian character throughout Europe. In England, many Presbyterian radicals interpreted the French Revolution as leading to the fall of the popish antichrist, and embraced the regenerative opportunities of creating a new society based on fraternity. When the experience went sour in the mid-1790s some crossed to the United States, like Joseph Priestley, who ended his life at Northumberland, Pennsylvania. Conspiracy explanations of events were popular. Barruel in his four volumes on the history of Jacobinism went back to the early thirteenth century to trace the origins of conspiracy directed against throne and altar, with the Albigensian heretics of Languedoc cast as the first Protestants.

Priestley and Barruel were middle-aged men. The reaction of a younger generation tended to be quite different. As William Hazlitt said in 'The Feeling of Immortality in Youth', the example of France excited an enormous hope in men in early manhood to whom the most inspiring and limitless prospects were suddenly disclosed. Frenchmen in their twenties and thirties tended to embrace the cause (or fight against with equal fervency) and were conscripted to the colours. It was the army not the clubs that were the primary means of republican socialisation. In a European context, the Revolution was inseparable from over two decades of incessant and worldwide fighting which, directly or indirectly, affected the lives of everyone from prince to pauper. The Revolution offered disruption rather than opportunity, death rather than life. It had a dramatic scale that put in the shade the localised revolutions of the 1780s in Geneva, the Austrian Netherlands and the United Provinces. It permanently changed the map of Europe and, for the first time since the classical world, revived the viability of republicanism as a form of government at the same time as it showed that a European state need not be confessionally Christian, indeed could be confessionally anti-Christian. If one seeks to be in at the birth of the modern world it is hard to avoid starting with the French Revolution.

# Notes

**Introduction**

1. For the debates before 1989 see Steven L. Kaplan, *Farewell, Revolution. The Historians' Feud, France, 1789–1989* (Ithaca, 1995).
2. This controversial book has at last been translated into English just when the debate has moved on. Reynald Secher, *A French Genocide: The Vendée*, trans. George Holoch (Notre-Dame, IN, 2003).
3. Schama's work resonates with earlier echoes of revolutionary remorse. As Bakunin wrote: 'Bloody revolutions are often necessary, thanks to human stupidity; yet they are always an evil, a monstrous evil and a great disaster, not only with regard to the victims, but also for the sake of purity and the perfection of the purpose in whose name they take place'. Quoted in George Woodcock, *Anarchism. A History of Libertarian Ideas and Movements* (Harmondsworth, 1962), 13. Thanks to Penny Simmons for this reference.
4. See Jeremy D. Popkin, 'Not Over After All: The French Revolution's Third Century', *Journal of Modern History* 74 (2001), 801–21.
5. For Jones's work see infra, chap. 9, n. 1. Hirsch's *Les deux reves du commerce. Entreprise et institution dans la région lilloise, 1780–1860* (Paris, 1991) is seminal.

**1 The End of the Monarchy, 1789–1792**

1. Vivian Gruder, 'A Mutation in Elite Political Culture: The French Notables and the Defense of Property and Participation', *Journal of Modern History* 56 (1984), 598–634.

2. Quoted in George Armstrong Kelly, *Victims, Authority, and Terror: The Parallel Deaths of d'Orléans, Custine, Bailly, and Malesherbes* (Chapel Hill, 1982), 259.
3. Jeremy J. Whiteman, *Reform, Revolution and French Global Policy, 1787–1791* (Aldershot, 2003), 43–70; O. Murphy, *The Diplomatic Retreat of France and Public Opinion on the Eve of the French Revolution, 1783–1789* (Washington, DC, 1998). Whiteman interestingly highlights the failure of the monarchy's prestigious Cochinchina project in the Far East in 1788 (one intended to counterbalance British dominance in India) as 'the humiliating low point of French power' outside Europe, 91–6.
4. Bailey Stone, 'Geopolitical Origins of the French Revolution Reconsidered', *Proceedings of the Consortium on Revolutionary Europe* (1988), 256.
5. For recent work on public opinion as a legitimating force in the polity see *inter alia*, Sarah Maza, 'Politics, Culture and the origins of the French Revolution', *Journal of Modern History* 61 (1989) 704–23; Dale Van Kley, 'In search of eighteenth-century Parisian public opinion', *French Historical Studies* 19 (1995), 215–26 Harvey Chiswick, 'Public opinion and Political Culture in France during the Second Half of the Eighteenth Century', *English Historical Review* 107 (2002), 48–77. J. Sawyer, *Printed Poison: Pamphlet Propaganda, Faction Politics and the Public Sphere in Seventeenth-Century France* (Berkeley, 1990) argues that the ingredients of the public sphere existed in French debate and contention as early as 1614–17.
6. Arthur Young, 21 June 1789. *Young's Travels in France during the years 1787, 1788, 1789*, ed. M. Betham-Edwards (London, 1913), 172.
7. Lord Hawkesbury to duke of Dorset, Centre for Kentish Studies, Sackville MSS U269/C182.
8. *Correspondance de Louis-Philippe-Joseph d'Orléans* etc. (Paris, 1800).
9. Evelyn Lever, *Louis XVI* (Paris, 1985); John Hardman, *Louis XVI* (New Haven, CT, 1993).
10. Cf. the discussion in Munro Price, *The Fall of the French Monarchy: Louis XVI, Marie Antoinette, and the Baron de Breteuil* (Basingstoke, 2002), 218–19.
11. Philip Mansel, *The Court of France, 1789–1830* (Cambridge, 1988). See also *La famille royale à Paris. De l'histoire à la légende [Musée Carnavalet]* (Paris, 1993).
12. National Library of Scotland, Dep. 313/744, Countess of Sutherland to Lady Douglas, 28 July 1790.
13. Durand Echeverria, *Mirage in the West: A History of the French Image of American Society to 1815* (New York, 1966), 163–8; Bernard Fäy, *The*

*Revolutionary Spirit in France and America: A Study of the Moral and Intellectual Relations between France and the United States at the End of the Eighteenth Century* (New York, 1927), 252–60.
14. Edna Lemay, *Revolutionaries at Work 1789–1791* (Oxford, 1996).
15. John McManners, *The French Revolution and the Church* (London, 1969), 38.
16. Price, *The Fall of the French Monarchy*, 202.

## 2 The Convention, 1792–1795

1. Michael Kennedy, *Middle Years of the Jacobin Clubs* (Princeton, 1988), 239, 244.
2. Approximately 15 per cent of the adult male population, all those who had signed for jury and national guard service.
3. Quoted in Jon Cowans, *To Speak for the People: Public Opinion and the Problem of Legitimacy in the French Revolution* (London, 2001), 91.
4. See Leigh Whaley, 'The Emergence of the Brissotins in the French Revolution', D.Phil., York University 1989.
5. Beinecke Rare Book and Manuscript Library, Yale University, Osborn Shelves c299, abbé Villard MS. For Burkean comparisons of Louis XVI to Christ, see Frans de Bruyn, *The Literary Genres of Edmund Burke* (Oxford, 1996), 188, 191.
6. *Northampton Mercury*, 26 January 1793.
7. Alison Patrick, *The Men of the First French Republic* (Baltimore, 1972).
8. Watkin Tench, *Letters from Revolutionary France: Letters Written in France to a Friend in London, between the Month of November 1794, and the Month of May 1795*, ed. Gavin Edwards (Cardiff, 2001), 50, Feb. 1795.
9. Morris Slavin, *The Hébertistes to the Guillotine: Anatomy of a 'Conspiracy' in Revolutionary France* (Baton Rouge, 1994).
10. W. Edmonds, *Jacobinism and the Revolt of Lyon, 1789–1793* (Oxford, 1990); W. Scott, *Terror and Repression in Revolutionary Marseilles* (London, 1973); Malcolm Crook, *Toulon in War and Revolution* (Manchester, 1991).
11. Recent books in English on Robespierre include: ed. William Doyle and Colin Haydon, *Robespierre* (Cambridge, 1999); John Hardman, *Robespierre* (London, 1999); Norman Hampson, *Robespierre* (London, 1975), the latter written in the form of an extended conversation between three characters about their subject's career, character and convictions.
12. Ken Alder, *Engineering the Revolution: Arms and Enlightenment in France 1763–1815* (Princeton, 1999), 255.

13. See in particular the post-war era writings of J. M. Talmon, particularly *The Origins of Totalitarian Democracy* (London, 1956). He argued that Robespierre's personal dominance of government anticipated the era of the twentieth-century dictators.
14. Hardman, *Robespierre*, 131–2.
15. P. Gueniffey, *La Politique de la Terreur. Essai sur la violence révolutionnaire* (Paris, 2000), 344.

## 3 An Attempt at Moderation: the Directory and the Consulate, 1795–1804

1. On the Two-Thirds decree one deputy opined that the real reason for it was that the *conventionnels* feared they would all be arrested if elections were genuinely free. Simon Burrows, *French Exile Journalism and European Politics 1792–1814* (London, 2001), 156.
2. Alexandre de Calonne. *The Political State of Europe at the beginning of 1796: or, Considerations on the most effectual means of procuring a solid and permanent peace* (Dublin, 1796), 70ff.
3. James Livesey, *Making Democracy in the French Revolution* (Cambridge, MA, 2001).
4. Jules Simon, *Une Académie sous le Directoire* (Paris, 1885), 111.
5. Quoted in Chery B. Welch, *Liberty and Utility: The French Ideologues and the Transformation of Liberalism* (New York, 1984), 37.
6. Cf. Howard G. Brown, 'From Organic Society to Security State: the War on Brigandage in France, 1797–1802', *Journal of Modern History* 69 (1997), 661–95.
7. The point is lucidly made by Michael Broers, *Europe under Napoleon 1799–1815* (London, 1996), 17–18.
8. One scholar, scarcely able to conceal his pleasure at the overthrow of the Jacobins, has even claimed that 'They [the Directors] managed to achieve a level of political civilization, which, for France in that age, seems remarkable'. J. F. Bosher, *The French Revolution: A New Interpretation* (London, 1989), 228.
9. Paul Barras, *Mémoires* (Paris, 1829), iii. 634–7. He claimed he was playing a double game.
10. Isser Woloch, *Napoleon and his Collaborators: The Making of a Dictatorship* (New York, 2001), draws attention to those whose co-operation was vital to the success of the Consulate.
11. Felix Markham, *Napoleon and the Awakening of Europe* (London, 1954), 44.

12. This arrangement was ended in 1802 when the Senate became a dependent institution and the First Consul presided.
13. Broers, *Europe under Napoleon*, 20.
14. Duchesse d'Abrantès, *Mémoires* (Paris, 1831). He was, for many on the Right, the next best thing to the Bourbons: 'One does not love Bonaparte, one prefers him.' Cited in Godechot, *The Counter-Revolution*, 362.
15. A decree reducing the number of Parisian political journals from approximately 60 to 13 had been passed the previous January. Burrows, *French Exile*, 106.
16. See *infra*, Chapter 5, 112.

## 4 The Language and Signs of Revolution and Counter-Revolution

1. Peter Gay, *Art and Act: On Causes in History* (New York, 1976), 16.
2. An important exception would be William Doyle, *The French Revolution: A Very Short Introduction* (Oxford, 2001).
3. It can lead to some clumsiness. Thus Keith Baker, keen to retain the link between discourse and action, ends up describing the Declaration of the Rights of Man as 'a speech-act' with 'illocutionary force', in ed. Keith Baker and François Furet, *The French Idea of Freedom: The Old Régime and the Declaration of Rights of 1789* (Stanford, CA, 1994), 157.
4. Diary, 13 July 1789 quoted in Patricia Taylor, *Thomas Blaikie, The 'Capability' Brown of France 1751–1838* (East Linton, 2001), 115.
5. Baker and Furet, eds, *The French Idea of Freedom*, 238.
6. Daniel Mornet, *Les Origines intellectuel de la Révolution française* (Paris, 1933), 297.
7. Roger Barny, *Rousseau dans la Révolution; Le Personnage de Jean-Jacques et les débuts du culte révolutionnaire* (Oxford, 1986); Norman Hampson, *Will and Circumstance: Montesquieu, Rousseau and the French Revolution* (London, 1983).
8. Henry Kett, *History the Interpreter of Prophecy, or, a view of scriptural prophecies and their accomplishment in the past and present occurrences of the world; with conjectures respecting their future completion* ( 3 vols., Oxford, 1799), iii, 117.
9. One important exception is Hillel Schwartz, 'The Napoeozoic Era: Revolution and the 1790s', in *Century's End: An Orientation Manual towards the Year 2000* (New York and London, 1996), 102ff. See also ed. Frances Carey, *The Apocalypse and the Shape of Things to Come* (London, 1999), 244–9.
10. Franco Venturi, *Utopia and Reform in the Enlightenment* (Cambridge, 1971).

11. For Priestley's belief in the Apocalypse see Jack Fruchtman Jr., 'The Revolutionary Millennialism of Thomas Paine', in ed. O. M. Brack, *Studies in Eighteenth-Century Culture* vol. 13 (Madison, 1984), 67.
12. Adrian Hastings, *The Construction of Nationhood: Ethnicity, Religion and Nationalism* (Cambridge, 1997), 27. See, generally, David A. Bell, *The Cult of the Nation in France: Inventing Nationalism 1680–1800* (Cambridge, MA, 2001).
13. Jack Censer, *The French Press in the Age of the Enlightenment* (London, 1994), 7.
14. J. R. Censer and J. D. Popkin, eds., *Press and Politics in Pre-Revolutionary France* (Berkeley, CA, 1987), viii.
15. Joseph Ritson to Mr Harrison, 26 Nov. 1791, Gray's Inn, in *The Letters of Joseph Ritson, Esq.* (2 vols., London, 1833), i, 204. Ritson was a radical antiquarian. He adopted the French Revolutionary calendar early in 1793 and used the word 'citizen' in letters to his nephew and intimate friends.
16. Quoted in P. M. Jones, *Reform and Revolution in France: The Politics of Transition, 1774–1791* (Cambridge, 1995), 228.
17. Jeremy D. Popkin, *Revolutionary News: The Press in France, 1789–1799* (Durham, NC, and London, 1990), 106–88.
18. Quoted in Evelyne Lever, *Marie Antoinette* (Paris, 1991), 282.
19. Richard Wrigley, *The Politics of Appearances: Representations of Dress in Revolutionary France* (Oxford, 2002).
20. Raymond Jonas, *France and the Cult of the Sacred Heart: An Epic Tale for Modern Times* (Berkeley, CA, 2000).
21. See William L. Pressly, *The French Revolution as Blasphemy: Johan Zoffany's Paintings of the Massacre at Paris, August 10, 1792* (Berkeley, CA, 1999).
22. Thomas Crowe, *Emulation: Making Artists for Revolutionary France* (New Haven, CT, 1995), 177.
23. Ewa Lajer-Burcharth, *Necklines: The art of Jacques-Louis David after the Terror* (New Haven, CT, 2000).
24. Anita Brookner, *Jacques-Louis David* (London, 1980), 135. See also David L. Dowd, 'Art and Politics during the French Revolution: A Study of Three Artist Regicides', in ed. Frederick J. Cox, Bernard C. Weber, Richard M. Brace and John F. Ramsey, *Studies in Modern European History in Honor of Franklin Charles Palm* (New York, 1956), 105–28.
25. Beatrice Hyslop, 'The Theater during a Crisis: the Parisian Theater during the Reign of Terror', *Journal of Modern History* 17 (1945), 333–55.
26. Quoted in Marie-Hélène Huet, *Mourning Glory: The Will of the French Revolution* (Philadelphia, 1997), 30.

27. George Wilson, hotel du roi, au Carousel, 21 Sept. 1791, *Memoirs of the Life of Sir Samuel Romilly, written by himself; with a Selection from his Correspondence*. Edited by his sons (3 vols., London, 1840).
28. See the essay by M. Elizabeth C. Bartlet in ed. Malcolm Boyd, *Music and the French Revolution* (Cambridge, 1992).
29. Laura Mason, *Singing the French Revolution: Popular Culture and Politics, 1787–1799* (Ithaca, 1996).
30. James Leith, *Space and Revolution: Projects for Monuments, Squares, and Public Buildings in France, 1789–1799* (Montreal, 1991).
31. Joseph Rykwert, *Times Literary Supplement*, 2 November 2001, p. 7, review of Daniel Rabreau, *Claude-Nicolas Ledoux (1736–1806). L'architecture et les fastes du temps* (Paris, 2001). See also Anthony Vidler, *Claude-Nicolas Ledoux: Architecture and Social Reform at the End of the Ancien Régime* (Cambridge, MA, and London, 1990).
32. Ken Alder, *The Measure of All Things: the Seven-Year Odyssey that Transformed the World* (London, 2002).
33. See Mona Ozouf, 'Le Panthéon', in ed. Pierre Nora, *Les Lieux de Mémoire*, 7 vols (Paris, 1984), i, 139–66.
34. Robert L. Herbert, *David, Voltaire, Brutus and the French Revolution: an Essay in Art and Politics* (New York, 1973).
35. Napoleon's brother, Lucien, drew on the parallel explicitly in his anonymous *A Parallel between Caesar, Cromwell and Bonaparte* (1800). It argued that the office must be made permanent and hereditary if the prize of political stability in France was to be secured.
36. Quoted Burrows, *French Exile Journalism*, 186.
37. Quoted in Jacques Bourgeat, *Napoléon, lettres à Josephine* (Paris, 1941).

## 5 The Transformation of Institutions

1. Gilbert Shapiro and John Markoff, eds, *Revolutionary Demands: A Content Analysis of the Cahiers de Doleances of 1789* (Stanford, CA, 1998).
2. Michael P. Fitzsimmons, *The Remaking of France: The National Assembly and the Constitution of 1791* (Cambridge, 1994).
3. *The Attic Miscellany; or, Characteristic Mirror of Men and Things* (London, Feb. 1790), i, 239.
4. Lynn Hunt, *Politics, Culture, and Class in the French Revolution* (London, 1986), ch. 3
5. Murray Forsyth, *Reason and Revolution: The Political Thought of the Abbé Sieyes* (Leicester, 1987). Sieyes was a bogeyman for adversaries of the

Revolution. Another British critic referred to 'that detestable apostle of the present plot against human civilisation and happiness, the abbé Sieyes. He and Condorcet are, or have been, the two grand movers of the great levelling machine'. Walter Sichel, ed., *The Glenbervie Journals* (London, 1910), 81, 19 Nov. 1793.

6. Clive Church, *Revolution and Red Tape: the French Ministerial Bureaucracy, 1770–1850* (Oxford, 1981); J. F. Bosher, *French Finances, 1770–1795: From Business to Bureaucracy* (Cambridge, 1970).
7. E. A. Whitcomb, 'Napoleon's Prefects', *American Historical Review* 69 (1974), 1089–118.
8. George Armstrong Kelly, *The Humane Comedy: Constant, Tocqueville and French liberalism* (Cambridge, 1992); Biancamaria Fontana, *Benjamin Constant and the Post-Revolutionary Mind* (New Haven, CT, 1991).
9. William Murray, *The Right-Wing Press in the French Revolution* (Woodbridge, 1986?).
10. Quoted in Jones, *Reform and Revolution in France*, 1789–92, 39.
11. P. M. Jones, 'Reforming Absolutism and the Ending of the Old Regime in France', *Australian Journal of French Studies*, 29 (1992).
12. Quoted in Pierre Duclos, *La notion de constitution dans l'oeuvre de l'assemblée constituante de 1789* (Paris, 1932), 94.
13. The vital text is Ted W. Margadant, *Urban Rivalries in the French Revolution* (Princeton, 1992).
14. M.-V. Ozouf-Marignier, *La Formation des départements: La Représentation du territoire française à la fin du dix-huitième siècle* (Paris, 1989), 166.
15. Colin Lucas, *The Structure of the Terror: The Example of Javogues in the Loire* (Oxford, 1973); R. R. Palmer, *Twelve who Ruled: The Committee of Public Safety During the Terror* (Princeton, 1941); Jean Tulard, *Joseph Fouché* (Paris, 1998).
16. Claude Langlois and Timothy Tackett, 'À l'épreuve de la Révolution (1770–1830)', in ed. François Lebrun, *Histoire des catholiques en France du XV siècle à nos jours* (Toulouse, 1980), 243.
17. *An Historical Sketch of the French Revolution from its Commencement to the Year 1792* (London, 1792), 124.
18. *The Attic Miscellany* (London, Jan. 1791), ii, 187.
19. Order by Mgr Toussaint Duvernin, suffragan bishop of Strasbourg, Lent 1782, quoted in Louis Châtellier, *Tradition chrétienne et renouveau catholique dans le cadre de l'ancien diocèse de Strasbourg (1650–1770)* (*Paris*, 1981), 409.

20. Publ. 10 May 1791: Abbé Guillaume, *Histoire du diocèse de Toul et de celui de Nancy* (5 vols, Nancy, 1866–7), III, 409–10.
21. John Wesley Etheridge, *The Life of the Rev Thomas Coke* (London, 1860), 227–30; Richard Treffry the Elder, *Memoirs of the Rev Joseph Benson* (London, 1840), 269.

## 6 Changing Patterns of Political Participation

1. See generally Ronald Schechter, 'The Jewish Question in Eighteenth-Century France', *Eighteenth-Century Studies* 32 (1998), 84ff.
2. Extracts from the debate are taken from Robert Badinter, *Libres et égaux. L'émancipation des Juifs (1789–1791)* (Paris, 1989), 149–54.
3. Kathleen Dahl, ' "Les Amies et les citoyennes": Two Women's Clubs During the French Revolution', in ed. Marie-France Brive, *Les femmes et la Révolution française*. Vol. 1, *Modes d'action et d'expression, nouveaux droits – nouveaux devoirs* [Actes du colloque international 12–13–14 avril 1989, université de Toulouse-Le-Mirail] (Toulouse, 1989), 77.
4. Quoted in Madelyn Gutwirth, 'Citoyens, Citoyennes: Cultural Regression and the Subversion of Female Citizenship in the French Revolution', in ed. Renée Waldinger, Philip Dawson and Isser Woloch, *The French Revolution and the Meaning of Citizenship* (Westport, 1993), 17–28, at 23.
5. Georges Fournier, 'Les femmes dans la vie politique locale en Languedoc pendant la Révolution française', in ed. Brive, *Les femmes et la Révolution*, 115–22, at 117.
6. Olwen Hufton, 'Femmes, religion et contre-révolution. L'expérience de sept diocèses', in ed. Brive, *Les femmes et la Révolution*, 231–8, at 234.
7. Ed. Betham-Edwards, *Young's Travels in France during the years 1787, 1788, 1789*, 294.
8. Keith Michael Baker, 'Public Opinion as Political Invention', in ed. K. M. Baker, *Inventing the French Revolution: Essays on French Political Culture in the Eighteenth Century* (Cambridge, 1990), 167–99.
9. Henri Carré, ed., *Correspondance inédite du marquis de Ferrières, 1789, 1790, 1791* (Paris, 1932), 45.
10. It has been argued that attitudes towards the binding mandate in 1789 was the earliest significant manifestation of the division between revolutionaries and counter-revolutionaries. Paul Friedland, *Political Actors. Representative Bodies & Theatricality in the Age of the French Revolution* (Ithaca, 2002), 100.

11. Ibid., 154.
12. Quoted in Jon Cowans, *To Speak for the People*, 50.
13. R. R. Palmer, *Twelve who Ruled* (new edn, Princeton, 1959), 128.
14. Michael P. Fitzsimmons, 'The National Assembly and the invention of citizenship', in ed. Waldinger etc., *The French Revolution and the meaning of citizenship*, 29–41, at 37.
15. Pierre Rosanvallon, *Le sacre du citoyen. Histoire du suffrage universel en France* (Paris, 1992)
16. Malcolm Crook, *Elections in the French Revolution: An Apprenticeship in Democracy, 1789–1799* (Cambridge, 1996), 103–5; Malcolm Crook, 'The Uses of Democracy: Elections and Plebiscites in Napoleonic France', in ed. Maire F. Cross and David Williams, *The French Experience from Monarchy to Republic, 1792–1824: New Dawns in Politics, Knowledge and Culture* (Basingstoke, 2000), 58–71.
17. See Claude Langlois, 'The voters', in ed. Frank Kafker and James Laux, *Napoleon and His Times: Selected Interpretations* (Malabar, 1989), 57–65.
18. Malcolm Crook, 'Confidence from Below? Collaboration and Resistance in the Napoleonic Plebiscites', in ed. Michael Rowe, *Collaboration and Resistance in Napoleonic Europe: State-Formation in an Age of Upheaval, c.1800–1815* (Basingstoke, 2003), 19–36. See generally J. Y. Coppolani, *Les Elections en France à l'époque napoléonienne* (Paris, 1980).
19. M. Edelstein, 'Integrating the French Peasants into the Nation-State: The Transformation of Electoral Participation, 1789–1870', *History of European Ideas* 15 (1992), 321.
20. Patrice Gueniffey, *Le Nombre et la raison. La Révolution française et les élections* (Paris, 1993), 513.
21. Richard Bowery Andrews, 'Social structures, political elites and ideology in Revolutionary Paris, 1792–94: a critical evaluation of Albert Soboul's Les Sans-Culottes Parisiens en I'An II', *Journal of Social History*, 19 (1985), 71–112; Michael Sonenscher, 'Artisans, Sans-culottes and the French Revolution', in ed. Alan Forrest and Peter Jones, *Reshaping France: Town, Country and Region During the French Revolution* (Manchester, 1991), 105–21, at 108, 115.
22. The term 'anti-revolution' owes much to C. Lucas, 'Resistances populaires à la Révolution dans le sud-est', in *Mouvements populaires et conscience sociale* (Paris, 1985), 473ff; Claude Mauziac, 'Autopsie d'un échec, la résistance à 'Anti-Révolution et la défaite de la Contre-Révolution', in François Lebrun and Roger Dupuy, *Les résistances à la Révolution* (Paris, 1987), 237ff.

23. Gwynne Lewis, *The Second Vendée: The Continuity of Counter-Revolution in the Department of the Gard, 1789–1815* (Oxford, 1978), 86–102.
24. A. Bendjebbar, 'Les problèmes des alliances politiques, sociales et économiques dans la Contre-Révolution angevine (1797–1799)', in Lebrun and Dupuy, *Les résistances à la Révolution*, 87–96.

## 7  The Militarisation of France: the Nation in Arms

1. Alan Forrest denies that Napoleon set up military dictatorship. He terms it 'a civilian government of a hierarchical and authoritarian kind' with Napoleon assuming in himself the sovereignty of the nation. 'The Military Culture of Napoleonic France', in ed. Philip G. Dwyer, *Napoleon and Europe* (Harlow, 2001), 43–59 at 58.
2. J. C. D. Clark, ed., *Edmund Burke: Reflections on the Revolution in France* (Stanford, CA, 2001), 388.
3. Stanley Weintraub, *George Washington's Christmas Farewell: A Mount Vernon Homecoming, 1783* (New York, 2003).
4. Gary Wills, *George Washington and the Enlightenment* (London, 1986).
5. Beineke Rare Book and Manuscript Library, Yale University, Osborn Shelves c408. Letter of an American Traveller to his friend in Connecticut. New Haven July 1794. (A pencil note suggests that the author is actually Lord Wycombe, son of the former British Premier, Lord Lansdowne. This may be doubted.)
6. [Stephen Weston], *Letters from Paris, during the summer of 1791* (London, 1792), and *Letters from Paris, during the summer of 1792* (London, 1793), ii. 206. See also 291–4.
7. Barry M. Shapiro, *Revolutionary Justice in Paris, 1789–1790* (New York, 1993).
8. For instance by the British diplomat, Lord Auckland. Bishop John Butler of Hereford to Lord Onslow, 6 April 1793, Surrey History Centre, Onslow MS G173/2/2, p. 76.
9. Quoted in A. Chuquet, *Les Guerres de la Révolution*, vol. 5, *La trahison de Domouriez* (Paris, n.d.), 178–9.
10. J. P. Bertaud, *La Vie quotidienne des soldats au temps de la Révolution* (Paris, 1985).
11. Rafe Blaufarb, *The French Army, 1750–1820: Careers, Talents, Merit* (Manchester, 2002). Blaufarb goes so far as to say that the army even stood back at Brumaire.

12. [Lord Auckland], *Some remarks on the apparent circumstances of the war in the fourth week of October 1795* (3rd edn, London, 1795), 42.
13. Elizabeth Sparrow, 'Secret Service under Pitt's Administrations', 1792–1806', *History* 83 (1998), 280–94.
14. Quoted in Jeremy Black, *British Foreign Policy in an Age of Revolutions 1783–1793* (Cambridge, 1994), 241.
15. Claude C. Sturgill, 'The French army's budget in the eighteenth century: A Retreat from Loyalty', in ed. David G. Troyansky, Alfred Cismaru and Norwood Andrews Jr., *The French Revolution in Culture and Society* (Westport, 1991), 125, 127.
16. Price argues that the timorous Broglie was incapable of staging a counter-revolutionary coup. Price, *Fall of the French Monarchy*, 76, 97–8.
17. Samuel Scott, *The Response of the Royal Army to the French Revolution* (Oxford, 1978), 106–8. Only 18 per cent of army officers active in 1789 were still in service in September 1792, but the figures for the artillery were 42 per cent. Alder, *Engineering the Revolution*, 83.
18. Calonne, now living in England, reported that, in all seriousness, Lafayette had offered to make him king of Madagascar. See George Selwyn to Lady Carlisle, 23 (?) Aug. 1790, HMC Carlisle, 686.
19. David Andress, *Massacre at the Champs de Mars: Popular Discontent and Political Culture in the French Revolution* (Woodbridge, 2000).
20. General James Grant [of Ballindaloch, 1720–1806] to Countess of Sutherland, 14 Nov 1792, NLS Dep 313/739B.
21. Beinecke Rare Book and Manuscript Library, Yale University, Osborn MS file 13483, Lord Sheffield to Auckland, 21 Oct 92. Sheffield Place.
22. Alan Forrest, *Soldiers of the French Revolution* (Durham, NC,1990), 140–1.
23. Beinecke Rare Book and Manuscript Library, Yale University, Osborn MSS 25, French Revolutionary Wars. Letters and Documents. Folder 16, Cananas du Muzanne to Col. James Henry Craig, adjutant, Nijmegen, late 1794.
24. Quoted in Cuneo d'Ornano, *Hoche*, 249–50. See generally Robert Garnier, *Lazare Hoche, ou l'honneur des armes* (Paris, 1986).
25. W. S. Cormack, *Revolution and Political Conflict in the French Navy, 1789–1794* (Cambridge, 1995); M. Acerra and J. Meyer, *Marines et Révolutions* (Rennes, 1988).
26. Alan Forrest, *The French Revolution* (Oxford, 1995), 132.
27. Jean-Paul Bertaud *La Revolution armée; les soldats-citoyens et la Révolution Française* (Paris, 1979), 194.

28. Florin Aftalion, *The French Revolution: an Economic Interpretation* (Cambridge, 1990).
29. Alder, *Engineering the Revolution*; J. F. Bosher, *The French Revolution*, 205.

## 8  Violence, Vandalism and Coercion

1. Simon Schama, *Citizens: a Chronicle of the French Revolution* (New York, 1989), 154.
2. Patrice Gueniffey, *La Politique de la Terreur: Essai sur la violence révolutionnaire, 1789–1794* (Paris, 2000), esp. 50. But cf. John Markoff, who calculates that there were approximately 4700 insurrectionary events between June 1789 and June 1793, many of which took place after the Constitution of 1791 was promulgated: 'Violence, Emancipation, and Democracy: the Countryside and the French Revolution', *American Historical Review* 100 (1995), 360–86.
3. Apart from Aruc J. Mayer, *The Furies: Violence and Terror in the French and Russian Revolutions* (Princeton, 2000), see also Richard D. E. Burton, *Blood and the City: Violence and Revolution in Paris, 1789–1944* (Ithaca, 2002); Eli Sagan, *Citizens and Cannibals: The French Revolution, the Struggle for Modernity and the Origins of Ideological Terror* (Oxford, 2003).
4. Classically examined in George Rudés pioneering study, *The Crowd in the French Revolution* (Oxford, 1959).
5. Welbore Ellis to the archbishop of Cashel, 23 July 1789, Hampshire Record Office, Normanton Papers, 21M57C29.
6. *The Contrast; Or, a Comparative View of France and England at the present period. A Poem addressed to the Right Honourable William Pitt* (London, 1790), 13.
7. Timothy Tackett, *Becoming a Revolutionary: The Deputies of the French National Assembly and the Emergence of a Revolutionary Culture* (Princeton, c.1996), 197. Colin Lucas has pointed out that in Nov. 1789 Marat produced the first unambiguous theory of revolutionary violence. The people only rose up when pushed beyond the limit of endurance; the fact of insurrection was evidence of its necessity: 'its vengeance is always just in principle'. 'Talking about urban popular violence in 1789', in ed. Forrest and Jones, *Reshaping France*, 122–36, at 133–4.
8. Steven Reinhardt, 'Peasant unrest in the Périgord 1789–90', in ed. Steven G. Reinhardt and Elisabeth A. Cawthorn, *Essays on the French Revolution: Paris and the Provinces* (College Station, TX, 1992).
9. Fitzsimmons, *The Remaking of France, passim.*

10. Earl Fife to Lord Amherst. Centre for Kentish Studies, Amherst MSS U1350/C78/3 Another British critic noted that the vastly experienced imperial diplomat, Mercy Argenteau, and other friends of the French royal family in Brussels agreed. It was 'too long, and says too much about the king'; Col. William Gardiner to Duke of Dorset, 12 Aug. 1792, Centre for Kentish Studies, Sackville MSS U269/C180.

   The Brunswick Manifesto was drawn up by Fersen, the queen's lover, in association with the marquis de Limon, 'an emigré of dubious reputation'. See Price, *The Fall of the French Monarchy*, 295–6. Brunswick himself (who privately distrusted the *émigrés* and his Austrian allies) later deprecated his own unhappy association with the document. 'Ah, that unlucky manifesto! I shall repent it to the last day of my life. What would I not give never to have signed it!' Quoted in Lord Edmond Fitzmaurice, *Charles William Ferdinand, Duke of Brunswick: An Historical Study, 1735–1806* (London, 1901), 57.
11. Quoted in Taylor, *Thomas Blaikie*, 167.
12. Edinburgh University Library, La II. 652. Letters from Cardinal de Bernis in Rome, 1792, to Limon in Brussels, f.24. 19 Sept. 1792.
13. An immediate aim of the September Massacres was to force the LA to withdraw its decree of 30 Aug 1792 abolishing the insurrectionary *commune*, otherwise it could not manage the elections. This duly happened on 2 September at the height of the Massacres.
14. See especially the work of Pierre Caron, *Les Massacres de Septembre* (Paris, 1935), 103–20, 363–410, 435, 469.
15. Lynn Hunt, *The Family Romance of the French Revolution* (London, 1992), 193.
16. Patrice Higonnet, *Goodness beyond virtue: Jacobins during The French Revolution* (Cambridge, MA, 1998) 38.
17. Patrice Gueniffey, *La Politique de la Terreur*. See also n,.2
18. Colin Lucas, *The Structure of the Terror, passim*.
19. Donald Greer, *The Incidence of the Terror* (Cambridge, MA, 1935), 25–37.
20. William Doyle, *The Oxford History of the French Revolution* (Oxford, 1989), 154.
21. Greer, *Terror*, 161–4.
22. Ivan Gobry, *Joseph Le Bon: La Terreur dans le nord de la France* (Paris, 1991), 69.
23. Quoted in Jacques Godechot, *The Counter-Revolution: doctrine and action*, trans Salvator Artanasio (Princeton, 1971), 222.
24. Y.-M. Bercé et al., eds, *La Vendée dans l'histoire* (Paris, 1994), 415, which notes (113) republican gloating at the damage done in the west.

25. See also Secher's study of the way the violence affected one particular community, *La Chapelle-Basse-Mer, village vendéen. Révolution et contre-révolution* (Paris, 1986).
26. For a sober assessment of the statistics, see F. Lebrun, 'Reyanald Secher et les morts de la guerre de Vendée', *Annales de Bretagne* 93 (1986). See also C. Petitfrère, 'The Origins of the Civil War in the Vendée', *French History* 2 (1988), 187–207. Gueniffey, *La Politique de la Terreur*, 235, estimates 140,000–190,000 rebel deaths in the Vendée.
27. Alain Gerard, *'Par principe d'humanité...' La Terreur et la Vendée* (Paris, 2000).
28. See generally R. Dupuy, *Les Chouans* (Paris, 1997).
29. Quoted in Georges Lefebvre, *The Thermidorians*, trans. Robert Bladick (London, 1965), 63.
30. Philippe Bourdin, 'La Basse-Auvergne, une seconde Vendée?', in ed. Jean-Clément Martin, *La Contre-Révolution en Europe, XVIIIe–XIXe Siècles* (Rennes, 2001), 35–59, at 36. See also Philippe Bourdin, *Le Puy-de-Dôme sous le Directoire. Vie politique et esprit public* (Clermont-Ferrand, 1990).
31. Quoted in Godechot, *The Counter-Revolution*, 344.
32. Robert Fellowes, *An Address to the People, on the present relative situations of England and France; with reflections on the genius of democracy, and on parliamentary reform* (London, 1799), 11.
33. Doyle, *Oxford History*, 258–9, 343.
34. John McManners, *French Ecclesiastical Society under the Ancien Régime: A Study of Angers in the Eighteenth Century*, 288.
35. Simone Bernard-Griffiths, Marie-Claude Chemin and Jean Ehrard, eds *Révolution française et 'vandalisme révolutionnaire'* [Actes du colloque international de Clermont-Ferrand, 15–17 décembre 1988] (Paris, 1992). The cathedrals of Chartres, Amiens and Strasbourg were singled out by Grégoire as masterpieces deserving special consideration.
36. 'Journal d'un bourgeois de Moulins', published by F. Claudon, La Quinzaine bourbonnaise (1898), t.7, quoted in Elizabeth Liris, 'Vandalisme et Régénération dans la mission de Fouché à l'automne 1793', in *supra* 217–25, at 222. In most cases, it was individuals or little groups who were the authors of this destruction or thefts. Christian Bonnet, 'Les pillages d'abbayes dans le Nord et leur signification (1789–1793)', in *supra* 169–73, at 172.
37. 'The new expression created by me was at once naturalised in all the languages used in Europe' (Grégoire, *Mémoires*, 348).
38. Edouard Pommier, *L'art de la Liberté. Doctrines et débats de la Révolution française* (Paris, 1992).

39. E. Champion, 'J.-J. Rousseau et le vandalisme révolutionnaire', *Révolution française*, 55 (1908), 26.
40. John Bacon erected a monument to Dundas in St Paul's cathedral, London. It shows Britannia defending Liberty from a violent attack by figures representing Anarchy and Hypocrisy. Alison Yarrington, *The Commemoration of the Hero, 1800–1864: Monuments to the British Victors of the Napoleonic Wars* (New York and London, 1988), 66.

## 9 The Economy and Society

1. See, for instance, Colin Jones, 'Bourgeois Revolution Revivified: 1789 and Social Change', in ed. Colin Lucas, *Rewriting the French Revolution* (Oxford, 1991), 69–118; idem., 'The Great Chain of Buying: Medical Advertisement, the Bourgeois Public Sphere, and the French Revolution', *American Historical Review* 101 (1996), 13–40. Cf. Sarah Maza, *The Myth of the French Bourgeoisie: An Essay on the Social Imaginary, 1750–1850* (Cambridge, MA, 2003).
2. See, for instance, M. Stuermer, 'An Economy of Delight: Court Artisans of the Eighteenth Century', *Business History Review* 53 (1979), 93, 109.
3. Ambrose Saricks, *Pierre Samuel de Nemours* (Lawrence, KS, 1965). He was an active Fayettiste in the National Assembly, and went to ground in 1792 after the defection of the general to the Austrians.
4. Beckford to (his agent) Thomas Wildman, quoted in ed. D. E. Ostergard, *William Beckford, 1760–1844: An Eye for the Magnificent* (New Haven, 2001).
5. J. F. Bosher, *French Finances, 1770–1795: From Business to Bureaucracy* (Cambridge, 1970), 273–4.
6. Beinecke Rare Books and Manuscripts Library, Yale University, Osborn Files 3966, Sir Grey Cooper to Sir Ralph Payne, 9 Oct 1794, 10 Feb 1796. The view that financial exigencies would drive France to sue for peace was quite common in the mid-1790s. See, for instance, a pamphlet by the former Genevan colleague of Clavière's, Sir Francis d'Ivernois, *Reflections on the War. In answer to Reflections on Peace, addressed to Mr Pitt and the French Nation* [by Mme de Staël] (London, 1795).
7. Jean-Pierre Gross, *Fair Shares for All: Jacobin Egalitarianism in Practice* (Cambridge, 1997).
8. R. C. Cobb's, 'The Revolutionary Mentality in France, 1793–1794', *History* 42 (1957), 181–96, remains full of insights on the mentality of the *sans-culottes*.

9. See R. B. Rose, *Gracchus Babeuf: The First Revolutionary Communist* (Stanford, CA, 1978).
10. Quoted in James Joll, *The Anarchists* (New York, 1964), 40.
11. Jean Boutier, 'Jacqueries en pays croquant: les révoltes paysannes en Aquitaine, décembre 1789–mars 1790', *Annales Economies Sociétés Civilisations* 34 (1979), 760–86.
12. Peter Jones, *Reform and Revolution in France*, 242.
13. Peter McPhee, *Revolution and Environment in Southern France, 1730–1830: Peasants, Lords, and Murder in the Corbières* (Oxford, 1999). He claims that the Revolution produced a political culture consisting of 'pragmatic republicanism primarily hostile to the seigneurial regime' (117); Peter Jones, *The Peasantry in the French Revolution* (Cambridge, 1988), 94–7.
14. In Quercy this was a new departure. The courts had been used for settling disputes before 1789 rather than any resort to violence.
15. See John Markoff, *The Abolition of Feudalism: Peasants, Lords and Legislators in the French Revolution* (University Park, PA, 1996).
16. Ibid., 160; Crook, *Elections in the French Revolution*, 59–61.
17. Higonnet, *Goodness beyond Virtue*, 83.
18. J. R. Dalby, *Les Paysans cantaliens et la Révolution française, 1789–1794* (Clermont-Ferrand, 1989), 60–2.
19. Quoted in Higonnet, *Goodness beyond Virtue*, 114.
20. J. M. Roberts, *The French Revolution* (Oxford, 1978), 96.
21. M. Benabou, *La Prostitution et la police des moeurs au XVIIIe siècle* (Paris, 1986), 274–314.
22. Quoted in Daniel Roche, *The Culture of Clothing: Dress and Fashion in the Ancien Régime*, trans. Jean Birrell (Cambridge, 1994), 148.
23. Ibid., 149.

## 10 The Impact on Europe

1. Price to Jefferson, Hackney, 3 August 1789, ed. W. Bernard Peach, *The Correspondence of Richard Price* (3 vols, Durham, NC, and Cardiff, 1983–1994), iii, 247.
2. Quoted in D. V. Erdman, *Commerce des Lumières: John Oswald and the British in Paris, 1790–1793* (Columbia, MO, 1987), 104.
3. Fellowes, *An Address to the People*, 56.
4. James Allan Park, *Memoirs of William Stevens Esq. Treasurer of Queen Anne's Bounty* (London, 1825), 107.
5. *Journal of William Cochrane, Capt of the 1st Rgt of the Foot*, aka the Royals (d. 1797). Edinburgh University Library, La.III.792, p. 1.

6. Staffordshire Record Office, Bagot papers D5121/1/16/15. Ld Bagot to Thomas Townson, Blithfield, 22 July 1789.
7. Quoted in C. B. Jewson, *Jacobin City* (Glasgow and London, 1975), 18.
8. Henry W. Meikle, *Scotland and the French Revolution* (Glasgow, 1912), 247–8.
9. H. Gough and D. Dickson, eds., *Ireland and the French Revolution* (Dublin, 1990); Nancy Curtin, *The United Irishmen* (Oxford, 1994); Jim Smyth, *The Men of no Property. Irish Radicals and Popular Politics in the late Eighteenth Century* (Basingstoke, 1992); E. W. McFarland, *Ireland and Scotland in the Age of the Revolution: Planting the Green Bough* (Edinburgh, 1994); A. T. Q. Stewart, *A Deeper Silence: The Hidden Origins of the United Irishmen* (London, 1993).
10. Quoted in Richard Herr, *The Eighteenth-Century Revolution in Spain* (Princeton, 1958), 253.
11. John Dunn, *Times Literary Supplement* 16 June 2000, p. 7, review of Mayer, *The Furies*.
12. Marilyn Morris, *The British Monarchy and the French Revolution* (New Haven, 1998).
13. Thomas Crawford, *Boswell, Burns and the French Revolution* (Edinburgh, 1990).
14. Richard A. Lebrun, *Joseph de Maistre: An Intellectual Biography* (Kingston, 1988).
15. Windham's speech in 1794 opposing Flood's motion for parliamentary reform tells one much about his view of France: 'I must still enter my protest against the strange mixture of metaphysics with politics, which we are witnessing in the neighbouring country, where it would seem as if the ideal world were about to overrun the real.' *Speeches in Parliament of the Right Honourable William Windham* (London, 1812), i. 193.
16. Johann Gottfried Seume, quoted in Ernst Wangermann, *The Austrian Achievement 1700–1800* (London, 1973), 184.
17. Kenneth R. Johnston, *The Hidden Wordsworth* (London, 1998).
18. Sparrow, 'Secret Service under Pitt's Administrations', 283.
19. Harvey Mitchell, *The Underground War against Revolutionary France: The Missions of William Wickham, 1794–1800* (Oxford, 1965); W. R. Fryer, *Republic or Restoration in France? 1794–97: The Politics of French Royalism* (Manchester, 1965)
20. J. M. Sherwig, *Guineas and Gunpowder: British Foreign Aid in the Wars with France, 1793–1815* (1969).
21. Marianne Elliott, 'French Subversion in Britain in the French Revolution', in ed. Colin Jones, *Britain and Revolutionary France: Conflict, Subversion and Propoganda* (Exeter, 1983), 40–52.

22. John A. Murphy, ed., *The French are in the Bay. The Expedition to Bantry Bay 1796* (Cork and Dublin, 1997).
23. J. Grossbart, 'La politique polonnaise de la Révolution française', *Annales historiques de la Révolution Française* 6 (1929) 35–55, 242–55, 476–85; 7 (1930) 129–51.
24. For Cloots and much more see Michael Rapport, *Nationality and Citizenship in Revolutionary France: The Treatment of Foreigners, 1789–1799* (Oxford, 2000).
25. Norman Hampson, *The Perfidy of Albion: French Perceptions of England During the French Revolution* (Basingstoke, 1998) is indispensable on its subject.
26. Laurence Cole, 'Nation, Anti-Enlightenment, and Religious Revival in Austria: Tyrol in the 1790s', *Historical Journal*, 43 (2000), 475–97, at 487.

## 11  The French Diaspora and the Wider World

1. The phrase is George Steiner's. See his 'Aspects of Counter-Revolution', in ed. Geoffrey Best, *The Permanent Revolution: The French Revolution and its Legacy, 1789–1989* (London, 1988), 129–53, at 150.
2. Beinecke Rare Book and Manuscript Library, Yale University, Osborne MS file 13483. Lord Sheffield to Lord Auckland, 21 Oct 92. Sheffield Place.
3. See the essays in Kirsty Carpenter and Philip Mansel, eds, *The French Emigrés in Europe and the Struggle against Revolution, 1789–1814* (London, 1999).
4. Kirsty Carpenter, *Refugees of the French Revolution. Emigrés in London* (1999), 21.
5. Col. William Gardiner to duke of Dorset, 9 Sept., 13 Nov. 1791, Centre for Kentish Studies, Sackville MSS U269/C180.
6. Quoted in J. Vidalenc, *Les Emigrés français 1789–1825* (Caen, 1963), 206, 397.
7. *Memoirs of General Dumourier, written by himself* (2 vols, London, 1795), ii. 142
8. Boisgelin to Lord Herbert, 24 October 1793. Hampshire Record Office, Carnarvon Papers 75M91/A6, reporting a long conversation with Lord Chancellor Loughborough. Boisgelin knew that if Monsieur went to Toulon or Provence, he himself would certainly be called to the council there by dint of his archbishopric and his local administrative experience over 20 years.
9. Harvey Mitchell, *The Undeground War against Revolutionary France* (Oxford, 1965), 205–11.

10. Aidan Bellenger, *The French Exiled Clergy in the British Isles after 1789* (Bath, 1986), 4.
11. Herr, *The Eighteenth-Century Revolution in Spain*, 302.
12. Quoted in Jean Tarrade, ed., 'Les Assemblées révolutionnaires et le problème de l'esclavage', *La Révolution française et les colonies* (Paris, 1989).
13. See Yves Bénoit, *La Révolution française et la fin des colonies* (Paris, 1988).
14. David Geggus, 'Racial Equality, Slavery, and Colonial Secession During the Constituent Assembly', *American Historical Review* 94 (1989), 1291.
15. Lester D. Langley, *The Americas in the Age of Revolution 1750–1850* (New Haven, 1996), 112.
16. There were various commemorative events. In Bourg-en-Bresse (*Bourg-régnéré*) the abolition of slavery was commemorated by 20 youths dressed as warriors with women preceded by a float with a young citizenness representing equality. On another float white women breastfed black babies and vice versa. Michael J. Kennedy, *The Jacobin Clubs in the French Revolution* (Princeton, 1988), ii. 189. With embarrassing timing, Peicam de Bressoles produced his *Fête Américaine* at the Opéra Comique in August 1794. The assortment of symbols included a black and a white man, a black and a white baby, the Tree of Liberty, and busts of Jacobin leaders. Frederic Cople Jaher, *The Jews and the Nation: Revolution, Emancipation, State Formation and the Liberal Paradigm in America and France* (Princeton, 2002), 190.
17. See David Geggus, *Slavery, War and Revolution: the British Occupation of Saint Domingue 1793–98* (Oxford, 1982); idem, 'The Anglo-French conflict in the Caribbean in the 1790s', in ed. Jones, *Britain and Revolutionary France*, 27–39.
18. C. James, *The Black Jacobins: Toussaint Louverture and the San Domingo Revolution* (3rd edn, London, 1980); Robin Blackburn, *The Overthrow of Colonial Slavery, 1776–1848* (London, 1988); D. Geggus and B. Gaspar, eds, *The French Revolution and the Greater Caribbean* (Bloomington, 1997).
19. Quoted in Thomas O. Ott, *The Haitian Revolution, 1789–1804* (Knoxville, 1973), 157.
20. Langley, *The Americas in the Age of Revolution*, 134–5.
21. T. Walsh, *Journal of the late campaign in Egypt* (London, 1803), 253.
22. Joanne B. Freeman, *Affairs of Honor. National Politcs in the New Republic* (New Haven, 2001), 5, 6–10.
23. Kramer in Joseph Klaits and Michael Haltzel, *The Global Ramifications of the French Revolution* (Cambridge, 1994), 53.
24. See Charles E. Bennett, *Florida's 'French Revolution', 1793–1795* (Gainsville, 1981).

25. Langley, *The Americas in the Age of Revolution*, 167–9. See also William Spence Robertson, *France and Latin American Independence* (Baltimore, 1939); David Robinson, 'Liberty, Fragile Fraternity, and Equality: Assessing the Impact of French Revolutionary Ideals on early Republican Spanish America', *Journal of Historical Geography* 16 (1990), 51–75. He argues that the French Revolution was less influential as a model for most Spanish-American revolutionaries than the classic liberty, republican model.
26. J. Holland Rose, *Napoleon I* (2 vols, London, 1902), i, 371.
27. Quoted in Philip Ziegler, *Addington: A Life of Henry Addington, First Viscount Sidmouth* (London, 1965), 182.

## Conclusion

1. Patrice Higonnet is an eloquent example. He argues beguilingly that 'Jacobinism was the quintessence of a single (if always changing), complex, divided, but ultimately liberal sensibility – or *esprit révolutionnaire* – ', *Goodness beyond Virtue*, 8.
2. Patrice Higonnet, *Sister Republics: The Origins of French and American Republicanism* (Cambridge, MA, 1988), 8.
3. Quoted in A. M. Williamson, *Thomas Paine: His Life, Work and Times* (London, 1973), 202, 296.
4. *A Sketch of the Reign of George the Third, from 1780, to the close of the year 1790* (2nd edn, 1791), p. 145, Oct. 1789.
5. Burke, *Letters on a Regicide Peace*, 98–9.
6. Watkin Tench, *Letters from Revolutionary France*, 124.
7. Bronislaw Baczko, *Ending the Terror: The French Revolution after Robespierre*, trans. Michel Petheram (Cambridge, 1994), 29. Cf. Jon Cowans, *To Speak for the People*, 114. 'The Revolution, in short, was in many ways a contest waged by minorities speaking for and posing as a majority.'
8. N. M. Karamzin, *Letters of a Russian Traveller, 1789–1790*, trans. Florence Jonas, (Princeton, 1957), 193. Paris, April 1790.
9. Lynn Hunt *Politics, Culture and Class in the French Revolution* (Berkeley, CA, 1985).
10. J. K. Lavater to his former friend, Hérault de Séchelles, Zurich, 21 Nov. 1793, quoted in George Armstrong Kelly, *Victims, Authority, and Terror*, 21.
11. *Moniteur*, vol. 25, pp. 81–2, quoted in John R. Ballard, *Continuity during the Storm: Boissy d'Anglas and the Era of the French Revolution* (Westport, CT, 2000), 514.

# Glossary

| | |
|---|---|
| *babouviste* | a supporter of, or one sympathetic to, the reform platform of Babeuf. |
| *Armées révolutionnaires* | armies of pro-revolutionary militants established in 1793 to take the terror into provincial France. |
| *Assignats* | paper currency introduced in 1790. |
| *biens nationaux* | national lands, most commonly lands once belonging to the clergy and the *émigrés*. |
| *Cahiers de doléances* | grievances by members of the three historic Orders of the kingdom for the meeting of the Estates-General in 1789. |
| *cercles constitutionnels* | moderate, anti-royalist clubs of the Directory era with branches in Paris and the provinces. |
| **Chancellor** | head of the legal profession in pre-revolutionary France. |
| *colonnes infernales* | republican troops in the Vendée used to ravage the countryside and intimidate the population in winter 1793–4. |
| *commissaires* | commissioners sent into the provinces during the Republic with specific responsibilities. |
| **Commission des Onze** | committee to draw up a new Constitution formed in the Convention in April 1795. |
| *commune* | unit of urban government established by the reforms of 1790, often associated with Paris. |
| *Décadi* | the tenth day (of rest) in the Revolutionary Calendar replacing Sunday. |

| | |
|---|---|
| **desacralisation** | the process of removing the divine sanction of kingship and thereby reducing its institutional legitimacy. |
| **'dry guillotine'** | the ironic name given to the punishment that sent prisoners to French Guiana, often priests during the 'Second Terror', 1797–8. |
| *émigrés* | men and women who left France because of their opposition to the Revolution. |
| **Erastian** | the relationship of Church and State in which the former is subordinate to the latter. |
| **federalism** | term usually given to republicans in the provinces opposed to the Jacobin coup of 31 May and who frequently resorted to armed struggle against it. |
| *fédérés* | those pro-revolutionaries from the provinces who were in Paris for the Festival of the Federation in 1792 and were subsequently involved in the storming of the Tuileries on 10 August. |
| *franc de Germinal* | stable unit of metallic currency introduced by Napoleon Bonaparte in 1803. |
| ***Fronde*** | a movement against the Bourbon Crown of 1648–53 involving townsmen, lawyers and nobles, i.e. *frondeurs*. |
| *gabelle* | pre-revolutionary tax on salt. |
| **Gallicanism** | emphasis on the independence and national character of the Roman Catholic Church in France. |
| **Governors** | the king's principal representative (usually a nobleman) in one of the pre-1790 provinces. |
| **Ideologues** | progressive, 'scientific' thinkers belonging to a club in existence in the later 1790s. |
| *indulgents* | name given to Danton, Desmoulins and their supporters. |
| *intendants* | senior royal official in a generality before 1789 and key link between centre and locality. |
| *journée* | a day of revolutionary action at a popular level often precipitating regime change. |
| **Keeper of the Seals** | deputy to the Chancellor (*supra*), often the *de facto* head of the judiciary if a Chancellor was in disgrace. |

| | |
|---|---|
| *levée en masse* | a ballot-based scheme of selection for military service for men aged 18 to 25. |
| *livres* | a pre-1789 currency unit. |
| *mandats territoriaux* | a form of paper currency designed to replace the *assignat* and available between 1796 and 1797. |
| *métayer* | a widespread form of land tenancy in pre-1789 France. |
| *noyades* | execution by drowning as practised in Nantes and district following the crushing of the Vendée revolt. |
| plebiscite | a consultative referendum on a particular issue. |
| presidial court | middle-tier of pre-1790 law court. |
| Provincial Assemblies | an assembly representative of propertied opinion first devised by Necker in 1778 and widely adopted in 1787. |
| Provincial Estates | like Provincial Assemblies but with wider powers and often having medieval origins. |
| refractories | clergy who refused to take the oath of loyalty to the Civil Constitution (1790–1). |
| *remonstrances* | protests that could be entered against edicts proposed by the Crown for registration in the *parlements*. |
| *salonnières* | female members of salons. |
| *senatus–consultum* | a device established during the Consulate permitting the First Consul to rule on the basis of senatorial decree. |
| *sections* | administrative divisions of Paris established in the municipal reforms of 1790. |
| theophilanthropy | an eclectic, emotional pantheism supported during the second Directory. |
| *vingtième* | a direct tax, periodically renewable, levied on members of both the Third and Second Estates pre-1789. |

# Select Annotated Bibliography of Publications in English

Aftalion, Florin, *The French Revolution: an Economic Interpretation* (Cambridge, 1990). A product of the late Reagan–Thatcher era.

Alder, Ken, *Engineering the Revolution: Arms and Enlightenment in France, 1763–1815* (Princeton, 1999).

——, *The Measure of All Things: the Seven-Year Odyssey that Transformed the World* (London, 2002).

Andress, David, *Massacre at the Champs de Mars: Popular Discontent and Political Culture in the French Revolution* (Woodbridge, 2000).

Aston, Nigel, *Religion and Revolution in France, 1780–1804* (Basingstoke, 2000).

Baker, K. M., ed., *Inventing the French Revolution: Essays on French Political Culture in the Eighteenth Century* (Cambridge, 1990). Collected articles of one of the pioneering revisionist cultural historians.

Baker, Keith and François Furet, eds, *The French Idea of Freedom: The Old Régime and the Declaration of Rights of 1789* (Stanford, CA, 1994).

Bell, David A., *The Cult of the Nation in France: Inventing Nationalism, 1680–1800* (Cambridge, MA., 2001). A rich text that shows the maturity of notions of nationhood in pre-revolutionary France.

Bellenger, Aidan, *The French Exiled Clergy in the British Isles after 1789* (Bath, 1986). Assesses the interaction of the exiles with their hosts and contains a checklist of names.

Best, Geoffrey, ed., *The Permanent Revolution: The French Revolution and Its Legacy, 1789–1989* (London, 1988). Essays by divers hands produced for the bicentenary.

Black, Jeremy, *British Foreign Policy in an Age of Revolutions, 1783–1793* (Cambridge, 1994). The definitive work.
Blanning, T. C. W., *The Origins of the French Revolutionary Wars* (London, 1986). Emphasis falls on diplomacy rather than ideology.
Blaufarb, Rafe, *The French Army, 1750–1820: Careers, Talents, Merit* (Manchester, 2002).
Bosher, J. F., *French Finances, 1770–1795: From Business to Bureaucracy* (Cambridge, 1970). Scholarship of an order that confirmed the author's reputation.
——, *The French Revolution: A New Interpretation* (London, 1989). Revisionist textbook strongest on the growth of the state and public finance.
Boyd, Malcolm, ed., *Music and the French Revolution* (Cambridge, 1992).
Broers, Michael, *Europe under Napoleon, 1799–1815* (London, 1996). A fine attempt to see Napoleonic Europe from the perspective of the ruled rather than the rulers.
Brookner, Anita, *Jacques-Louis David* (London, 1980). Remains the most accessible presentation of the leading artist of the 1790s and his studio.
Brown, Howard G., 'From Organic Society to Security State: the War on Brigandage in France, 1797–1802', *Journal of Modern History* 69 (1997), 661–95.
Burton, Richard D. E., *Blood and the City: Violence and Revolution in Paris, 1789–1944* (Ithaca, 2002).
Carlson, Marvin A., *Theatre of the Revolution* (Ithaca, 1966).
Carpenter, Kirsty, *Refugees of the French Revolution: Emigrés in London* (Basingstoke, 1999). Stresses the variety of the revolutionary experience for those who left France.
Kirsty Carpenter and Philip Mansel, eds, *The French Emigrés in Europe and the Struggle against Revolution, 1789–1814* (Basingstoke, 1999).
Censer, Jack, *The French Press in the Age of the Enlightenment*, (London, 1994). Writing from the world's leading specialist on the subject.
Censer, J. R. and J. D. Popkin, eds, *Press and Politics in Pre-Revolutionary France* (Berkeley, CA, 1987).
Church, Clive, *Revolution and Red Tape: the French Ministerial Bureaucracy, 1770–1850* (Oxford, 1981). Particularly useful when read in conjunction with Bosher.
Cobb, R. C., 'The Revolutionary Mentality in France, 1793–1794', *History* 42 (1957), 181–96.
Cormack, W. S., *Revolution and Political Conflict in the French Navy, 1789–1794* (Cambridge, 1995). Fine scholarship on a neglected topic.
Cowans, Jon, *To Speak for the People. Public Opinion and the Problem of Legitimacy in the French Revolution* (London, 2001).

Crook, Malcolm, *Toulon in War and Revolution* (Manchester, 1991).
——, *Elections in the French Revolution: an Apprenticeship in Democracy, 1789–1799* (Cambridge, 1996). The key text in English on one of the most important new scholarly lines opened up in the 1990s.
——, *Napoleon Comes to Power: Dictatorship and Democracy in Revolutionary France* (Cardiff, 1998). A balanced assessment with a handy selection of primary documents included.
Crowe, Thomas, *Emulation: Making Artists for Revolutionary France* (New Haven, CT, 1995).
Curtin, Nancy, *The United Irishmen* (Oxford, 1994).
Doyle, William, *The Origins of the French Revolution* (3rd edn, Oxford, 1999). An updated, standard text.
——, *The French Revolution: a Very Short Introduction* (Oxford, 2001). Masterly summary.
——, *The Oxford History of the French Revolution*, (Oxford, 1989). Easily the best moderately revisionist account now in its second edition (2003).
Doyle, William and Colin Haydon, eds, *Robespierre* (Cambridge, 1999).
Dwyer, Philip G., *Talleyrand* (Harlow, 2002). The best assessment of Talleyrand's life and times currently available in English.
Edmonds, W., *Jacobinism and the Revolt of Lyon, 1789–1793* (Oxford, 1990).
Elliott, Marianne, 'French Subversion in Britain in the French Revolution', in ed. Jones, *Britain and Revolutionary France*, 40–52.
Ellis, Geoffrey, *Napoleon* (Harlow, 1997). Measured, acute, well-written.
Farge, A., *Subversive Words: Public Opinion in Eighteenth-Century France*, trans Rosemary Morris (London, 1994). A fine starting point for students wanting to check on the emergence of public opinion as well as an original work in its own right.
Fäy, Bernard, *The Revolutionary Spirit in France and America: a Study of the Moral and Intellectual Relations between France and the United States at the End of the Eighteenth Century* (New York, 1927).
Fitzsimmons, Michael P., *The Remaking of France: the National Assembly and the Constitution of 1791* (Cambridge, 1994). An upbeat view of 1789–91 grounded in the sources.
Fontana, Biancamaria, *Benjamin Constant and the Post-Revolutionary Mind* (New Haven, CT, 1991). A study in the emergence of liberalism.
Forrest, Alan, *Soldiers of the French Revolution* (Durham, NC,1990). Forrest is one of the world's leading experts on the French army in the 1790s.
——, *The French Revolution* (Oxford, 1995).
——, 'La patrie en danger. The French Revolution and the First *Levée en Masse*', in *The People in Arms: Military Myth and National Mobilization since the*

*French Revolution*, ed. Daniel Moran and Arthur Waldron (Cambridge University Press: Cambridge, 2002), 8–32.

Forsyth, Murray, *Reason and Revolution: The Political Thought of the Abbé Sieyes* (Leicester, 1987). A fine case study on the thinking of one of the most profound politicians of the 1790s.

Friedland, Paul, *Political Actors: Representative Bodies & Theatricality in the Age of the French Revolution* (Ithaca, 2002). Slightly overstates the resemblances between theatre and politics.

Fruchtman Jr., Jack, 'The Revolutionary Millennialism of Thomas Paine', in O. M. Brack, Jr, ed., *Studies in Eighteenth-Century Culture*, vol. 13 (Madison, 1984), 65–78.

Fryer, W. R., *Republic or Restoration in France? 1794–1797* (Manchester, 1965). One of the first historians to take spying networks seriously, in this instance that operated by William Wickham in Switzerland.

Furet, François, *Revolutionary France, 1770–1880* (Oxford, 1992). The late leading revionist lays his emphasis on discourse and places the Revolution in a long timeframe.

Geggus, David, *Slavery, War and Revolution: the British Occupation of Saint Domingue 1793–98* (Oxford, 1982).

Geggus, D. and B. Gaspar, eds, *The French Revolution and the Greater Caribbean* (Bloomington, 1997).

Godechot, Jacques, *The Counter-Revolution: Doctrine and Action*, trans. Salvator Artanasio (Princeton, 1971). A canonical study.

Godineau, Dominique, *The Women of Paris and their French Revolution* (Berkeley, CA, 1998).

Gough, Hugh, *The Newspaper Press in the French Revolution* (London, 1988). A reliable, detailed study.

Gough, Hugh and D. Dickson, eds, *Ireland and the French Revolution* (Dublin, 1990). Several useful essays.

Greer, Donald, *The Incidence of the Terror* (Cambridge, MA, 1935). Despite its age, Greer did his work well and this book is still inevitably cited 70 years on.

——, *The Incidence of the Emigration During the French Revolution* (Cambridge, MA, 1951).

Gross, Jean-Pierre, *Fair Shares for All: Jacobin Egalitarianism in Practice* (Cambridge, 1997).

Hampson, Norman, *Robespierre* (London, 1975). Approaches its subject through the novel scheme of a four-way conversation between imaginary subjects all with quite different approaches to Robespierre.

——, *Will and Circumstance: Montesquieu, Rousseau and the French Revolution* (London, 1983). Divides the revolutionaries into followers of either of these two apparently irreconcilable *philosophes*.

——, *The Perfidy of Albion. French Perceptions of England during the French Revolution* (Basingstoke, 1998). Charts and assesses the falling out of the two neighbours after the initial hopes of 1789 gave way to two decades of warfare.

Hardman, John, *Louis XVI* (New Haven, CT, 1993).

Harris, J. and François Crouzet, *Industrial Espionage and Technology Transfer in Eighteenth-Century France and Britain* (Aldershot, 1998).

Harris, R., *Politics and the Rise of the Press: Britain and France, 1620–1800* (London and New York, 1996). An invaluable comparative summary.

Hastings, Adrian, *The Construction of Nationhood: Ethnicity, Religion and Nationalism* (Cambridge, 1997). One of the first recent studies to emphasise the importance of religion in the formation of national consciousness.

Herbert, Robert L., *David, Voltaire, Brutus and the French Revolution: an Essay in Art and Politics* (New York, 1973).

Higonnet, Patrice, *Goodness beyond Virtue: Jacobins During the French Revolution* (Cambridge, MA, 1998). A fascinating and learned attempt at rehabilitation that finally fails to persuade.

Hyslop, Beatrice, 'The Theater During a Crisis: the Parisian Theater During the Reign of Terror', *Journal of Modern History* 17 (1945), 333–55.

Huet, Marie-Hélène, *Mourning Glory: The Will of the French Revolution* (Philadelphia, 1997).

Hunt, Lynn, *Politics, Culture, and Class in the French Revolution* (London, 1986). A classic revisionist text.

——, *The Family Romance of the French Revolution* (London, 1992).

Hunt, L., D. Lansky and P. Hanson, 'The Failure of the Liberal Republic in France, 1795–1799: the Road to Brumaire', *Journal of Modern History* 51 (1979), 734–59.

Hutt, Maurice, *Chouannerie and Counter-Revolution: Puisaye, the Princes and the British Government in the 1790s* (2 vols, Cambridge, 1983). An outstanding in-depth look at the organisational mismanagement of the counter-revolutionaries.

Jaher, Frederic Cople, *The Jews and the Nation: Revolution, Emancipation, State Formation and the Liberal Paradigm in America and France* (Princeton, 2002).

James, C., *The Black Jacobins: Toussaint Louverture and the San Domingo Revolution* (3rd edn, London, 1980).

Jones, Colin, ed., *Britain and Revolutionary France: Conflict, Subversion and Propaganda* (Exeter, 1983).

Jones, Colin, 'Bourgeois Revolution Revivified: 1789 and Social Change', in ed. Colin Lucas, *Rewriting the French Revolution* (Oxford, 1991), 69–118. The bourgeoisie rejoin the Revolution but not in a Marxist context.

——, 'The Great Chain of Buying: Medical Advertisement, the Bourgeois Public Sphere, and the French Revolution', *American Historical Review* 101 (1996), 13–40.

Jones, P. M., *The Peasantry in the French Revolution* (Cambridge, 1988). A definitive work on this topic.

——, 'Reforming Absolutism and the Ending of the Old Regime in France', *Australian Journal of French Studies*, 29 (1992).

——, *Reform and Revolution in France: The Politics of Transition, 1774–1791* (Cambridge, 1995). Assured overview stressing the continuity of reform between the 'old' and 'new' regimes.

Kelly, George Armstrong, *Victims, Authority, and Terror: The Parallel Deaths of d'Orléans, Custine, Bailly, and Malesherbes* (Chapel Hill, 1982).

——, *The Humane Comedy. Constant, Tocqueville and French Liberalism* (Cambridge, 1992).

Kennedy, Michael, *The Jacobin Clubs in the French Revolution* (3 vols, Princeton, 1982–99). An exhaustive survey.

Joseph Klaits and Michael Haltzel, *The Global Ramifications of the French Revolution* (Cambridge, 1994).

Lajer-Burcharth, Ewa, *Necklines: The art of Jacques-Louis David after the Terror* (New Haven, CT, 2000).

Landes, Joan, *Women and the Public Sphere in the Age of the French Revolution* (Ithaca, 1988).

Langley, Lester D., *The Americas in the Age of Revolution, 1750–1850* (New Haven, CT, 1996). Takes in southern and central America as well as the United States.

Langlois, Claude, 'The Voters', in ed. Frank Kafker and James Laux, *Napoleon and His Times: Selected Interpretations* (Malabar, FL, 1989), 57–65.

Lefebvre, Georges, *The Thermidorians*, trans. Robert Baldick (London, 1965). A measured and neglected summary by comparison with Lefebvre's other writings.

Leith, James, *Space and Revolution: Projects for Monuments, Squares, and Public Buildings in France, 1789–1799* (Montreal, 1991).

Lemay, Edna, *Revolutionaries at Work 1789–1791* (Oxford, 1996).

Livesey, James, *Making Democracy in the French Revolution* (Cambridge, MA, 2001). Makes strong progressive claims for the political cultural of the later 1790s (cf. Crook above).

Lucas, Colin, *The Structure of the Terror: the Example of Javogues in the Loire* (Oxford, 1973). Looks at the Terror in its local provincial setting.

——, 'The First French Directory and the Rule Of Law', *French Historical Studies* (1977), 231–60.

——, 'The Rules of the Game in Local Politics under the Directory', *French Historical Studies* 16 (1989), 345–71.
Lyons, Martyn, *France under the Directory* (Cambridge, 1973). The book which inaugurated modern scholarship on the subject.
——, *Napoleon Bonaparte and the Legacy of the French Revolution* (Basingstoke, 1994).
McFarland, E. W., *Ireland and Scotland in the Age of the Revolution: Planting the Green Bough* (Edinburgh, 1994).
McManners, John, *The French Revolution and the Church* (London, 1969). A classic text.
McPhee, Peter, *Revolution and Environment in Southern France, 1730–1830: Peasants, Lords, and Murder in the Corbières* (Oxford, 1999).
Mansel, Philip, *The Court of France, 1789–1830* (Cambridge, 1988). Shows how Bonapartists were no less committed to court society and etiquette than the Bourbons.
Margadant, Ted W., *Urban Rivalries in the French Revolution* (Princeton, 1992).
Markham, Felix, *Napoleon and the Awakening of Europe* (London, 1954). Remains one of the best studies of Napoleon.
Markoff, John, *The Abolition of Feudalism: Peasants, Lords and Legislators in the French Revolution* (University Park, PA, 1996). The definitive study of its subject to-date.
May, Gita, *Madame Roland and the Age of Revolution* (New York, 1970).
Melzer, Sara E. and Leslie W. Rabine, *Rebel Daughters: Women and the French Revolution* (New York, 1992).
Mitchell, Harvey, *The Underground War against Revolutionary France: The Missions of William Wickham, 1794–1800* (Oxford, 1965).
Morris, Marilyn, *The British Monarchy and the French Revolution* (New Haven, CT, 1998). Some interesting comparisons between Louis XVI and George III.
Murphy, O., *The Diplomatic Retreat of France and Public Opinion on the Eve of the French Revolution, 1783–1789* (Washington, DC, 1998).
Murray, William, *The Right-Wing Press in in the French Revolution* (Woodbridge, 1986).
Outram, Dorinda, *The Body and the French Revolution: Sex, Class, and Political Culture* (New Haven, CT, 1989).
Ozouf, Mona, *Festivals and the French Revolution*, trans. Alan Sheridan (Cambridge, MA, 1988). Perhaps the single most original work on the Revolution since 1970.
Palmer, Robert, 'The National Idea in France before the Revolution', *Journal of the History of Ideas* 1 (1940), 95–111.

——, *Twelve who Ruled: The Committee of Public Safety During the Terror* (Princeton, 1941). Still repays consultation.

Patrick, Alison, *The Men of the First French Republic* (Baltimore, 1972). Girondins and Jacobins in context.

Petitfrère, C., 'The Origins of the Civil War in the Vendée', *French History* 2 (1988), 187–207.

Price, Munro, *The Fall of the French Monarchy: Louis XVI, Marie Antoinette, and the Baron de Breteuil* (Basingstoke, 2002). Argues for the primary importance of Sweden in supporting the Counter-Revolution and for the royal family's unbending distaste for the Revolution.

Rapport, Michael, *Nationality and Citizenship in Revolutionary France: The Treatment of Foreigners, 1789–1799* (Oxford, 2000).

Roberts, J. M., *The French Revolution* (Oxford, 1978). A fine short introduction.

Robinson, David, 'Liberty, Fragile Fraternity, and Equality: Assessing the Impact of French Revolutionary Ideals on early Republican Spanish America', *Journal of Historical Geography* 16 (1990), 51–75.

Rose, R. B., *Gracchus Babeuf: The First Revolutionary Communist* (Stanford, CA, 1978).

Rudé, George, *The Crowd in the French Revolution* (Oxford, 1959).

Sagan, Eli, *Citizens and Cannibals: The French Revolution, the struggle for Modernity and the Origins of Ideological Terror* (Oxford, 2003).

Scarfe, F., *André Chénier, His Life and Work, 1762–94* (London, 1965).

Schama, Simon, *Citizens: a Chronicle of the French Revolution* (New York, 1989). Caused a stir on publication for its uncompromising insistence on the Revolution's violent character. Actually has more on the pre-1789 years than the Revolution proper.

Scott, Samuel, *The Response of the Royal Army to the French Revolution* (Oxford, 1978). Meticulous treatment and the inspiration for subsequent military studies.

Scott, W., *Terror and Repression in Revolutionary Marseilles* (London, 1973). Detailed account of the Terror in one provincial city.

Shapiro, Barry M., *Revolutionary Justice in Paris, 1789–1790* (New York, 1993).

Shapiro, Gilbert and John Markoff, eds, *Revolutionary Demands: a Content Analysis of the Cahiers de Doleances of 1789* (Stanford, CA, 1998). An exhaustive survey of this literature.

Sherwig, J. M., *Guineas and Gunpowder: British Foreign Aid in the Wars with France, 1793–1815* (1969).

Slavin, Morris, *The Hébertistes to the Guillotine: Anatomy of a 'Conspiracy' in Revolutionary France* (Baton Rouge, 1994).

Sparrow, Elizabeth, 'Secret Service under Pitt's Administrations, 1792–1806', *History* 83 (1998), 280–94.
——, *Secret Service: British Agents in France, 1792–1815* (Woodbridge, 1999). Authoritative.
Stone, Bailey, *The Genesis of the French Revolution: a Global-Historical Interpretation* (Cambridge, 1994). Argues for the monarchy's foreign policy failures as a dissolvent of its prestige in the 1780s.
Sutherland, D. M. G., *The French Revolution and Empire: The Quest for Civic Order* (Oxford, 2003). Full coverage of both the Counter-Revolution and the Consulate.
Tackett, T., *Religion, Revolution and Regional Culture in Eighteenth-Century France: the Ecclesiastical Oath of 1791* (Princeton, 1986). The best account and analysis of the response to the Civil Constitution of the Clergy.
——, *Becoming a Revolutionary: The Deputies of the French National Assembly and the emergence of a revolutionary culture (1789–1790)* (Princeton, 1996).
Van Kley, Dale, eds, *The French Idea of Freedom: The Old Regime and the Declaration of Rights of 1789* (Stanford, CA, 1994).
Vidler, Anthony, *Claude-Nicolas Ledoux: Architecture and Social Reform at the End of the Ancien Régime* (Cambridge, MA, 1990).
Waldinger, Renée, Philip Dawson and Isser Woloch, eds, *The French Revolution and the Meaning of Citizenship* (Westport, CT., 1993).
Whitcomb, E. A., 'Napoleon's Prefects', *American Historical Review* 69 (1974), 1089–118.
Welch, Chery B., *Liberty and Utility. The French Idéologues and the Transformation of Liberalism* (New York, 1984).
Whiteman, Jeremy J., *Reform, Revolution and French Global Policy, 1787–1791* (Aldershot, 2003).
Woloch, Isser, *Jacobin Legacy: The Democratic Movement under the Directory* (Princeton, 1970).
——, *The New Régime: Transformations of the French Civic Order, 1789–1820* (New York, 1994).
——, *Napoleon and his Collaborators: The Making of a Dictatorship* (London, 2001).
Wrigley, Richard, *The Politics of Appearances: Representations of Dress in Revolutionary France* (Oxford, 2002).
Young, Arthur, *Young's Travels in France during the years 1787, 1788, 1789*, ed. M. Betham-Edwards (London, 1913).

# Index

*Note*: The notes section has not been indexed.

Abercromby, Sir Ralph, 249
Abrantes, duchesse d', 64
Académie Royale, 85
Act of Union, 214
Adams, John, US president, 251
Addington, Henry, 1st viscount Sidmouth, 229, 248
Adelaide, Madame, 238
Agoult de Bonneval, d', bishop, 238
Alexander the Great, 90
Aliens Act, 243
Aligre, Etienne-François, marquis d', 238
American War of Independence, 9, 10–11, 14, 126, 147, 152, 163
*ancien régime*, 15, 74, 127, 162, 192, 208, 218, 236
Ancients, 48
Andress, D., 1
Andrews, Richard Mowery, 136
Angivillier, comte d', 80
antiquity, 89–92
Aranda, Conde de, 228
Aristotle, 54
Arms and Powder Commission, 165
Army of Coburg, 36

Army of the Ocean Coasts, 158–9
Army of the Princes, 239
Arno Meyer, J., 169
Artois, Charles Philippe, comte d' 21, 27, 152, 238, 241, 255
arts, 82–9
Assembly of Notables, 11–13, 18, 126, 127, 128, 132, 195
Atlantic area, Revolution in, 245–53
Auckland, Lord, 149
Augustins, 184
Austria, 32, 216, 223, 229, 237, 249, 259
  Directory and Consulate, 68
  institutions, transformation of, 112
  language and signs of revolution and Counter-Revolution, 80
  militarisation, 145, 148, 154, 156, 161
  National Convention, 36
  violence, vandalism and coercion, 173–4
'Austrian committee', 154
Austrian Netherlands, 22, 155, 162, 219, 224, 227, 242
authoritarianism, 225–32
autocracy, 145–50

# INDEX

Babeuf, Gracchus
  (François-Noël), 56, 100,
  138, 199–200
Baecque, Antoine de, 169
Bagot, William, 1st baron, 220
Bank of England, 14, 229
Bank of France, 65, 208
Bara, Joseph, 85, 91
Barbé-Marbois, 56
Barère, Bertrand, deputy,
  43, 219, 231
Barnave, 28
Barras, Paul-François,
  viscomte de, 51–3, 56,
  58–61, 131, 135
Barruel, Augustin,
  abbé, 259
Barthélemy, François, 54, 56
Bazas, 108
Beckford, William, 193
Belgium, 22, 36, 50, 155, 162,
  204, 223, 244
Bell, David, 76
Bergasse, Nicolas, 104, 110
Bernadotte, marshal, Charles XV
  of Sweden, 62
Bernis, Cardinal, 27, 174
Bertaud, Jean-Paul, 157, 164
Bill of Rights, 2
Billaud-Varenne, Jean-Nicolas,
  42–3
Biron, Antoin de Gontaut,
  duc de, 18
Blaikie, Thomas, 174
Blanning, T.C.W., 162
Boisgelin de Cucé, archbishop,
  239, 241
Boissy d'Anglas, François-Antoine
  de, 57, 105, 213, 259
Bolingbroke, Lord, 31
Bon, Joseph Le, 177
Bonald, Louis de, 239
Bonaparte, Lucien,
  62–3, 102
Bonaparte, Napoleon,
  58, 61–9, 86, 89, 91, 92,
  93–5, 96, 254–5, 257
  economy and society, 209

Europe, impact of Revolution
  on, 234
global impact of Revolution,
  242, 244, 247–9,
  252–3
institutions, transformation of,
  98, 100, 102–4, 112,
  117–18
militarisation, 145–7, 150–1,
  159, 162–7
political participation, 124,
  131–4, 138
violence, vandalism and
  coercion, 183, 186, 190
Bosher, J.F., 233
Bouillé, Etienne-Louis, 88
Bouillé, François, marquis de,
  general, 27, 153, 240–1
Bourbon Family Compact,
  29, 101
Bourbon, Louis, duc de, 238
Bourbon monarchy, 15, 16, 32,
  79, 82, 105
Bourbons, 96, 163, 208, 244
Bourgoing, Jean-François, 224
Bowood Circle, 216
Breteuil, Louis Charles de
  Tonnelier, baron de, 21, 244
Brienne, Loménie de, 13–14, 15,
  16, 27, 127
Brissot de Warville, Jacques–
  Pierre, 29–30, 35–6, 39,
  81, 134, 155, 217, 245–6
Brissotins, 31, 33–4, 36–46, 100,
  111, 135, 149, 160, 173
Britain, 2, 10, 14, 15, 17, 23,
  29, 255, 257, 259
  and American War of
    Independence, 9
  Bill of Rights, 2
  constitutional settlement, 19
  Directory and Consulate, 50
  economy and society, 191–2,
    193, 205, 206, 207, 209
  Europe, impact of revolution
    on, 214, 217, 219–23,
    227–31
  finance, 65

Britain – *continued*
  global impact of Revolution, 237, 239–41, 243, 245–50, 252–3
  institutions, transformation of, 98, 104, 112
  language and signs of revolution and Counter-Revolution, 73, 79, 80, 85
  militarisation, 146, 147, 150, 151, 158, 161, 163, 167
  National Convention, 32, 35, 36, 41
  Parliament, 119
  political participation, 126, 133, 134
  'Revolutionary' settlement, 14
Broglie, Charles François, duc de, general, 152
Brumaire, 98
Brunswick, duke of, 36, 155, 174
Brutus, 92
Bull, John, 229
Buonarotti, Filippo Michele, 56, 199
Burgundy, duke of, 90
Burke, Edmund, 100–1, 146, 151, 171, 189, 216–17, 225–6, 239, 243, 256
Burke, Richard, 217
Burns, Robert, 225–6

Cabanis, Georges, 54–5
Caesar, Augustus, 90, 92
*Cahiers*, 128, 129, 200
Calonne, (Charles) Alexandre de, 11, 12–13, 14, 15, 17, 49, 126, 193
Cambacérès, chancellor, 62–3
Campo-Formio Treaty, 150
Caribbean, 206
Carlos IV, 218, 224
Carnot, Lazare, 52, 54, 56, 68, 165
Carrier, J.-B., 112, 178–9
Cashel, archbishop of, 170
Castries, Charles-Gabriel de la Croix, marquis de, 11

Cathelineau, *generalissimo*, 160
Catholicism, 25, 256
  Directory and Consulate, 54, 66–7
  economy and society, 202
  Europe, impact of revolution on, 222, 223, 226, 232, 234
  global impact of Revolution, 237, 243
  institutions, transformation of, 114, 115, 117, 118
  language and signs of revolution and Counter-Revolution, 78, 79, 82, 83, 85, 95
  militarisation, 160
  National Convention, 37
  political participation, 120, 122, 124, 139, 140
  violence, vandalism and coercion, 172, 187
central government power and performance, 101–5
*Cercle Sociale*, 134, 216
Chabot, François, 130
Chalier, Marie-Joseph, 83, 91
Chambord, comte de, 96
Championnet, general, 162
Chapelier, Le law, 28
Charette, François-Athanase, 179
Charles I, 20
Charles II, 148
Charles IV, 29
Chateaubriand, François-Auguste, viscomte de, 234, 239–40
Cháteauvieux Regiment, 153
Chaudet, Antoine, 184
Chemin, 54
Chénier, André-Marie de, 86
Chénier, Marie-Joseph, 86–7, 88
Choiseul, Etienne François, duc de, 157
*Chouans*, 180

# INDEX

Church
  subordination of, 113–18
  *see also* Catholicism; Civil
    Constitution of the Clergy;
    Gallican Church;
    Presbyterians;
    Protestantism
Cicero, 90
Civil Constitution of the
    Clergy, 25–6, 27, 256
  Directory and Consulate, 53
  global impact of
    Revolution, 237, 238, 244
  institutions, transformation
    of, 114, 115, 116, 118
  political participation, 133,
    139
  violence, vandalism and
    coercion, 172–3, 184–5
Clavière, Etienne, 33, 39, 216
Clerisseau, 186
Clermont-Tonnerre, Stanislas,
    comte de, deputy, 104,
    120, 134, 174
Cloots, Anacharsis, baron
    von, 215, 231
*Club de Salm*, 135
*Club des Amis de la Constitution
    monarchique*, 134
*Club des Clichyens*, 135
*Club des Impartiaux*, 134
*Club du Manège*, 135
*clubbistes*, 137
Coalition, 17, 228
  First, 161, 229
  Second, 60, 68, 145, 229
  Third, 209, 229
Cobb, Richard, 2–3, 74, 157
Cobban, Alfred, 2
Cobbett, William, 258–9
Coburg, Army of, 36
Coke, Thomas, 117
Colley, Linda, 79
Collot d'Herbois, Jean-Marie, 43
*Commission des Onze*, 39, 48, 49,
    50, 52
Committee of General Defence *see*
    Committee of Public Safety

Committee of General
    Security, 102
Committee of Instruction, 54
Committee of Public Safety, 33
  Directory and Consulate, 52
  economy and society, 194,
    198, 199
  institutions, transformation
    of, 102, 103, 109
  language and signs of revolution
    and Counter-Revolution, 91
  militarisation, 149, 156–7, 159,
    165, 166
  National Convention, 37, 40,
    42, 43, 46
  violence, vandalism and
    coercion, 176, 179, 184–5
Committees, 110, 136
'Commons', 20
Company of Jesus, 180
Company of the Sun, 180
*Compte rendu*, 14
Concordat, 67, 93, 95, 118,
    124, 242
Condé, Louis Henri de
    Bourbon, duc de,
    157, 238–9
Condorcet, Marie Jean de
    Caritat, 41, 54, 125, 134
*Conseil des Anciens*, 48
*Conseil des Cinq-cents*, 48
Constant, Benjamin, 105
Constituent Assembly, 246
Constitution, 29, 61, 63
  1791, 23, 30, 32, 33, 51,
    87–8, 101, 111
  economy and society, 196
  Europe, impact of revolution
    on, 214
  institutions, transformation
    of, 103
  political participation,
    121, 129
  1793, 41, 123, 137
  1795, 48, 49, 57, 59, 100
  global impact of
    Revolution, 245
  militarisation, 153

Constitution – *continued*
  National Convention, 39–40
  Poland, 214
  political participation, 134
  *see also under* Years
Constitutional Church,
  27, 54, 75, 78, 113,
  115–16, 117, 256
Consul, 95
  First, 63, 68, 86, 89, 93,
    94, 100, 255
  global impact of
    Revolution, 244,
    248, 253
  institutions, transformation
    of, 117
  militarisation, 145
  political participation, 132
  Second, 63
  Third, 63
Consular Commission, 62
Consulate, 4, 60–4, 90, 92, 96
  economy and society, 205,
    208, 209
  Europe, impact of revolution
    on, 235
  global impact of Revolution,
    236, 242, 247, 252
  institutions, transformation
    of, 98, 103, 104, 110,
    112, 118
  militarisation, 146,
    163, 167
  political participation, 123,
    133, 134, 141
  success and stability, 64–8
Conti, Louis-François de
  Bourbon, prince de, 238
Convention *see* National
  Convention
*conventionnels*, 137
Cooper, Sir Grey, 195
Corday, Charlotte, 40, 123
Cordeliers, 26, 40, 122,
  135, 175
Corporation Act, 221
Corresponding Societies, 222

Côte-d'Or, Prieur
  de la, 165–6
Council of, 500, 65, 89
Councils, revolutionary, 56, 58,
  60, 62, 177
Counter-Revolution, 2, 4,
  140, 207
  Europe, impact of revolution
    on, 217, 226
  global impact of Revolution,
    241, 244
  *see also* language and signs
    of Revolution and
    Counter-Revolution
Couthon, Georges-Auguste,
  43, 99
Crafts, Nicholas, 192
Crook, Malcolm, 58, 132
Crouzet, François, 191–2
Custine, comte de, 36, 149

Danton, Georges Jacques, 34, 40,
  99, 130, 177
Darthé, Augustin-Alexandre, 199
Daunou, Pierre, 38, 60
David, Jacques-Louis, 40, 80,
  85–6, 92, 207
Declaration of Fraternity, 161
Declaration of the Rights of
  Man, 2, 5, 24, 49
  economy and society, 203
  Europe, impact of revolution
    on, 222
  global impact of
    Revolution, 245
  institutions, transformation
    of, 110
  militarisation, 154
  National Convention, 38
  political participation, 120
  violence, vandalism and
    coercion, 168
Defenders, 222
Delambre, Jean-Baptiste-Joseph, 89
Denmark, 163
Denon, Dominique Vivant de,
  baron, 209

# INDEX

Desmoulins, Lucie Camille Simplice de, 40, 82, 99, 177
Dessalines, Jacques, 248
Destutt de Tracy, 54
Directory, 47–59, 255, 258
  economy and society, 195, 199, 200, 204
  Europe, impact of revolution on, 228, 230
  global impact of Revolution, 249, 251
  institutions, transformation of, 100, 102, 104, 105, 109, 112, 117
  language and signs of revolution and Counter-Revolution, 83, 90, 91, 93
  militarisation, 147, 150, 158, 160, 161, 163, 165, 167
  National Convention, 46
  political participation, 123, 129, 131, 134, 135, 137, 138
  Second, 146, 229
  violence, vandalism and coercion, 182, 186, 190
Douglass, John, vicar apostolic, 243
Doyle, William, 1, 183
Ducos, Roger, 58, 60, 62, 104
Dugommier, general, 159
Dumont, André, 216
Dumouriez, Charles-François du Pévier, general, 36, 148–9, 155, 241
Dundas, Henry, 217, 246
Dundas, Sir David, 247
Dundas, Thomas, major general, 189
Dundee Whig Club, 215
Dupont de Nemours, 193
Duport, Adrien, 28
Duqueylar, Paulin, 91
Dutch United Provinces, 14, 219
'Duties of Man', 49

East Indies, 193
economy and society, 191–209
  economic egalitarianism, 196–200
  economic liberalism and market economy, 192–5
  property, predominance of, 195–6
  rural society, 200–5
  war, impact of, 205–8
Eden, William, 1st baron Auckland, 155
egalitarianism, 196–200
Egypt, 61–2, 163, 167, 236, 249, 253
Emigrants' Relief Committee, 243
'Emigration', 27
*emigrés*, 237–45
Enghien, duc d', 66, 238
Enlightenment, 15–16, 18
  Europe, impact of revolution on, 214, 218, 222, 223, 228
  institutions, transformation of, 98, 100, 110, 115
  language and signs of revolution and Counter-Revolution, 73, 78, 80, 88
  militarisation, 151
  National Convention, 41
  violence, vandalism and coercion, 173, 189
Estates-General, 4, 11, 37, 170, 200
  institutions, transformation of, 97, 98, 103, 106
  language and signs of revolution and Counter-Revolution, 75, 87
  meeting, 19–24
  political participation, 119, 127, 128, 129
  prelude to, 9–19
Europe, 28, 29, 254, 255, 259, 260
  Directory and Consulate, 51
  economy and society, 206, 209

Europe – *continued*
  global impact of
    Revolution, 236, 237,
    244, 245, 252
  institutions, transformation
    of, 98, 99, 104, 113
  language and signs of
    revolution and Counter-
    Revolution, 85, 87, 93, 94
  militarisation, 151, 152, 154–5,
    156–7, 161, 162, 167
  National Convention, 34, 37
  political participation, 121,
    127, 139
  violence, vandalism and
    coercion, 173
  *see also* Europe, impact of
    revolution on
Europe, impact of revolution
  on, 213–35
  authoritarianism, 225–32
  international dimension,
    214–24
Expilly, Louis-Alexandre, 116

Fabre d'Eglantine, 81, 91
Fauchet, François-Claude,
  bishop, 78, 134, 251
Federalists, 108, 159, 177,
  181, 251
Federation, 82
Fénelon, archbishop, 76, 90
Fersen, Hans Axel, count
  von, 82, 242
Festival of Liberty, 83
Feuillants, 28, 122, 149
Fifth Republic, 168, 179
Finance Bill, 229
First Estate, 17, 19, 20, 21, 25, 67
  global impact of
    Revolution, 238
  institutions, transformation
    of, 113, 114
  political participation, 128
First Republic, 81
First World War, 188
Fitzgerald, Edward,
  lord, 222

Fitzsimmons, Michael, 172
Fitzwilliam, William Wentworth,
  2nd earl, 217
Five Hundred, 48
Fleuriot-Lescot, Jean-Baptiste-
  Edmond, 42
Floridablanca, condé de, 224
Fontaine, 89
Forrest, Alan, 157, 163
Fouché, Joseph, duke of
  Otranto, 42, 60–1, 66, 95,
  102, 109, 131, 135, 185
Fouquier-Tinville, public
  prosecutor, 112, 177
Fox, Charles James, 17, 222, 225
Francis II, Holy Roman Emperor
  of Austria, 150, 155, 217–18,
  223–4, 228
Franco–Prussian War, 96
Frederick William II, 29,
  154, 218
French Guiana, 182, 248, 249
French Revolutionary
  Gospel, 219
French West Indies, 245,
  246, 248
Fréron, Louis-Stanislas, 81
Friedrich, Karl, 155
Frimaire, law of, 42, 103
Furet, François, 2, 26, 73,
  169, 254

Gallican Church, 26, 66, 67, 78
  global impact of Revolution,
    242, 243
  institutions, transformation
    of, 113, 114, 117
  language and signs of
    revolution and Counter-
    Revolution, 83, 95
Garat, Dominique-Joseph,
  Minister of Justice, 54
Gardiner, William,
  colonel, 254
Gaudin, Martin, 65
Gay, Peter, 73
General Maximum,
  Law of, 194, 198

## INDEX

Genêt, Edmund Charles, 250–1
George III, 23–4, 50, 189, 218, 225, 247
Gerard, Alain, 180
Gérard, François, 85
Gerle, Dom, deputy, 78, 172
Germany, 52, 154, 217, 234
Girondins, 35, 39, 166, 189, 194, 231, 250
  political participation, 123, 125, 134, 136
Gisors, 89
global impact of Revolution, 236–53
  Atlantic area, 245–53
  *emigrés*, 237–45
'Glorious Revolution', 25, 221
glossary, 282–4
Godechot, Jacques, 219
Godoy, Manuel de, principe de la paz, 228
Gohier, Louis-Jérome, 58, 60
Gossec, 88
Gouge, Olympe de, 122
Gower, Earl, 23
Grand Elector, 63
Grant, 155
Great Fear, 107, 171
Great Terror, 41, 102, 175–81, 182
  implementation, 177–81
  machinery, 176–7
  objectives, 175–6
  violence, vandalism and coercion, 169
Greece, 32, 88
Greer, Donald, 238
Grégoire, Henri, bishop, 54, 116–17, 175, 186
Grenville, George, 1st baron, 229, 239
Grétry, André Ernest Modeste, 87
Grey, Charles, 2nd earl, 222
Grey, Sir George, 247
Grimaldi of Noyen, bishop, 238
'Grub Street', 76

Guadeloupe, 189, 248
Gual, Pedro, 252
Gueniffey, Patrice, 44, 169, 176
Gustavus III, 242
Guyana, 59

Habeas Corpus Act, 227
Habsburg Empire, 213, 223
Habsburgs, 29, 154, 155, 217
Hampson, Norman, 75–6
Hanriot, François, 39, 184
Hardman, John, 23
Hardy, Thomas, 168
Harrington, James, 31
Hassenfratz, Jean-Henri, 166–7
Hastings, Adrian, 78
Hazlitt, William, 259
Hébert, Jacques-René, 40, 81, 99, 123, 198
Hébertistes, 177, 199
Helvetic Club, 216
Helvetic Republic, 234
Henri IV, 32, 86
Herbert, Henry, 239
Hirsch, Jean-Pierre, 3
Hoche, Lazare, general, 61, 150, 158–9, 163, 165, 179, 230
Holland *see* Netherlands
Hood, Lord, admiral, 41, 159
Hostages, Law of, 60
Huguenots, 120
Hugues, Victor, 247
Hungary, 219, 223
Hunt, Lynne, 3, 74, 100, 257
Hussars, 21

ideologies, 75–82
Ideologues, 54, 55, 59
*Impartiaux*, 26
India, 250
Institut de France, 85
institutions, transformation of, 97–118
  central government power and performance, 101–5
  Church, subordination of, 113–18

institutions – *continued*
  justice, machinery of, 110–13
  local government, renewal of, 106–10
Insurrectionary Committee, 56, 199
'Intermediary Orders', 18
international dimension, 214–24
Ireland, 163, 219, 223, 230
Irish Rebellion, 214, 228
Italy, 32, 88, 91, 118, 186
  Directory and Consulate, 52, 58, 61
  Europe, impact of revolution on, 224, 229, 232, 234
  militarisation, 150, 162

Jackson, Rev. William, 230
Jacob, Georges, 207
Jacobin Club, 28, 30, 31, 44, 123, 130, 198, 216
Jacobin Republic, 254
Jacobins, 26, 255, 259
  Directory and Consulate, 49, 50, 56, 57, 66
  economy and society, 194, 198, 202–3, 204, 208
  Europe, impact of revolution on, 214, 218, 219, 227, 231, 232, 234
  global impact of Revolution, 242, 247, 250, 251
  institutions, transformation of, 99, 109, 112
  language and signs of revolution and Counter-Revolution, 77, 81, 82, 85, 86, 87, 90, 92, 95
  militarisation, 146, 148, 149, 156–7, 159, 160, 161, 163–4, 167
  National Convention, 38, 39, 40, 41, 43, 44, 45
  political participation, 122, 123, 124, 132, 135, 136, 138
  violence, vandalism and coercion, 176, 177, 180, 181, 184, 185, 189

Jamaica, 247
James II, 220
Jansenists, 79
Javogues, Claude, 109
Jay Treaty, 251
Jefferson, Thomas, 24, 215, 250–1
Jews, 67, 120–1, 122
Jones, Colin, 3, 191
Jones, Peter, 200–1
Jones, Robert, 220
Joseph II, Emperor, 9, 22, 154, 219, 223, 242
Josephine, Marie-Josephe-Rose Tascher de la Pegerie, Empress, 67, 93
Joubert, general, 62
Jourdan, general, 231
Juigné de Paris, archbishop, 238
justice, machinery of, 110–13
Justices of the Peace, 111, 128, 228

Kellerman, general, 150

La Fare, bishop, 120
La Révellière-Lépeaux, Louis-Marie de
Labroussée, Suzette, 78
Lacombe, Claire, 123
Lafayette, Marie Joseph-Motier, marquis de, 18, 28, 29, 36, 147–8, 153, 256
Lally-Tollendal, Trophime-Gérard, marquis de, deputy, 26, 237
Lamballe, Marie-Thérèse-Louise de Savoie-Carignan, princesse de, 169, 174
Lameth, Alexandre, comte de, 28, 148
Lameth, Charles de, 28, 29
Lamoignon, 13, 15
Lamourette, Adrien, Bishop, 78
language and signs of Revolution and Counter-Revolution, 73–96
  antiquity, 89–92

arts, 82–9
language, ideologies and
  Revolution, 75–82
Napoleon and signs and
  symbols, 93–5
Lansdowne, William Petty-
  FitzMaurice, 1st marquess
  of, 216
Launey, Bernard-René,
  marquis de, governor
  of the Bastille, 170
Lavater, Johann Kaspar, 258
Law of the Maximum, 166
Law of Suspects, 41, 176
lawlessness, 181–3
Lebrun, Charles-François,
  39, 62–3
Leclerc, Charles, general,
  199, 248
Lecointre, Laurent, 89
Ledoux, Claude-Nicolas, 88–9
Lefebvre, Georges, 2, 134
Legislation Committee, 46, 102
Legislative Assembly, 29, 30,
  32, 173, 217, 246
  economy and society, 197, 201
  institutions, transformation
    of, 101, 108
  militarisation, 148, 154,
    155, 165
Legislative Body, 63
Leopold II, 29, 154, 216–17, 223
Lepeletier de Saint-Fargeau,
  Louis-Michel, 83, 91
Lever, Evelyn, 23
liberalism, 192–5
Liberty-Equality oath, 54
Lindet, Robert-Thomas,
  116, 166
Livesy, James, 50, 58
Livy, 92
local government, renewal
  of, 106–10
London Corresponding
  Society, 134, 228
Louis XIII, 17
Louis XIV, 68, 90, 162
Louis XV, 10, 79, 90, 113, 126

Louis XVI, 9, 14, 16, 17,
  19, 21–4, 27–30, 255
  Convention, the, 31, 34–6
  Directory and the
    Consulate, 51
  economy and society, 193
  Europe, impact of revolution
    on, 214, 219–20, 230
  global impact of
    Revolution, 237, 240,
    244, 250
  institutions, transformation
    of, 104–5, 115
  language and signs of
    revolution, 79–80, 82,
    84–5, 86, 90, 93
  militarisation, 148, 153
  political participation,
    119, 125
  violence, vandalism and
    coercion, 169
Louis XVII, 148
Louis XVIII, 66, 158, 226,
  239, 241–2, 255
Low Countries, 229
Lucas, Sir Colin, 135
Luxembourg, 51
Luzerne, la, bishop, 171
Lyons, Martin, 50

Mably, abbé, 31, 83
Machiavelli, Niccolò, 31
McManners, John, 1, 26
McPhee, Peter, 1, 201
Maistre, Joseph de, 226, 239
Malesherbes, Chrétien-Guillaume
  de Lamoignode, 13
Mallet du Pan, Jacques,
  82, 105, 226
Malouet, Pierre-Victor,
  deputy, 66, 105, 134
Malta, 163
Mansel, Philip, 23
Marat, Jean-Paul, 40, 81, 83,
  85, 91
  economy and society, 198
  global impact of
    Revolution, 246

Marat – *continued*
  political participation, 123
  violence, vandalism and
    coercion, 175
Marceau, 165
Marche, Jean-François de la,
  bishop, 243
Maréchal, Sylvain, 87
María Louisa, queen of
  Spain, 228
Marie-Antoinette, 22, 154,
  174, 216
Markoff, John, 201
Maroon War, 247
Martinique, 163, 248
Marxism, 2–3, 44, 46, 168,
  169, 254
Masonic lodges, 18
Maupeou, René-Charles-
  Augustine de, 10
Maurepas, Jean-Frédérice de
  Phélypeaux, comte de, First
  Minister, 9, 11, 12, 119
Maury, Jean-Siffrein, abbé,
  120–1
May Edicts, 13, 15–16
Méchain, Pierre-François-
  André, 89
Mediterranean, 253
Mélas, general, 145
Mercier, Louis-Sébastien,
  125, 257
Méricourt, Theoroigne de, 123
Merlin 'de Douai', Philippe-
  Antoine, 52, 58, 104
Meyer, Arnold, 188, 254
Michelet, Jules, 44
militarisation, 145–67
  army and autocracy, 145–50
  going to war, 154–7
  unmartial opening of
    Revolution, 151–2
  warfare, consequences of, 163–7
  Wars of the Revolution, 158–63
Ministry
  for Ecclesiastical Affairs,
    67, 118
  of the 'hundred hours', 22

  of the Interior, 55, 111
  of Justice, 111
Mirabeau, Honoré-Gabriel
  Riquetti, comte de, 105,
  216, 256
Miranda, Francisco de, 252
Miromesnil, Armand-Thomas
  Hue de, Keeper of the Seals,
  11–12, 119
Mitterand, François,
  2, 168, 179
Monarchy, end of, 9–30
  Estates-General, meeting
    of, 19–24
  Estates-General, prelude to,
    9–19
  National Assembly, reform
    agenda of, 24–30
Montagnards, 33–4, 137, 149,
  159, 160, 184
Montbrion, Jacques, 203
Montesquians, 76
Montesquieu, Charles-Louis,
  10, 12, 16, 18, 50, 214
  language and signs of
    revolution, 75, 76, 80
Montlosier, 65, 93
Montmorin, Armand-Marc
  Montmorin de Saint-Hérem,
  comte de, Foreign
  Minister, 22–3, 101,
  125, 151, 174
More, Hannah, 225
Moreau, Jean-Victor, general,
  16, 61–2, 68,
  80, 150
Morellet, abbé, 216
Morveau, Louis-Bernard Guyton
  de, 166–7
Moulin, Jean, 58, 61
Mounier, Jean–Joseph,
  deputy, 26, 66, 104–5,
  171–2, 220
Mountain, 33, 34, 35, 108

Napoleonic Wars, 188
Narbonne, Louis, comte de,
  Minister for War, 29

National Assembly, 14, 20, 21,
    22, 23, 29, 33, 35
  economy and society,
    193–4, 201
  Europe, impact of revolution
    on, 214, 215, 221
  global impact of
    Revolution, 245–6
  institutions, transformation
    of, 99, 101, 103, 104, 106–8,
    110, 113, 114–15, 118
  language and signs of
    revolution and Counter-
    Revolution, 75
  militarisation, 151, 152,
    153, 159
  National Convention, 37
  political participation, 120,
    121, 122, 129, 131, 133
  reform agenda, 24–30
  violence, vandalism and
    coercion, 170, 171,
    172, 186
National Convention,
    31–46, 259
  Brissotins, destruction of,
    36–46
  economy and society, 194–5,
    196–8, 199, 202, 205
  establishment of, 31–6
  Europe, impact of revolution
    on, 218, 230, 231
  global impact of
    Revolution, 246–7
  institutions, transformation
    of, 100, 102, 103–4, 108
  language and signs of
    revolution and Counter-
    Revolution, 81, 83,
    85, 88
  militarisation, 145, 148, 149,
    159, 160–1, 166
  political participation, 123,
    130–1, 132, 136, 137, 138
  violence, vandalism and
    coercion, 178–9, 186
National Food Commission,
    166, 198, 199

National Guard, 28, 39, 44,
    149, 153, 196
  violence, vandalism and
    coercion, 172, 173,
    181, 184
National Institute of Arts and
    Sciences, 54
Necker, Jacques, 9, 11, 14,
    16–22, 25, 256
  institutions, transformation
    of, 100, 103, 106
  language and signs of
    revolution, 79
  political participation, 119,
    125–9, 133
Nelson, Horatio, 1st viscount,
    admiral, 58, 163, 249
Netherlands, 35, 126, 255, 259
  Europe, impact of revolution
    on, 220, 223, 232, 234
  global impact of
    Revolution, 244
  language and signs of
    revolution and Counter-
    Revolution, 80
  militarisation, 163, 166
  *see also* Austrian Netherlands
Neufchâteau, François de,
    Minister of the Interior,
    52, 204
Newton, Isaac, 88
North, 17
North America, 234

O'Brien, Patrick, 192
Ocean Coasts, Army of, 158–9
October Days, 170–1
'Old Order', 24, 89
opinion, power of, 125–30
Orders, 20, 21, 25, 114, 128, 241
Organic Articles, 67, 93, 118
Orléanists, 149
Orléans, Louis-Philippe,
    duc d', 22–3, 31, 68, 77, 105,
    119, 148, 240
Oswald, John, 216
Ottoman Empire, 29, 249
Ozouf, M., 74

Padua Circular, 154
Paine, Thomas, 216, 255
Palmer, R.R., 130
Panthéon Club, 135, 199
Paris *commune*, 81
Payan, Claude-François, 87
Peace
  of Amiens, 68, 209
  of Basle, 229
  of Lunéville, 68
Peninsula War, 232
Percier, 89
Pergen, Minister of Police, 223–4, 227
Philadelphia Convention, 147
Philanthropic Institute, 135
Pichegru, general, 56, 150
Pillnitz, Declaration of, 217
Pitt, William, the Younger, Prime Minister, 29, 50, 163, 193, 239, 243, 250
  Europe, impact of Revolution on, 214, 217, 222, 227, 229, 231
Pius VI, 27, 116–18, 224, 232, 234, 238
Pius VII, 66–7, 95
Plutarch, 80
Poincaré, 238
Poland, 29, 154, 214, 230
political participation, 119–41
  opinion, power of, 125–30
  patterns, 130–8
  political nation defined, 119–24
  revolutionary involvement, limits to, 139–41
Poniatowski, Stanislas, king of Poland, 230
Popkin, 81
Portland, William Cavendish Bentinck, 3rd duke of, 217, 222
Poyet, 89
Prairial, law of, 41, 44, 112, 137, 177
Prefect, 65
Presbyterians, 259

Price, Richard, 215–16
Priestley, Joseph, 78, 215–16, 259
Princes, Army of, 239
property, predominance of, 195–6
Protestantism, 67, 120
  Europe, impact of revolution on, 222
  global impact of Revolution, 243
  institutions, transformation of, 117
  language and signs of revolution and Counter-Revolution, 79
  political participation, 120
  violence, vandalism and coercion, 172, 187
Provence, Louis Stanislas Xavier, comte de, 27, 28, 255
Provincial Assemblies for the Berry and the Limousin, 106
Provincial Estates, 17, 106
Prussia, 14, 32, 34, 255
  Europe, impact of revolution on, 213, 229
  global impact of Revolution, 237
  militarisation, 154, 155, 156, 162
  violence, vandalism and coercion, 173–4
Puisaye, comte de, 239, 241

Quai, Maurice, 91

Rasdatt, Treaty of, 232
Reformed Church, 79
Regency (1715–23), 17
Religious Committee, 114
Representatives-on-Mission, 102, 109, 137, 177, 184–5
Reubell, Jean François, 51–3, 56, 61

Révellière-Lépeaux, Louis Marie La, 51–4, 56, 58–9
Revolutionary
  Armies, 160, 161, 185, 232, 244
  Government, 102, 103
  settlement, 14
  Tribunal, 41, 44, 176
  Wars, 150, 161, 162, 164, 188, 228
Rey, Claude Antoine, 227
Rhineland, 36, 162, 229, 232, 234
Richet, Denis, 73
Rigaud, André, 247
Rivarol, Antoine, 105, 226
Roberts, John, 206
Robespierre, Maximilien-François-Isidore, 30, 33, 34, 40–5
  Directory and the Consulate, 48, 52
  economy and society, 194, 198
  Europe, impact of revolution on, 219, 231
  global impact of Revolution, 244, 246
  institutions, transformation of, 99, 103
  language and signs of revolution, 77, 83, 85–6, 90, 92, 93
  militarisation, 165
  political participation, 131, 136
  violence, vandalism and coercion, 176–7, 186
Rochambeau, general, 248
Rochefoucauld, Louis Alexandre, duc de la, 18, 28, 125
Rochefoucauld-Liancourt, François Alexandre, duc de la, 174
Roederer, Pierre Louis, deputy, 69
Roland, Jean Marie, de la Platière, 33, 125, 134
Roland, Jeanne Mamon, madame de la Platière, 125

Rousseau, Jean-Jacques, 16, 54, 75–7, 83, 87, 90, 92, 99, 121–2
Rousseauians, 76
Roux, Jacques, priest, 198–9
Royal and Catholic Army, 158, 160
'Royal Session', 21
Rural Code, 201
rural society, 200–5
Russia, 29, 193, 230, 249
  Revolution, 169

Saint-André, Jeanbon, 166
Saint-Just, Louis-Antoine-Léon de, 40, 43, 92, 99, 131, 184
Saint-Louis, 32
Saintes, 108
'Salmigondis', 135
San Domingo, 163, 245, 246–7, 248, 253
Sans-culottes, 136, 137, 138, 149, 184–5, 188
Sapinaud, 179
Saurau, deputy Minister of Police, 227
Schama, Simon, 2, 148, 169, 254
Schiller, 215
Secher, Reynauld, 2, 179–80
Second Estate, 17, 21, 152, 191–2
'Second Hundred Years War', 79
'Second Revolution', 32
Sedillot, René, 169
Ségur, Philippe Henri, marquis de, Minister for War, 193
Ségur-Ordinance, 152
Selwyn, George, 213
Senate, 63, 69, 100, 104, 678
Servan, Joseph, Minister for War, 33
Seven Years War, 14, 15, 245
Sheridan, Richard Brinsley, 222, 225
Sieyes, Emmanuel Joseph, abbé, 18, 58, 60–3, 100–1
Simmoneau, mayor, 197
Sinking Fund, 65

Smith, Adam, 193
Soboul, 2
Socialists, 168
society *see* economy and society
Society
 of the Friends of the People, 221, 222
 of Republican Revolutionary Citizennesses, 123
 of Thirty, 18, 28
Socrates, 54
Sonenscher, Michael, 136
Sonnenfels, 223
South America, 252
Spain, 29, 101
 Europe, impact of revolution on, 213, 224, 228, 229
 global impact of Revolution, 242, 243, 246, 250, 251, 252
 militarisation, 151, 163, 166
Special Tribunals, 112
Spencer, 2nd earl, 1st lord of the Admiralty, 163
St-Just, 34, 43, 45
Staël, Anne-Louise-Germaine Necker, Madame de, 105, 239
Stevens, William, 219
Stofflet, Nicolas, 179
Stone, Bailey, 14
Supreme Beings, festival of, 42
Suspects, Law of, 111, 231
Sutherland, Countess of, 23
Sutherland, Don, 1
Sweden, 242
Swiss Guards, 218
Switzerland, 80, 126, 162, 219, 259

Tacitus, 80
Tackett, Timothy, 256
Talleyrand, Charles Maurice de, 27, 52, 60, 62, 102, 239, 252–3
Tallien, Jean-Lambert, 43
Target, Guillaume-Jean-Baptiste, 110

Taylor, William, of Norwich, 221
Terror, 40, 59
 economy and society, 204
 Europe, impact of revolution on, 231
 first reign of, 54
 institutions, transformation of, 109, 111, 113
 language and signs of revolution and Counter-Revolution, 84, 88
 militarisation, 156–7
 National Convention, 41, 42, 43, 45
 political participation, 133
 second reign of, 54
 violence, vandalism and coercion, 183, 187
 *see also* Great Terror; White Terror
terrorism, 181–3
Test Act, 221
Thatcher, Margaret, 2
Theophilanthropy, 54, 59
Thermidorians, 34, 43, 44, 47, 76, 181, 187, 199
Third Estate, 18–19, 20, 21, 22, 238
 institutions, transformation of, 97, 106, 113, 114
 political participation, 127, 128
Thouret, Jacques-Guillaume, 107
Tierney, George, 222
Tipoo Sahib, 250
Tone, Wolf, 163, 222, 230
Tour du Pin, Madame de la, 239
Toussaint l'Ouverture, 247–8
Treaty
 of Amiens, 248, 253
 of Basle, 162, 228
 of Eden, 193
 of Paris, 15
Treilhard, Jean-Baptist, deputy, 58
Trémoille, Prince Louis de la, 241

Tribunal, 112, 182
Tribunate, 63, 68
Trimmer, Sarah, 225
Triumvirate, 28
Triumvirs, 53, 57
Turenne, general, 93
Turgot, Anne-Robert-Jacques, 9, 11, 125, 192
Turkey, 216–7
Turreau, general, 41, 161, 179
'Twelve who ruled', 176
Two-Thirds, Law of, 47, 53, 100, 138

United Bishops, 117
United Irishmen, 163, 222, 223, 228, 230
United Provinces, 162, 213, 259
United States, 2, 15, 17, 214, 215, 217, 259
  constitution, 13, 50
  Declaration of Independence, 20
  global impact of Revolution, 247, 250, 251, 252
  Historical Association, 3
  institutions, transformation of, 98
  language and signs of revolution and Counter-Revolution, 73
  militarisation, 147, 167
  Supreme Court, 214
  *see also* American War of Independence
Unity and Indivisibility of the Republic, 40

Vadier, Marc-Guillaume-Alexis, 43
Van Kley, Dale, 125
Vandal, Albert, 1
Varennes, 28
Varlet, Louis de la, prince, 199
Veau, Athanase, 83
Vendémaire, 150
Ventôse, Laws of, 194, 203

Vergennes, Charles Gravier, comte de, Foreign Minister, 9, 12, 80
Vermond, Matthieu Jacques, abbé de, 127
Verona, Declaration of, 226
Versailles Treaty, 15
Victoire, Madame, 238
Villard, abbé, 34
violence, vandalism and coercion, 168–90
  Great Terror, 175–81
  terrorism and lawlessness, 181–3
  vandalism, 183–8
  violence, 168–75
Volney, Constantin-François Chasseboeuf, comte de, 54
Voltaire, François Marie Arouet de, 10, 17, 83, 88, 92, 169
Vovelle, M., 74, 179

Wallace-Hadrill, J.M., 1
war, impact of, 205–8
War Office, 156
War of the Spanish Succession, 10
War of the Third Coalition, 209
Wars of Religion, 172, 187
Washington, George, 146–7, 214
Wellesley, Arthur, 1st duke of Wellington, 250, 252
Wellesley, Richard, 1st marquess, 250
West Indies, 163, 189, 236, 237
White Terror, 44, 55, 160, 180, 182, 204
Wilmot, John, 243
Windham, William, 217, 227, 239
Windward Islands, 246
Wiscar, J.B., 184
Wordsworth, William, 220, 227

'XYZ affair', 251

Year
  I, 89, 98
    Constitution, 132, 137, 194, 199

Year – *continued*
  II, 52, 60, 83, 87, 103,
    165, 177
    Constitution, 259
  III, 46, 117, 132, 133, 199
    Constitution, 47, 48, 49, 54,
      56, 57, 58, 60, 68, 90,
      138, 140
    institutions, transformation
      of, 100, 102, 103,
      104, 105, 112
  IV, 48
  V, 56
  VI, 57, 186
  VII, 48, 57, 132
  VIII, 64, 90, 132
    Constitution, 102, 103, 134
York, army of, 36
York, duke of, 157
Young, Arthur, 20, 125, 220

Zoffany, Johan, 85